MOTIVATION:
THEORY AND RESEARCH

MOTIVATION:
THEORY AND RESEARCH

Edited by
HAROLD F. O'NEIL, JR.
University of Southern California
MICHAEL DRILLINGS
Army Research Institute

LEA LAWRENCE ERLBAUM ASSOCIATES, PUBLISHERS
1994   Hillsdale, New Jersey   Hove, UK

Lawrence Erlbaum Associates, Inc., Publishers
365 Broadway
Hillsdale, New Jersey 07642

Library of Congress Cataloging-in-Publication Data

Motivation : theory and research / edited by Harold F. O'Neil, Jr.,
  Michael Drillings.
       p. cm.
  Includes bibliographical references and indexes.
  ISBN 0-8058-1286-5. — ISBN 0-8058-1287-3 (pbk.)
  1. Motivation (Psychology) 2. Motivation in education.
  3. Motivation (Psychology)—Social aspects. I. O'Neil, Harold F.,
  1943– . II. Drillings, Michael.
  BF503.M685   1994
  153.8—dc20   94-4848
                                                      CIP

Books published by Lawrence Erlbaum Associates are printed
on acid-free paper, and their bindings are chosen for strength
and durability.

Printed in the United States of America
10   9   8   7   6   5   4   3   2   1

Contents

Preface

The U.S. military is a major funder of basic research in the United States in the social and behavioral sciences. In the 1980s, military-funded basic research was marked by a reduced interest in the areas of organizational and individual variables that are commonly associated with motivational concepts. Even leadership, a traditional military interest, was studied mostly from the point of view of the leader, rather than from that of the individual soldier. Military research, instead, focused to a large extent on ideas emerging from cognitive psychology and computer science. Thus, research focused on the cognitive aspects of human functioning and not on motivational aspects.

In the early nineties, however, it became apparent that the military services' capabilities to draw large numbers of high quality, career-oriented recruits might not be able to be sustained in the future. Further observations during the U.S./Allies vs. Iraq conflict in the Middle East (Operation Desert Storm/Desert Shield) appeared to indicate that maintaining soldier motivation was critical to the success of a wide range of responsibilities in a large scale military operation, particularly one whose start was drawn out over several months. Applied research being conducted in environments that realistically simulate combat (e.g., the Army's National Training Center) identified unit cohesion and motivation as important variables in successful combat performance.

Motivation is particularly important to the U.S. Army. The Army is composed of many individuals of diverse backgrounds and aptitudes who are expected to perform both individually and collectively to meet performance standards. Despite this diversity, each soldier is expected to perform his or her particular job and to be interchangeable with other soldiers performing that same job. Soldiers also differ in their initial motivation for joining the Army. Some soldiers join to serve their nation, others to learn a skill, and still others because they have few better options. Soldiers in battle have at least one powerful and obvious source of motivation. However, the great majority of military tasks are performed neither on the battlefield nor during wartime. In this sense, the Army is similar to a service-oriented multinational company. Moreover, because the Army trains for battle and yet fights so rarely, it is a continuing challenge to maintain combat skills.

Military life is also filled with education and training of varying contexts, content, length, quality, and expense. Institution-based training includes the basic combat skills that are taught after entry from the civilian sector and advanced technical skills that are trained later in a soldier's career. Throughout one's career there are also a variety of skills that soldiers are expected to learn informally, on the job. The environment in which the performance occurs also varies from the sterile, high-tech surroundings of a research center to the mud and darkness of changing a tank's track at night under fire. Occasionally, jobs must be performed despite great physical and mental exhaustion and considerable stress.

Thus, the military, particularly the Army, have increased interest in identifying factors underlying the motivation of their personnel. As a result of this interest, the U.S. Army Research Institute for the Behavioral and Social Sciences contracted with a number of basic and applied researchers in order to pull together various ideas and trends in motivation research to assist in R&D program planning. The results of this effort are documented in this volume. As a secondary result, we hope to stimulate renewed interest in the motivation area by both basic and applied researchers. This book is designed for professionals and graduate students in the personality/social, educational psychology, military psychology, assessment/evaluation communities. It explores the state of the art in motivational research for individuals and teams from multiple theoretical viewpoints. Further, the effect of motivation in both educational and training environments is explored.

This volume could not have happened without the help and encouragement of many people. Our thanks to our editor, Hollis Heimbouch of LEA, for her support and guidance in the publication process. We thank Katharine Fry for her assistance in preparing the manuscript.

ACKNOWLEDGMENTS

Support for this work was provided in part by the Army Research Institute for the Behavioral and Social Sciences. However, the views, opinions and findings contained in this article are the authors' and should not be construed as an official position, policy, or decision unless so designated by other, official documentation.

Harold F. O'Neil, Jr.
Michael Drillings

MOTIVATION:
THEORY AND RESEARCH

1 Introduction to *Motivation: Theory and Research*

Michael Drillings
Army Research Institute for the Behavioral and Social Sciences

Harold F. O'Neil, Jr.
University of Southern California/CRESST

There are several well-documented trends that will affect education and training now and in the future: introduction of large numbers of immigrants into the United States; a reduction in the 17–20 year-old group between 1980 and 1996; an increased participation rate by women and minorities in the labor force; increasing use of English as a second language; increased requirements for second language learning; and a possible increased use of robotics to accomplish unskilled jobs (Johnston & Packer, 1987; O'Neil, Allred, & Baker, 1992). Further, several issues specific to the Armed Forces also magnify these general trends for Department of Defense education and training. These issues include reduction in force structure, reduction in manpower and personnel, decreasing budgets for training, increasing equipment complexity, and increased use of the Reserves (Office of the Assistant Secretary of Defense, 1992; National Research Council, 1992).

Thus, students will have to master an increased variety of complicated subject material, to master an increased set of sophisticated skills, and to perform these skills at higher standards in ever-changing contexts. We expect that these trends will continue well into the 21st century for both the military and civilian sectors.

A FRAMEWORK FOR MOTIVATION

The great majority of education and training research and development is focused on the cognitive dimensions of learning, for instance, the acquisition and retention of declarative and procedural knowledge. Less attention has been given in the literature and in the design of education and training itself to motivational

1

variables and their influence on performance. Motivational variables, such as effort, anxiety, and curiosity, play a significant role in performance at all stages. They influence the rate and ease with which individuals acquire new competencies, the quality of inference that can be made from testing trainee achievement, the likelihood that the individual will actually use trained skills in the target context, and the resistance of knowledge and skills to degradation under conditions of stress and other unanticipated changes in situation.

In this volume, we view motivational variables in a fairly traditional framework of individual differences (addressing the predisposition of individuals to have particular feelings and reactions) and environmental factors (addressing the likelihood that given conditions will engender particular feelings).

Individual Differences

Individual differences have been conceived to vary along two dimensions: (a) the *trait* of the individual, that is, the predisposition to manifest a state across a wide range of contexts and conditions; and (b) the *state* of the individual, that is, affective reactions that vary in intensity, fluctuate over time, and result from specific environmental conditions and level of the trait that an individual possesses. A common example of this distinction is in the area of anxiety (O'Neil, Baker, & Matsuura, 1992; Sieber, O'Neil, & Tobias, 1977; Spielberger, 1975, 1980), where first an individual's propensity to be anxious is determined (trait anxiety); then, his or her general disposition to be anxious in a specific setting of taking achievement tests (trait test anxiety); and finally, the individual's actual anxiety levels in the situation when taking tests of different sorts (state test anxiety).

Although the formulation of descriptive typologies for analyzing individual differences has occupied many psychologists (Snow, 1989a, 1989b; Snow & Jackson, this volume), others have concentrated their attention on documenting the influence of such variables, such as anxiety, on performance (e.g., Franken & O'Neil, this volume; Morris, Davis, & Hutchings, 1981; O'Neil & Fukumura, 1992), on assessing the interactions between such individual differences, such as visualization, and training conditions (Duesbury, 1992; Kyllonen, Lohman, & Snow, 1984), and on enhancing positive effects of such motivational variables as curiosity (Spielberger & Starr, this volume) or ameliorating through interventions the negative effects of such affective variables (e.g., anxiety) on performance (Hembree, 1988; Meichenbaum & Butler, 1980).

Environmental Factors

A number of environmental factors can influence motivational states. Perhaps most obvious for training environments are task characteristics such as content, difficulty, pacing, ambiguity, and so on. For many researchers, however, the most powerful agents in the environment are other people. The social mediation of motivational variables, self-confidence, persistence, risk-taking, and anxiety has been well acknowledged in the literature of social psychology for the last half-century. But the specific functions of teamwork and strategies for team-building are less well known (Swezey, Meltzer, & Salas, this volume), although analysts have proposed largely unvalidated frameworks for investigation (Fleishman & Zaccaro, 1992).

Boundary Conditions

Although it is common to conceptualize motivation as feelings connoting emotional or visceral reactions versus cognitive dimensions such as thinking, the boundaries between these two classes are in fact rather blurry and may be explained from a number of perspectives. First, the fragility of the distinctions is due in part to the documented relationships between certain affective and cognitive variables. For example, the relationship between need achievement and performance (Atkinson, 1974; Spangler, 1992) is well known as is the relationship between will (volition) and cognition (Snow & Jackson, this volume). A second reason for the blurring of categories is the view that many affective states are driven by cognitive control by the individual (Locke & Latham, this volume). Researchers and clinicians have also documented the impact of various strategies to develop the individual's control of affective states. These strategies include anxiety training programs (O'Neil & Richardson, 1977; Spielberger & Vagg, 1987), creativity training programs (e.g., Glynn, Britton, Semrud-Clikeman, & Muth, 1989), cognitive restructuring (Wise & Haynes, 1983), and attribution training programs (Graham, this volume). The fact that cognitive processes are conceived to operate to enhance or inhibit affective states raises questions about the inherent separation of the dimensions.

A third element in the erosion of boundaries inheres in the conceptualization of particular variables themselves. For example, is curiosity a cognitively enabled construct? How much do you need to know (prior knowledge) to be curious? How do puzzling or other logically dissonant task characteristics stimulate will? How much of curiosity is under direct cognitive control? Consider the variable of creativity. How much of creativity is knowledge-driven? How much do risk-taking and self-confidence contribute to creative behavior? The area of self-regulation also illustrates the merging of affective and cognitive dimensions (O'Neil, Sugrue, Abedi, Baker, & Golan, 1992). For example, is the propensity to plan and check principally an affective characteristic (finickiness) or a cognitive one (application of procedural knowledge)? Another set of questions deserving of more serious research concerns the impact of cultural factors on motivational states including differential effects of child-rearing and role expectation on motivational variables (e.g., Hawkins, this volume; Rueda & Moll, this volume).

Needs

If our goal is to develop individuals and groups that are capable, willing, and able to perform complex tasks under a wide range of conditions, attention must be devoted to determining training and maintenance conditions that will promote such abilities. While there are well known competing frameworks and strategies for the design of education and training to achieve cognitive outcomes, no comparable framework exists for training on the motivational dimension.

Alternative "training" strategies that emphasize extremely short interventions are much admired and applied by the business community. One common strategy is the use of motivational speakers to inspire and inculcate aspirations and values. These events are epitomized by Dodger coach Tommy Lasorda, who routinely provides the message "Ya' really gotta wanna" and other pithy comments to communicate the importance of motivation, caring, quality control, and other virtues. Motivation by quick, charismatic fix is the general idea. A related and similarly brief intervention involves the workshop focused on the transmission of a few basic precepts for application, such as the six steps to improve customer satisfaction, creativity and pride, etc. Rare, of course, is the availability of evidence, other than testimonial, about the impact of such strategies.

Yet, questions about training goals and strategies in the area of motivation and related motivational variables remain to be addressed in a coherent way, with a view to applications. This is one reason this volume on motivation was created.

ABOUT THIS VOLUME

This volume is divided into three major sections: Theoretical Approaches, Motivation of Groups, and Motivation of Individuals. What follows is a brief description of each chapter within the three major sections. The descriptions are meant to provide a "roadmap" for readers of different interests.

Theoretical Approaches

In their chapter, Locke and Latham provide a historical backdrop for the entire section. They identify goals as a powerful motivator. They present convincing evidence that the simplest reason for why some people perform better than others, controlling for ability and knowledge, is that they have different performance goals. Their exposition of this topic suggests ways to use goals effectively in applied settings. In general, the best performance is generated by assignment or adoption of challenging but achievable goals.

In the second chapter of this section, Sandra Graham presents some of her recent motivational research in the context of attribution theory (Weiner, 1992). The basic premise of this theory is that people attribute reasons to their performance, and such reasons determine the subsequent performance. This social cognitive approach to motivation is concerned with an individual's representation of his or her environment as a determinant of how he or she strives for achievement. In the context of this theory, Graham has investigated the implications of different feedback (e.g., praise vs. blame) that teachers give minority students and how this feedback influences self-perceived ability and effort. She also addresses various discipline problems, showing here, too, that attribution theory makes meaningful predictions. She describes her school-based cognitive instructional program to reduce peer-directed aggression.

In Chapter 4, McCombs explores the role of reflective self-awareness and understanding of self as an agent, which, she states, underlies performance and motivation. She focuses on beliefs as a basic set of filters (schemata) through which all information is acted on. She also discusses how various theoretical approaches can be used to design measures of motivation, and she suggests interventions to enhance such motivation. Research findings with military populations are also presented.

Snow and Jackson (Chapter 5) expand on the often neglected role of volition (e.g., will) in motivation. They review the constructs and measures that seem promising for research and evaluation. Such constructs include achievement orientation, anxiety, interests and styles, action controls, and effort. For example, in the area of achievement motivation, persistence and value are key constructs in the general area of conative constructs in this chapter. Persistence relates to the energy with which an individual pursues a goal. Value relates to the significance of the goal that the individual is seeking. An individual will pursue a highly valued goal with greater diligence. The authors present several taxonomies that both help to structure the literature in the area and suggest various R&D activities.

Both Hawkins (Chapter 6) and Rueda and Moll (Chapter 7) address how characteristics of individuals are based on social and cultural contexts, and, further, how such experiences help to determine people's ability to profit from learning. In both cases, the authors address the role of the greater society in which the individual lives and its subsequent effect on learning. Hawkins discusses how motivational factors in Asia differ from those in Western society and the subsequent effect on learning. He provides a cultural rationale of why Westerners may stereotype Asians, especially Japanese, as harder working, more disciplined, quiet, overachievers. He suggests that a main cultural influence is Confucianism in both its traditional and modern expressions. Rueda and Moll offer a sociocultural approach to motivation, suggesting that it is socially negotiated, socially distributed, and context specific. The influence of Vygotsky on their ideas is acknowledged. What a person finds motivating may depend on the culture in which the individual develops and the situation in which he or she acts. The authors provide examples from their work with Latino children. This work is an interesting blend of both qualitative and quantitative methodologies.

Motivation of Groups

In Chapter 8, Swezey, Meltzer, and Salas provide an intellectual framework for the entire Section II. One of the notable characteristics of the military and industry is the degree to which tasks are performed in teams. The area of collaborative learning in the civilian sector is a similar context. Although the role of individual motivation is certainly important to team performance, the interaction with other individuals completes the concept of motivation. Swezey, Meltzer, and Salas are among the first to study team motivation. They describe three issues of team motivation and goals: First, the goals of an individual team member may not be the goals of the team itself; second, individuals may not share the same goals; and third, there are varying interdependencies among team and individual goals. The authors provide both theoretical and empirical research on the factors that affect team motivation (e.g., team structure, cohesion).

The Army has generally assumed that both good leadership and highly motivated troops are necessary for effective combat operations. However, there was little understanding of the underlying relationship between motivation and leadership. Siebold (Chapter 9) describes research conducted with small groups of combat soldiers performing combat tasks in simulated battles. Siebold found that highly motivated troops were effective only when well-led. In fact, surprisingly, motivated troops actually performed less well than less motivated troops when they were poorly led. A further understanding of these relationships will be of immense importance to organizations in general.

In Chapter 10, Banks describes his research designed to better understand why motivational interventions sometimes fail to be reflected in performance gains. He identifies resistance as being a significant factor in defining the effectiveness of performance. This construct addresses the issue of why some individuals with sufficient ability and strong motivation do not perform well under certain supervisory conditions. Banks also describes a series of effects that he has observed when the similarity between individuals and their supervisors is systematically varied across gender and across race.

Franken and O'Neil (Chapter 11) examine to what degree trait and state anxiety influenced the performance of individuals and teams during high and low stress scenarios in a Navy team simulator. The environment of their research involved simulation in which performance of teams was assessed in lieu of the actual system. The simulator used in their research is the U.S. Navy's means of qualifying its antisubmarine warfare teams as combat-ready. The authors discuss their findings in terms of both cognitive (e.g., metacognition) and affective (e.g., anxiety) processes for both individuals and teams.

Motivation of Individuals

Spielberger and Starr (Chapter 12) provide a review of theory and research in curiosity. They view curiosity as reflecting an intense desire to seek out, explore, and understand new things in the environment. They review procedures for measuring curiosity as both a trait and state. Further, they offer a new theoretical position, an optimal stimulation/dual process theory of exploratory behavior. Finally, they report the findings of several empirical studies investigating the interactive effects of curiosity and anxiety.

In their chapter on measuring creativity, O'Neil, Abedi, and Spielberger review the literature on the nature, measurement and teaching of creativity, and suggest some necessary research activities to facility the teaching of creativity. With regard to measuring creativity, they suggest that the *Torrance Tests of Creative Thinking* (Torrance, 1974) is the best off-the-shelf measure. However, because many of the test items are open-ended, the test takes a considerable amount of time to administer and score. They also provide some suggestive evidence for a multiple-choice version of a creativity test. With regard to the teaching of creativity, there is no single off-the-shelf program that can be easily modified for teaching creativity to students. An R&D approach to create such a program is suggested.

Many organizations are concerned with the problem of motivating and educating students who have a history of poor performance in school (i.e., at-risk students). Pogrow and Londer (Chapter 14) suggest that for an educational program to have major effects, it must be carefully designed, highly systematic, creative, and provide extensive services. The Higher Order Thinking Skills (HOTS) program is an attempt to design such a program. This program is intensive in that it takes 35 minutes per day, 4–5 hours a week, for 2 years, including a higher order thinking approach to remedial education of disadvantaged children. Pogrow and London describe and review the research bases for the program and the hypotheses underlying motivational factors.

In the final chapter, Mael and White present a method to use motivational information to inform decisions regarding the downsizing of the Army (fewer people and less equipment). This downsizing requires that selection and classification be done with greater precision to utilize personnel more effectively. Their chapter attempts to measure the "will do" aspect of performance, rather than the "can do." The measures that they present are gathered from bio-data and temperament questionnaires. Motivational measures may also provide a means to more effectively select those recruits who do not otherwise meet current intellectual requirements.

ACKNOWLEDGMENTS

The research reported in this chapter was supported in part by the U.S. Army Research Institute for the Behavioral and Social Sciences through a subcontract with Battelle Institute. However, the views, opinions and/or findings contained in this report are the authors' and should not be construed as an official ARI position, policy, or decision, unless so designated by other official documentation.

Partial support was also provided by the National Center for Research on Evaluation, Standards, and Student Testing (CRESST) under the Educational

Research and Development Center Program cooperative agreement R117G10027 and CFDA catalog number 84.117G as administered by the Office of Educational Research and Improvement, U.S. Department of Education. The findings and opinions expressed in this chapter do not reflect the position or policies of the Office of Educational Research and Improvement or the U.S. Department of Education.

REFERENCES

Atkinson, J. W. (1974). Strength of motivation and efficiency of performance. In J. W. Atkinson & J. P. Raynor (Eds.), *Motivation and achievement* (pp. 193–218). Washington, DC: Winston.

Duesbury, R. T. (1992). *The effect of practice in a 3D CAD environment on a learner's ability to visualize objects from orthographic projections.* Unpublished doctoral dissertation, University of Southern California, Los Angeles.

Fleishman, E. A., & Zaccaro, S. J. (1992). Toward a taxonomy of team performance functions. In R. W. Swezey & E. Salas (Eds.), *Teams: Their training and performance* (pp. 31–56). Norwood, NJ: Ablex.

Glynn, S. M., Britton, B. K., Semrud-Clikeman, M., & Muth, K. D. (1989). Analogical reasoning and problem solving in science textbooks. In J. A. Glover, R. R. Ronning, & C. R. Reynolds (Eds.), *Handbook of creativity* (pp. 383–198). New York: Plenum Press.

Hembree, R. (1988). Correlates, causes, effects and treatment of test anxiety. *Review of Educational Research, 58*(1), 47–77.

Johnston, W. B., & Packer, A. (1987). *Workforce 2000. Work and workers for the 21st century.* Indianapolis, IN: Hudson Institute.

Kyllonen, P. C., Lohman, D. F., & Snow, R. E. (1984). Effects of aptitudes, strategy training, and task facets on spatial task performance. *Journal of Educational Psychology, 76*(1), 130–145.

Meichenbaum, D. N., & Butler, L. (1980). Towards a conceptual model for the treatment of test anxiety: Implications for research and treatment. In I. G. Sarason (Ed.), *Test anxiety, theory, research and application* (pp. 187–208). Hillsdale, NJ: Lawrence Erlbaum Associates.

Morris, L. W., Davis, M. A., & Hutchings, C. H. (1981). Cognitive and emotional components of anxiety: Literature review and a revised worry-emotionality scale. *Journal of Educational Psychology, 73*(4), 541–555.

National Research Council. (1992). *STAR 21. Strategic technologies for the Army of the twenty-first century.* Washington, DC: National Academy Press.

Office of the Assistant Secretary of Defense. (1992, June). *Military manpower report FY 1993.* Washington, DC: Office of the Assistant Secretary of Defense (Force Management & Personnel).

O'Neil, H. F., Jr., Allred, K., & Baker, E. L. (1992). *Measurement of workforce readiness competencies: Review of theoretical frameworks* (CSE Tech. Rep. 343). Los Angeles: University of California, Center for Research on Evaluation, Standards, and Student Testing. (ERIC Document Reproduction Service No. TM019392)

O'Neil, H. F., Jr., Baker, E., & Matsuura, S. (1992). Reliability and validity of Japanese trait and state worry and emotionality scales. *Anxiety, Stress, and Coping, 5*(3), 225–239.

O'Neil, H. F., Jr., & Fukumura, T. (1992). Relationship of worry and emotionality to test performance in a Juku environment. *Anxiety, Stress, and Coping, 5*(3), 241–251.

O'Neil, H. F., Jr., & Richardson, F. C. (1977). Anxiety and learning in computer-based learning environments: An overview. In J. Sieber, H. F. O'Neil, Jr., & S. Tobias (Eds.), *Anxiety, learning and instruction* (pp. 133–146). Hillsdale, NJ: Lawrence Erlbaum Associates.

O'Neil, H. F., Jr., Sugrue, B., Abedi, J., Baker, E., & Golan, S. (1992). *NAEP TRP Task 3a: Experimental motivation study. Final report of experimental studies on motivation and NAEP test performance* (Deliverable to NCES, Contract #RS90159001). Los Angeles: University of California, Center for Research on Evaluation, Standards, and Student Testing.

Sieber, J. E., O'Neil, H. F., Jr., & Tobias, S. (Eds.). (1977). *Anxiety, learning and instruction.* Hillsdale, NJ: Lawrence Erlbaum Associates.

Snow, R. E. (1989a). Aptitude-treatment interaction as a framework for research on learning and individual differences. In P. L. Ackerman, R. J. Sternberg, & R. Glaser (Eds.), *Learning and individual differences* (pp. 13–59). New York: Freeman.

Snow, R. E. (1989b). Toward assessment of cognitive and conative structures in learning. *Educational Researcher, 18*(9), 8–14.

Spangler, W. D. (1992). Validity of questionnaire and TAT measures of need for achievement: Two meta-analyses. *Psychological Bulletin, 112*(1), 140–154.

Spielberger, C. D. (1975). Anxiety: State-trait process. In C. D. Spielberger & I. G. Sarason (Eds.), *Stress and anxiety* (Vol. 1, pp. 115–143). Washington, DC: Hemisphere.

Spielberger, C. D. (1980). *Test anxiety inventory, preliminary professional manual.* Palo Alto, CA: Consulting Psychologists Press.

Spielberger, C. D., & Vagg, P. V. (1987). The treatment of test anxiety: A transactional model. In R. Schwarzer, H. M. Van der Ploeg, & C. D. Spielberger (Eds.), *Advances in test anxiety research* (Vol. 5, pp. 179–186). Lisse/Hillsdale, NJ: Swets & Seitlinger/Erlbaum.

Torrance, E. P. (1974). *Norm-technical manual: Torrance Tests of Creative Thinking.* Lexington: MA: Personnel Press.

Weiner, B. (1992). *Human motivation: Metaphors, theories, and research.* Newbury Park, CA: Sage Publications.

Wise, E. H., & Haynes, S. N. (1983). Cognitive treatment of test anxiety: Rational restructuring versus attentional training. *Cognitive Therapy and Research, 7*, 69–78.

I

THEORETICAL
APPROACHES

2 Goal Setting Theory

Edwin A. Locke
University of Maryland

Gary P. Latham
University of Toronto

In the 1960s, three approaches to the study of human motivation were dominant:

1. *Drive Theory.* Hull (1952), and others, asserted that motivation stemmed from physiological need deprivation which "drove" organisms to engage in random activity until, by chance, the need was satisfied and the drive was thus reduced. On subsequent occasions, cues in the situation would be recalled so that organisms would take suitable action rather than engage in random trial and error. This theory encountered numerous difficulties. For example, it was found that not all motivation stems from physiological needs (e.g., curiosity, self-efficacy). Second, not all need deprivation leads to an increase in drive (e.g., certain vitamin deficiencies). Third, partial need satisfaction sometimes leads to increased drive (e.g., as when the appetite is "whetted"). Finally, organisms, including people, often are motivated to engage in activities that increase rather than decrease tension (e.g., many purposeful human activities).

2. *Reinforcement Theory.* Skinner's (1953) approach to motivation was similar to drive theory except that the concept of an internal drive state was eliminated. Skinner asserted that behavior was controlled by reinforcements, which were consequences that followed behavior, making subsequent, similar responses more likely to occur in similar situations. Reinforcers were defined solely in terms of their effects. This behaviorist approach (along with that of drive theory) dominated the field of psychology for decades. It was based on the premise that human action could be understood without reference to consciousness. This premise was wrong (Binswanger, 1991) and led ultimately to the demise of behaviorism as a major intellectual force in psychology. Reinforcers (consequences of behavior) only affect subsequent action if the individual:

(a) anticipates that the reinforcer will follow future actions; (b) desires or values the reinforcer; (c) understands what actions need to be taken to get it; and (d) believes that he or she can take the requisite actions (Bandura, 1986; Locke, 1977). All of these contingencies entail the operation of consciousness, the very attribute which behaviorists denied or negated by arguing that thinking was an epiphenomenon caused by external forces.

3. *Subconscious Motives.*   An alternative approach to motivation was taken by David McClelland (1961). McClelland acknowledged the role of consciousness in human action—but stressed the subconscious part of consciousness in his own work. (We use the term consciousness to designate both the conscious and subconscious minds. By the subconscious we mean all of the person's knowledge, values, motives, beliefs, memories, etc. which are not, at any given time, in conscious awareness.) Thus he argued that human action was guided, in part, by subconscious motives (such as the achievement motive) which regulate human action over the long term. People with a strong achievement motive, for example, were said to choose activities in which: They can control the outcome through their own efforts, they believe the risks are moderate, they can obtain clear feedback concerning their progress, and they can experience the successful attainment of standards of excellence. According to McClelland, such a motive plays a crucial role in the success of people in entrepreneurial occupations, including sales. There is evidence to support McClelland's predictions with respect to entrepreneurship, and he and his colleagues have also studied other motives such as power and affiliation. A practical problem with this approach, however, is that every occupation presumably has a different motive pattern; thus a very large number of motives would have to be studied in order to make predictions of action in specific situations. Furthermore, this approach takes virtually no account of the individual's conscious convictions despite the introspectively verifiable fact that such convictions regulate our actions on a daily basis.

The approach to motivation via conscious goal setting was begun in the mid-1960s as an alternative to these approaches (though it had earlier precursors; see Ryan, 1970). Goal setting theory was based on the premise that much human action is purposeful, in that it is directed by conscious goals. Actually, goal directedness characterizes the actions of all living organisms including those of plants (Binswanger, 1991). At the lowest (vegetative) level of life, goal-directed action is physiologically controlled. The next highest level is present in the lower animals and entails conscious self-regulation through sensory-perceptual mechanisms including pleasure and pain. Human beings possess the highest form of consciousness, the capacity to reason. They have the power to choose their own goals and pursue long-range purposes (Locke, 1969). Purposeful action in human beings, unlike the lower animals, is volitional (Binswanger, 1991).

Goal setting theory,[1] as we have developed it within the realm of work, lies within the domain of purposefully directed action. Our theory addresses the question of why some people perform better on work tasks than others. Controlling for ability and knowledge, the answer must lie in the realm of motivation. Goal setting theory (most fully presented in Locke and Latham, 1990) approaches the issue of motivation from a conscious, first-level perspective (Ryan, 1970). The theory's core premise is that the simplest and most direct motivational explanation of why some people perform better on work tasks than others is because they have different performance goals.

Goal Attributes

The two attributes of goals that have been most extensively studied are *content* and *intensity*. Two aspects of content have been the main focus of the research to date, specificity and difficulty.

With regard to *specificity*, goal content can be vague ("work on this") or specific ("try for a score of 25 on this task within the next 10 minutes"). With regard to *difficulty*, goals can be easy ("try to get 10 items completed in the next 20 minutes"), moderate ("try to get 20 . . ."), difficult ("try to get 30 . . ."), or impossible ("try to get 100 . . ."). Difficulty pertains to a relationship between the person and the goal. The same goal can be easy for one person and hard for another depending on ability and experience. Generally, however, the higher the absolute *level* of the goal, the more difficult it is for people to attain it.

Over 400 studies have examined the relationship of difficulty and specificity to performance. It has been found consistently that performance is linearly related to goal level. Given sufficient ability and high commitment to the goal, the harder the goal the better the performance. This is because people adjust their effort to the difficulty of the task undertaken.

This linear function is different in shape than is predicted by Atkinson's (1958) version of achievement motivation theory which predicts a performance drop at the highest level of difficulty, thus yielding an inverse-U function. Goal theory predicts and finds a performance drop at high goal difficulty levels only if there is a large decrease in goal commitment (or a poor task strategy was used). Performance levels out, of course, when the limits of ability are reached.

A second consistent finding pertaining to goal content is that goals which are both specific and difficult lead to higher performance than vague but challenging goals such as "do your best," vague but unchallenging goals, or the setting of no goals. The superiority of specific, hard goals is due to the fact that vague goals are compatible with many different performance outcomes, including those that

---

[1]For further details on goal setting theory, see Latham and Locke (1991) and Locke and Latham (1990).

are less than the person's actual best. For example, Mento, Locke, and Klein (1992) found that people with "do best" goals anticipated more satisfaction from virtually every level of possible future performance than did people with specific, hard goals. The ambiguity inherent in do best goals allows people to give themselves the benefit of the doubt in evaluating their performance, that is, to feel satisfaction with low or modest performance. This is one reason do best subjects do not perform as well as those with specific hard goals.

There is substantial evidence for the generalizability of these core findings (Locke & Latham 1990). Goal setting studies have been conducted with 88 different tasks including bargaining, driving, faculty research, health promoting behaviors, logging, technical work, managerial work, management training, safety, and sports performance. Laboratory findings regarding goal setting replicate well in field settings. Nearly 40,000 subjects have been used in the goal setting studies, including males, females, Blacks, Whites, managers, students, engineers and scientists, and college professors. Although most studies were conducted in the United States and Canada, significant findings have been obtained as well in Australia, the Caribbean, England, Germany, Israel, and Japan. Thus it would appear that goal setting is applicable in different cultures; this should not be surprising in that purposeful action is characteristic of all humans beings.

A third finding pertaining to goal content, based on two studies, is that goal specificity divorced from difficulty, affects the variability of performance (Locke, Chah, Harrison, & Lustgarten, 1989). That is, people with very specific goals show less variation in performance than people with vague goals. As noted earlier, vague goals allow for many possible outcomes as compared to specific goals.

A second attribute of goals that has been studied is *intensity*. Intensity refers to the scope, clarity, and mental effort involved in mental processes (Rand, 1990). For example, Gollwitzer, Heckhausen, and Ratajczak (1990) found that subjects who thought most intensely about how to solve a problem (which involved attaining a personal goal) were most likely to become committed to solving it and subsequently to actually solve it.

The aspect of goal intensity that has been studied most frequently is *commitment*. Commitment refers to the degree to which an individual is attracted to the goal, considers it important, is determined to attain it, and sticks with it in the face of obstacles. The feeling of commitment does not automatically lead one to act. The ultimate proof of goal commitment is the taking of action. This reflects the thinking (or lack thereof) which preceded it and the volitional choice to act on the thinking (Binswanger, 1991). High commitment, is more likely to lead to goal attainment than low commitment.

There has been considerable controversy in the literature concerning the effectiveness of assigned (by the person in authority) versus participatively set goals (that is, set by mutual agreement) in achieving goal commitment and increasing performance on the part of subordinates. Ultimately it was discovered that goals that are assigned with a rationale (as to why the goal is desirable and/or reachable) are just as motivating as goals that are set participatively. Both procedures are more effective than curtly assigning a goal with no rationale as to why it should be attained (Latham, Erez, & Locke, 1988).

Commitment is enhanced when people believe that achieving the goal is *possible,* and that achieving the goal is *important* (Klein, 1991). The first class of factors raise what Bandura (1986) has labeled self-efficacy (task-specific self-confidence). These include ability, experience, training, information about appropriate task strategies, past success, and internal attributions (Locke & Latham, 1990). Those in authority can affect the second class of factors by explaining why the goal is important, exerting reasonable pressure for performance, being knowledgeable about the task and job, and serving as a role model for the behavior they desire in the subordinate (Locke & Latham, 1990).

It should be stressed that persuasive requests by authority figures do not compel commitment. Commitment is still a choice process; commitment from a subordinate is often easy for a manager to obtain precisely because the assigned goal *is* appraised as legitimate by the subordinate.

Peers can influence goal commitment by conveying normative information and inspiring competition. Agreeing publicly to strive for a goal can also enhance commitment relative to private agreement (Hollenbeck, Williams, & Klein, 1989).

Recent research (Lee, Locke, & Phan, 1992) has found that the role of incentives in generating commitment is a complex one. Offering bonuses for pursuing unreachable goals can actually lower performance. Offering bonuses for reaching easy goals can aid commitment, but the commitment is to *low* performance due to the fact that the goals are easy. Bonuses for moderate goals appear most likely to promote high performance.

Goal Choice

The factors that affect goal choice are similar to those that influence goal commitment. The probability of choosing to pursue a given goal is increased if the person thinks that it can be attained. People with high self-efficacy are more likely than those with low self-efficacy to choose hard goals (Locke, Frederick, Lee, & Bobko, 1984).

Choice is also affected by the person's belief that a given goal is important or desirable. The perceived importance or desirability is enhanced when a person is provided with normative information, role models, competition, or pressure (Locke & Latham, 1990). However, the most direct method of influencing choice is simply for a legitimate authority figure to assign the goal.

FIG. 2.1.   Relation of ability, self-efficacy, goals, and performance.

Goals, Self-Efficacy, and Performance

It has been shown consistently that self-efficacy (task-specific self-confidence) has direct effects on performance (Bandura, 1986). This finding holds for goals as well. Thus, both goals and self-efficacy have direct, independent effects on performance. Self-efficacy also can affect performance indirectly by affecting goal choice and commitment. Further, assigning goals influences both personal goals and self-efficacy: People who are assigned challenging goals are more likely to have high self-efficacy than those who are assigned low goals since the assignment of high goals is in itself an expression of confidence (Salancik, 1977). The foregoing relationships are summarized in Fig. 2.1.

Goals, Valences, and Instrumentalities

Garland (1985) reported a *negative* relationship between goal level and valence. The latter was defined as anticipated satisfaction with attaining each of a number of performance levels. This finding was also obtained by Klein (1991) as well as in a series of studies by Mento et al. (1992). The explanation for this finding is that goals are at the same time both targets to shoot for and standards for evaluating one's performance (Bandura, 1986). If one views one's goals as minimally acceptable levels of performance, we can see that a person with low goals will be satisfied with reaching a low level of performance and thus even more satisfied if more than this minimal level is attained. A person with high goals, on the other hand, will be only minimally satisfied with reaching a high goal and thus will be quite dissatisfied with reaching a low goal.

Although high goals make it harder to gain success and therefore satisfaction, such goals are more instrumental in gaining practical as well as psychological benefits than are low goals. MBA students, for example reported that the higher their grade point average, the greater the anticipated benefits with respect to personal pride, as well as school, future job, and life outcomes (Mento et al., 1992).

Goals and Feedback

Goals and feedback together are more effective in motivating high performance or performance improvement than either is alone (Locke & Latham, 1990). The goal identifies what object or outcome one should aim for and is the standard by which one evaluates one's performance; feedback provides information as to the degree to which the standard is being met. If performance meets or exceeds the standard, performance is typically either maintained or increased. If performance falls below the standard, subsequent improvement will occur to the degree that: (a) the individual expects to be dissatisfied with that level of performance in the future; (b) the individual has high self-efficacy; and (c) the individual sets a goal to improve over his past level of performance. The joint effect of these three factors is shown in Fig. 2.2, based on research by Bandura and Cervone (1986).

Goal Mechanisms

There are three direct mechanisms by which goals regulate performance. First, goals *direct* activity toward actions that are goal relevant to it at the expense of actions that are not relevant. Second, goals regulate *effort* expenditure in that people adjust their effort to the difficulty level of the task or goal. Third, goals affect the *persistence* of action in situations where there are no time limits. An aspect of persistence is tenacity—the refusal to quit, despite setbacks, until the goal is reached. Tenacity is affected by *both* commitment and goal difficulty.

When these direct mechanisms are insufficient to attain a goal, individuals

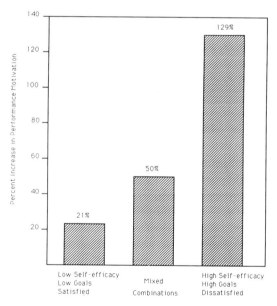

FIG. 2.2. The joint effects on performance improvement of self-efficacy, goals, and anticipated satisfaction. From Locke and Latham (1990).

typically search for new task strategies in order to attain their goals. This is especially the case on complex tasks where effort, direction of attention, and persistence alone are not sufficient unless accompanied by suitable strategies.

Goals and task strategies are related in the following ways:

1. Specific, challenging goals stimulate planning in general and sometimes higher quality planning than is the case with do best goals (Smith, Locke & Barry, 1990).

2. People may lower quality as an implicit strategy to attain hard, quantitative goals.

3. The most challenging area for goal setting theory from the point of view of task strategies pertains to the realm of complex tasks. On complex tasks there are many more possible strategies than in the case of simple tasks and many of these strategies may be poor ones. Thus choosing a good strategy becomes more critical if goal success and high performance are to be attained. In support of this reasoning, Chesney and Locke (1991) found in a management simulation that goal difficulty was more strongly related to task performance among subjects who used more suitable strategies than among those who used less suitable strategies. They also found that, in general, task strategies (measured as frequency of use of suitable strategies) were more highly related to performance than were goals.

What is not well understood so far are the conditions under which people working on complex tasks are most likely to formulate effective strategies under different types of goals. For example, sometimes people working for hard goals will choose poor strategies and as a result will perform no better than or even more poorly than people working for easy or do best goals. In such cases the hard goal subjects appear to *panic* in the face of trying frequent but unsystematic strategy changes; as a result they never learn the best way to perform the task. Under less stringent goals subjects may be more patient in developing and testing strategy hypotheses. This failure of goal difficulty to facilitate performance seems especially likely to occur when subjects are asked to perform a complex task in which they have had no prior training (Earley, Conolly, & Ekegren, 1989; Huber, 1985; Kanfer & Ackerman, 1989). On the other hand, when subjects *are* given training in the proper strategies, they are more likely to actually *use* them subsequently when given specific hard goals than when given easy or vague goals. Thus while hard goals might retard strategy discovery, they may facilitate strategy implementation (Locke & Latham, 1990). The latter finding makes sense if one considers that using the trained strategies may be the only way to attain the hard goals.

If we were to speculate on the conditions that would be most likely to facilitate the *discovery* of suitable strategies on complex tasks, we would predict that the key factors would include:

(a) past experience, so that there is a base of knowledge on which suitable strategies can be built;

(b) formal training in techniques for discovering strategies, that is, meta-strategy training (e.g., showing people how to vary one factor at a time when there are multiple possible causes of an effect; showing them how to break large tasks into smaller ones, etc.);

(c) giving subjects a learning period, without any pressure for results, during which they could feel free to try out various possibilities;

(d) raising subjects' initial self-efficacy by persuading them that highly effective task strategies exist and that they were highly capable of discovering them;

(e) allowing or encouraging subjects to search for effective strategies from sources external to the group (e.g., outside experts, business competitors). These hypotheses, of course, remain to be tested.

In situations in which effective task strategies are already known, naturally the most efficient procedure is formal training in those strategies.

Other Moderators

In addition to commitment, feedback, and task complexity, there are at least two additional moderators of the goal-performance relationship. Obviously, ability limits the goal-performance relationship at very high goal levels because such goals exceed the reach of most people (Locke, 1982). A second additional moderator involves situational constraints (Peters, Chassie, Lindholm, O'Connor, & Kline, 1982).

Goals and Affect

The basic model for understanding the relationship between goals and affect comes from Locke's (1976) satisfaction theory (based on Rand, 1964) which states that emotional responses are the result of automatic, subconscious value appraisals (Locke & Latham, 1990). Goals are valued or desired outcomes. Thus, the greater the degree of success experienced, the greater the degree of satisfaction with performance. When a person works toward an end goal across a number of trials, satisfaction with performance on any given trail is a joint function of (a) the degree of discrepancy between goals and performance for that trial; and (b) the perceived instrumentality of performance on that trial for attaining the end goal (Locke, Cartledge, & Knerr, 1970). Small discrepancies are usually more instrumental for long-term success than are large ones. The more important the goal, the more intense the affect experienced after both success and failure (Locke, 1976). Goals may also increase task interest and reduce boredom, at least on those tasks that are initially boring (Latham & Kinne, 1974; Locke & Bryan, 1967).

Because goal success is more frequent when goals are easy, it means that easy goals produce more satisfaction than hard goals. In contrast, higher performance is achieved when goals are difficult. This poses a dilemma: How does one balance the two outcomes? There are several possible solutions:

1. Set moderate goals so that the net total of satisfaction and productivity is maximized.

2. Give credit for partial goal attainment, rather than only for goal success.

3. Apply the Japanese principle of *Kaizen* or continuous improvement (Imai, 1986). Make goals moderately difficult at any given time, but insist on constantly raising the goals by small amounts.

4. Use multi-level goal and reward structures, so that increasingly greater rewards are given for attaining increasingly higher goal levels. As yet there has been no research comparing the effectiveness of these four procedures.

The High Performance Cycle

The integrated goal setting model has been called the high performance cycle (Locke & Latham, 1990). The model starts with challenge in the form of specific, difficult goals. If there is high commitment to these goals, feedback, high self-efficacy (and ability) and appropriate task strategies, high performance will result. If high performance leads to desired rewards (including self-rewards) high satisfaction will result. Job satisfaction is, in turn, highly associated with commitment to the job (Locke & Latham, 1990). High commitment in turn is associated with an increased propensity to stay on the job (Mowday, Porter, & Steers, 1982). People who are satisfied and stay on the job are then willing to accept new challenges. Deviations from the requirements of the high performance cycle (e.g., low challenge, lack of rewards) lead to a low performance cycle.

Self-Regulation

The need for reducing management layers in today's organizations in order to reduce costs, and the simultaneous need to meet employee demands for jobs that will challenge and motivate them has resulted in an ongoing interest by both management and employees in the principles of self-regulation. Self-regulation refers to the fact that people do more than simply react to external influences in that they select, organize, and transform the stimuli that impinge upon them (Bandura, 1977, 1986). Through self-set goals and self-administered incentives, people learn how to exert control over their own actions.

Self-regulation is implicit in goal setting theory because, as noted throughout this chapter, the setting of goals and their translation into action is a volitional process (Binswanger, 1991). However, most goal setting experiments have not emphasized self-regulation explicitly because the goals were assigned in order to ensure sufficient variation in goal type and level.

The predominant theory of self-regulation in psychology is Bandura's (1986) social cognitive theory. Unlike Skinner's philosophy of behaviorism discussed in our introduction, social cognitive theory recognizes that people choose goals and that goals influence how they act. This theory, therefore, is congruent with goal setting theory. Both theories acknowledge that certain properties of goals influence self-evaluation. For example, goal specificity enhances one's awareness of the type and amount of effort required to attain the goal. Further, a goal that is specific provides a clear benchmark for judging personal accomplishment. In contrast to specific goals, general goals provide much less basis for regulating effort or evaluating performance.

A second property of goals that affects the self-evaluation that accompanies variations in one's performance is the level of difficulty at which the goals are set. When goals are too difficult for the individual to attain, performance is likely to be self-evaluated as disappointing. Efforts that produce repeated failure can weaken one's self-efficacy. Consequently, Bandura (1977) concluded that goals of "moderate difficulty are therefore likely to be most motivating and at the same time satisfying" (p. 162). This conclusion is consistent with applications of goal setting theory in field settings, namely the setting of goals that are difficult but attainable (e.g., Latham & Kinne, 1974), because satisfaction as well as performance is desired in those settings.

Bandura's (1982) concept of self-efficacy, as noted earlier, is an integral part of goal setting theory. Self-efficacy is a judgment of "how well one can execute courses of action required to deal with prospective situations" (p. 122). It is based on one's assessment of all personal factors that could affect one's performance such as past performance, ability, adaptability, capacity to coordinate skilled sequences of actions, resourcefulness, etc.

Because self-efficacy ratings are always performance based, it does not apply to goals as such. However, commitment to a hard goal is obviously higher when self-efficacy for a task is high as opposed to low. This is because high self-efficacy keeps people committed to a course of action, especially when pursuing that course of action involves overcoming setbacks, failures, and obstacles. For example, Bandura and Cervone (1986) found that when people were given feedback indicating their performance was below their goal, subsequent effort was higher for those with high than for those with low self-efficacy.

Proximal Goals.   The extant research on the relative effectiveness of proximal versus distal goals has yielded inconsistent results (Locke & Latham, 1990). However, a recent study by Stock and Cervone (1990) suggests that proximal goals do indeed affect self-regulatory processes, which in turn affect performance in at least four ways.

1. The assignment of a proximal goal increases the strength of the person's self-efficacy for completing a complex task. People who had been assigned a proximal goal in addition to the distal goal of task completion had significantly higher initial ratings of self-efficacy than did those people who only had a distal goal. Mentally "breaking down" the task makes it appear manageable which in turn enhances the person's perception that he is capable of performing effectively.

2. Reaching the proximal goal enhances one's self-efficacy. As people attained the subgoal they became more confident of their capability to complete the task. Those people who reached the same level of performance without knowing that they had achieved a proximal goal showed no increase in self-efficacy.

3. The attainment of the proximal goal also positively affects *self-evaluative reactions*. Those who achieved the proximal goal were more satisfied with their progress than were those people who did not attain the subgoal of those people who had not been assigned one to attain.

4. Those people with proximal goals persisted on the task significantly longer than did those people who did not have proximal goals. Stock and Cervone (1990) concluded that when individuals are uncertain of their ability to perform a complex challenging endeavor, setting proximal goals can influence positively self-referent thought, motivation, and performance.

There are circumstances, however, where proximal goals may fail to enhance performance. In long-term programs of behavior change, where the person has a high degree of interest in it, moderately distal goals can allow greater flexibility in use of tactics than proximal goals (Kanfer & Grimm, 1978; Manderlink & Harackiewicz, 1984). The demanding standards represented by specific proximal goals on such tasks can impair thinking and problem solving activities by diverting attention to only task-outcome related activities (Bandura & Wood, 1989).

Using a complex computer simulation game over 10 weeks of business activity, Cervone, Jiwani, and Wood (1989) investigated whether different goal structures affected the strength of relations between self-regulatory processes and performance. To optimize performance, the subjects were required to learn a large number of nonlinear and compound rules that are especially difficult to master.

Consistent with goal setting theory, the assigned goals, which in this study were distal, affected the subjects' use of analytic strategies. Specifically, those people who were assigned a specific distal goal were more systematic in their testing of analytic strategies for managing the simulated organization than were the people who were not assigned goals. Those people with moderate versus very difficult distal goals did not differ on this dimension.

Again, consistent with goal setting theory, the higher goals led to higher levels of performance than did the moderately difficult goals. In both goal conditions, higher levels of self-efficacy, self-satisfaction with performance, and personal (self-set) goals predicted higher levels of performance. In contrast, the authors found no evidence of a positive relation between performance and either self-efficacy or self-evaluative reactions within the no-goal condition. When subjects were trying "to do their best," variations in performance feedback were unrelated to either self-evaluative reactions or self-efficacy judgments. The authors concluded that assigned goals imposed a standard for performance that strongly affected self-reactions and their role in the self-regulation of task performance.

The emphasis thus far in this chapter has been primarily on motivation. However, performance is a function of ability as well as motivation. Ability, as noted earlier, is a moderator of the effects of goals on performance. Training is often needed to give people skills in self-regulation. For example, Brief and Hollenbeck (1985) found that salespeople, in the absence of training, failed to demonstrate adequate skills in this area. The benefit of such training is discussed next.

Training in Self-Management.   Training in self-management focuses on goal setting and its moderators: ability, commitment, feedback, task complexity, and situational constraints. For example, skills in self-management have been taught to unionized state government employees to use to increase their job attendance (Frayne & Latham, 1987; Latham & Frayne, 1989).

The training program consisted of 8 weekly 1-hour group sessions. In the first week, an orientation session was conducted to explain the principles of the training program. In the second session, trainees listed the reasons why they had difficulty getting to work. The third session focused on the setting of specific attendance goals. In the fourth session, trainees were taught the importance of self-monitoring their attendance through the use of graphs and to record in diaries the reasons for missing a day of work, as well as the steps that were followed to subsequently get to work. In the fifth session, trainees identified rewards and punishers to self-administer as a result of attaining or failing to attain the proximal goal. In the sixth session, trainees wrote a behavioral contract with themselves that specified the goals to be achieved, the time frame for achieving them, the consequences for attaining or failing to attain them, and the behaviors necessary for attaining the goals. The seventh training session emphasized the importance of maintenance. The discussion focused on issues that might result in a relapse in absenteeism, planning for such situations should they occur, and developing coping strategies for dealing with these situations. During the final (eighth) week of training, the trainer reviewed each technique presented in the training, answered questions from the trainees regarding these skills, and clarified expectations for the self-management of the training program's effectiveness.

The moderating variable, ability, was strengthened in the group discussion where employees brainstormed strategies for overcoming obstacles to coming to work. Thus it is not surprising that the study showed that there was a main effect of training on self-efficacy, and that self-efficacy correlated positively with subsequent job attendance. The effect of training on self-efficacy is shown in Fig. 2.3. Latham, Winters, and Locke (1991) found that the benefit of participating in decision making is completely mediated by these two cognitive variables, namely task strategies and self-efficacy. This is especially true when the task is perceived as complex by the individual. By pooling different ideas, individuals can increase their ability to solve problems, which in turn increases their conviction that the problems can be solved by them. Task complexity and situational constraints were focused on in sessions 2 and 7 of the Frayne and Latham (1987) studies.

Goal commitment, the focus of the fifth and sixth sessions occurred through the self-selection and self-administration of rewards and punishers and the writ-

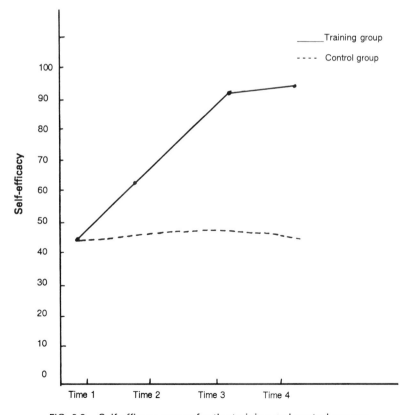

FIG. 2.3. Self-efficacy scores for the training and control groups.

ing of the behavioral contract. Such consequences affect behavior largely through their informative and incentive value. Thus, they influence behavior antecedently by creating expectations of outcomes on future occasions (Bandura, 1977). In this way the likelihood of particular actions was increased by anticipated reward and reduced by anticipated punishment.

The moderating variable, feedback, was the focus of training in the fourth session. Knowledge of results, as mentioned earlier, takes on significance in relation to the person's goals. Feedback, which shows that a person's performance is in alignment with one's goals not only sustains effort and creates self-satisfaction, but it often results in the raising of goals for subsequent performance (Bandura, 1977).

With the goal setting programs in place, Frayne and Latham (1987) found that 3 months later employee attendance was significantly higher in the training than in the control group. Latham and Frayne (1989) conducted a 6-month and 9-month follow-up study to determine the long-term effects of this training. Employees who had been trained in self-management continued to have higher job attendance than those in the control group. Moreover, when the people in the control group were subsequently given the same training in self-management, but by a different trainer, they too showed the same positive improvement in their self-efficacy with regard to coping with obstacles perceived by them as preventing them from coming to work. Moreover, their job attendance increased to the same level as that which the original training group had achieved 3 months after it had been trained.

CONCLUSION

More than 25 years of research have strongly supported the usefulness of approaching the study of motivation from the viewpoint of conscious goals (Locke & Latham, 1990). Current goal setting research is moving in many directions. Among the issues now being studied are: goals as performance mediators of the effects of monetary incentives on activity; factors affecting performance, including the choice of strategies, when goals are hard and the tasks complex; the relationship of conscious and subconscious motivation; and the effects of goal conflict on performance.

ACKNOWLEDGMENTS

The research reported in this chapter was supported in part by the U.S. Army Research Institute for the Behavioral and Social Sciences through a subcontract with Battelle Institute. However, the views, opinions and/or findings contained in this report are the authors' and should not be construed as an official ARI position, policy, or decision, unless so designated by other official documentation.

REFERENCES

Atkinson, J. W. (1958). Towards experimental analysis of human motivation in terms of motives, expectancies, and incentives. In J. W. Atkinson (Ed.), *Motives in fantasy, action and society.* Princeton, NJ: Van Nostrand.

Bandura, A. (1977). *Social learning theory.* Englewood Cliffs, NJ: Prentice Hall.

Bandura, A. (1982). Self-efficacy mechanism in human agency. *American Psychologist, 37,* 122–47.

Bandura, A. (1986). *Social foundations of thought and action: A social-cognitive theory.* Englewood Cliffs, NJ: Prentice Hall.

Bandura, A., & Cervone, D. (1986). Differential engagement of self-reactive influences in cognitive motivation. *Organizational Behavior and Human Decision Processes, 38,* 92–113.

Bandura, A., & Wood, R. E. (1989). Effect of perceived controllability and performance standards on self-regulation of complex decision-making. *Journal of Personality and Social Psychology, 56,* 805–814.

Binswanger, H. (1991). Volition as cognitive self-regulation. *Organizational Behavior and Human Decision Processes, 50,* 154–178.

Brief, A. P., & Hollenbeck, J. R. (1985). An exploratory study of self-regulating activities and their effects on job performance. *Journal of Occupational Behavior, 6,* 197–208.

Cervone, D., Jiwani, N., & Wood, R. (1989). *Goal-setting and the differential influence of self-regulatory processes on complex decision-making performance.* Paper presented at the Annual Convention of the American Psychological Association, New Orleans, LA.

Chesney, A. A., & Locke, E. A. (1991). Relationships among goal difficulty, business strategies and performance on a complex management simulation task. *Academy of Management Journal, 34,* 400–424.

Earley, P. C., Connolly, T., & Ekegren, G. (1989). Goals, strategy development and task performance: Some limits on the efficacy of goal setting. *Journal of Applied Psychology, 74,* 24–33.

Frayne, C. A., & Latham, G. P. (1987). Application of social learning theory to employee self-management of attendance. *Journal of Applied Psychology, 72,* 387–392.

Garland, H. (1985). A cognitive mediation theory of task goals and human performance. *Motivation and Emotion, 9,* 345–367.

Gollwitzer, P. M., Heckhausen, H., & Ratajczak, K. (1990). From weighing to willing: Approaching a change decision through prior or postdecisional mentation. *Organizational Behavior and Human Decision Processes, 45,* 41–65.

Hollenbeck, J. R., Williams, C. R., & Klein, H. J. (1989). An empirical examination of the antecedents of commitment to difficult goals. *Journal of Applied Psychology, 74,* 18–23.

Huber, V. L. (1985). Effects of task difficulty, goal setting, and strategy on performance of a heuristic task. *Journal of Applied Psychology, 70,* 492–504.

Hull, C. L. (1952). *A behavior system: An introduction to behavior theory concerning the individual organism.* New Haven, CT: Yale University Press.

Imai, M. (1986). *Kaizen: The key to Japan's competitive success.* New York: Random House.

Kanfer, F. H., & Grimm, L. G. (1978). Managing clinical change. *Behavior Modification, 4,* 419–444.

Kanfer, R., & Ackerman, P. L. (1989). Motivation and cognitive abilities: An integrative aptitude-treatment interaction approach to skill acquisition. *Journal of Applied Psychology, 74,* 657–690.

Klein, H. J. (1991). Further evidence on the relationship between goal setting and expectancy theories. *Organizational Behavior and Human Decision Processes, 49,* 230–257.

Latham, G. P., Erez, M., & Locke, E. A. (1988). Resolving scientific disputes by the joint design of crucial experiments by the antagonists: Application to the Erez-Latham dispute regarding participation in goal setting. *Journal of Applied Psychology* (Monograph), *73,* 753–772.

Latham, G. P., & Frayne, C. A. (1989). Self-management training for increasing job attendance: A follow-up and a replication. *Journal of Applied Psychology, 74,* 411–416.

Latham, G. P., & Kinne, S. B. (1974). Improving job performance through training in goal setting. *Journal of Applied Psychology, 59,* 187–191.

Latham, G. P., & Locke, E. A. (1991). Self regulation through goal setting. *Organizational Behavior and Human Decision Processes, 50,* 212–247.

Latham, G. P., Winters, D. C., & Locke, E. A. (1991). *Cognitive and motivational mediators of the effects of participation on performance.* University of Toronto, Unpublished manuscript.

Lee, T. W., Locke, E. A., & Phan, S. H. (1992). *Explaining the assigned goal-incentive interaction: The role of self-efficacy, and personal goals.* University of Washington, Unpublished manuscript.

Locke, E. A. (1969). Purpose without consciousness: A contradiction. *Psychological Reports, 25,* 991–1009.

Locke, E. A. (1976). The nature and causes of job satisfaction. In M. Dunnette (Ed.), *Handbook of industrial and organizational psychology,* Chicago: Rand McNally.

Locke, E. A. (1977). The myths of behavior mod in organizations. *Academy of Management Review, 2,* 543–553.

Locke, E. A. (1982). Relation of goal level to performance with a shortwork period and multiple goal levels. *Journal of Applied Psychology, 67,* 512–514.

Locke, E. A., & Bryan, J. F. (1967). Performance goals as determinants of level of performance and boredom. *Journal of Applied Psychology, 51,* 120–130.

Locke, E. A., Cartledge, N., & Knerr, C. (1970). Studies of the relationship between satisfaction, goal setting and performance. *Organizational Behavior and Human Performance, 5,* 135–58.

Locke, E. A., Chah, D. O., Harrison, D. S., & Lustgarten, N. (1989). Separating the effects of goal specificity from goal level. *Organizational Behavior and Human Decision Processes, 43,* 270–287.

Locke, E. A., Frederick, E., Lee, C., & Bobko, P. (1984). Effect of self-efficacy, goals, and task strategies on task performance, *Journal of Applied Psychology, 69,* 241–251.

Locke, E. A., & Latham, G. P. (1990). *A theory of goal setting and task performance.* Englewood Cliffs, NJ: Prentice-Hall.

Manderlink, G., & Harackiewicz, J. M. (1984). Proximal versus distal goal setting and intrinsic motivation. *Journal of Personality and Social Psychology, 47,* 918–928.

McClelland, D. C. (1961). *The achieving society.* New York: Van Nostrand.

Mento, A. J., Locke, E. A., & Klein, H. J. (1992). Relationship of goal level to valence and instrumentality. *Journal of Applied Psychology, 77,* 395–405.

Mowday, R. T., Porter, L. W., & Steers, R. M. (1982). *Employee-organization linkages.* New York: Academic Press.

Peters, L. H., Chassie, M. B., Lindholm, H. R., O'Connor, E. J., & Kline, C. R. (1982). The joint influence of situational constraints and goal setting on performance and affective outcomes. *Journal of Management, 8,* 7–20.

Rand, A. (1964). The Objectivist ethics. In A. Rand (Ed.), *The virtue of selfishness.* New York: New American Library.

Rand, A. (1990). *Introduction to Objectivist epistemology.* H. Binswanger & L. Peikoff (Eds.), New York: New American Library.

Ryan, T. A. (1970). *Intentional behavior.* New York: Ronald Press.

Salancik, G. R. (1977). Commitment and the control of organizational behavior and belief. In B. M. Staw & G. R. Salancik (Eds.), *New directions in organizational behavior.* Chicago: St. Clair Press.

Skinner, B. F. (1953). *Science and human behavior.* New York: Macmillan.

Smith, K. G., Locke, E. A., & Barry, D. (1990). Goal setting, planning and organizational performance: An experimental simulation. *Organizational Behavior and Human Decision Processes, 46,* 118–134.

Stock, J., & Cervone, D. (1990). Proximal goal setting and self-regulatory processes. *Cognitive Therapy and Research, 14,* 483–498.

3 Classroom Motivation From an Attributional Perspective

Sandra Graham
University of California, Los Angeles

Psychologists study motivation to understand why people think and behave as they do. Applied to achievement contexts like classrooms, we would be addressing motivational concerns if we were to ask, for example: Why do some children persist to task completion despite enormous difficulty, while others give up at the slightest provocation? Why do some individuals believe that effort pays off and others do not? Or, what accounts for the fact that some children set such unrealistically high goals for themselves that failure is bound to occur?

Rather than take a more traditional approach and focus on personality traits or specific behavior as a way of addressing questions such as these, in this chapter I adopt a social cognitive approach to the study of motivation. A social cognitive approach to motivation is concerned with an individual's cognitive representation of his or her environment—that is, perceptions, inferences, and interpretations of social experience as determinants of achievement strivings. For example, a cognitive social psychologist might investigate how a student interprets praise from her teacher as a guide to inferences about her own competence: Did my teacher praise me because she believes me to be a capable student? Or does she simply want to protect my feelings because she does not think much of my ability? The particular social cognitive representations addressed in this chapter are causal attributions, or inferences about why outcomes occur. Causal attributions are central to a theory of motivation that has proved to be exceedingly rich and applicable to a wide range of achievement-related concerns (see reviews in Graham, 1991; Weiner, 1985a, 1986). A major goal of this chapter is to demonstrate how this theory can be a useful conceptual framework for investigating motivational phenomena that often occur in classroom contexts.

The following sections begin with a brief introduction to causal attributions and their underlying properties. This will be followed by a review of research on both antecedents and consequences of causal ascriptions that my students and I have conducted over the past several years. On the antecedent side, I consider some of the situational factors, including teacher feedback, that influence self-perceived ability and effort. On the consequence side, I focus on some recent research on the effects of particular attributions on peer-directed aggression. Throughout the chapter, the implications of the research for understanding motivation in the classroom are highlighted.

CAUSAL ATTRIBUTIONS

"Why did I get a poor grade on the exam?" Why didn't I make the team? Why don't my classmates like me?" The answers to such queries are causal attributions. As implied in these examples, some categories of experience are particularly conducive to causal search. For example, we are more likely to want to know *why* following failure rather than success and in response to unexpected as opposed to anticipated outcomes (Weiner, 1985b). Causal search is therefore functional because it may impose order on a sometimes uncertain environment.

In achievement contexts, causal attributions are most directly concerned with the perceived causes of success and failure. A number of studies have documented that success and failure often are attributed to some ability factor that includes both aptitude and acquired skills, an exertion factor that includes both temporary and sustained effort, the difficulty of the task, luck, mood, family background, and help or hindrance from others. Among these causal ascriptions, in this culture at least, ability and effort are the most dominant perceived causes of success and failure. When explaining achievement outcomes, individuals attach the most importance to their perceived competencies and how hard they try. That is, when someone succeeds, they probably say, "I worked hard" or "I am smart"; and if they don't succeed, they are likely to conclude that "I did not work hard enough" or "I am not very smart."

Causal Dimensions

Attributional judgments are phenomenological; they depict the causal world as perceived by the actor. Thus, attributional content will certainly vary between individuals and there may be an infinite number of perceived causes for success or failure. It has therefore been necessary for the theory to focus on causal *meaning* in addition to specific causes per se.

It appears that meaning is determined in part by the underlying properties of perceived causes. Now what is meant by causal properties? Let me first illustrate with a nonsocial example. If we give students a variety of round objects that also differ in other ways such as color or size, and a variety of square objects that also differ in these other ways, and we ask our students to then sort these objects into

TABLE 3.1
Effort and Ability Attributions Related to Causal Dimensions

	Causes	
Causal Dimension	Effort	Ability
Locus	internal	internal
Stability	unstable	stable
Controllability	controllable	uncontrollable

two meaningful piles, the round objects will probably be put in one pile and the square objects in another. Shape is therefore one of the perceived underlying properties of these objects.

Causal attributions also have underlying properties, although these are psychological rather than physical representations. Three such properties, labeled causal dimensions, have been identified. They are locus, or whether a cause is internal or external to the person; stability, which designates a cause as constant or varying over time; and controllability (responsibility), or whether a cause is or is not subject to volitional influence.

All causes are classifiable within one of the eight cells of a locus × stability × controllability dimension matrix. To illustrate, Table 3.1 shows the dimensional placement of effort and ability, the two most dominant causal ascriptions. It can be seen that effort is perceived as internal, unstable, and controllable. Failure ascriptions to lack of effort thus indicate a personal characteristic that is modifiable by one's own volitional behavior. The dimensional placement of ability, on the other hand, indicates that this cause is internal, stable, and uncontrollable. That is, when we attribute failure to low ability, we tend to see this as a characteristic of ourselves, enduring over time, and beyond our personal control.

These conceptual distinctions between causes are central to an attributional theory of motivation because each dimension is uniquely related to a particular set of psychological consequences. I return to this issue in a later section where I discuss some recent findings on the consequences of perceived controllability in others among school aged boys labeled as aggressive. For now, however, I want to move backward in a motivational sequence to examine some of the antecedents or determinants of particular self-ascriptions.

ATTRIBUTIONAL ANTECEDENTS

How do students arrive at attributions about, for example, ability versus effort? It is evident that teachers are constantly asking themselves: "Did the student fail because she did not try hard enough or because she is not able?". And students are constantly asking themselves this same question. Therefore one implication of these kinds of self-reflective processes is that what one learns in the classroom is not only related to subject matter. Equally important, one learns about oneself when they ask such questions as: Am I smart? Am I willing to do what it takes? *Can* I succeed?

Attribution research has identified a number of informational cues, such as prior performance history and social norm information, that influence causal attributions (Kelley & Michela, 1980). If I as a student have been doing poorly in a course all semester, or if I fail a test and everyone else gets an "A," both of these are very salient sources of information that I might use to infer that I have low ability.

Indirect Attributional Cues

In contrast to these more straightforward causal cues, other sources of attributional information may be more subtle and indirect. This appears to be particularly the case when the source of the information is the teacher. Teachers no doubt often directly and intentionally tell their students that they did not put forth enough effort, for trying hard has moral implications and is certainly compatible with the work ethic espoused in school. On the other hand, although teachers typically do not intentionally tell their students that they are low in ability, this attributional information may subtly, indirectly, and even unknowingly be conveyed. This unintended communication of low ability information appears particularly likely when the teacher wishes to protect the self-esteem of the failure prone student. In the following sections, I review evidence regarding three prevalent and seemingly positive teacher behaviors that can indirectly function as low ability cues. The operation of these messages has not been sufficiently recognized by educators. The particular behaviors included in this category are: (a) communicated pity following failure; (b) the offering of praise following success, particularly at easy tasks; and (c) unsolicited offers of help (see Graham, 1990). Thus, the indirect sources of attributional information are found in a full range of teacher behaviors and in situations of success as well as imminent failure.

Pity Versus Anger.   In attribution research, it has been documented that student failure perceived as caused by low ability elicits pity or sympathy in teachers (Weiner, Graham, Stern, & Lawson, 1982). Imagine, for example, the teacher's reaction to the mainstreamed retarded child who continuously experiences academic difficulty. In contrast, failure perceived as due to lack of effort gives rise to teacher anger (think of your reaction to the gifted child who chronically does not complete homework assignments). Now suppose that a teacher does respond with pity or anger toward a failing student. It might be the case that the student will then use this affective display to infer, first, the teacher's attribution, and second, his or her own self-ascription for failure. In other words, failing students can gain information about the causes of their achievement outcomes based on the affective displays of teachers.

A few years ago, I was able to document the role of pity and anger as indirect attributional cues in a laboratory study where sixth-grade participants were induced to fail at a novel puzzle solving task (Graham, 1984). Following failure, a female experimenter posing as a teacher communicated either pity, anger, or no affective reaction. These emotional displays were conveyed through appropriate verbal responses, facial expressions, and postural gestures. Subjects then reported their causal attributions for failure. As predicted, the findings revealed that children were most likely to attribute their failure on the puzzles to low ability when pity was conveyed and most likely to report lack of effort as the cause of failure when anger was conveyed. That is, the students used the emotional communications of the teacher to infer why they themselves failed.

Although based on laboratory experimental research, these findings do have applications to classroom motivation. Searching for real world analogues to the laboratory investigation, it appears that pity can also be indirectly displayed in the classroom through certain gestures, postures, or subtle verbal content. In other instances this emotion, while privately experienced, may be the motivator of particular teacher behaviors. In the teacher expectancy literature, for example, Brophy and Good (1974) suggest that a set of well-documented teacher behaviors toward low expectancy students, such as teaching less difficult material or setting lower mastery levels, may be determined, in part, by what they call "excessive sympathy for the student" (p. 311). Of all the subtle attributional cues in classroom contexts, the emotional reactions of teachers may be among the most important antecedents of perceived personal competence.

Praise Versus Blame.   Praise and the absence of blame can also function as indirect low ability cues. This may seem somewhat counterintuitive since traditional conceptions of praise suggest that this feedback should have positive motivational consequences. Why should such feedback serve as a low ability cue?

According to attribution principles, praise and the absence of blame are related to perceived effort expenditure (Weiner & Kukla, 1970). The successful student who tries hard is maximally praised or rewarded, whereas the failing student who puts forth little effort elicits the most blame or punishment. Thus, praise and blame from others can allow us to make inferences about effort as a cause of success and failure. Furthermore, among adults and older children, ability and effort are often perceived as compensatory (Nicholls, 1978). In both success and failure, the higher one's perceived effort, the lower one's perceived ability and vice versa. This is why they are perceived as compensatory: As one increases, the other decreases. Applied to the cue value of praise and blame, these attribution principles suggest the following: Praise, relative to neutral feedback, leads to the inference of high effort, and the higher one's perceived effort, the lower one's perceived ability. In contrast, blame, relative to neutral feedback, leads to the inference of low effort, and the lower one's perceived effort, the higher one's perceived ability.

As cognitive social psychologists, my colleagues and I again took these ideas and studied them in the laboratory. In a study that I conducted with George Barker (Barker & Graham, 1987), children between the ages of 4 and 12 watched videotaped teaching sessions depicting a pair of students solving a set of objectively easy math problems. In one videotape, both students successfully solved easy problems. One student was praised by the teacher with such enthusiastically positive statements as: "Good thinking!" or "Great job!" The other student received only neutral feedback such as "Correct." In the second videotape, both students failed the easy problems, but one student was criticized, whereas the other student merely received feedback that his answer was not correct. Subjects then rated the effort and ability of the two videotaped students.

The data revealed that as children increased in age, the student praised for success and the student not blamed for failure were inferred to be *lower* in ability than their neutral feedback or blamed counterparts. In other words, the presence of praise and the absence of blame functioned as antecedents to low ability attributions.

These relations documented in the laboratory have been shown to be relevant to actual classroom settings. For example, Parsons and her colleagues recorded extensive classroom observations of feedback patterns between teachers and students in nearly 20 fourth-, fifth-, and sixth-grade math classrooms (Parsons, Kaczala, & Meece, 1982). These researchers found that frequent blame or criticism for quality of one's work was positively related to high self-concept of math ability and high future expectancies among students. Praise, on the other hand, was unrelated to math self-concept, although boys who were not praised believed their teachers held high expectations for them. Parsons et al. (1982) concluded that:

> To suggest that teachers should avoid criticism or give praise more freely overlooks the power of the context in determining the meaning of any message. A well chosen criticism can convey as much positive information as a praise; abundant or indiscriminant praise can be meaningless; insincere praise which does not covary with teachers' expectations for the student can have detrimental effects on many students. (p. 336)

With the growing influence of attribution theory, the multifaceted effects of praise have become more evident. Thus, one of the advantages of this theoretical work is that it points out relationships that heretofore have not been recognized. I turn now to a third teacher behavior that is positive, but at the same time might have aversive consequences.

Help Versus Neglect.   As in the case of praise, simple reinforcement principles underscore the desirable consequences of help. Being the recipient of aid usually results in some tangible gain, at least when compared to undesirable alternatives such as failure. Why, then, might the offering of help have unintended effects on perceptions of ability?

The fact that help can be a cue to low ability is based on an attributional analysis of helping behavior (Schmidt & Weiner, 1988). According to this analysis, we are more likely to help others when the cause of their need is due to uncontrollable factors like low ability than when the need is due to controllable factors such as insufficient effort.

If a teacher's attributions determine likelihood of help, then one can argue, as with pity and praise, that these behaviors might function as a low ability cue. George Barker and I also investigated the cue function of help versus neglect in a recent study (Graham & Barker, 1990). Drawing on the videotape methodology that we used in the praise study, we filmed a classroom sequence depicting two male students solving a set of math problems in the presence of their teacher. As the students worked, the teacher circulated around their desks, much as she might do in a regular classroom, stopping unobtrusively to gaze at their papers. With one of the problem solvers (the nonhelped student) the teacher casually looked over his shoulder and then moved on without comment. With the other problem solver (the helped student), the teacher also looked over his shoulder and then without apparent knowledge of the student's immediate performance, leaned down to offer help. Unsolicited help was administered when the teacher said: "Let me give you a hint. Don't forget to carry your tens." The help manipulation was therefore intended to coincide with the early stages of problem solving when the outcome was unknown and it was unclear whether the student would have solved the problem successfully on his own. After viewing the videotape, 6–12-year-old research participants rated the two students' ability and effort.

The results of this study were exactly as predicted. All age groups, including the youngest children, perceived the helped student to be lower in ability than his counterpart who received no such assistance. Thus unsolicited help, like pity and praise, can function as an antecedent to low ability, just as relative neglect, like anger and blame, can be a cue to lack of effort ascriptions.

Of course, it is not being suggested that the teacher behaviors described here always function as low ability cues. Sympathetic affect, generous praise, minimal criticism, and helping behavior are useful instructional strategies that often neutralize some of the immediate impact of failure, such as public embarrassment or frustration. Furthermore, it is important to distinguish between what we might label "instrumental help," such as probing when appropriate, from "gratuitous help," such as supplying answers outright, for it is only this latter form of premature unsolicited help that is thought to be detrimental to ability self-perception. Therefore, I am not advocating that teachers should never help their students or that they should always be angry rather than sympathetic or critical as opposed to complimentary. The appropriateness of any of these feedbacks will depend on many factors, including the general classroom climate and the relationship between teacher and students. Rather, the general message I wish to convey is that attribution principles can facilitate our understanding of how some well-intentioned teacher behaviors may, at times, have unexpected or even negative effects on classroom motivation.

Task and Ego Involvement

In addition to indirect communications from teachers, certain environmental variables are also likely to influence attributions to ability and effort. One such environmental variable can be described in terms of Nicholls' (1984) distinction between task-involving and ego-involving contexts. Task-involving situations are those where one's goal is to master the task: Greater understanding or acquisition of new skills is considered an end in itself. This is contrasted with ego-involving contexts where one's primary goal is to demonstrate high ability relative to others or to conceal low ability. Unlike a task-focused context which emphasizes personal accomplishment and preference for moderately challenging tasks, an ego-focused context connotes highly evaluative situations in which the emphasis is on competition with others.

Research drawing on these distinctions has documented that task-involving and ego-involving situations can be antecedents to effort and ability attributions respectively (Butler, 1987; Jagacinski & Nicholls, 1984, 1987). In a study with elementary school children, for example, Butler (1987) reported that a task-focused learning context resulted in higher attributions to effort as well as more interest in the task and better performance. This was in contrast to an ego-focused situation which resulted in greater attributions to low ability, less interest, and poorer overall performance. The general premise underlying these findings is that because task-involved subjects believe more in the efficacy of effort, they work harder and therefore experience more positive outcomes.

My colleagues and I recently examined the effects of task-versus ego-involvement on fifth- and sixth-grade children's attributions and performance on a memory task (Graham & Golan, 1991). The task consisted of remembering a set of 60 words manipulated to be encoded at either shallow or deep levels of processing (Craik & Lockhart, 1972). Children engaged in this activity under either task- or ego-involving conditions, as manipulated by specific instructions from an experimenter posing as a teacher. To elicit task involvement, subjects were told to "concentrate on the task, try to see it as a challenge, and enjoy mastering it." Ego involvement was evoked by telling the subjects that "people are either good at these activities compared to other kids their age or they are not, so how you do will tell me something about how good you are at this kind of task." The children were presented with an unexpected test of word recall and they were asked to indicate whether their performance was mostly due to ability or effort.

The findings documented the role of task and ego involvement as antecedents to particular attributions, as well as the effects of these distinct motivational states on performance. Ego-focused children were more likely to endorse ability as the cause of their performance on the recall task than were their task-focused counterparts. Thus the ego-focused manipulation enhanced attention to ability, whereas the task-focused manipulation promoted an emphasis on trying hard.

The results for word recall as a function of the task-ego manipulation are shown in Fig. 3.1 (there was also a control condition where children received no specific motivational instructions). Note that for words processed at shallow or superficial levels of encoding, there were no effects of motivational state. None of the children remembered many words that they were only required to attend to superficially. However, when the task necessitated deeper levels of processing, ego-involved children showed poorer word recall. It has been assumed that shallow processing requires little cognitive effort: There are relatively few demands on one's limited processing capacities when attending to surface features of incoming stimuli. Deep processing, on the other hand, entails greater elaboration and thus greater cognitive effort (Craik & Lockhart, 1972). If this analysis is accepted, then it appears that ego involvement may well interfere with the cognitive effort needed for deeper levels of information processing.

These findings have important implications for both learning and instruction. With its emphasis on competition, grades, and various other kinds of normative evaluation, much of school learning has become synonymous with an ego-focused context, the very motivational state that we have found to have detrimental consequences for both attributions and performance. Furthermore, contemporary approaches to instruction, guided by cognitive views of learning, attach ever greater importance to meaningfulness, elaboration, and various other cognitive activities that require deep rather than shallow processing (see Glover, Ronning, & Bruning, 1990). As our data indicate, these are the kinds of learning activities that might be most vulnerable to the effects of a maladaptive motivational state.

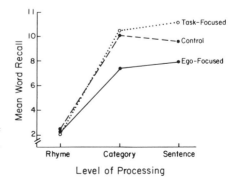

FIG. 3.1. Word recall as a function of motivational state and level of processing. From Graham and Golan (1991). Reprinted by permission.

To summarize, in the preceding sections I have discussed some of the determinants of causal ascriptions such as low ability and lack of effort. Communicated sympathy from teachers, excessive praise, unsolicited offers of help, and ego-focused learning environments can sometimes foster low ability self-ascriptions. In contrast, communicated anger from teachers, blame for failure, relative neglect, and task-focused learning environments often function as antecedents to attributions about effort. In the next part of this chapter, I move forward in a motivational sequence and consider some of the consequences of particular kinds of causal attributions.

CAUSAL CONSEQUENCES

To examine attributional consequences, it is necessary to return to causal dimensions, or the underlying properties of causal attributions. Recall that three dimensions have been identified with some certainty: *locus, stability,* and *controllability.* Each of these dimensions, moreover, is linked to particular psychological and emotional consequences (see Weiner, 1986). For example, the locus dimension is linked to esteem-related affect. Individuals feel greater pride when success is attributed to internal causes such as ability or effort, but greater shame when failures are attributed to these same factors. The stability dimension is linked to expectancy for future success. When achievement failure is attributed to a stable cause such as low ability, one is more likely to expect the same outcome to occur again than when the cause of failure is due to an unstable factor like lack of effort. Thus the failing student who believes she did not try hard enough can be bolstered by the expectation that failure need not occur again, whereas a self-ascription for failure to low ability tends to lower one's expectation for future success. Guided by these known consequences of ability vs. effort based on the stability-expectancy linkage, a number of attribution retraining studies have attempted to change the failing student's attributions from low ability to lack of effort (see review in Forsterling, 1985).

Thus far the discussion of attributional consequences (and antecedents) has focused on self-perceived causes and their influence on achievement strivings. But as a social psychological model of motivation, attribution theory also has some well-established relations between the dimension of controllability and particular emotional and behavioral reactions toward *others* (Weiner, 1990). Attribution researchers prefer to label the dimension causal *responsibility* when referring to perceived controllability in others, for this better captures the naive understanding of the construct when applied to other-perception rather than self-perception. That is, individuals typically view their own outcomes as personally controllable or not, whereas they tend to hold others responsible or not for what they do. We also do not distinguish between perceived responsibility in others and intentionality as dimensional labels, and these terms are used interchangeably here.

According to attribution theory, responsibility inferences influence behavior toward others through the mediating influence of emotion. To illustrate, consider the evidence supporting these linkages that has been gathered in the domain of helping behavior. When people are perceived as not responsible for negative outcomes, this tends to elicit pity and prosocial behavior such as help. (These principles are, of course, complementary with the earlier discussion of pity and help from teachers as indirect low ability cues.) In contrast, individuals judged as responsible for negative events often elicit anger and help tends to be withheld. Furthermore, a very reliable finding in this attribution literature is that emotions of pity and anger, more so than responsibility attributions, directly influence prosocial versus antisocial behavior (Schmidt & Weiner, 1988). Thus, attribution theorists propose a particular thought-emotion-action sequence whereby causal thoughts determine feelings and feelings, in turn, guide behavior.

The consequences for emotional and behavioral reactions of perceiving others as responsible have been documented across a range of situations and motivational domains; indeed, this set of principles are among the most robust in attribution theory (see Weiner, 1990). Next I focus on some recent research that my colleagues and I have conducted on responsibility inferences among school-aged males labeled as aggressive.

Perceived Responsibility in Others and Aggression

One of the most robust findings in the contemporary peer aggression literature is that aggressive children have biased perceptions about others' responsibility for negative outcomes. Guided largely by the work of Kenneth Dodge and his colleagues, a number of studies report that aggressive children display a marked attributional bias to infer hostile intent following a peer-instigated negative event, particularly when the cause of the event is portrayed as ambiguous (Dodge, 1993). For example, imagine a situation where a target child experiences a negative outcome, such as having his lunch milk spilled or being pushed while waiting in line. It is known by the target that this outcome is caused by a peer but the reason for the peer's actions remain ambiguous. Dodge and his colleagues have found that aggressive children are more likely than their nonaggressive counterparts to infer that the peer did this "on purpose"; in other words, they see the other person as responsible for what happened. Such biased responsibility attributions are then thought to lead to aggressive retaliation. Even among normal populations, the child who believes that another acted with malicious intent can feel justified in the endorsement of aggressive behavior. The problem with aggressive children, however, is that either through some process of social cue distortion or selective recall of available information, they often inappropriately assume hostile peer intent in situations where the causes of outcomes are ambiguous.

It follows logically from attribution principles that perceived responsibility results in more anger toward peers and that anger, in turn, leads to aggressive behavior. If attributions to peer responsibility instigate a set of reactions that leads to aggression, then it might be possible to train aggression-prone children to see peer provocation as unintended (i.e., the peer is not responsible for what happened). This should mitigate anger in others as well as the tendency to react with hostility. The notion of altering causal thinking to produce changes in behavior has been the guiding assumption of attributional retraining programs in the achievement domain that I referred to earlier. So there are good theoretical and empirical precedents for considering attributional change as a way to alleviate peer-directed aggression.

Guided by our own theoretical analysis as well as the clinical literature on the treatment of childhood aggression (e.g., Kazdin, 1987), my colleague Cynthia Hudley and I developed a school-based cognitive intervention program designed to alter responsibility attributions of aggression-prone children (Hudley & Graham, 1993). The intervention was a 6-week, 12-session program with activities designed to be appropriate for the late elementary grades. A variety of instructional strategies were employed, including group discussion, role play, and paper and pencil exercises.

One component of the program was designed to strengthen aggressive children's ability to accurately detect responsibility in others. Through role play and discussion of personal experiences, the children were trained to search for, interpret, and properly categorize the verbal and behavioral cues emitted by others in social dilemmas. In addition, they produced short videotaped scenarios to demonstrate their understanding of the difference between prosocial, accidental, ambiguous, and hostile peer intent.

A second component was designed to increase the cognitive availability of attributions to nonresponsibility or nonintentionality when the causal situation was portrayed as ambiguous. For example, children wrote endings to unfinished stories on social dilemmas of ambiguous causal origin, which then served as a vehicle for training them to judge accidental and uncertain outcomes as unintended by peers. They were also given practice in the interpretation of ambiguous nonverbal social cues through use of photographs and pantomime games.

Our research participants were 66 African American fifth and sixth grade boys identified as aggressive according to the standard criteria in the peer aggression literature (i.e., peer nominations and teacher ratings). We specifically selected our sample to be African American boys, given the severity of the problem of deviancy and antisocial behavior among young Black males (see Gibbs, 1988). Approximately one third of the boys were targeted for the experimental intervention; one third participated in an attention training program of the same scope and duration as the intervention, but unrelated to attributional change; and one third of the boys constituted the control group who participated in no intervention of any kind. Assignment of aggressive children to one of these groups was done on a completely random basis. The experimental and attention training groups met twice weekly for 6 weeks in small groups of six to eight.

We collected data on a number of different dependent variables, only some of which are described here (see Hudley & Graham, 1993). On one measure, subjects were administered an attributional questionnaire, developed for this study, both before and after the experiment. In the questionnaire, participants read short vignettes where they were asked to imagine that they experienced a negative outcome, such as damage to one's property or social rejection, which was initiated by a hypothetical peer provocateur. The cause of the peer provocations were portrayed as ambiguous, as in the following "homework paper" scenario:

> Imagine that as you are walking to school one morning, you look down and notice that your shoelace is untied. You put the notebook that you are carrying down on the ground to tie your shoelace. An important homework paper that you worked on for a long time falls out of your notebook. Just then, another kid you know walks by and steps on the paper, leaving a muddy footprint right across the middle. The other kid looks down at your homework paper and then up at you.

For each scenario, subjects made attributions about the peer's intent (e.g., "Did he do it on purpose?") and they indicated how angry they would feel if the outcome indeed happened to them. They also judged the likelihood that they would engage in six behaviors that varied along a continuum from prosocial ("do something nice for the other kid") to hostile ("do something to get even" and "have it out right then and there").

Figure 3.2 shows the pre- and postexperimental data on intentionality attributions, reported anger, and endorsement of aggressive behavior in these hypothetical situations. Intent and anger judgments were made on 7-point scales, whereas the behavioral choices were converted to 6-point scales. For the three variables, high numbers indicate greater perceived responsibility on the part of the peer provocateur, more anger, and more hostile behavioral preference.

It is evident in Fig. 3.2 that the attributional intervention had its intended effect. The first panel of data shows ratings of peer intent as a function of treatment group, both before and after the experimental intervention. All aggressive children perceived that the peer was responsible for the provocation before the intervention. Posttest measures, however, indicate that only the boys exposed to attributional change altered their judgments in the direction of less perceived hostile intent. The same pattern prevailed for the anger and behavioral data, as shown in the second and third panels of Fig. 3.2. Following the intervention, only experimental subjects reduced the amounts of reported anger and endorsed hostile behavior. Across all three variables, the differences between experimental

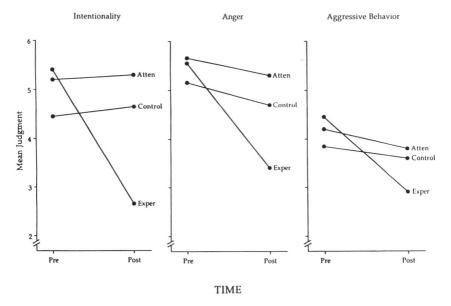

FIG. 3.2. Pre- and postexperimental intent attributions, anger, and aggressive action, by treatment group. From Hudley and Graham (1993). Reprinted by permission.

subjects compared to attention training and control groups were significant, and in no case did the latter two groups differ from one another.

Did the attributional change program generalize to situations of actual behavior? Ethical constraints did not allow us to create *in vivo* the kinds of social dilemmas depicted in the hypothetical scenarios. Our compromise was to use a laboratory analogue task in the second part of this study that would simulate ambiguously caused peer provocation. We devised a situation where the aggressive child would interact with an actual peer whose actions resulted in the subject's failure to obtain a desired goal. The reasons for this outcome were designed to be perceived as ambiguous. Measures of perceived responsibility, amount of felt anger, and behavioral reactions were obtained.

More specifically, about 1 month after the training program ended, all subjects participated in a problem-solving task that was supposedly unrelated to the earlier intervention. The task required the subject to communicate with an unseen peer who was seated on the other side of a barrier. Using simple grid maps, the peer was to give directions to the subject so that he could complete a maze, with the goal of winning a prize. But in fact, the task was designed to be frustrating. Unbeknownst to either child, the peer's map was different from the subject's. Thus, incorrect directions were necessarily given, the maze was not completed, and no prize was awarded. While the two children engaged in the task, the experimenter unobtrusively observed and recorded the subject's behavior in the wake of nonattainment of the goal. After the first trial, when it was clear that the subject had not successfully completed the maze, he was asked a series of questions about the outcome. Embedded in these questions were attributions about the peer's intent (e.g., "Do you think your partner meant to give you bad directions so you wouldn't win a prize?") and feelings of anger toward the peer. These questions were answered using 7-point rating scales.

Aggressive children's intent attributions, reported anger, and recorded verbal behavior during the frustrating task are shown in Table 3.2 as a function of experimental group. Notice that children who participated in the attributional intervention were significantly less likely than the other two groups to infer that the peer intentionally caused them to fail. They also expressed less anger, although the difference between groups on the emotion variable was less strong.

Verbal behaviors during the communication task were classified into one of four types: *neutral*, defined as nonjudgmental statements to the adult experimenter (e.g., "That's not possible."); *complaining*, which captured negative comments directed toward the experimenter about the subject's own performance (e.g., "I can't do this"); *criticizing*, defined as negative remarks to the peer about his performance (e.g., "You obviously don't know how to read a map"); and *insulting*, which described negative personal comments directed toward the peer (e.g., "You're dumb").

If boys who participated in the attributional intervention inferred less responsibility and reported less anger, then they should also engage in less of the kind of

TABLE 3.2
Intentionality Attributions, Reported Anger, and Verbal Behavior in an Analogue Task, by
Treatment Group

	Treatment Group		
Variable	Experimental (n = 20)	Atten. Training (n = 24)	Control (n = 24)
Intentionality	2.3	4.5	4.7
Anger	1.7	2.5	2.6
Behavior (% total)			
Neutral	61%	29	31
Complain	20	25	31
Criticize	19	29	23
Insult	0	17	15

From Hudley and Graham (1993). Reprinted by permission.
Note. Rating scales for intent and anger range from 1 to 7. High numbers indicate greater perceived hostile intent and more intense anger.

verbally aggressive behavior (i.e., criticizing and insulting) that might accompany goal frustration in this context. The behavioral data in Table 3.2 show that this was indeed the case. Neutral comments were far and away the preferred verbal behavior of experimental subjects (61%) and not one of these children resorted to insult. For the two groups of nontrained aggressives, in contrast, the four classes of behavior were more evenly evoked, with about one of every six responses classified as an insult.

In summary, peer-directed aggression by young Black males is, to at least a modest degree, predictable by these children's causal thoughts and consequent emotions. Furthermore, it is possible to reduce their tendency to respond with hostility by changing the way they causally construe a social dilemma. Even in the achievement change literature there are few studies that report such clear cognitive and behavioral change based on an attributional intervention. This may be one of few, if not the only documented study with children that shows positive effects of specific attribution retraining on *social* behavior.

GENERAL SUMMARY

I have been guided in this chapter by a conception of a motivational sequence that includes the antecedents and consequences of attributional thoughts. A partial representation of this sequence is depicted in Fig. 3.3 which also serves as a useful framework to briefly review the material presented here. The sequence begins with an achievement outcome such as success or failure. A causal search might then be instigated to determine why the outcome occurred. A number of antecedent cues guide particular self-ascriptions. I documented several principles relating communicated sympathy, praise, unsolicited offers of help, and ego-focused learning contexts to low ability self-ascriptions. These were contrasted with principles relating communicated anger, blame, the withholding of help, and task-focused contexts to lack of effort self-ascriptions.

Given a list of antecedents, the next linkage in Fig. 3.3 shows the relatively

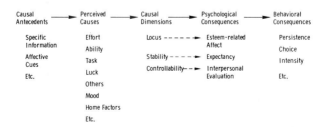

FIG. 1.3. Partial representation of an attributional model of motivation.

small set of dominant perceived causes for success and failure and their underlying properties, labeled causal dimensions. Once a particular cause is endorsed, it theoretically is located in dimensional space (see Table 3.1) and these dimensions then have particular psychological and behavioral consequences. Here I focused on the linkage between perceived controllability (responsibility, intentionality) in others and the likelihood of behaving aggressively. It was shown that changes in cognitions about controllability of negative outcomes led to reductions in anger and antisocial behavior among African American boys labeled as aggressive. Thus at the heart of this temporal sequence comprising an attributional theory of motivation is the specification of complex interrelationships between thinking, feeling, and acting that apply across both achievement and social domains.

If there is one message I wish to convey with what has been presented in this chapter, that message is that classroom motivational life is complex. No single word or principle such as reinforcement or intrinsic motivation can possibly capture this complexity. Much of the practical significance of attribution theory lies in its recognition of the complexity of human motivation and its attempts to address some of the real-world concerns of educators.

ACKNOWLEDGMENTS

Preparation of this chapter was supported in part by the U.S. Army Research Institute for Behavioral and Social Sciences through a subcontract with Battelle Institute. However, the views, opinions and/or findings contained in this report are the authors' and should not be construed as an official ARI position, policy, or decision, unless so designated by other official documentation.

REFERENCES

Barker, G., & Graham, S. (1987). A developmental study of praise and blame as attributional cues. *Journal of Educational Psychology, 79,* 62–66.

Brophy, J., & Good, T. (1974). *Teacher-student relationships: Causes and consequences.* New York: Holt, Rinehart, & Winston.

Butler, R. (1987). Task-involving and ego-involving properties of evaluation: Effects of different feedback conditions on motivational perceptions, interest, and performance. *Journal of Educational Psychology, 79,* 474–482.

Craik, F., & Lockhart, R. (1972). Levels of processing: A framework for memory research. *Journal of Verbal Learning and Verbal Behavior, 11,* 671–684.

Dodge, K. (1993). Social-cognitive mechanism in the development of conduct disorder and depression. In L. Porter & M. Rosenzweig (Eds.), *Annual review of psychology* (Vol. 44, pp. 559–584). Palo Alto, CA: Annual Reviews.

Forsterling, F. (1985). Attribution retraining: A review. *Psychological Bulletin, 98,* 495–512.

Gibbs, J. (Ed.). (1988). *Young, black, and male in America: An endangered species.* Dover, MA: Auburn House.

Glover, J., Ronning, R., & Bruning, R. (1990). *Cognitive psychology for teachers.* New York: Macmillan.

Graham, S. (1984). Communicating sympathy and anger to black and white students: The cognitive (attributional) antecedents of affective cues. *Journal of Personality and Social Psychology, 47,* 40–54.

Graham, S. (1990). On communicating low ability in the classroom: Bad things good teachers sometimes do. In S. Graham & V. Folkes (Eds.), *Attribution theory: Applications to achievement, mental health, and interpersonal conflict* (pp. 17–36). Hillsdale, NJ: Lawrence Erlbaum Associates.

Graham, S. (1991). A review of attribution theory in achievement contexts. *Educational Psychology Review, 3,* 5–39.

Graham, S., & Barker, G. (1990). An attributional-developmental analysis of help-giving as a low ability cue. *Journal of Educational Psychology, 82,* 7–14.

Graham, S., & Golan, S. (1991). Motivational influences on cognition: Task involvement, ego involvement, and depth of information processing. *Journal of Educational Psychology, 83,* 187–194.

Hudley, C., & Graham, S. (1993). An attributional intervention to reduce peer-directed aggression among African-American boys. *Child Development, 64,* 124–138.

Jagacinski, C., & Nicholls, J. (1984). Conceptions of ability and related affects in task involvement and ego involvement. *Journal of Educational Psychology, 76,* 909–919.

Jagacinski, C., & Nicholls, J. (1987). Competence and affect in task involvement and ego involvement. *Journal of Educational Psychology, 79,* 107–114.

Kazdin, A. (1987). *Conduct disorders in childhood and adolescence.* Newbury Park, CA: Sage.

Kelley, H., & Michela, J. (1980). Attribution theory and research. In M. Rosenzweig & L. Porter (Eds.), *Annual review of psychology* (Vol. 31, pp. 457–501). Palo Alto, CA: Annual Reviews.

Nicholls, J. (1978). The development of the concepts of effort and ability, perceptions of own attainment, and the understanding that difficult tasks demand more ability. *Child Development, 49,* 800–814.

Nicholls, J. (1984). Achievement motivation: Conceptions of ability, subjective experience, task choice, and performance. *Psychological Review, 91,* 328–346.

Parsons, J., Kaczala, C., & Meece, J. (1982). Socialization of achievement attitudes and beliefs. *Child Development, 53,* 322–339.

Schmidt, G., & Weiner, B. (1988). An attribution-affect-action theory of motivation: Replications examining help-giving. *Personality and Social Psychology Bulletin, 14,* 610–621.

Weiner, B. (1985a). An attributional theory of achievement motivation and emotion. *Psychological Review, 92,* 548–573.

Weiner, B. (1985b). "Spontaneous" causal thinking. *Psychological Bulletin, 97,* 74–84.

Weiner, B. (1986). *An attributional theory of motivation and emotion.* New York: Springer-Verlag.

Weiner, B. (1990). On perceiving the other as responsible. In R. Dientsbier (Ed.), *Nebraska symposium on motivation* (Vol. 38, pp. 165–198). Lincoln: University of Nebraska Press.

Weiner, B., Graham, S., Stern, P., & Lawson, M. (1982). Using affective cues to infer causal thoughts. *Developmental Psychology, 18,* 278–286.

Weiner, B., & Kukla, A. (1970). An attributional theory of achievement motivation. *Journal of Personality and Social Psychology, 15,* 1–20.

4 Strategies for Assessing and Enhancing Motivation: Keys to Promoting Self-Regulated Learning and Performance

Barbara L. McCombs
Mid-continent Regional Educational Laboratory
Aurora, Colorado

We learned in other chapters that research on motivation within the Armed Forces is directed at two primary goals: (a) to motivate soldiers (as both individuals and teams) to learn and do their jobs well; and (b) to contribute to selection, classification, and retention decisions (Drillings, 1991; Drillings & O'Neil, this volume). In this context, what we know from basic and applied research on human motivation is used to enhance both individual and group or team performance as well as generally contribute to organizational effectiveness and creative leadership. Particularly important in military training systems are individual and unit job proficiency and job readiness to carry out national security missions when called upon—in times of peace or war (Office of the Assistant Secretary of Defense, 1992; O'Neil, Anderson, & Freeman, 1986). A major motivational issue for the military is essentially one of maintaining a proficient force of soldiers who are satisfied and happy with their jobs and who reenlist.

In this chapter, recent research on strategies for enhancing and assessing motivation is discussed, with a focus on the relationship of these strategies to the promotion of self-regulated learning and performance. While other chapters have dealt with particular aspects of motivation (e.g., goals, expectations, intentions, commitment) important to individual and unit performance, my purpose is to integrate these components of motivation within the larger context of the nature of human psychological functioning. In this context, motivation is fundamentally a function of the degree to which individuals are aware of themselves as agents in the construction of their thoughts, beliefs, goals, expectations, attributions, or any other thought systems. By looking at where the content of thought originates—in the knower or person as agent—thought becomes the common denominator for understanding human functioning and motivation. How aware

49

individuals are that they have voluntary control over their thinking, including being able to step outside the boundaries of their own constructed thoughts, is what fundamentally fuels or motivates self-regulated behaviors. In turn, to the degree that individuals can exercise natural self-regulatory capacities, basic needs for personal control and competence are met and performance is enhanced.

Building on my work on motivation in the schools (McCombs, 1992; McCombs & Whisler, 1989) as well as work with military training (McCombs, 1984, 1987, 1988), I discuss the importance of supportive interpersonal interactions and a match of organizational goals with individual's primary needs for personal control and competence for the generation of positive motivation. I begin with a review of current theoretical assumptions regarding human motivation and self-regulated learning, followed by a discussion of how these theories can be used in the assessment and enhancement of primary motivational variables. Results of my work with military populations in these areas are summarized, and I conclude by deriving implications for future research and development in motivation relevant to military training and retention.

THEORETICAL ASSUMPTIONS

The Self and Motivation

The past 20 to 30 years of research in motivation has led to some profound changes in how motivation is defined and the constructs that are assumed to underlie motivation to learn, perform, or make important life decisions (Weiner, 1992). One of the most significant changes has been a focus on internal processes and self-constructions rather than on external reinforcements or environmental determinants. Even among those who have argued that there is an interaction between person and environment variables in motivation, current theories have tended to emphasize the importance of individuals' internal constructions, interpretations, and generated meanings as the impetus for motivation. An exception to this general trend has been the research by Rueda and Moll (this volume). Moreover, research on the prediction of complex human behavior—including job performance as well as career decision making—has increasingly looked to various classes of motivational variables to account for variance not explained by ability, background, or prior performance variables.

In general, the classes of motivational variables that have taken on particular importance as predictors of performance in military and educational research include intentions, expectations, goals, and commitment. In addition to these variables, however, a number of motivational and self theorists have argued that attention needs be given to various self-system structures and processes, and particularly to personal evaluations of self-competence and self-agency. Furthermore, to explain behavior that seems to fall outside what is considered predictable by past histories, personal characteristics, and constructed belief systems, there has been a search for ways to account for the self-determining aspects of human nature or higher order self-processes by which individuals direct and control learning, motivation, and performance.

Deci and Ryan (1991), for example, define self-determination as an aware-ness or realization of one's source of agency and personal control. Agency is described as an inherent tendency of the self to originate behavior, to relate to and assimilate events, and to gain a sense of personal control and mastery of one's environment. In this view, an awareness of agency is the basis for self-determination; it is a basic motivational process of the self that goes beyond cognition. Deci and Ryan describe the self as having at its core an energizing component termed intrinsic or growth motivation. The "true self" is in operation when one's actions are endorsed by oneself—with integrity and cohesion. Au-thenticity is self-determination, with the person viewing him or herself as the locus of active development. The "I" is intrinsically motivated and actively engaged in knowing and directing itself at levels of functioning that lie outside the cognitive system. This higher order, metacognitive self is the originator and formulator of goals, intentions, and self-beliefs that underlie decisions, motiva-tions, and self-regulated performance.

Others beginning to argue for higher order self-processes as underlying mo-tivation and self-regulation include Susan Harter. Her recent work (Harter, 1990, 1992) describes the self "beyond the me in the mirror" and emphasizes the need to move away from descriptive and evaluative aspects of self-concept and self-esteem and focus on a deeper understanding of self as outside of or beyond these constructions. This work focuses on researching and understanding higher-order self-processes that explain how individuals can direct thoughts, affect, and be-havior outside the narrow bounds of self-concept. In researching causal relation-ships between self-processes, affect, motivation, and performance, Harter (1990) has discovered that individuals differ with respect to whether their judgments of personal adequacy or competence *precede* positive evaluations of self-worth or whether the opposite causal relationship is true. For some individuals, percep-tions of worth are conditional on the social approval of significant others, where-as for other individuals, perceptions of worth are internalized. That is, some individuals are not nearly as dependent on external sources in order to sustain a sense of self-esteem, and they experience more positive affect and intrinsic motivation to learn. This research points to individual differences in the internal-ization of higher-order self-processes that may have important theoretical and methodological implications in the prediction of performance.

The meaning and role of goals in directing and energizing behavior has also begun to focus on higher-order self-processes. In Locke and Latham's (this volume) work, the role of conscious goal setting and choice in generating com-mitment and enhancing the likelihood of selected actions is discussed. Consistent with this research, Showers and Cantor (1985) cite the importance of personal self-goals for individuals' development of what they perceive to be appropriate strategies for processing information and planning how to act in specific situations. Cantor's (1990) more recent research on life tasks posits dynamic processes to account for how individuals actively attempt to understand the world, take control, and reach personal goals. In a similar vein, work by Markus and her colleagues (Inglehart, Markus, Brown, & Moore, 1987; Markus & Ruvulo, 1990) indicates that "possible selves"—one's future self-goals—help both to structure behavior and to energize that behavior. This research also suggests that the very process of working toward valued self-goals enhances well-being and positive affect.

In addition, research by Ridley (1991, 1992) points to the importance of reflective self-awareness as a self-system process related to intentions, performance goals, effort, task perseverance, and performance. In this work, reflective self-awareness is defined as a higher level or metacognitive awareness of thoughts, beliefs, and actions that mediates the consistency between one's intentions and actions. According to Ridley (1992), this reflectively intentional consistency between what a student wants and what a student does is the essence of self-regulation. Ridley's research verifies that higher level awareness and understanding of one's personal agency over lower order cognitive processes, thoughts, and beliefs positively impacts goals selected, affect, motivation, and performance in a learning situation involving complex problem solving.

In an integration of recent work on self-system variables and their causal relationships, I have argued that such models assume that individuals' understanding of "self-as-agent" and their beliefs about personal competence and control form the base set of filters (schemas) through which all information is acted upon (McCombs, 1991a, 1992). The self is both causal agent and the object of self-system processes, the most important of which are self-awareness, self-evaluation, and self-monitoring. The outputs of these self-system processes are perceptions, self-goals, expectations, and judgments about self-capabilities to perform specific kinds of tasks. The global and specific nature of self-evaluations of competence and control reciprocally influence the resulting perceptions, self-goals, expectations, and judgments. If the output of self-evaluations engaged in as individuals begin a task is positive, the processes of self-regulation and self-reinforcement follow naturally and provide positive feedback to subsequent self-evaluation.

Within this framework, the self makes use of and controls the entire set of processing capacities available (including metacognitive, cognitive, and affective processes)—first directing these processes inward at the self and then outward at the required task activities. The role of the self-system is thus one of creating and maintaining positive self-evaluations before, during, and after task activities that contribute to the motivation to employ necessary self-regulated learning processes and activities. When the result is enhanced feelings of competence and control, a sense of personal relevance for learning results that facilitates learning and retention, including deep processing approaches.

The Self and Self-Regulation

From research in the area of the self and self-processes, we can see that the self-referent nature of information processing activities forms a set of filters (self-schemas) that can enhance or deter individuals' abilities to feel efficacious or in control of the mental and physical processes necessary to accomplish task or performance requirements. However, without an understanding of the role of self-as-agent in generating positive self-perceptions, expectations, goals, feelings, and motivation, the stage cannot be set for the emergence of self-regulation processes or for the generation of intrinsic motivation to engage these processes (McCombs, in press; McCombs & Marzano, 1990). Furthermore, without capabilities for what Sternberg (1986) calls mental self-management and practical intelligence, individuals are unable to capitalize on their strengths and minimize their weaknesses.

Just as goals are important to engaging self-motivation, once motivation is elicited, the facilitative context for the emergence of self-regulation is one of positive socioemotional support in the form of quality interpersonal relationships and interactions. Recent research by Ryan and his colleagues (Ryan & Powelson, 1991; Ryan & Stiller, 1991) clarifies how quality teacher-student relationships and environmental supports can foster higher order motivation, autonomy, and self-regulated learning. Although conducted in school and classroom settings, the following research findings, as reported by Ryan and Stiller (1991), have several important implications for other contexts, including military training or performance situations.

1. Teachers who are more autonomy-oriented (vs. controlling) elicit student reports of more curiosity, desire for challenge, independent mastery attempts, greater perceived competence, and higher general self-worth.

2. Students experiencing more controlling and externally set performance goals engage in less active assimilation and integration of what is read and demonstrate lower long-term retention than students in less directed and pressured learning environments.

3. Teachers' capacity to promote self-regulation and internalization of value for learning in students is inexorably intertwined with teachers' opportunities to regulate their own activities and be creative, innovative, and intrinsically motivated on a day-to-day basis.

4. Policies that pressure teachers toward externally imposed standards or performance requirements for their students result in more controlling vs.

autonomy-supported styles in teachers which, in turn, leads to student performance decrements and lower level cognitive outcomes (e.g., less creative and critical thinking) as well as deepening feelings of alienation and disengagement from learning.

5. Changing teacher and student perceptions of autonomy support as well as their perceptions of the quality of relatedness facilitates positive relationships which, in turn, promote more active student engagement, volition, and confidence in learning.

Ryan and his colleagues conclude that an understanding of the psychological needs of individuals clearly points to the fact that both autonomy and relatedness are fundamental to learning and, thus, facilitating environments are those that provide interpersonal involvement and support for autonomy—for students and their teachers.

Our own work with the Reciprocal Empowerment Model (McCombs, 1990, 1992; McCombs & Marzano, 1990; McCombs & Whisler, 1989; Whisler, 1991) corroborates these findings. Our model focuses on promoting the development of higher order self-processes and self-regulated learning skills through addressing will, skill, and social support components of motivation. Within this model, *will* is defined by (a) a recognition of one's innate or self-actualized state of motivation, an internal state of well-being, in which individuals are in touch with their natural self-esteem, common sense, and intrinsic motivation to learn; (b) an understanding that the authentic self is a psychological vantage point as defined by qualities of self-determination and autonomy—an agent in the orchestration of thinking, feelings, motivation, and behavior; and (c) operation from conscious awareness and an enhanced understanding of one's inherent self-directing capacities such that the motivational processes of choice, volition, intention, and commitment originate from the authentic or true self rather than from conditioned beliefs about self, others, or reality.

Skill is defined as an acquired cognitive or metacognitive competency (relative to the enactment of self as defined by the will component) that develops with training and/or practice and that results in enhanced (a) self-control and regulation of cognition, affect, motivation, and behavior; (b) metacognitive strategies for shifting one's level of consciousness and developing self-evaluation skills and higher level awareness of one's agency over thoughts or conditioned ways of thinking; and (c) abilities to elicit or facilitate in others their intrinsic motivation and healthy functioning from the authentic self.

Social support is the enabling interpersonal context for the empowerment of will and development of skill components, specifically through quality relationships and interactions with others. In this context, support is provided for meeting needs for (a) relatedness, by creating a climate or culture of trust, respect, caring, concern, and a sense of community with others; (b) autonomy, by providing opportunities for individual choice, expression of self-determination and agency, and freedom to fail or take risks; and (c) competence, by providing informational feedback, various forms of challenge to elicit creative and critical thinking, and opportunities to grow and to see growth in one's capacities and skills over time.

All three components—will, skill, and social support—are assumed to be essential for maximum motivation. It is the will component, however, that lies at the center of an individual's capacity for understanding "self-as-agent" and for thereby realizing potentials for self-regulation. As shown in the work of Mills and his colleagues (Mills, 1990, 1991; Mills, Dunham, & Alpert, 1988; Mills, Olson, & Bailey, 1992; Suarez, Mills, & Stewart, 1987), once individuals see their own inherent potential for personal control over their thinking processes and define positive future self-possibilities, they are able to step outside prior cognitive constructions defined by external standards, and become self-determining and self-regulatory. A key, then, in the emergence of self-regulation is the support of quality relationships and relevant skill training in aligning personal and externally defined instructional or training goals. As shown in the research of Schunk and Swartz (1991), when students are helped to learn a strategy they believe is useful for accomplishing their own performance goals, they exhibit higher levels of motivation, effort, persistence, and judgments of self-efficacy.

Another recent area of research has focused on strategies for enhancing self-regulation and perceptions of agency by modifying belief systems. Dweck and her colleagues (Dweck, 1991; Dweck & Leggett, 1988), for example, have found that adopting learning goals leads to positive beliefs about efficacy and agency. In this research, both classroom goal structures (noncompetitive vs. competitive, i.e., goals that emphasize cooperation with others or working to better personal outcomes vs. goals that emphasize competing with others to obtain performance outcomes) and goal orientations (learning vs. performance goals where the object is to increase competence vs. gain favorable judgments of competence) were strongly related to adaptive vs. nonadaptive motivational patterns.

Within self-as-agent perspectives, however, constructed self-knowledge and beliefs play a primary role in motivation and behavior only to the extent that individuals are not aware of their role in choosing how to view the influence of these thoughts and beliefs (McCombs, 1991b; McCombs & Marzano, 1990). Supporting research by Suarez (1988) shows that if individuals do not recognize the choice to selectively use their thought system (e.g., choosing the level of influence specific beliefs will have in a given situation), they operate unconsciously within the limits of that thought system (e.g., experiencing high anxiety and low performance as a result of beliefs that they cannot learn math). Higher level processes such as insight, creativity, and common sense operate outside the cognitive system and are accessed at higher levels of awareness. In addition, Suarez argues that it is the *function* of thought (voluntary control over one's thinking) that provides a more primary level of agency than the *content* of thought (results of thinking such as beliefs, goals, expectations). Thought is both the immediate cause of all beliefs and can be controlled consciously and voluntarily. Self-regulation then becomes a self-confirming cycle of personal agency. Thus, new conceptions of motivation see self-regulation as a natural outgrowth of individuals' realization of personal agency in the context of positive interpersonal support and a match of personal and organizational goals.

Emerging Models of Motivation and Self-Regulation

Early theories of motivation saw humans as starting off with certain basic biological "urges" that drove behavior, or saw motivation as a function of external conditioning (McCombs, 1991b; McCombs, in press). Current theories of motivation (Meece, in press; Ryan, 1992; Weiner, 1992) are increasingly recognizing the self-determining and agentic aspects of human motivation. Individuals are not seen as simply responding to and being manipulated by internal drives or external stimuli; they are seen as being motivated by personal goals, self-constructions of reality, and personal evaluations of their worth and agency. Strategies that maximize individual motivation and performance are those that respect individual needs for autonomy, self-determination, and personal control. Although adults, like young children, can be "motivated" by external rewards and punishments, researchers are consistently discovering that higher levels of functioning result when evolving principles of human motivation and the role of self-as-agent are taken into account (Deci, 1992; McCombs, 1992; Rigby, Deci, Patrick, & Ryan, 1992; Ryan, 1992). These principles emphasize that people can operate outside the boundaries of their thoughts and conditioned belief systems, and see these cognitions as personal constructions of reality. It is when individuals get trapped into conditional self-concepts (e.g., my self-worth depends on the opinions of others) or negative evaluations of self-worth and competence that motivation and higher levels of performance suffer.

In spite of trends to define motivation within more self-determining frameworks, many current conceptualizations of motivational functioning remain deterministic and mechanistic (McCombs, 1991b). For example, Bandura's (1989) account of human agency places the locus of agency within a system of "triadic reciprocal causation" in which self-generated influences are only one source of human action; other personal factors (such as background) and the environment also have determining influences on action. Bandura (1989) contends that persons are neither autonomous agents nor mechanical conveyors of environmental influences, but because self-generated influences are contributing factors, personal agency operates within an interactional causal structure. In his recent presentation at the Nebraska Symposium on Motivation, Bandura (1991) stresses that it anticipatory cognitive mechanisms (e.g., expectations) and generative cognitive control (e.g., goals) as self-generated or emergent influences, construed and cognitively represented in consciousness, are what activate and regulate human behavior.

A number of other researchers view cognitive beliefs (about self, task, others) as "driving" the rest of the cognitive/motivational system, such as in the expectancy-value models of motivation of Eccles (1983) and Pintrich and de Groot (1990). In these models, the primary variables that predict motivation are beliefs about (a) ability to perform a task and personal responsibility for performance (expectancy competent), and (b) goals and beliefs about the importance and interest of the task (value component). Graham (this volume) is representative of this approach with her emphasis on the meaning students give to teacher actions. Her research validates that thoughts lead to feelings and feelings lead to behavior. What is missing, however, in all of these attempts from my perspective is a focus on the "I"—the self-as-agent—who steps outside the boundaries of thoughts or beliefs and exercises control at a higher level of awareness, perspective taking, and choosing to redirect the thinking processes in healthier ways.

Robinson (1987) argues that current psychological theories discount the importance of self-phenomena, particularly the explanatory value of "authentic agency" in motivation and behavior. Authentic agency is said to be in operation to the extent that individuals self-select and define those external influences that appear most nurturing of self. Theories emphasizing personal control and authentic agency over not just the contents of thought but the actual thought processes are, however, becoming more prevalent. Brandtstadter (1989) stresses the important impact for adults that self-percepts of control over personal development have on actual development in adulthood, helping individuals realize their personal development options. Iran-Nejad (1990) argues for higher-order self-regulation that not only involves conscious executive control in the internalization of external knowledge, but also involves understanding one's role in orchestrating the whole system and reconceptualizing previously learned knowledge in dynamic, holistic, active, creative, and flexible ways. Thus, we are coming to understand that as individuals develop higher levels of understanding of their agency, they see that they have the capability within themselves to be self-regulatory (i.e., authentic agency).

In my own work (McCombs & Marzano, 1990), this general framework that puts the self-as-agent at the beginning of the motivational sequence has been translated into a real-time processing model that can be used to explain an individual's variance in performance across homogeneous tasks. As shown in Fig. 4.1, when an individual is either implicitly or explicitly presented with a task, if that individual lacks an understanding of self-as-agent ("I" Self), he or she will initially filter perceptions of the task through cognitive self-system structures (beliefs about self or "Me" Self, others, and the external world) to determine the task's relationship to self-goals and its possible effect on self-beliefs and self-evaluations. If no match with self-goals is found, the task is rejected by the individual as irrelevant. If the task is judged as a threat or detrimental to self-beliefs or self-evaluations, it is rejected as a high-risk situation. Once a task is rejected, the cognitive self-system of constructed beliefs

SELF-SYSTEM

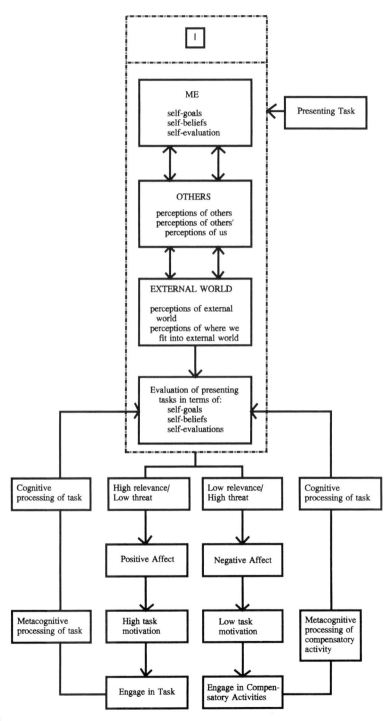

considers other presenting tasks or engages in compensatory behavior that also includes cognitive processing activities. Although compensatory activities are engaged in to protect self-beliefs and evaluations and increase situational relevance to self-goals, they are continually screened for relevance and level of threat and may, themselves, be rejected. Evaluations of tasks solely from the level of the cognitive self-system results in aversive emotions and unmotivated behavior, to the degree that the task is relevant to, or conflicts with, learned self-concept.

Performance on a task, however, is not solely a function of the extent to which an individual engages in self-evaluative, metacognitive, or cognitive construction processes. Overseeing the whole system of interpretation relative to presenting tasks is the self as agent—the self as "I." Operationally, this implies that at any point in time, the individual can gain a recognition of self as agent, a recognition that the self has fundamental control over the processes and content of thinking. With this recognition, the self as "I" overrides the more automatic interpretation of the self as "me." Thus, although uncommon, the self as "I" can cast off the interpretations of the self as "me" and engage intensely in a task even though it is not related to self-goals and is a threat to self-beliefs and evaluations. This explains such illogical acts as the self as "me" sacrificing my life to save another's.

A fundamental difference, therefore, between constructivist and self-as-agent perspectives is the understanding that individuals not only actively create and construe their personal realities, but they also fundamentally control all cognitions or thoughts. As Suarez (1988) and Mills et al. (in press) have argued, it is the *function* of thought that provides a more primary level of agency than the *content* of thought (beliefs, values, expectancies, etc.). Thought is both the immediate origin of all cognitions and amenable to conscious voluntary control. By looking at where the content of thought originates—in the person as agent—we gain an understanding that thought is the common denominator for understanding human functioning, not the content which is the product of thought.

In summary, emerging models of motivation are grappling with the concepts of authentic agency, free will, and self-determination. The source of motivation is increasingly being seen as something inside the person, as an intrinsic part of human nature to learn and grow in positive ways, that needs to be *supported or elicited* rather than *established*. There is an emerging understanding that to elicit natural motivation requires supportive interpersonal interactions and environments that provide for autonomy support and a match of personal and organizational goals. In such environments, motivation is increased to acquire and/or use higher order strategies for self-regulation of learning and learning processes. The issue in the assessment of primary motivational processes becomes one of capturing those higher-order perceptions and understandings of personal agency and

FIG. 4.1. Real-time self-as-agent processing framework. From McCombs and Marzano (1990).

future self-goals, including evaluations of personal control over and responsibility for achieving learning and performance goals.

NEW DIRECTIONS IN MOTIVATIONAL ASSESSMENT AND INTERVENTION

To capture the array of variables underlying motivation and decision making in complex situations, it is necessary to assess higher-order self-system processes and understandings of self-as-agent. It is also necessary to operationally define constructs such as reflective self-awareness, volition, and future self-goals as well as specify the reciprocal and dynamic interrelationships of domains of variables causally related to various performance outcomes. Assessment of motivation thus must be multi-dimensional and based on emerging theories of motivation that adequately define the basis of behavior.

Within my own work on assessing primary motivational variables underlying self-regulated learning (McCombs, 1987, 1991a), the following measurement goals were specified: (a) to carefully identify and define self-system structures and processes most important in self-regulated learning; (b) to use these construct definitions to evaluate the appropriateness of existing measures and to design new measures where needed; (c) to delineate a causal model of hypothesized relationships between self-system constructs and criterion variables of interest; and (d) to specify a systematic validation process establishing the psychometric properties of the measures and verifying their predictive relationships. The result was the construction of global and domain-specific, trait and state evaluations of competence and control, and domain-specific trait evaluations of the importance of being competent and exercising personal control in specific contexts. Construct definitions of control and competence were as follows:

Control is generally defined as individuals' judgments and perceptions of their capabilities to be self-determining, as well as their understanding of the contingencies responsible for success and failure. More specifically, these cognitive self-evaluation processes include (a) locus of control—underlying understandings regarding the locus of responsibility for events as internal (self) vs. external (others, fate); (b) personal control—perceptions of being able to exercise agency and personal responsibility over thoughts, feelings, and actions; and (c) attributions—tendencies to attribute reasons for successes and failures to internal (ability, effort) vs. external (luck, others) factors.

Competence is generally defined as individuals' perceptions or judgments about their capabilities to interact effectively with their environments and to execute the courses of action that are required to effectively handle particular situations. More specifically, these cognitive self-evaluation processes include (a) self-confidence—judgments of personal confidence with respect to specific capabilities or competencies; (b) adaptability—perceptions of capabilities to easily adjust to new requirements; (c) self-worth—judgments and perceptions of one's inherent value; and (d) competence—perceptions of capabilities to exercise adequate control over one's thoughts, feelings, and actions.

The development process used in the construction of scales to measure these constructs consisted of reviewing available measures, selecting items that on the basis of conceptual analyses taped the constructs of interest, revising or adapting items as necessary, and writing new items as appropriate. Separate global and domain-specific (job-related) versions were created. Trait and state versions of the global and domain-specific scales were developed to contain the same items, but with different response formats (frequency vs. intensity, respectively) and different directions to reflect how individuals generally felt vs. felt right now, respectively. That is, trait and state items differed only in terms of their response categories. Trait items asked subjects to pick responses that describe *how you generally feel* on a frequency dimension (almost never, sometimes, often, almost always). State items asked subjects to pick responses that describe *how true each statement is for you, right now, at this moment* on an intensity dimension (not at all, somewhat, moderately so, very much so). The resulting measures of competence and control consisted of a total of 320 items, with not less than 10 items per subscale (see Fig. 4.2). In addition, 30 items that assessed the importance of being competent and in control were developed as a way to refine assessments of competence and control (cf. McCombs, 1987). Sample items for each subscale are shown in Table 4.1.

Other variables important in a study of primary motivational variables based on emerging theories include: awareness of personal values and goals; psychological and vocational maturity; self-esteem and self-efficacy; expectations about the demands of the military, technical training, and ability to take responsi-

RESULTING MEASURES AND NUMBER OF ITEMS PER SUBSCALE

Scale/ Subscales	Control				Competency			
	Global		Domain-Specific		Global		Domain-Specific	
	Trait	State	Trait	State	Trait	State	Trait	State
Control Scale								
1-Locus of Control	10	10	10	10				
2-Personal Control	19	19	10	10				
3-Attributions	11	11	10	10				
Competence Scale								
1-Self-Confidence					13	13	10	10
2-Adaptability					10	10	10	10
3-Self-Worth					15	15	10	10
4-Competence					12	12	10	10
Total Number of Items: (320)	40	40	30	30	50	50	40	40

FIG. 4.2.   Construction of battery of primary motivational variables.

TABLE 4.1
Sample Items From Primary Motivational Battery

Scale	Sample Items
	Global Control
Locus of Control	Becoming a success is a matter of hard work; luck has little or nothing to do with it.
	Most people don't realize the entext to which their lives are controlled by accidental happenings.
Personal Control	I have little influence over the things that happen to me.
	My successes and failures are my own doing.
Attributions	When unfortunate things happen to me it is due to bad luck.
	Being a success is mostly a matter of hard work.
	Domain-Specific Control
Locus of Control	Getting promoted depends on how much ability you show on the job.
	Getting a good job is mostly a matter of being lucky enough to be at the right place at the right time.
Personal Control	When someone criticizes my performance at work, I feel there is nothing I can do about it.
	I do believe I can do whatever I want in my career.
Attributions	There is a direct connection between how hard I work and the promotions/successes I get.
	When I am rewarded for my performance, it is because I deserved it.
	Global Competence
Self-Confidence	I am pretty sure of myself.
	I don't have much confidence in my abilities.
Adaptability	I like to be sure I will be able to do something well before I even try doing it.
	When things don't go well, I don't give up because I know I can reach my goal eventually.
Self-Worth	I feel I am a person of worth, and at least on an equal basis with others.
	I have a low opinion of myself.
Competence	I know how to go after what I want.
	I often fail to do things as well as I would like.
	Domain-Specific Competence
Self-Confidence	I feel confident I can perform most tasks required of me on my job.
	I lack confidence in my ability to perform well in my job.
Adaptability	Facing unexpected problem situations at work doesn't bother me a lot.
	When faced with a difficult problem at work, I know I can solve it if I try.
Self-Worth	I feel stupid when I don't understand something about my job.
	I am satisfied with my job skills and abilities.
Competence	I feel competent at my job.
	I cannot complete my job tasks as quickly as others.
	Importance
Control	It is ijmportant to me to be able to change things I don't like about my job.
	It is important to me to be able to do things I can have control over.
Competence	It is important to me to be able to figure out difficult problems.
	It is important to me to be able to do the best I can in my job.

bility for learning; perceptions of ability to deal with various sources of stress; achievement motivation; success/failure attributions; and learning-related self-verbalizations. All of these variables represent various self-system processes and structures identified as related to motivation and performance. The challenge, then, is to systematically explore the dynamic and reciprocal relationships among these variables and performance outcomes. The promise within the context of military research on motivation is that attention to primary motivational variables that relate to fundamental, higher-order self-system structures and processes can both enhance performance predictions and help define effective interventions for enhancing job proficiency, readiness, and retention. The next section describes some preliminary research evidence from a study of career-decision making with Army enlisted personnel.

RESEARCH ON THE ASSESSMENT OF PRIMARY MOTIVATIONAL VARIABLES

Despite advances that have been made in the identification of variables predictive of reenlistment decisions, improvements in models of the career decision making process, and new developments in tests and measurement, the best predictive models of military enlistment decisions account for no more than 40% to 60% of the variance (McCombs, 1987). Based on the preceding conceptualization of self-system variables, McCombs, Doll, Baltzley, and Kennedy (1987) attempted to operationalize this conceptual framework in a research project for the Army Research Institute. The role of motivational and metacognitive variables in predicting reenlistment decisions was explored relative to more traditional aptitudes and abilities. In addition, the research explored the underlying causal relationships among various classes of self-system variables and between more traditional aptitude and ability measures. Classes of self-system variables included in the model were: general perceptions of personal agency, perceived control over success and failures, perceived competence in general and in specific performance domains, job satisfaction, expectancies for reenlisting or leave the Army, organizational commitment, and intentions and goals related to reenlistment. The battery of competence and control measures described in the preceding section was used to assess what was conceptualized as primary motivational variables. These more fundamental self-evaluations were the focus of the study in terms of their contribution to the prediction of career decision making as compared with more traditionally explored variables (job satisfaction, expectancies, commitment, intentions, goals).

Concurrent with the administration of the primary motivational measures, criterion data (information regarding whether and what reenlistment decision was made) were collected on 124 U.S. Army enlisted personnel, primarily males, from Ft. Rucker, Alabama. Armed Services Vocational Aptitude Battery

(ASVAB) composite scores were also retrieved on all subjects, and controlled interviews were conducted to provide alternative measures of competency and control as compared with self reports per the battery of primary motivational measures. Subjects were selected for the study on the basis of whether they were (a) within 3–6 months of a reenlistment decision, (b) within two Military Occupational Specialties (helicopter crewman, administrative specialist), and (c) first-term soldiers coming to the end of their first tour who were considered by the Army as desirable in terms of their performance and skill levels. The battery of measures (see Fig. 4.2) was administered twice in order to obtain test/retest reliability estimates. Research questions of primary interest were: (a) Can the constructs of competency and control be reliably measured? (b) Do measures of competency and control predict criteria reflecting decisions to reenlist or not reenlist? (c) Do measures of commitment add to the predictive capability of other measures? and (d) Do motivationally related measures (competency, control, commitment, intentions) add uniquely to the predictive capability presently offered by ASVAB?

The preliminary model explored via multiple stepwise regression techniques was one that placed needs for self-determination and individuals' perceptions of control and competence at the beginning of the causal chain. To the degree that needs for control and competence were being met, job satisfaction was predicted to be high, along with intentions to reenlist and organizational commitment. Findings of theoretical and practical importance included: (a) the motivational measures and their subscales demonstrated high internal consistencies, with alpha coefficients ranging from .85 to .97 on total scales and .66 to .94 on subscales (see Fig. 4.3); (b) test/retest reliabilities ranged from .58 to .86 on the total scale scores for the competence and control measures (see bottom of Fig. 4.3;

RELIABILITY INFORMATION ON EACH SUBSCALE

Scale/ Subscales	Control								Competency							
	Global				Domain-Specific				Global				Domain-Specific			
	Trait		State		Trait		State		Trait		State		Trait		State	
	α	Test/ Retest	α	Test/ Retest	α	Test/ Retest	α	Test/ Retest	α	Test/ Retest	α	Test/ Retest	α	Test/ Retest	α	Test/ Retest
Control Scale																
1-Locus of Control	.75		.68		.86		.85									
2-Personal Control	.64		.75		.67		.85									
3-Attributions	.78		.85		.70		.79									
Competence Scale																
1-Self-Confidence									.90		.92		.89		.94	
2-Adaptability									.82		.94		.81		.66	
3-Self-Worth									.90		.85		.66		.75	
4-Competence									.78		.92		.89		.92	
Total Scales	.85	.69	.94	.59	.86	.81	.91	.61	.89	.76	.94	.62	.87	.81	.82	.58

FIG. 4.3. Reliability information on each subscale.

(c) motivational variables uniquely contributed to the prediction of reenlistment decisions, accounting for between 12% and 16% of the adjusted variance; (d) there were predominantly low, nonsignificant correlations between the self-system variables and ASVAB scores, indicating that these variables may contribute unique variance to the prediction of retention-related criteria; and (e) preliminary causal modeling via path analyses of alternative logical models revealed non-linear relationships between the self-system variables and criterion variables, indicating further enhancements to prediction may be possible with innovative models (e.g., nonrecursive models) that make allowances for interactive effects and that capture dynamic, reciprocal, and complex relationships between variables. In addition, the self-system variables (personal control and competence) added predictive power to equations that included previously explored motivation variables (job satisfaction, organizational commitment, reenlistment intentions).

These preliminary findings regarding the contributions of primary motivational variables to the prediction of complex decisions are encouraging in several respects. First, we can have some confidence that these variables can be reliably measured. Second, these variables add unique variance to predictions of criterion variables of interest. Finally, the descriptive information available from specific item responses (e.g., My job is so regimented there's not much room for personal choice, It is frightening to have a lot of job responsibility) suggests that they might play a role in career counseling or other intervention programs for selection and retention of desirable military personnel (e.g., person–job matches). Of perhaps the most significance, theoretically, is the potential of systematically evaluating the motivational characteristics of those who stay in vs. leave the military service and the implications for system or policy changes that enhance the quality of personnel, skill training, and resource supports offered within the military system.

IMPLICATIONS FOR FUTURE RESEARCH AND DEVELOPMENT

As with all individuals and organizations facing the 21st century, important changes in skills and knowledge will be required. The Armed Forces is no exception, and it is expected that future emphases will include significant organization change (downsizing), career and leadership development, group training, and technological competence. Enlisting and retaining high quality personnel will continue as a need, with motivational issues taking on increasing importance. From this perspective, I believe it will be important for future research and development to continue to capitalize on higher order motivational processes and emerging theories of self-as-agent in system refinement efforts in the areas of training, selection, and retention.

To capitalize on newer theoretical assumptions regarding motivation and self-regulated learning, there will be a need to continue research on assessing higher order motivational processes that underlie more traditional measures of attitudes, beliefs, expectations, and goals. Continued research in this direction promises to add to the understanding and prediction of important performance variables. Additional directions of importance will include (a) examining alternative models of causal relationships between primary motivational variables and criterion variables of interest; and (b) exploring new paradigms of performance assessment that capture the richness of cognitive, metacognitive, and self-system and motivational variables that contribute to optimal individual and group effectiveness. For example, simulated complex team decision making tasks that model current work being done on authentic performance assessments (e.g., Shavelson, Baxter, & Pine, 1992) may prove valuable in research on the relationships of higher order motivational processes to performance. Furthermore, with a clearer understanding of individual differences in perceptions of personal agency and awareness of future self-goals, as well as the relationship of these self-system variables to environmental supports, it will be possible to establish both individual and contextual variables that can enhance the match of personal and organizational goals. These matches can then be assessed as a way to better predict those most likely to be happy and satisfied with their jobs and to reenlist.

Humans are self-determining and goal-directed, with further needs for belonging and relatedness. Motivation becomes an issue when basic needs for personal control, autonomy, and relatedness are not met. Understanding these needs and ways to enhance natural potentials for motivation and self-regulation is a key to meeting military goals for the 21st century. We are seeing demands for a transformed society while at the same time, new paradigms are emerging that capture the nature of human psychological functioning. The stage is set for designing those organizational structures within the systems supporting our society—including the military—that will elicit the highest levels of human productivity, motivation, and involvement in complex thinking and problem solving. As shown in current research on motivation, attention needs to be given to those organizational structures and quality interpersonal relationships that address individuals' basic psychological needs. In contexts that respect higher order needs for personal agency and self-determination while also addressing relatedness issues, motivation, self-regulation, and higher levels of individual and group performance can emerge.

ACKNOWLEDGMENTS

The research reported in this chapter was supported in part by the U.S. Army Research Institute for Behavioral and Social Sciences through a subcontract with Battelle Institute. However, the views, opinions and/or findings contained in this report are the authors' and should not be construed as an official ARI position, policy, or decision, unless so designated by other official documentation.

REFERENCES

Bandura, A. (1989). Human agency in social cognitive theory. *American Psychologist, 44*(9), 1175–1184.

Bandura, A. (1991). Self-regulation of motivation through anticipatory and self-reactive mechanisms. In R. Dienstbier (Ed.), *Nebraska symposium on motivation: Vol. 38. Perspectives on motivation.* Lincoln: University of Nebraska Press.

Brandtstadter, J. (1989). Personal self-regulation of development: Cross-sequential analyses of development-related control beliefs and emotions. *Developmental Psychology, 25*(1), 96–108.

Cantor, N. (1990). From thought to behavior: "Having" and "doing" in the study of personality and cognition. *American Psychologist, 45,* 735–750.

Deci, E. L. (1992). Interest and intrinsic motivation of behavior. In K. A. Renninger, S. Hidi, & A. Krapp (Eds.), *The role of interest in learning and development* (pp. 43–70). Hillsdale, NJ: Lawrence Erlbaum Associates.

Deci, E. L., & Ryan, R. M. (1991). A motivational approach to self: Integration in personality. In R. Dienstbier (Ed.), *Nebraska symposium on motivation: Vol. 38. Perspectives on motivation.* Lincoln: University of Nebraska Press.

Drillings, M. (1991, August). *ARI's basic research program.* Keynote address presented at the Motivation Conference, Sponsored by the Army Research Institute for Behavioral and Social Sciences, San Francisco, CA.

Dweck, C. S. (1991). Self-theories and goals: Their role in motivation, personality and development. In R. Dienstbier (Ed.), *Nebraska symposium on motivation: Vol. 38. Perspectives on motivation.* Lincoln: University of Nebraska Press.

Dweck, C. S., & Leggett, E. L. (1988). A social-cognitive approach to motivation and personality. *Psychological Review, 95,* 256–273.

Eccles, J. (1983). Expectancies, values and academic behaviors. In J. T. Spence (Ed.), *Achievement and achievement motives* (pp. 75–146). New York: Wiley.

Harter, S. (1990, November). *Visions of self: Beyond the me in the mirror.* Presentation as University Lecturer of the Year, University of Denver.

Harter, S. (1992). *Affective and motivational correlates of self-esteem.* In R. Dienstbier (Ed.), *Nebraska symposium on motivation: Vol. 40. Developmental perspectives on motivation.* Lincoln: University of Nebraska Press.

Inglehart, M. R., Markus, H., Brown, D. R., & Moore, W. (1987, May). *The impact of possible selves on academic achievement: An institutional analysis.* Paper presented at the Mid Western Psychological Association, Chicago.

Iran-Nejad, A. (1990). Active and dynamic self-regulation of learning processes. *Review of Educational Research, 60*(4), 573–602.

Markus, H., & Ruvulo, A. (1990). Possible selves: Personalized representations of goals. In L. Pervin (Ed.), *Goal concepts in psychology* (pp. 211–241). Hillsdale, NJ: Lawrence Erlbaum Associates.

McCombs, B. L. (1984). CAI enhancements to motivational skills training for military technical training students. *Training Technology Journal, 1*(4), 10–16.

McCombs, B. L. (1987, August). *Preliminary validation of a battery of primary motivational process variables.* Paper presented at the annual meeting of the American Psychological Association, New York.

McCombs, B. L. (1988). Motivational skills training: Combining metacognitive, cognitive, and affective learning strategies. In C. E. Weinstein, E. T. Goetz, & P. A. Alexander (Eds.), *Learning and study strategies: Issues in assessment, instruction, and evaluation.* New York: Academic Press.

McCombs, B. L. (1990). *The reciprocal empowerment model: A key to positive motivation and development.* Denver, CO: Unpublished manuscript.

McCombs, B. L. (1991a). The definition and measurement of primary motivational processes. In M. C. Wittrock & E. Baker (Eds.), *Testing and cognition.* Englewood Cliffs, NJ: Prentice Hall.

McCombs, B. L. (1991b). Overview: Where have we been and where are we going in understanding human motivation? *Journal of Experimental Education, 60*(1), 5–14.

McCombs, B. L. (1992, April). *What are the parameters of a new paradigm of motivation?* Paper presented at the annual meeting of the American Educational Research Association, San Francisco.

McCombs, B. L. (in press). Alternative perspectives for motivation. In L. Baker, O. Afflerbach, & D. Reinking (Eds.), *Developing engaged readers in school and home communities.* Hillsdale, NJ: Lawrence Erlbaum Associates.

McCombs, B. L., Doll, R. E., Baltzley, D. R., & Kennedy, R. S. (1987). *Predictive validities of primary motivation scales for reenlistment decision-making.* (ARI Final Report). Alexandria, VA: Army Research Institute for the Behavioral and Social Sciences.

McCombs, B. L., & Marzano, R. J. (1990). Putting the self in self-regulated learning: the self as agent in integrating will and skill. *Educational Psychologist, 31,* 819–833.

McCombs, B. L., & Whisler, J. S. (1989). The role of affective variables in autonomous learning. *Educational Psychologist, 24*(3), 277–306.

Meece, J. L. (in press). The role of motivation in self-regulated learning. In D. H. Schunk & B. J. Zimmerman (Eds.), *Self-regulation of learning and performance: Issues and educational applications.* Hillsdale, NJ: Lawrence Erlbaum Associates.

Mills, R. C. (1990, June). *Substance abuse, dropout and delinquency prevention: An innovative approach.* Paper presented at the 8th annual conference of the Psychology of Mind, St. Petersburg, Florida.

Mills, R. C. (1991). A new understanding of self: The role of affect, state of mind, self understanding, and intrinsic motivation. In B. L. McCombs (Ed.), Unraveling motivation: New perspectives from research and practice. Special issue of the *Journal of Experimental Education,* Fall 1991.

Mills, R. C., Dunham, R. G., & Alpert, G. P. (1988). Working with high-risk youth in prevention and early intervention programs: Toward a comprehensive model. *Adolescence, 23*(91), 643–660.

Mills, R. C., Olson, P., & Bailey, J. (1992). *Treatment effects of short term therapy based on psychology of mind.* Minneapolis-St. Paul: University of Minnesota, School of Professional Psychology.

Office of the Assistant Secretary of Defense (1992, April). *Military manpower training report for FY 1993.* Washington, DC: Department of Defense.

O'Neil, H. F., Jr., Anderson, C. L., & Freeman, J. A. (1986). Research in teaching in the armed forces. In M. C. Wittrock (Ed.), *Handbook of research on teaching* (3rd Edition, pp. 971–987). New York: Macmillan.

Pintrich, P. R., & de Groot, E. V. (1990). Motivational and self-regulated learning components of classroom academic performance. *Journal of Educational Psychology, 82*(1), 33–40.

Ridley, D. S. (1991). Reflective self-awareness: A basic motivational process. In B. L. McCombs (Ed.), Unraveling motivation: New perspectives from research and practice. Special issue of the *Journal of Experimental Education,* Fall 1991.

Ridley, D. S. (1992, April). *What do theories of self-regulated learning have to offer teachers? Toward an integration of theory and practice.* Paper presented at the annual meeting of the American Educational Research Association, San Francisco.

Rigby, C. S., Deci, E. L., Patrick, B. C., & Ryan, R. M. (1992). Beyond the intrinsic-extrinsic dichotomy: Self-determination in motivation and learning. *Motivation and Emotion, 16*(3), 165–185.

Robinson, D. N. (1987, August). *What moves us? A note on human motives.* Paper presented at the annual meeting of the American Psychological Association, New York.

Ryan, R. M. (1992). A synthetic view of the role of motivation in development. In R. Dienstbier (Ed.), *Nebraska symposium on motivation: Vol. 40. Developmental perspectives on motivation.* Lincoln: University of Nebraska Press.

Ryan, R. M., & Powelson, C. L. (1991). Autonomy and relatedness as fundamental to motivation and education. In B. L. McCombs (Ed.), Unraveling motivation: New perspectives from research and practice. Special issue of the *Journal of Experimental Education,* Fall 1991.

Ryan, R. M., & Stiller, J. (1991). The social contexts of internalization: Parent and teacher influences on autonomy, motivation, and learning. In M. L. Maehr & P. R. Pintrich (Eds.), *Advances in motivation and achievement* (Vol. 7, pp. 115–149). Greenwich, CT: JAI Press.

Schunk, D. H., & Swartz, C. W. (1991, April). *Process goals and progress feedback: Effects on children's self-efficacy and skills.* Paper presented at the annual meeting of the American Educational Research Association, Chicago.

Shavelson, R. J., Baxter, G. P., Pine, J. (1992). Performance assessments: Political rhetoric and measurement reality. *Educational Researcher, 21*(4), 22–27.

Showers, C., & Cantor, N. (1985). Social cognition: A look at motivated strategies. *Annual Review of Psychology, 36,* 275–305.

Sternberg, R. J. (1986). Three heads are better than one. *Psychology Today, 20*(8), 56–62.

Suarez, E. M. (1988). A neo-cognitive dimension. *The Counseling Psychologist, 16*(2), 238–244.

Suarez, R., Mills, R. C., & Stewart, D. (1987). *Sanity, insanity, and common sense.* New York: Fawcett Columbine.

Weiner, B. (1992). *Human motivation: Metaphors, theories, and research.* London: Sage Publications.

Whisler, J. S. (1991). The impact of teacher relationships and interactions on self-development and motivation. In B. L. McCombs (Ed.), Unraveling motivation: New perspectives from research and practice. Special issue of the *Journal of Experimental Education,* Fall 1991.

5 Individual Differences in Conation: Selected Constructs and Measures

Richard E. Snow
Douglas N. Jackson III
Stanford University

In recent years, a plethora of psychological constructs and their associated measures have been proposed for attention in instructional research and evaluation. These constructs are attempts to capture in one way or another, aspects of human learning and performance relevant to instruction that go beyond conventional constructs of cognitive ability. Some are old concepts in psychology that have not received much attention in contemporary work. Some are quite new, with relatively little foundation in prior research. Some represent the inventions of educational practitioners. Many are designed to identify potentially important individual differences among students that influence learning in instructional situations. Many also can be used to assess outcomes from such learning.

Among the most interesting and potentially useful of these constructs are those reflecting motivational and volitional aspects of human behavior; we call these *conative* constructs. There are of course also important *cognitive* constructs and *affective* constructs, both old and new. The distinction between cognition, conation, and affection is convenient and historically well-founded in psychology, though it should be regarded as a matter of emphasis rather than a true partition; all human behavior, especially including instructional learning and achievement, involves some mixture of all three aspects (Hilgard, 1980). But the conative side of school learning has been largely ignored in instructional assessment until very recently (Snow, 1980; Snow & Farr, 1987).

By way of formal definition, *conation* represents:

> That aspect of mental process or behavior by which it tends to develop into something else; an intrinsic "unrest" of the organism . . . almost the opposite of homeostasis. A conscious tendency to act; a conscious striving. . . . Impulse, desire,

volition, purposive striving all emphasize the conative aspect. (English & English, 1958, p. 104)

Among the constructs we place in this category today are: several kinds of achievement motivational distinctions, including need for achievement and fear of failure, but also various beliefs about one's own abilities and their use, feelings of self-esteem and self-efficacy, and attitudes and interests concerning particular subject-matter learning; volitional aspects pertaining to persistence, academic work ethic, will to learn, mental effort investment, and mindfulness in learning; intentional constructs reflecting control or regulation of actions leading toward chosen goals, attitudes toward the future, and self-awareness about proximal and distal goals and consequences; and many kinds of learning styles and strategies hypothesized to influence cognitive processes and outcomes of instruction. Many other more traditional personality or style constructs, such as intellectual flexibility, conscientiousness, extraversion, or reflection-impulsivity, could also be added to the list. And many of these constructs and measures may prove extremely useful in understanding student commitment to learning, or lack thereof.

Unfortunately, most of the research on conative constructs in education has been limited to small-scale, isolated and piecemeal studies. Measures have usually been limited to questionnaires, often hastily developed and inadequately evaluated. No programmatic validational research has yet been mounted to determine what theoretical and practical distinctions and what kinds of assessments will best serve the needs of instructional research, evaluation, and improvement.

The purpose of this chapter is to review briefly some of the constructs and measures that seem most promising as useful for future research and evaluation in instructional psychology. We include examples of innovative assessment methods where possible. We also discuss questions and criticisms relating to construct validation in hopes of promoting more programmatic research in this direction. However, we cannot here provide a comprehensive review of literature on any particular construct or on conative functions in general. More general discussions of the problems and prospects of conative assessment in instruction, and details on various aspects are available elsewhere (see, for example, Snow, 1989a, 1989b, 1990; Snow & Farr, 1987; Snow, Corno, & Jackson, in press, and Snow & Jackson, 1992).

THEORETICAL FRAMEWORK

A Provisional Taxonomy

It should be helpful as an overview to provide some rationale for our selection of the constructs included, and for their organization into categorical order here. This may help explain terminology and ultimately step toward a more standardized taxonomy for use in further research. Our categorization is admittedly rough and provisional, and in some instances rather arbitrary. However, we do see some proximities and symmetries we think worth preserving and considering further as suggestions for research, even if they are not ultimately retained in a more formal or complete theory.

Figure 5.1 shows our present schematic taxonomy of conative constructs and its place in relation to the cognitive and affective domains. We see the conative domain as "located" in some sense between affect and cognition, and there is some theoretical justification for this (see Kuhl & Beckman, 1985, in press). We also see motivation and volition as forming a continuum within the conative category—a kind of commitment pathway from wishes to wants to intentions to

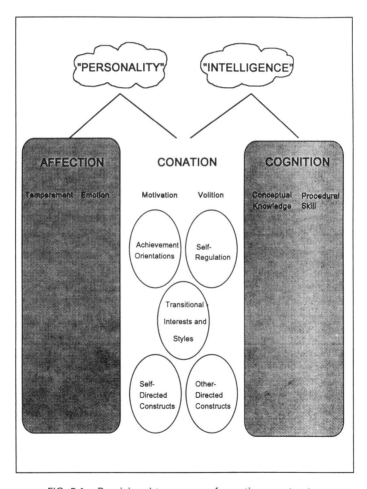

FIG. 5.1. Provisional taxonomy of conative constructs.

actions, again following other theory (Heckhausen & Kuhl, 1985). However, we do not extend this continuum to the temperament and emotion constructs of the affective domain or to the ability and knowledge constructs of the cognitive domain, which would be located in the shaded regions of Fig. 5.1. Nor do we enter the old and continuing theoretical debates about the priority or primacy of cognitive versus affective influences (see, for example, Izard, Kagan, & Zajonc, 1984; Lazarus, 1991; Reisenzein & Schönpflug, 1992). For the most part, we shade these domains out of consideration here. Finally, we note that conation as a category seems to include aspects of both *personality* and *intelligence*. We avoid these cloudy concepts as too molar and vague for our purposes here.

The first two categories of conative constructs identified in Fig. 5.1 are the main concern in this chapter. The first includes the various constructs of achievement motivation and anxiety. Related motivational constructs address individual differences in wishes, wants, needs, or goals, and either positive or negative expectations with respect to them. The second category contains volitional, self-regulatory constructs addressing individual differences in intentions and the control of effort and action with respect to them. Here are constructs representing action control, effort investment, and the like.

But there are also interest constructs that seem to have intrinsic motivational significance in either short or long-range connection to performance in instructional learning. There is voluminous research on long-range, career goal interests and also scattered new work on particular subject-matter or kinds of activities or situations. There are also dozens of personal and learning style constructs, some of which seem to reflect characteristic volitional differences. Some interest and style constructs should relate to one another, in that particular kinds of instructional methods and content seem to call for and promote development of characteristic interests and styles of work. Also, both kinds of constructs represent preferences. We include reference to some examples in this chapter as transitional constructs between the motivational and volitional categories, but we cannot review the whole category here.

Finally, on the motivational side, we locate the category of self-directed constructs, self-esteem, self-efficacy, etc. and on the volition side we form a category of other-directed constructs. This would include beliefs and perceptions about subject-matter domains, instructional situations, instructors, and other students, but also such constructs as persuasibility, leadership, social competence, need for social approval, and Machiavellianism. We omit discussion of these altogether.

Each of our categories touches one or another or our domain boundaries in some way. This underscores the fuzzy character of many distinctions and reminds us that some investigators prefer cognitive interpretations of what we call volitional constructs and affective interpretations of what we call motivational constructs. Thus, aspects of self-regulation, style and strategy, and knowledge and belief structure are often described as strictly cognitive, or metacognitive.

Achievement motivation, anxiety, some interest factors and self concepts are often interpreted as temperamental dispositions. There is also sometimes a state-trait distinction in the interpretive contrast as well. We emphasize the conative aspect here because it is so often ignored. But only time and much validational research will show us what kinds of interpretations we are entitled to. In the interim, promoting research in this direction will at least enrich the psychological spectrum with which instructional research and evaluation contends.

A Performance Commitment and Assembly Pathway

As noted earlier, we imagine a commitment pathway from wishes to wants to intentions to actions along which the distinction between motivation and volition can be made (following Heckhausen & Kuhl, 1985). We also think it useful to imagine a parallel assembly pathway along which the production of cognitive performance can be traced (Snow, 1989b). A condensed representation of the result is shown in Fig. 5.2. Although highly speculative and schematic, such a view may help suggest how some conative constructs can be distinguished from one another in process terms.

In brief, the Heckhausen–Kuhl (1985; see also Kuhl, 1986 and Kuhl & Beckman, in press) theory concerns the processes that transform wishes to wants, to intentions, to actions, and that regulate the progress of actions in relation to goals. A wish is essentially a value attached to a goal. These values are valences or incentives with respect to anticipated end states, which can be positive or negative. The individual's basic emotional needs and interests presumably dictate these wishes or goal values, at least in part. There are also expectancies with respect to the attainment of any particular goal. The expectancy-value theories of Atkinson and Feather (1966) and Heckhausen (1977) then predict what goal will be chosen in a given situation. However, there is also a goal hierarchy, and lower-order or more proximal goals can differ in their instrumentality with respect to higher-order or more distal goals. A wish becomes a want when there is sufficient expectancy and instrumentality (i.e., when it exceeds a certain threshold of potency). Also, proximal or lower goals receive valence and potency from distal or higher goals. So, for example, some learners want to learn from today's instruction, because they want to do well on the next achievement test, because they want to pass the course, etc., ultimately, to graduate and reach a higher level of education. We see most kinds of individual differences classed as achievement orientations in Fig. 5.1 as related mainly to processes in this wish-want segment of the pathway.

Then, for a want to become an intention, it must also be relevant to action conditions expected in the future. That is, conditions will need to favor the intended action goals in terms of opportunity, time, and means, as well as importance and urgency. Achievement orientations or styles that concern preferences for some kinds of learning conditions over others should be related to this

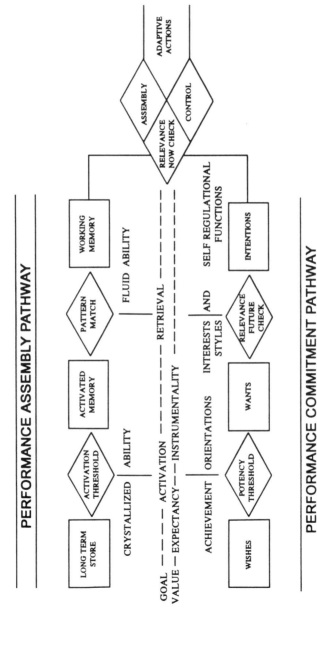

FIG. 5.2. Performance commitment and assembly pathway.

want-intention segment. So also should interests in particular learning activities, though broad subject matter or career interests would presumably be relevant throughout the wish–want–intention region.

Lastly, for an intention to become an action it must also be immediately relevant in the present situation, under control in the person-situation interaction, and maintained or protected against competing intentions and action tendencies in the ongoing flow of performance. The category of individual difference constructs called action controls seems most related to this intention-action segment. Various personality and learning style constructs should also be connected here.

Figure 5.2 also depicts a cognitive performance assembly pathway, as noted. This part of the schema is intended to represent the retrieval of cognitive knowledge and skill components and their assembly and reassembly into performance programs in a particular sequence of learning tasks (see Snow 1989b, 1992). Consistent with available theory and evidence, it suggests that crystallized cognitive abilities are more associated with the long-term store and activation region of the assembly pathway, because they are thought to be triggered and retrieved as units given appropriate stimulus conditions. Fluid ability is more associated with the pattern matching and assembly functions in working memory because it is thought to reflect more fine-grain adaptation to the flow of person-task interaction as well as inferential reasoning therein. Although it may seem fanciful to suggest parallels and connections of this sort at this stage of research, there is evidence to suggest that crystallized ability interacts with some achievement orientations and fluid ability correlates with some kinds of action controls and styles, at least under some instructional conditions.

ACHIEVEMENT ORIENTATIONS

Need for Achievement

Perhaps the oldest standing conative construct relevant to instruction is Need for Achievement, traditionally defined in terms of competition with a standard of excellence in relation to particular goals. Until the late 1940s, the prevailing view was that human motivational phenomena could be explained by an analysis of the primary needs (such as hunger) of all animals. But psychologists influenced by Murray (1938) had accumulated a corpus of data on complexities of human motivation that seemed difficult to account for by reference to basic organismic factors. Atkinson and McClelland (1948) sought a new approach to the study of human motivation that went beyond the reductionism of the time (Heckhausen, Schmalt, & Schneider, 1985). Their measure was Murray's (1938) Thematic Apperception Test (TAT), a projective technique using ambiguous pictures as stimuli about which respondents generate stories. The stories are then scored for particular themes.

The assessment technique assumes that if a person is motivated to achieve a particular goal, then thoughts concerning that motive should be readily accessible in the person's memory and should be reflected in their stories and scores. Although the TAT had been used in clinical work, evidence for its validity and theoretical viability was weak. Atkinson and McClelland (1948) successfully demonstrated validity for the TAT as a measure of need for food in a food deprivation experiment and as a measure of experimentally induced need for achievement. In further studies, they and their colleagues investigated individual differences in need for achievement in a variety of experiments guided by the Lewinian notion that achievement behavior would be influenced by characteristics of both person and environment (Lewin, 1926). But questions about the validity of the TAT remained (Entwistle, 1972).

McClelland later distinguished two dimensions of achievement motivation: fear-of-failure and hope-of-success. Some persons are primarily motivated to avoid failure, whereas others are primarily motivated to achieve success. Both aspects of motivation can lead to effort investment and success. But persons with different profiles differ in the kinds of risks they prefer to take. Those seeking success choose moderately difficult tasks where the payoff is also moderate. Those wishing to avoid failure choose either easy, low payoff tasks where failure is unlikely, or very difficult, high payoff tasks where failure is probable and expected.

Assessment of both dimensions is possible using McClelland, Atkinson, Clark, and Lowell's (1953) adaptation of the TAT, scored for hope of success and fear of failure, and deriving measures of net hope (the difference) and total achievement motivation (the sum). Another measure of the same variables from the TAT was devised by Schmalt (1976) called the Achievement-Motive Grid.

Numerous questionnaire measures have been devised to measure need for achievement (see Lens & DeCruyenaere, 1991). Proponents of TAT procedures (e.g., McClelland, 1972; McClelland, Koestner, & Weinberger, 1989) argue that TAT more validly measures different aspects of achievement motivation than questionnaire procedures. Over the years, proponents of questionnaires have disputed the reliability and validity of TAT, citing the various concerns about projective assessment techniques in general (for discussion, see Cronbach, 1990). Most recently, in a meta-analysis of 105 empirical research articles, Spangler (1992) compared TAT and questionnaire measures, to conclude that:

> the correlations between TAT measures of need for achievement with outcomes were on average positive; that these correlations were particularly large for outcomes such as career success measured in the presence of intrinsic, or task-related, achievement incentives; that questionnaire measures of need for achievement were also positively correlated with outcomes, particularly in the presence of external or social achievement incentives; and that on average TAT-based correlations were larger than questionnaire-based correlations. (p. 140)

In other words, Spangler found an interaction between the type of measure (TAT vs. questionnaire) and the environmental stimuli (task-related vs. social achievement incentives). Furthermore, Spangler found a low correlation of .09 between TAT and questionnaire measures of need for achievement. This supports the notion that TATs and questionnaires are validly measuring different aspects of achievement motivation. However, Spangler's meta-analysis compared TAT results to those obtained from what must be a diverse set of questionnaire measures of variable reliability and test construction standards. The correlations between questionnaire measures and achievement outcomes might well have differed depending on the particular questionnaire measures used in the studies included; Spangler did not discuss these measures in detail.

Lens and DeCruyenaere (1991) reported educational achievement relations for several of the most widely used questionnaire measures. It does seem that these measures offer useful prediction in educational settings. Both TAT and questionnaire measures have also been used with success in research on aptitude-treatment interactions in instruction, most notably by McKeachie and his colleagues (see summaries of these and other studies by Cronbach & Snow, 1977). Of particular note is Lens's (1983) demonstration of curvilinear relations with educational achievement measures for both need for achievement and fear of failure. Maximum achievement was shown by students in the middle range on both questionnaires, on average. Achievement declined as students were scored more toward either end of either dimension. These relations are consistent with the classical theory of arousal and serve as a warning against thoughtless use of linear models in conative measurement.

Fear of Failure and Test Anxiety

The fear of failure dimension of achievement motivation is essentially the same construct widely referred to as test anxiety but more properly interpreted as evaluation anxiety. The typical measures are questionnaires designed to reflect individual differences in proneness to fear of failure in evaluative situations generally, not just on tests.

Mandler and Sarason (1952) began the study of test anxiety, interpreting differences in performance of high- and low-test-anxious students on the basis of learned psychological drives. Two kinds of drives were said to be evoked by test situations: task-directed drives and learned anxiety drives. These stimulate two opposite and incompatible kinds of behavior: task-relevant efforts to finish the task and thereby reduce the anxiety and self-directed, task-irrelevant responses, manifested by insecurity, anticipation of negative outcomes or diminished self-worth and status, and implicit attempts to leave the evaluative situation (Mandler & Sarason, 1952).

Alpert and Haber (1960) labeled these task-directed and task-irrelevant drives as facilitating and debilitating anxieties, respectively, and devised a questionnaire to distinguish these components in subscales. Mandler and Sarason provided their questionnaire with only a debilitating scale, inferring the presence of one anxiety from the absence of the other. From factor analyses of this scale, Liebert and Morris (1967) proposed that debilitating test anxiety is itself bidimensional, consisting of separate components for worry and emotionality. They defined worry as cognitive concerns about the consequences of failure and emotionality as reactions of the autonomic nervous system that are evoked by evaluative stress. This evaluative stress can be associated with particular content domains or performance situations, such as learning mathematics or using computers. Spielberger (1980) has applied these concepts of worry and emotionality in the construction and development of another questionnaire system that also provides the distinction between trait and state anxiety.

The research literature on test anxiety is voluminous (Hembree, 1988) and in addition to much correlational and experimental evidence, there are strong demonstrations of test anxiety operating in interaction with ability differences and instructional treatment variations to influence educational learning (see Cronbach & Snow, 1977; Snow, 1989a, 1989b). There are also indications that test anxiety interacts with test format and test taking strategy to influence student performance (Schmitt & Crocker, 1981). Unfortunately, it is also the case that most of this research fails to distinguish among the components of test anxiety or to recognize it as only the negative side of motivation, that is, only half the story of performance in evaluative situations. The positive side of motivation (e.g., need for achievement) is also aroused in evaluative situations and makes a contribution that needs to be included when explaining differences in test performance (Rand, Lens, & Decock, 1989; Naveh-Benjamin, McKeachie, Lin, & Tucker, 1986).

Also important are information processing approaches to the study of test anxiety, as discussed by Hunsley (1987), Naveh-Benjamin, McKeachie, and Lin (1987), Tobias (1985), and Sieber, O'Neil, and Tobias (1977), among others. Tobias (1985), for example, discusses competing hypotheses concerned with how anxiety might hinder information processing in learning and performance at different stages of processing. The interference hypothesis suggests that the evaluative threat posed in testing situations impedes the retrieval of already learned information for high-anxious students by reducing their cognitive processing resources. The deficit-skills hypothesis argues that inadequate initial preparation and poor test-taking skills account for the reduced performance of high anxious students. Tobias cites evidence suggesting that these competing hypotheses are not mutually exclusive, and that both can yield instructionally relevant research. Other work along these lines by Naveh-Benjamin, McKeachie, and Lin (1987) has used nonevaluative situations to distinguish students with retrieval problems from students having organizational and other problems. Identifying the nature of the relationship between anxiety and information processing could serve as a foundation for designing differential treatment programs for high anxious students that might be more effective in improving learning and performance than global test anxiety reduction programs or study skill improvement programs. It might also lead to measurement techniques based on performance indicators as well as questionnaires.

Other Components of Achievement Motivation

Just as fear of failure seems composed of distinct parts, the original positive, hope for success aspect of achievement motivation has also been decomposed. The many measures noted earlier may well tap different aspects. Ray (1982) listed over 70 different achievement measures, and Fineman (1977) listed 22. As noted before, projective and questionnaire measures have often been found uncorrelated (e.g., Spangler, 1992; Weinstein, 1969). Sometimes different questionnaire measures seem to be linked by little more than the use of the word *achievement* in their descriptors.

Jackson, Ahmed, and Heapy (1976) sought to explore the multidimensional nature of achievement motivation using a multitrait multimethod design. Following a conceptual analysis of the achievement construct, they postulated six distinct components: Concern for Excellence (motivation for competition with a standard of excellence, to do one's best, as the component originally defined by McClelland et al., 1953); Competitiveness (motivation for competing with others in order to win); Acquisitiveness (motivation based on the reinforcing properties of material rewards); Status with experts (motivation associated with the rewarding aspects of striving for social recognition with experts); Status with peers (motivation associated with the rewarding aspects of striving for social recognition with one's peers); Achievement via independence (motivation to do well in tasks and environments where individual initiative is rewarded).

Factor analytic results supported these distinctions. For example, the emergence of acquisitiveness as distinct from achievement is important because it stands in contrast to McClelland (1961, p. 47) who views wealth as a symbol and secondary to achievement. Jackson et al.'s (1976) work suggests that achievement and acquisitiveness do not necessarily covary. Furthermore, Jackson et al. and Atkinson have slightly different views on the nature of achievement behavior. According to Jackson et al. (1976), achievement-oriented behavior is "the resolution of the six primary vectors interacting with a given situation" (p. 19), whereas Atkinson views achievement-oriented behavior as the resultant of hope for success minus fear of failure plus various extrinsic influences. For a methodological treatment of the Jackson et al. (1976) study, see Messick (1989). Cassidy and Lynn (1989) report a questionnaire measure of multidimensional achievement motivation combining the Jackson et al. (1976) questionnaire with questionnaires from Lynn, Hampson, & Magee (1983), Spence and Helmreich (1983) and others.

Other perspectives on achievement motivation could also be included here. For example, attribution theory offers another approach to this analysis (Weiner, 1986). Although work in this line often ignores individual differences, there have been attempts to develop usable assessment instruments from this perspective. A main example is Anderson's (1983) work on attributional styles.

In a similar vein, Nicholls, Patashnick, and Nolen (1985) examined high-school students' perceptions of the causal attributions related to school success. For example, students who believed that school should enable them to enhance their wealth and status were less likely to be committed to learning for its own sake than students who believed schools should teach commitment to society, understanding of the world, and high standards. Nicholls et al.'s work is important because it links students' personal goals with their educational ideologies and causal attributions for success. A related approach assesses a broad array of personal goals and personal agency beliefs to capture the multifaceted character of achievement motivation (see Ford & Ford, 1987; Ford & Thompson, 1985). For other approaches to personal goals, see Ames (1992); Ames and Ames (1984); Ames and Archer (1988); Blumenfeld (1992), and Nicholls, Cheung, Lauer, and Patashnick (1989).

Achievement via Independence Versus Achievement via Conformance

It was noted earlier that achievement via independence has been identified as a component of achievement motivation. A related approach to subdividing achievement motivation is to contrast achievement via independence from achievement via conformance. The former was defined as a drive to do well in tasks and environments where individual initiative is rewarded. A high scoring person here is described as mature, foresighted, demanding, and self-reliant. In contrast, the latter refers to a drive to do well when tasks and environment are well defined. A high scoring person is described as capable, efficient, organized, responsible, and sincere. These constructs have been measured by scales of the California Psychological Inventory, a well-known self-report personality inventory that has been subjected to extensive research. Factor analytic studies tend to group the two scales with other scales to create more general personality constructs; the independence scale is grouped with intellectual efficiency and flexibility, whereas the conformance scale is grouped with conformity, responsibility, compliance, and conscientiousness.

Morris and Snyder (1978) reported strong correlations between one achievement motivation scale and both achievement via conformance and achievement via independence. But another achievement motivation measure correlated only moderately. Morris and Snyder also experimented with several a priori scoring procedures that differed from the standard procedures, and these dramatically changed the relationships observed among the measures. Ac and Ai have also been included in several Aptitude-Treatment-Interaction studies designed to test whether students who are high Ac or Ai would be more successful when presented with instruction that was structured and demanding of conformity versus instruction that emphasized student initiative and independence, respectively (Domino, 1968, 1971). In these studies, better student work was produced when the instructor's teaching style was matched to the student. High Ac's did better with formal instruction, and high Ai's excelled when allowed initiative and self-direction. Other studies at the high school level (see Snow, 1977, for a summary) have confirmed the importance of the Ai–Ac distinction and its relation to achievement in these different instructional situations. Furthermore, the two measures seem unrelated to ability or anxiety.

TRANSITIONAL INTERESTS AND STYLES

Intrinsic Motivation

Researchers often use the terms intrinsic motivation and interest interchangeably, even thought it appears that the two may be different though closely related constructs. Persons engage in tasks and activities that are intrinsically motivating for their own sake, not to receive some external reward or avoid some negative consequence. "Intrinsically motivated learning is learning that occurs in a situation in which the most narrowly defined activity from which the learning occurs would be done without any external reward or punishment" (Malone & Lepper, 1987, p. 229). Interest in the concept of intrinsic motivation was stimulated in part by White (1959), who argued that curiosity, exploration, and attempts at mastery can be considered expressions of an intrinsic need to deal competently with one's environment (Harter & Connell, 1984). Recent cognitive evaluation theory (Deci & Ryan, 1985) strikes a similar tone. According to Deci and Ryan, intrinsically motivated behavior is based in an individual's need to be competent and self-determining and arises from an internal locus of causality in which individuals undertake behavior for its "internal rewards," including interest and mastery. Deci and Ryan (1985) view interest as an emotional outcome or reward of intrinsic motivation. Factor analytic studies of school motivation have obtained factors for curiosity and interest in school work, and intrinsic motivation (Snow, 1989b).

A few self-report scales have recently been constructed to measure aspects of intrinsic motivation. One by Ryan and Connell (1989) for late elementary and middle school students contains subscales for intrinsic motivation and three forms of extrinsic motivation. The same scales are provided by Vallerand, Blais, Briere, and Pelletier (1989) for use with college students. This instrument also adds a scale for lack of interest or poor motivation for academic material. Harter's (1981) instrument is a forced choice measure of intrinsic vs. extrinsic motivation including subscales for preference for challenge versus easy work; incentive to work to satisfy one's own interest and curiosity versus to please the teacher and obtain good grades; attempts at independent mastery versus dependence on the teacher; independent judgment versus reliance on teacher's judgment; and internal versus external criteria for success and failure. These subscales clustered, and can be scored for constructs labeled Autonomous Judgment and Intrinsic Mastery Motivation.

Measures used to assess the presence or degree of intrinsic motivation for a particular person and situation at a particular time need to be designed to represent the person-situation interactional character of the construct, as well as its state vs. trait aspect. More than most other achievement motivation constructs, intrinsic motivation seems more interstitial between person, situation, and time, and thus less accessible by conventional questionnaire. Given the theoretical as well as practical importance of the construct, much more extensive assessment research is needed.

Another line of work refers to motives directed towards specific content areas or subject-matter oriented interests which may also vary within learning situations. Nenniger (1987) describes a content motive in learning as "an enduring, highly general and very stable personality trait that determines the person's sensitivity to situational determinants" (p. 159). He contrasts content motives with achievement motives, which he regards as "highly general and a very stable result of the socialization process" (p. 159). In contrast to achievement motives, content motives may need to be considered as individual difference variables which are modified, even as they affect learning. In several studies, Nenniger has used a questionnaire to assess content-oriented motive toward mathematics. There are separate scales for interest in mathematics, and readiness for work in mathematics.

Individual Interest

Individual interest is a relatively enduring and stable preference for certain topics, subject areas, or activities (Schiefele, 1991). In an attempt to provide a theoretical definition of individual differences in interest, Schiefele and Krapp (1988) proposed an "Educational Interest Theory," which regards interest as a "specific form of relationship between a person and an object." This relationship is characterized by a concrete interaction between the person and the object and an enduring, stable disposition or orientation toward the object. They suggest that this interest relationship is expressed in cognitive, emotional, and value terms, in which there is strong subjective meaning and self-intentionality towards the object. Prenzel (1988) added to the definition qualities of persistence (the maintenance of the relationship by repeated engagements with the object) and selectivity (the stability of content in consecutive engagements over time). Observing the need for a theoretically based means of assessing interest, Schiefele,

Krapp, and Winteler (1988) described the development of a questionnaire by Winteler and Sierwald (1987) yielding scores for both interest and cognitive competence. Further developments focus on assessing the combined "tendency or the willingness to acquire knowledge about the object of interest" (Schiefele, Krapp, & Winteler, 1988, p. 7).

There is evidence that high interest learners achieve deeper understanding than low interest learners. But it is not clear how the learning of high interest learners differs from that of extrinsically motivated learners, or how interest and the quality of learning outcome relate (Schiefele, 1991). Further research needs to address the relationship between learning processes and strategies and interest, but also the emotional aspect or valence associated with interest. Further, since working on interesting tasks improves the quality of the learning experience, interest should be considered a desired outcome of learning as well as a factor that motivates learning.

Deep Versus Surface Approaches to Learning

There are very long lists of learning styles and strategies proposed as distinct constructs of use in instructional research, and there are also many multiscale questionnaires available (see, for example, Curry, 1990; Keefe, 1987; Keefe & Monk, 1988; Pintrich, Smith, Garcia, & McKeachie, 1991; Schmeck, 1988; Weinstein, Goetz, & Alexander, 1988). Styles are usually defined as characteristic ways in which individuals prefer to learn, and strategies are particular information processing activities habitually applied in learning situations with the aim of promoting more efficient or effective performance. Rather than address the complex definition, measurement, and validation problems involved in this category, we adopt the pervasive style distinction between deep and surface approaches to the processing of information in learning situations proposed by Marton and Säljö (1976) and Entwistle (1987a, 1987b), and their coworkers (Entwistle & Ramsden, 1983; Marton, Hounsell, & Entwistle, 1984). We think this distinction summarizes the effective result in learning activities of a large number of other style and strategy differences. Also, although this result may be interpreted in cognitive information processing terms, it clearly reflects differences in intention or commitment to learn, which is a broader conative construct.

In the deep approach, learners regard the learning material (text, problem, etc.) as the means through which to gain an understanding of the underlying meaning found in the material. In the surface approach, learners regard the particular learning material as what needs to be learned, without attempting to link it to a larger conceptual framework. Students who are intrinsically motivated and learning for its own sake with less concern about their performance, and particularly others' evaluations of their performance, are more likely to use a deep approach. Learning is viewed primarily as constructing meaning and as an interpretive process of understanding reality. A surface approach is likely to occur when students are motivated to fulfill the demands placed on them by others, so it relates more to extrinsic motivation and evaluation anxiety and is particularly sensitive to assessment procedures. Learning is regarded as a passive transmission of what is found in learning materials to the head of the learner, with particular emphasis on memorization in knowledge acquisition. The deep vs. surface dichotomy has elements that are both state- and trait-like. Marton, Hounsell, and Entwistle (1984) described it as not ". . . a stable characteristic of the student, but rather . . . a relation between the student's perception of a task and his approach to it" (p. 135). Yet research has implied that it "was to some extent a stable characteristic of the student—or at least that some students adopted consistent approaches across a range of different study tasks." (p. 213). The relationship between deep vs. surface approach and performance is of course indirect. Successful performance can be achieved through either approach with effort, but the deep approach will lead to far greater understanding than the surface approach.

Both questionnaire and interview assessment methods have been developed, and there is now solid evidence on the deep vs. surface distinction as important in learning. There is also evidence for another distinct approach, called *strategic,* to represent learners whose activities aim mainly at impressing instructors and obtaining the highest possible grade by whatever means or process is necessary. Unfortunately, there has not yet been sufficient work on relating these distinctions to the many other style and strategy constructs previously noted. Deep vs. surface processing ought to correlate with measures of subject-matter interests and intrinsic motivation, but also with other components of achievement motivation. The strategic approach may also be close to what others have called a performance as opposed to a deeper mastery orientation (Dweck & Leggett, 1988). This distinction is one of our volitional constructs taken up next.

ACTION CONTROLS

Action Versus State Orientation

According to action control theory, volitional control processes are called on to maintain intended actions and inhibit competing actions or distractions when a desired intention is perceived to be difficult to enact. The difficulty of enacting an intention is influenced by the strength of competing intentions, the amount of social pressure to engage in alternative activities, and the extent to which the individual is currently "state oriented." State orientation is simultaneously both an ability-like and state-like construct hypothesized to influence self-regulatory efficiency. State oriented persons are characterized by a "fixation on past, present, or future states, for example, on a past failure to attain a goal, on the present emotional consequences of that failure, or on the desired goal state itself" (Kuhl & Kraska, 1989, p. 366).

A second factor leading to volitional control is that the students perceived ability or sense of personal agency or self-efficacy (Bandura, 1977; Ford & Thompson, 1985) to enact an intention must exceed some critical level. That is, they must both perceive that they can implement the intention and also perceive that the environment or situation will allow them to implement it.

Kuhl's theory includes a taxonomy of six volitional strategies that allow students to protect selected intentions from competing action tendencies (see Kuhl, 1984 and Corno, 1986, 1989 for presentations of the complete taxonomy). To illustrate these strategies, suppose that a student needs to support the intention to do homework and inhibit the preference to watch television. The student could use *selective attention* strategies to try to avoid visual contact and engagement with the television set, or *motivation control* strategies involving self-reinforcement and punishment to emphasize the sense of satisfaction that comes from completing the homework. *Emotion control* strategies (such as reassuring self-speech) could also be used to limit anxiety about the difficulty in starting the homework. *Environmental control* strategies, such as choosing a work environment away from the distraction of the television, could also be used.

Kuhl and Kraska (1989) have developed a standardized measure of these strategies called the Metamotivational Knowledge Test for Children (MKTC). This measure consists of three pictures that depict situations in which it is difficult to maintain an intention. For example, one picture shows a student working on homework while friends play outside the window. Respondents are asked questions about alternative strategies for maintaining desired intentions and avoiding distractions. Scores increase almost linearly from Grade 1 to Grade 4 for motivation control, attention control, and coping with failure, but scores on emotion control remain flat, suggesting that emotion control might develop later in childhood. Scores also correlate positively with teacher ratings of compliance with classroom rules and overall adjustment to school.

Action control theory led to empirical research on an individual difference construct labeled action orientation (vs. state orientation). The action-oriented individual "is characterized by an intentional focus on a situationally appropriate action plan" (Kuhl & Kraska, 1989, p. 366). He or she is able to attend successively or even simultaneously to all of the following: (a) the present state; (b) some future state; (c) a discrepancy between the present and future states; and (d) an appropriate action that will lead to the transformation of the present state into the desired future state (Kuhl, 1987). Action oriented individuals tend to take immediate action to achieve their goals. In contrast, state oriented individuals tend to focus on past difficulties and situationally inappropriate intentions. The state-oriented individual is unable to deal effectively with these four elements. His or her behavior is marked by the overmaintenance of an intention that is either unrealistic or should be postponed. This overmaintenance can result in a "fixation on past, present, or future states, for example, on a past failure to attain a goal, on the present emotional consequences of that failure, or on the desired goal state itself" (Kuhl & Kraska, 1989, p. 366).

Kuhl (1981, 1984) developed a self-report measure of action vs. state orientation. Each item specifies a situation followed by an action oriented and a state oriented response. This measure yields scores on three types of action vs. state orientation: performance related, failure related, and decision related, and does not yield a combined score. A sample item from the decision-related subscale is: "When I have work to do at home: (a) It is often hard for me to get the work done, (b) I usually get it done right away." Kuhl (1984) reports moderate correlations between action orientation subscale scores and personality variables such as test anxiety, extroversion, self-consciousness, achievement motivation, future orientation, and cognitive complexity. These correlations reflect the theoretically expected overlap and at the same time indicate that a sizable proportion of variance in action-orientation scores cannot be accounted for by these variables.

In addition to the self-report measure, more recent work by Kuhl and Kraska (1989) has emphasized a computerized performance-based assessment of the efficiency of action control. In the children's version, respondents complete a choice-reaction-time task in the lower left portion of the screen. Successful performance earns them money to buy a toy after the experiment. Occasionally, while they are working on the speeded task, an interesting and uncontrollable distraction appears in the upper right portion of the screen. The distraction affects the amount of money they will earn. Children readily understand that interrupting their performance on the speeded task to watch the distraction will reduce their earnings, so they form an intention to avoid looking at the distraction. Children having low strategy knowledge, as measured by Kuhl's Metamotivational Knowledge Test for Children, tend to have much higher variances in their response times, although they often do not show longer average response times on distracter trials. Had Kuhl found different mean response times for distracter vs. non-distracter trials, he would have been unable to determine whether the decreased task performance was the result of an inability to maintain the intention or a change in the intention to view the race. According to Kuhl, when children become distracted, they notice that their performance has decreased, so they try to make up for it by increasing their speed on later trials. The development of a performance-based measure of volitional efficiency and its convergence with scores from the strategy knowledge measure is significant and provides a valuable source of validity evidence for both measures.

Mastery Versus Performance Orientation

Similar to Kuhl's distinction between action and state orientation, mastery and performance learning orientations result in different patterns of response to failure on achievement tasks (Dweck & Leggett, 1988). A mastery orientation is characterized by the seeking of challenging tasks and the maintenance of effective striving under failure (Dweck & Leggett, 1988). In achievement tasks, mastery oriented individuals exhibit solution-oriented self instruction and sustained performance in challenging situations (Diener & Dweck, 1978, 1980).

Unsolved problems are seen as challenges, and attention becomes focused on strategy and effort. A performance orientation is characterized by avoidance of challenge, impaired performance, and negative affect in the face of failure (Elliott & Dweck, 1988). Individuals who are performance oriented seek to maintain positive judgments of their ability and avoid negative judgments (Nicholls & Dweck, 1979).

Dweck's research program places motivational measures within the context of general theories of achievement goals, showing how attributions and anxiety follow from a focus on particular goals. Dweck and Leggett (1988) suggest that these differences arise from implicit theories of intelligence. An individual with an entity theory of intelligence believes that social and personality attributes are fixed. Such a theory leads to performance goals, and a performance-oriented response to failure. In contrast, an individual with an incremental theory of intelligence believes that social and personality attributes are malleable (Goodnow, 1980). An incremental theory is said to lead to learning goals and a mastery orientation. Implicit theories of intelligence help formulate goals. According to Elliott and Dweck (1988) goal orientation interacts with confidence in order to set in motion a sequence of specific processes that influence task choice, performance, and persistence.

Measurement of mastery vs. performance orientation depends on the age of the students. Dweck uses ten effort-related items taken from Crandall, Katkovsky and Crandall's (1965) attributional scale to classify primary school children as mastery- or performance-oriented. This scale was chosen because past research (Dweck, 1975) showed that the major difference between the mastery and performance orientations was in the respective tendency to neglect or emphasize the role of effort in determining failure. Mastery-oriented responses focus on effort as the major cause of failure, resulting in renewed attention toward the task. Performance-oriented responses, on the other hand, focus on failure as a result of ability, with additional effort not regarded as helpful. For older children and adolescents, Dweck administers questions that assess students theories about the nature of intelligence, and infers learning orientation from their responses. For a related approach that investigates the mastery, evaluation, prosocial and compliance goals that students pursue in relation to achievement, see Wentzel (in press, 1991).

Mindful Effort Investment Versus Effort Avoidance

Mindfulness involves intentional, purposeful metacognitively guided employment of nonautomatic, hence effort demanding, mental processes (Salomon, 1987). A learner rarely applies knowledge and skill automatically when needed or appropriate. There must be an intention to mobilize and apply knowledge and skill to a new situation. This intention mobilization is mentally taxing—it demands effort investment in mindful application of knowledge and skill. The difference between what a person can do and what a person actually does in a situation indicates the effect of mindful effort investment. The distinction between mindfulness and mindlessness seems parallel to that between controlled and automatic processing.

Mindfulness is a function of stable individual differences but also of situational, perceptual and instructional conditions. Persons differ in their tendency to engage in and enjoy effortful cognitive activity vs. to minimize mental effort in processing incoming information. Learners high in mindfulness perform better when given loose guidance and enough freedom to work on their own, but react negatively when given unduly specific and continuous guidance. The opposite is seen for learners low in mindfulness. High mindful learners perform better when working alone than in teams. However, in teams that also allow independent activity, highs are unaffected while low mindful learners tend to loaf. Mindful learners intentionally seek out opportunities to invest mental effort. They are selective—mindful about some aspects of a situation while ignoring others. Mindlessness occurs when a situation is perceived as familiar, undeserving of effort, or too demanding—the sequence of events is passively allowed to unfold without actively engaging it (see Salomon, 1981, 1983, 1984; Salomon & Leigh, 1984).

On the other hand, there also appears to be a mindful, volitional system aimed at actively avoiding the investment of effort in learning in achievement situations. The person's behavior seems motivated to escape from such situations, mentally or physically or both (Rollett, 1987). Effort avoidance can be distinguished from low need for achievement characterized by laziness or high fear of failure characterized by striving to achieve. But a person motivated by effort avoidance shows active mental or physical escape, that is, mindful avoidance, and no intention to succeed. The causes of effort avoidance seem to be frustrating early experiences in a task domain, so the construct is usually domain specific. But experiencing frustration in many school activities can presumably lead to generalized effort avoidance.

Unsupportive, restrictive intervention styles used by parents and teachers appear associated with the emergence of effort avoidance. The more teachers or parents use pressure to motivate such persons, the quicker effort avoidance appears. Effort avoiders use their intelligence to convince teachers they are not intelligent enough to cope with tasks given them. They tend to score lower in group tests than in individual intelligence tests. Their strategies for effort avoidance include: working very slowly; working very rapidly in slipshod fashion; stopping work when praised; producing feelings of resignation to induce teachers not to push them; generating various excuses for not working.

Further research needs to distinguish *debilitating* or *defensive* effort avoidance from *intelligent* effort avoidance, that is, intelligent budgeting of minimal effort to reach desired goals. Effort avoidance may at times be a healthy reaction to exhausting or extremely difficult tasks. Thus, discontinuing work or setting lower standards for performance in such situations needs more study as an adaptive device. Also, the nature of prior frustrations and the appraisal of situations that lead to effort avoidance are not yet well understood.

Assessment of both effort investment and effort avoidance relies on questionnaires. Effort investment is reflected in self-reports about the number and kind of nonautomatic mental elaborations a person uses in various situations (Salomon, 1981). The scale has been used successfully in instructional research on television viewing and reading. A related measure of need for cognition also exists (Cacioppo & Petty, 1982). The effort avoidance scale includes items such as: "I really can't understand why I should know the multiplication table by heart"; "I can't work when the sun is shining"; "when I'm supposed to write for a long time I get quite tired." The scale has been shown to be unidimensional and to contribute to prediction of learning criteria even with fear-of-failure partialled out. No research as yet seems to have included both investment and avoidance measures in the same study.

TOWARD IMPROVED ASSESSMENT: A SUMMARY

The preceding sections lay out our selection of important old and new conative constructs. We think these constructs and their interrelationships deserve research in instructional psychology because they represent important influences on learning and development in instructional situations but also because they themselves often represent intended or unintended goals and outcomes of instruction. A continuing focus for research aimed at either point needs to be the elaboration and deepening of definition and validation of each construct in relation to proximal others. This research, however, also badly needs improved assessment techniques. This brief concluding section therefore offers a summary of some lines of development toward improved measurement, with some added notes on related methodological issues.

Perhaps the first need for further work is to collect in one place what is known about questionnaire design, the strengths and weaknesses of different formats, the need for controls on different response styles, etc. So many of today's measures rely on questionnaires developed and used without adequate evaluation that a comprehensive review of this technology seems a logical place to start.

A related need is for review of the accumulated literature on particular assessment techniques and the contrasts between them. Spangler's (1992) review of TAT versus questionnaire measures of achievement motivation, noted above, provides an invaluable addition to the construct validity argument. Other accumulations of research on particular techniques, such as Smith's (1992) handbook on the TAT, are also extremely valuable. Expanding the catalogue of constructs, measures, and directly related studies beyond that now available (e.g., as in

Robinson, Shaver, & Wrightsman, 1991, and Snow & Jackson, 1992) is itself a useful early step.

But these reviews will suggest new lines of research that should advance and perhaps radically alter current approaches to assessment. One example is the work of Kline (1973) aimed at producing an information processing account of responses to some forms of projective assessments. Another line has sought to build process models of response to conventional personality inventory items and to analyze the subjective meaning of such items for different persons (see, for example, Cliff, 1977; de Boeck, 1978, 1981; Rogers, 1974).

A particularly important advance may come from a computer-based free response technique developed by a team of Belgian researchers (Claeys, de Boeck, van den Bosch, Biesmans, & Bohrer, no date). The free self-report gives the respondent only this instruction: "Describe your personality as completely as possible, using any personal adjectives you choose. Do not say how you want to be, but say how you really are. Try to use words of common usage." The adjectives are then scored for various personality dimensions, using a computerized dictionary of adjectives and system of weights for each of the personality dimensions, based on expert judgments previously obtained. A series of studies compared this free-response instrument with conventional, fixed format personality measures. Both a traditional inventory and a fixed list of adjectives for self-rating were used; each represented personality dimensions such as extraversion, agreeableness, conscientiousness, and neuroticism. The order of administration of fixed and free response instruments was also varied.

The results suggested that the validity of all of the personality measures may be substantially increased when a free-response self-description instrument is administered first in a battery including other, conventional instruments. Predictive validity coefficients were substantial with this order and near zero for the opposite order. These trends were strong in two studies with college students. Even in a study with military personnel, where the validity differences might be expected to be attenuated by several factors, the trend was notable at least for achievement motivation and self-confidence dimensions. The interpretation is that the free-response condition first activates the respondent's personal knowledge structure so that the content of active or working memory is enlarged and intensified in a state of free, self-focused attention. The effect is to improve the validity of the person's responses both to free-format instruments and to the fixed-format inventories that follow. When not preceded by free recall, conventional inventories, rating scales, and questionnaires may appear circumstantial, so response to them may be impulsive, superficial, and less valid.

The possibility that the personal knowledge structure that individuals bring to bear in self-reports of personality can be activated by free recall to increase the validity of ensuing reports deserves much further research. The rationale of conventional questionnaires is that individuals will reveal their personalities by recognizing themselves as fitting in some degree statements composed by researchers. Such an approach essentially ignores the individuality of personal self-concepts, as well as the possibility that such self-knowledge may not routinely be consciously available. Free response, on the other hand, allows individuality of response and may also provide a more intensive conscious search of personal knowledge. The free recall form of reporting personal conceptions is also akin to the open-ended self-report methods used in cognitive research on learner's conceptions of their own learning in particular instructional situations. And computerization of the technique makes it easily used as well as applicable to more focused domains than general personality dimensions. One can imagine descriptor systems designed along the lines of the Belgian free self-report, but focused on learning-related motivations, interests, perceptions, and action tendencies, as well as learning activities in particular situations. It might even be possible to collect such scaled descriptions periodically during learning from instruction. The coordination of these lines of research might produce a richer and more integrated view of the cognitive and conative psychology of personal knowledge, as well as practical improvements in assessment technology.

The computer performance task developed by Kuhl, as already noted, is an innovative prototype for many possible performance based assessments of conative constructs. There have been occasional attempts to develop performance tests and other objective measures in the history of personality research (Cattell & Warburton, 1967; Eysenck & Eysenck, 1985; Kline, 1973; Kline & Storey, 1978; Kline & Cooper, 1983; Strelau, 1983). We believe much basic research is needed in this direction.

ACKNOWLEDGMENTS

The research reported in this chapter was supported in part by the U.S. Army Research Institute for Behavior and Social Sciences through a subcontract with Battelle Institute. However, the views, opinions and/or findings contained in this report are the authors' and should not be construed as an official ARI position, policy, or decision, unless so documented by other official documentation.

REFERENCES

Alpert, R., & Haber, R. (1960). Anxiety in academic achievement situations. *Journal of Abnormal and Social Psychology, 61,* 207–215.

Ames, C. (1992). Classrooms: Goals, structures, and student motivation. *Journal of Educational Psychology, 84,* 261–271.

Ames, C., & Ames, R. (1984). Systems of student and teacher motivation: Toward a qualitative definition. *Journal of Educational Psychology, 76,* 535–556.

Ames, C., & Archer, J. (1988). Achievement goals in the classroom: Students' learning strategies and motivation processes. *Journal of Educational Psychology, 80,* 260–267.

Anderson, C. A. (1983). Motivational and performance deficits in interpersonal settings: The effects of attributional style. *Journal of Personality and Social Psychology, 45,* 1136–1147.

Atkinson, J. W., & Feather, N. T. (1966). A theory of achievement motivation. New York: Wiley.

Atkinson, J. W., & McClelland, D. C. (1948). The projective expression of needs: II. The effect of different intensities of the hunger drive on thematic apperception. *Journal of Experimental Psychology, 38,* 643–658.

Bandura, A. (1977). Self-efficacy: Toward a unifying theory of behavioral change. *Psychological Review, 84,* 191–215.

Blumenfeld, P. C. (1992). Classroom learning and motivation: Clarifying and expanding goal theory. *Journal of Educational Psychology, 84,* 272–281.

Cacioppo, J. T., & Petty, R. E. (1982). The need for cognition. *Journal of Personality and Social Psychology, 42,* 116–131.

Cassidy, T., & Lynn, R. (1989). A multifactorial approach to achievement motivation: The development of a comprehensive measure. *Journal of Occupational Psychology, 62,* 301–312.

Claeys, W., De Boeck, P., Van Den Bosch, W., Biesmans, R., & Bohrer, A. (no date). *A comparison of one free format and two fixed format self-report personality assessment methods.* Unpublished manuscript, Department of Psychology, University of Leuven, Belgium.

Cliff, N. (1977). Further study of cognitive processing models for inventory response. *Applied Psychological Measurement, 1,* 41–49.

Corno, L. (1986). The metacognitive control components of self-regulated learning. *Contemporary Educational Psychology, 11,* 333–346.

Corno, L. (1989). Self-regulated learning: A volitional analysis. In B. Zimmerman, & D. Schunk (Eds.), *Self-regulated learning and academic achievement: Theory, research and practice.* New York: Springer-Verlag.

Corno, L., & Mandinach, E. B. (1983). The role of cognitive engagement in classroom learning and motivation. *Educational Psychologist, 18,* 88–108.

Crandall, V. C., Katkovsky, W., & Crandall, V. J. (1965). Childrens' beliefs in their own control of reinforcement in intellectual-academic situations. *Child Development, 36,* 91–109.

Cronbach, L. J. (1990). *Essentials of psychological testing.* New York: Harper & Row.

Cronbach, L. J., & Snow, R. E. (1977). *Aptitudes and instructional methods: A handbook for research on interactions.* New York: Irvington.

Curry, L. (1990). *Learning styles in secondary schools: A review of instruments and implications for their use.* National Center on Effective Secondary Schools, University of Wisconsin, Madison, WI.

de Boeck, P. (1978). Validity of a cognitive processing model for responses to adjective and sentence type inventories. *Applied Psychological Measurement, 2,* 369–376.

de Boeck, P. (1981). Individual differences in the validity of a cognitive processing model for responses to personality inventories. *Applied Psychological Measurement, 5,* 481–492.

Deci, E. L., & Ryan, R. M. (1985). *Intrinsic motivation and self-determination in human behavior.* Plenum Press: New York.

Diener, C. I., & Dweck, C. S. (1978). An analysis of learned helplessness: Continuous changes in performance, strategy, and achievement cognitions following failure. *Journal of Personality and Social Psychology, 36,* 451–462.

Diener, C. I., & Dweck, C. S. (1980). An analysis of learned helplessness: II. The processing of success. *Journal of Personality and Social Psychology, 47,* 580–592.

Domino, G. (1968). Differential predictions of academic achievement in conforming and independent settings. *Journal of Educational Psychology, 59,* 256–260.

Domino, G. (1971). Interactive effects of achievement orientation and teaching style on academic achievement. *Journal of Educational Psychology, 62,* 427–431.

Dweck, C. S. (1975). The role of expectations and attributions in the alleviation of learned helplessness. *Journal of Personality and Social Psychology, 31,* 674–685.

Dweck, C. S., & Leggett, E. L. (1988). A social-cognitive approach to motivation and personality. *Psychological Review, 95,* 256–273.

Elliot, S., & Dweck, C. S. (1988). Goals: An approach to motivation and achievement. *Journal of personality and social psychology, 54,* 5–12.

English, H. B., & English, A. C. (1958). *A comprehensive dictionary of psychological and psychoanalytical terms.* New York: Longmans Green.

Entwistle, D. R. (1972). To dispel fantasies about fantasy-based measures of achievement motivation. *Psychological Bulletin, 77,* 377–391.

Entwistle, N. (1987a). A model of the teaching-learning process derived from research on student learning. In J. T. E. Richardson, M. W. Eysenck, & D. Warren Piper (Eds.), *Student learning: Research in education and cognitive psychology.* London: Society for Research into Higher Education and Open University Press.

Entwistle, N. (1987b). *Understanding classroom learning.* London: Hodder and Stoughton.

Entwistle, N., & Ramsden, P. (1983). *Understanding student learning.* London: Croom Helm.

Eysenck, H. J., & Eysenck, M. W. (1985). *Personality and individual differences.* New York: Plenum.

Fineman, S. (1977). The achievement motive construct and its measurement: Where are we now? *British Journal of Psychology, 68,* 122.

Ford, M. E., & Ford, D. H. (1987). *Humans as self-constructing living systems.* Hillsdale, NJ: Lawrence Erlbaum Associates.

Ford, M. E., & Thompson, R. A. (1985). Perceptions of personal agency and infant attachment: Toward a life-span perspective on competence development. *International Journal of Behavioral Development, 8,* 377–406.

Goodnow, J. J. (1980). Everyday concepts of intelligence and its development. In N. Warren (Ed.), *Studies in cross-cultural psychology* (Vol. 2, pp. 191–219). Oxford, England: Pergamon Press.

Harter, S. (1981). A new self-report scale of intrinsic vs. extrinsic orientation in the classroom: Motivational and informational components. *Developmental Psychology, 17,* 300–312.

Harter, S., & Connell, J. P. (1984). A model of children's achievement and related self-perceptions of competence, control and motivational orientation. *Advances in Motivation and Achievement, 3,* 219–250.

Heckhausen, H. (1967). *The anatomy of achievement motivation.* New York: Academic Press.

Heckhausen, H. (1977). Achievement motivation and its constructs: A cognitive model. *Motivation and Emotion, 1,* 283–329.

Heckhausen, H., & Kuhl, J. (1985). From wishes to action: The dead ends and shortcuts on the long way to action. In M. Frese & J. Sarini (Eds.), *Goal-directed behavior: Psychological theory and research on action* (pp. 134–159). Hillsdale, NJ: Lawrence Erlbaum Associates.

Heckhausen, H., Schmalt, H.-D., & Schneider, K. (1985). *Achievement motivation in perspective.* Orlando, FL: Academic Press.

Hembree, R. (1988). Correlates, causes, effects, and treatment of test anxiety. *Review of Educational Research, 58,* 47–77.

Hilgard, E. R. (1980). The trilogy of mind: Cognition, affection, and conation. *Journal of the History of Behavioral Sciences, 16,* 107–117.

Hunsley, J. (1987). Cognitive processes in Mathematics anxiety and test anxiety: The role of appraisals, internal dialogue, and attributions. *Journal of Educational Psychology, 79,* 388–392.

Izard, C. E., Kagan, J., & Zajonc, R. B. (Eds.). (1984). *Emotions, cognition and behavior.* New York: Cambridge University Press.

Jackson, D. N., Ahmed, S. A., & Heapy, N. A. (1976). Is achievement a unitary construct? *Journal of Research in Personality, 10,* 1–21.

Keefe, J. W. (1987). *Learning style theory and practice.* Reston, VA.: National Association of Secondary School Principals.

Keefe, J. W., & Monk, J. S. (1988). *Learning style profile technical manual.* Reston, VA: National Association of Secondary School Principals.

Kline, P. (1973). *New approaches in psychological measurement.* New York: Wiley.

Kline, P., & Cooper, C. (1983). The validity of the Objective Analytic Test Battery. *Personality and Individual Differences, 5,* 328–337.

Kline, P., & Storey, R. (1978). The dynamic personality inventory: What does it measure. *British Journal of Psychology, 69,* 375–383.

Kuhl, J. (1977). *Mess-und prozesstheoretische Analysen einiger Person- und Situationsparameter der Leistungmotivation* [Personal and situation determinants of achievement motivation: Computer simulation and experimental analysis]. Bonn: Bouvier.

Kuhl, J. (1981). Motivational and functional helplessness: The moderating effect of state versus action orientation. *Journal of Personality and Social Psychology, 40,* 155–170.

Kuhl, J. (1984). Volitional aspects of achievement motivation and learned helplessness: Toward a comprehensive theory of action control. In B. A. Maher (Ed.), *Progress in experimental personality research* (Vol. 12, pp. 99–170). New York: Academic Press.

Kuhl, J. (1986). Motivation and information processing: A new look at decision making, dynamic change, and action control. In R. M. Sorrentino & E. T. Higgins (Eds.), *Handbook of motivation and cognition: Foundations of social behavior* (pp. 404–434). New York: Guilford Press.

Kuhl, J. (1987). Feeling versus being helpless: Metacognitive mediation of failure-induced performance deficits. In F. Weinert & R. Kluwe (Eds.), *Metacognition, motivation, and understanding* (pp. 217–235). Hillsdale, NJ: Lawrence Erlbaum Associates.

Kuhl, J. (1990, July). *Self-regulation: A new theory for old applications.* Keynote address presented at the XXII international congress of applied psychology, Kyoto, Japan.

Kuhl, J., & Beckman, J. (Eds.). (1985). *Action control: From cognition to behavior.* Berlin: Springer.

Kuhl, J., & Beckman, J. (Eds.). (in press). *Volition and personality: Action versus state orientation.* Toronto/Göttingen: Hogrefe.

Kuhl, J., & Kraska, K. (1989). Self-regulation and metamotivation: Computational mechanisms, development, and assessment. In R. Kanfer, P. L. Ackerman, & R. Cudeck (Eds.), *Abilities, Motivation, and Methodology* (pp. 343–374). Hillsdale, NJ: Lawrence Erlbaum Associates.

Lazarus, R. S. (1991). *Emotion and Adaptation.* New York: Oxford.

Lens, W. (1983). Achievement motivation, test anxiety, and academic achievement. *Psychological Reports.* University of Leuven, Belgium.

Lens, W., & DeCruyenaere, M. (1991). Motivation and de-motivation in secondary education: Student characteristics. *Learning and Instruction, 1,* 145–159.

Lewin, K. (1926). Untersuchungen zur Handlungs- und Affekt-Psychologie: II. Vorsatz, Wille und Bedurfnis [Studies on action and affect psychology: Intention, will, and need]. *Psychologische Forschung, 7,* 330–385.

Liebert, R., & Morris, L. (1967). Cognitive and emotional components of test anxiety: A distinction and some initial data. *Psychological Reports, 20,* 975–978.

Lynn, R., Hampson, S. L., & Magee, M. (1983). Determinants of educational achievement at 16+: Intelligence, personality, home background and school. *Personality and Individual Differences, 4,* 473–481.

Malone, T. W., & Lepper, M. R. (1987). Making learning fun: A taxonomy of intrinsic motivations for learning. In R. E. Snow & M. J. Farr (Eds.), *Aptitude, learning and instruction: Vol. 3. Conative and affective process analysis* (pp. 223–253). Hillsdale, NJ: Lawrence Erlbaum Associates.

Mandler, G., & Sarason, S. (1952). A study of anxiety and learning. *Journal of Abnormal and Social Psychology, 47,* 166–173.

Marton, F., Hounsell, D. J., & Entwistle, N. J. (Eds.). (1984). *The experience of learning.* Edinburgh: Scottish Academic Press.

Marton, F., & Säljö, R. (1976). On qualitative differences in learning. I—Outcome and process. *British Journal of Educational Psychology, 46,* 4–11.

McClelland, D. C. (1961). *The achieving society.* Princeton, NJ: Van Nostrand.

McClelland, D. C. (1972). Opinions predict opinions: So what else is new? *Journal of Consulting and Clinical Psychology, 38,* 325–326.

McClelland, D. C., Atkinson, J. W., Clark, R. A., & Lowell, E. L. (1953). The achievement motive. New York: Appleton-Century-Crofts.

McClelland, D. C., Koestner, R., & Weinberger, J. (1989). How do self-attributed and implicit motives differ? *Psychological Review, 96,* 690–702.

Messick, S. (1989). Validity. In R. L. Linn (Ed.), *Educational Measurement* (Third Ed.). New York: Macmillan.

Morris, J. H., & Snyder, R. A. (1978). Convergent validities of the resultant achievement motivation test and the presatie motivatie test with Ac and Ai scales of the CPI. *Educational and Psychological Measurement, 38,* 1151–1155.

Murray, H. A. (1938). *Explorations in personality.* Cambridge, MA: Harvard University Press.

Naveh-Benjamin, M., McKeachie, W. J., & Lin. Y. G. (1987). Two types of test anxious students: Support for an information processing model. *Journal of Educational Psychology, 79,* 131–136.

Naveh-Benjamin, M., McKeachie, W. J., Lin, Y. G., & Tucker, D. G. (1986). Inferring students' cognitive structures and their development using the "Ordered Tree Technique." *Journal of Educational Psychology, 78,* 130–140.

Nenniger, P. (1987). How stable is motivation by contents? In E. de Corte, H. Lodwijks, R. Parmentier, & P. Span (Eds.), *Learning and instruction: European research in an international context Vol. 1* (pp. 159–179). London: Pergamon Press.

Nicholls, J. G., Cheung, P. C., Lauer, J., Patashnick, M. (1989). Individual differences in academic motivation: Perceived ability, goals, beliefs, and values. *Learning and Individual Differences, 1,* 63–84.

Nicholls, J. G., & Dweck, C. S. (1979). A definition of achievement motivation. *Unpublished manuscript.* University of Illinois at Champaign-Urbana.

Nicholls, J. G., Patashnick, M., & Nolen, S. B. (1985). Adolescents' theories of education, *Journal of Educational Psychology, 77,* 683–692.

Pintrich, P. R., Smith, D. A., Garcia, T., & McKeachie, W. J. (1991). A manual for the use of the motivated strategies for learning questionnaire. National Center for Research to Improve Postsecondary Teaching and Learning, School of Education, University of Michigan.

Prenzel, M. (1988). *Conditions for the persistence of interest.* Paper presented at the annual meeting of the American Educational Research Association, New Orleans, LA, April 1988.

Rand, P., Lens, W., & Decock, B. (1989). Negative motivation is half the story *(Tech. Report No. 41).* University of Leuven/Louvain Psychological Reports.

Ray, J. J. (1982). *Self-report measures of achievement motivation: A catalog* (Eric publication number ED237523).

Reisenzein, R., & Schönpflug, W. (1992). Stumpf's cognitive-evaluative theory of emotion. *American Psychologist, 47,* 34–45.

Robinson, J. P., Shaver, P. R., & Wrightsman, L. S. (1991). *Measures of personality and social psychological attitudes.* San Diego, CA: Academic Press.

Rogers, T. B. (1974). Ratings of content as a means of assessing personality items. *Educational and Psychological Measurement, 33,* 205–213.

Ryan, R. M., & Connell, J. P. (1989). Perceived locus of causality and internalization: Examining reasons for acting in two domains. *Journal of Personality and Social Psychology, 57,* 749–761.

Salomon, G. (1981). *Communication and education: Social and psychological interactions.* Beverly Hills, CA: Sage Publications.

Salomon, G. (1983). The differential investment of mental effort in learning from different sources. *Educational Psychologist, 18,* 42–50.

Salomon, G. (1984). Television is "easy" and print is "tough": The differential investment of mental effort in learning as a function of perceptions and attributions. *Journal of Educational Psychology, 76,* 647–658.

Salomon, G. (1987, September). Beyond skill and knowledge: The role of mindfulness in learning and transfer. *Invited address to the Second European Conference for Research on Learning and Instruction.* Tubingen FRG.

Salomon, G., & Leigh, T. (1984). Predispositions about learning from print and television. *Journal of Communication, 20,* 119–135.

Schiefele, U. (1991). Interest, learning, and motivation. *Educational Psychologist, 26,* 299–323.

Schiefele, U., Krapp, A., & Winteler, A. (1988, April). *Conceptualization and measurement of interest.* Paper presented at the annual meeting of the American Educational Research Association, New Orleans, LA.

Schiefele, U., & Krapp, A. (1988, April). *The impact of interest on qualitative and structural indicators of knowledge.* Paper presented at the annual meeting of the American Educational Research Association, New Orleans, LA.

Schmalt, H.-D. (1976). *Das LM—GITTER, Ein objectives Verfahren zur Messung des Leistungsmotivs bei Kendern: Handanweisung.* Gottingen: Hogrefe.

Schmeck, R. R. (Ed.). (1988). *Learning strategies and learning styles.* New York: Plenum Press.

Schmitt, A. P., & Crocker, L. (1981, April). *Improving examinee performance on multiple choice tests.* Paper presented at AERA, Los Angeles.

Sieber, J. E., O'Neil, H. F., & Tobias, S. (1977). *Anxiety, learning, and instruction.* Hillsdale, NJ: Lawrence Erlbaum Associates.

Smith, C. P. (1992). *Motivation and personality: Handbook of thematic content analysis.* New York: Cambridge University Press.

Snow, R. E. (1977). Research on aptitude for learning: A progress report. In L. S. Shulman (Ed.), *Review of research in Education (Vol. 4).* Itasca, IL: F. E. Peacock Publishers.

Snow, R. E. (1989a). Cognitive-conative aptitude interactions in learning. In R. Kanfer, P. L. Ackerman, & R. Cudeck (Eds.), *Abilities, motivation, and methodology.* Hillsdale, NJ: Lawrence Erlbaum Associates.

Snow, R. E. (1989b). Toward assessment of cognitive and conative structures in learning. *Educational Researcher, 18*(9), 8–14.

Snow, R. E. (1990). New approaches to cognitive and conative assessment in education. *International Journal of Educational Research, 14,* 455–473.

Snow, R. E. (1992). Aptitude theory: Yesterday, today, and tomorrow, *Educational Psychologist, 27,* 5–32.

Snow, R. E., Corno, L., & Jackson III, D. N. (in press). Individual differences in affective and conative functions. In D. C. Berliner & R. C. Calfee (Eds.), *Handbook of educational psychology.* New York: Macmillan.

Snow, R. E., & Farr, M. J. (1987). Cognitive-conative-affective processes in aptitude, learning, and instruction: An introduction. In R. E. Snow & M. J. Farr (Eds.), *Aptitude, learning, and instruction, Vol. 3: Conative and affective process analyses* (pp. 1–8). Hillsdale, NJ: Lawrence Erlbaum Associates.

Snow, R. E., & Jackson III, D. N. (1992). *Assessment of conative constructs for educational research and evaluation: A catalogue.* Unpublished report. National Center for Research on Evaluation, Standards, and Student Testing. University of California, Los Angeles.

Spangler, W. D. (1992). Validity of questionnaire and TAT measures of need for achievement: Two meta-analyses. *Psychological Bulletin, 112,* 140–154.

Spence, J. T., & Helmreich, R. L. (1983). Achievement related motives and behavior. In J. T. Spence (Ed.), *Achievement and achievement motives: Psychological and sociological approaches.* San Francisco: W. H. Freeman.

Spielberger, C. D. (1980). *Test Anxiety Inventory ("Test Attitude Inventory"),* Preliminary professional manual. Palo Alto, CA: Consulting Psychologists Press.

Strelau, J. (1983). *Temperament, personality, activity.* New York: Academic Press.

Tobias, S. (1985). Test anxiety: Interference, defective skills, and cognitive capacity. *Educational Psychologist, 20,* 135–142.

Vallerand, R. J., Blais, M. R., Briere, N. M., & Pelletier, L. G. (1989). Construction et validation de l'Echelle de Motivation en Education [Construction and validation of the Academic Motivation Scale]. *Canadian Journal of Behavioral Sciences, 21,* 323–349.

Weiner, B. (1986). *An attribution theory of motivation and emotion.* New York: Springer-Verlag.

Weinstein, M. S. (1969). Achievement motivation and risk preference. *Journal of Personality and Social Psychology, 13,* 153–172.

Weinstein, C. W., Goetz, E. T., & Alexander, P. A. (Eds.). (1988). *Learning and study strategies: Issues in assessment, instruction and evaluation.* San Diego, CA: Academic Press.

Wentzel, K. R. (1991). Social competence at school: Relation between social responsibility and academic achievement. *Review of Educational Research, 61,* 1–24.

Wentzel, K. R. (in press). Motivation and achievement in early adolescence: The role of multiple classroom goals. *Journal of Early Adolescence.*

White, R. W. (1959). Motivation reconsidered: The concept of competence. *Psychological Review, 66,* 297–333.

Winteler, A., & Sierwald, W. (1987). *Entwicklung und Uberprufung eines Fragebogens zum Studieninteresse (FSI).* Hochschulausbildung.

6 Issues of Motivation in Asian Education

John N. Hawkins
University of California, Los Angeles

Motivation in individuals, let alone cultures, is a complicated characteristic to measure or account for. Yet, over time, scholars have attempted to make sense of motivation factors among large clusters of people, sometimes nationally, other times ethnically or religiously; sometimes, all of the above. In the case of motivation among Asians the stereotypes are becoming increasingly common. "Asians" (by which is meant, typically, Japanese, Chinese and Koreans, although this leaves out large groups of Indochinese and South Asians—India, Pakistan, Bangladesh, Sri Lanka) work harder, are disciplined, quiet, overachievers, excel in mathematics and science, and so on. Furthermore, much of the data on these groups supports the stereotypical views mentioned before (Anderson, 1982; Chapey, 1983; Cogan, 1984; Cummings, 1986; Garmon, 1982; Leestma & Walberg, 1992; Lynn, 1988; Shields, 1989; White, 1987). Although it is relatively easy to measure achievement, it is less obvious what accounts for the observed high levels of motivation among students of Japanese, Chinese, and Korean descent.

What follows is a broad-stroked picture of some motivation factors attributed to students from the East Asian "Confucian," based cultures (Japan, China, and Korea), with a more specific focus on Japan. We adopt a broad definition of motivation, which states basically that motivation is "the most important determinant of the difference between what a person can do and what he or she will do" (Amabile, 1983, p. 366).

What must first be noted is that there are multiple explanations for the high motivation and, therefore, achievement of East Asians. These explanations have, for example, been characterized as being defined by either a "cultural" approach (Yao, 1985), or what Sue and Okayaki (1990) call "relative functionalism," or

Ogbu's (1987) notion of the "folk theory of success," and the overall concept of the "need to achieve," which is more predominant among some cultures than others (DeVos, 1983). All of these explanations (and others that are not explored in this chapter) offer some sense of why Asians, particularly those from the East Asian grouping, tend to be highly motivated with respect to formal schooling and, as a consequence, can be measured as higher achievers. Other less documented explanations have to do with the role of Confucian thought, the influence of an ideographic language, a tradition of rote memorization, and so on. Here, however, we focus on the historical context of education and motivation and on a literature review of the wide variety of educational and social factors that might contribute to high motivation in Asia, especially Japan.

EAST ASIA AND CONFUCIANISM

The role of the family is often seen as one important motivating factor. For example, how do ordinary, uneducated Chinese come to share common Confucian values? Willingness to work hard and defer rewards is often explained in reference to family organization. Authority relations, the success that the People's Republic of China has had in reestablishing educational institutions, a new state and so on can be traced in some respects to the structure of the family and the values that it promotes. One major term that came to be associated with this phenomenon is filial piety; this was stressed throughout Chinese society, in schools, in textbooks, in magistrate's lectures, plays, local religions, and so on. Gradually these values came to be shared throughout the population with a degree of homogeneity not found in other cultures and certainly not in Europe (Rozman, 1991). Indeed, the cultural arguments and the role of the family in accounting for high motivation seem to be strong throughout all of East Asia leading to the question: why has East Asia emerged as a model of motivation and achievement?

As one of the three regions of the world competing for world superiority (the others being Western and Northeast Europe including the newly developing Russian confederation, and North America) East Asia has Confucianism as a principal source of dynamism contained within a rich culture and history. On the other hand, the region has been insular and not very outward looking. Now many Westerners are taking notice of the region, not only because of its economic powers but family stability, low crime rates, high life expectancies, and superior educational motivation and performance. At the same time, there is some perception that with this level of achievement has come a cost: namely, individual personality. Although there are obvious differences between nations in the region (Korea, Japan, and China) Confucianism is the glue that holds them together (Rozman, 1991).

Core values emerged in the region in the second millennium B.C. in northern

China and over time spread to Korea and Japan. Rozman (1991) makes the point that a typology of societies that includes Confucianism makes more sense than the traditional capitalist and socialist notions that seem to have prevailed or conventional concepts of modernization and development. It is the brand and expression of Confucianism that needs explanation.

Although it is dangerous to utilize stereotypes based on culture and history, they are nevertheless useful in setting the tone of the discussion. Rozman (1991) and associates found many of the following stereotypes regarding East Asians to be ". . . relatively true: individuals are characterized by self-denial, frugality, patience, fortitude, self-discipline, dedication, rote learning, and an aptitude for applied sciences and mathematics" (pp. 28–29). Some educational implications for these statements are that individuals from the region excel in efforts that require patience and unstinting effort over long periods of time, with delayed gratification; memorization and repetition are rewarded; individualism is down-played both at home and in the school. In the school, motivation and achievement are highlighted by student diligence, rote learning, memorization (often reinforced by chanting in unison), emphasis on test-taking at an early age, and moral education.While all this may suggest uniformity, in fact the opportunity structure (merit based competition) was quite open both in China and Korea in the early periods (Rozman, 1991).

Other group stereotypes that help frame the discussion have to do with "group orientation, acceptance of authority, deference, dependence, conflict avoidance, interest in harmony, seniority consciousness, and dutifulness" (Rozman, 1991, p. 30). If one would want to locate a unit of analysis that best encompasses these traits, then probably the family and its extension, familism, would be a good place to start. Group organizations, whether they are the family proper, or an enterprise (e.g., a school), are more strict in the degree of commitment required to join or be admitted and their exclusivity, than is the case in other societies. Although there are certainly intraregional variations in East Asia, the similarities outweigh the differences.

All of these stereotypes are grounded to some degree in the philosophical mode of thought typically referred to as Confucianism. The modern expression of this system of thought varies between Japan, Korea, and China, however, with significant similarities.

In China, as far back as the Song dynasty (960 A.D.), the teaching of Confucianism through formal and nonformal educational means became established (Levenson, 1964). At this time the educated class expanded significantly, and schools could be found in most all market towns and certainly at least one at the county level. Ordinary peasants now came into contact with educated people, and even the highest ranking officials were by this time marrying into the local lower class families. Thus, Confucian values were spreading throughout the different classes of Chinese society and were not solely present in the privileged classes. The educational system played a powerful role in this expansion, particularly the memorization associated with the examination system; this became a widespread phenomenon and verses expressing Confucian values were memorized by people at all social levels. Thus, an indirect outcome of the spread of schools was the spread of Confucian ideas and values (Ebrey, 1991). The role of the family in spreading Confucian ideas was also significant, not only in China proper but in other areas populated by Chinese (e.g., the "three little Chinas— Hong Kong, Singapore, Taiwan).

The educational implications of the practice of filial piety are not often discussed. In brief, the hierarchy of family relations (obedience, rites, responsibilities, etc.), polite language toward superiors, and a variety of behaviors associated with superiors and inferiors found their way into the school environment once education became more widespread. In some respects, the family reflected the autocratic nature of traditional Chinese society: superiority of old over young, and males over females. This was modulated, however, by rules based on mutual responsibility and obligation; a high sense of security and predictability among family members made the system work. Just as the children and mother of a family (the inferiors) had to adhere to the decisions of the father (superior) so did younger siblings to the oldest son. These decisions would range from internal family matters, to property concerns to marriage. Just as there was a high degree of uniformity in the Chinese family by the end of the Qing dynasty (1911) there was a parallel high degree of uniformity of belief and behavior regarding learning, which if properly approached resulted in uniformally high motivation among students in the Chinese societies (Ebrey, 1991).

In Japan and Korea this was less the case, and the spread of Confucian values came more through the spread of formal education than through the family. In Japan it can be found in the modern period in Motoda's Imperial Rescript on Education, drafted in 1890 and memorized by millions of teachers and students of the time (Anderson, 1975). Within it are contained a blend of Western notions of utility and practicality and Confucian notions of moral value, particularly loyalty and filial piety. Although many would argue that there has been a postwar rejection of Confucianism in Japan (following its transformation into nationalism in the 1930s), it can equally be argued that it has survived in a modified form particularly in education. If it were asserted that Japan's current success had something to do with Confucianism, most Japanese would reject it out of hand. If, on the other hand, it were argued that certain values were critical to Japan's success—stability, order, belief in the family, harmony, hierarchy in the workforce, loyalty to employers and superiors, importance of diligence, self-cultivation—then there would generally be a high degree of consensus. In fact, these values can be characterized as "Confucian" and all contribute to a structure supporting high motivation and achievement (Collcutt, 1991; Davis, 1987).

The motivating rituals and values found in the workplace can also be found in the schools. As Rohlen (1983) notes: "Although schools in both cultures [Japan and the U.S.] have formulas for events, less depends on convention in the United States. School events and ceremonies are readily changed, and most are abandoned if student support lags. Japanese school events, on the other hand, appear uniform and constant. They depend on tradition and teachers. The Confucian appreciation for formality in ritual as expressive of the moral order lingers in Japan, just as our democratic and Protestant heritage inclines us to events with grass roots spontaneity that is informal and emotionally expressive" (p. 167). Schools thus become a kind of Confucian moral community expressing values, order and discipline, transmitted by moral example, usually with the teacher in the lead. High motivation is far easier to sustain if there is a common sense of purpose, ritually reinforced, and backed up by teacher behavior.

Korea, on the other hand, had little resemblance to a Confucian society until the 15th century when it began to exhibit many of the Confucian characteristics generally associated with Japan and China. In some ways, Koreans became more Confucian than the Chinese from whom they borrowed many of the forms. Despite the fact that it was an alien creed and in many ways in conflict with more indigenous animistic beliefs, it nevertheless took root and spread throughout Korean society, especially the lower classes, through the educational system and the innovation of the Korean alphabet (Hangul). Assumptions regarding the value of hard work, meritocratic rewards, and the significance of formal education became deeply imbedded in Korean society, much more rigidly than in either Japan or China. It has not been difficult for Korean educators and parents to reinforce the already high levels of motivation among Korean students given the commonly held convictions regarding the reward structure (Haboush, 1991). Koreans carried the notion of the power of education to transmit values to an extreme. Education was seen as being the central force in transforming society, and it was not long after the Confucian tradition became imbedded in Korean society that a comprehensive, nationwide state-run school system emerged (early 1400s). The formal study of officially approved texts (Elementary Learning, Classic of Filial Piety, The Four Books, and the Five Classics), rote memorization of critical passages, and a powerful belief in the value of learning and education characterized this early approach to formal education. The successful passing of crucial examinations led automatically to respectable official positions; one's future was assured (Haboush, 1991). All of these early predilections toward education carried forward into the modern period. As Robinson notes (1991) "The Confucian tradition has shaped other modern sectors of Korean life. In the 1950s and 1960s government service continued to be a prime goal for educated elites. The expansion of higher education (from 60,000 college students in 1960 to over one million in 1985) in the postwar era was matched by an increase in the size of the state bureaucracy. Based on its ability to attract the best and brightest students, the relative efficiency of the South Korean bureaucracy, in spite of its many flaws, has been singled out as a major contributor to economic growth" (p. 222). The very strong links between formal learning and education, guaranteed employment, and nation-building were powerful ties forming the web supporting high motivation at the individual level.

Overall, scholars of East Asian societies, and particularly those focusing on the philosophical traditions of this region, agree that assumptions about human nature gave great credence to the power and role of formal education and mental training (the notion that just as the body can be made physically fit through training, so too can the mind). This expressed itself in family rituals, work attitudes, study habits, the structure and organization of schooling and, finally, served as the foundation upon which individual motivation could be nurtured (Rozman, 1991). As Rozman (1991) states:

> It is particularly noteworthy that these societies channeled expectations toward schooling. In Korea the yangban (ruler) status was associated with education; this status was widely sought and, once attained, led to higher aspirations to pass exams. In Japan, literacy rates climbed steeply during the two and one-half centuries of the Tokugawa period (1603–1867). In China, the prestige of scholar-officials continued to draw vast numbers to the district-level examinations that might lead to higher-level examinations and elite social standing. Education to serve one's family, to help it rise in status within one's community, and, for some, to earn government recognition and office was a powerful magnet for the ambitious. (pp. 168–69)

One might also say that education served as a powerful motivator not only for the ambitious but for the ordinary as well, since it was the single societal sector where hard work paid off. Obviously, the system did not work flawlessly in any of these nations, and exceptions existed in all cases. However, the very powerful Confucian notion that successfully pursuing education leads to individual and social progress was deeply imbedded by the mid-20th century. As we begin to examine the modern period (1900 on), more empirical forms of evidence become available and provide us with additional sources of information regarding the issue of motivation in the East Asia region. Here, we look principally at Japan although much of what is argued here holds true for the Chinese cultures and Korea as well.

THE JAPAN CASE

The culture arguments, the notion that high achievement and motivation are a product of the peculiar social organization of a particular society, seem to be the most pervasive and in some respects, the most persuasive. In many studies, the authors convey a subtle sense that Japan's educational successes accompanied by high motivation are, perhaps, cultural specific and could not really be duplicated in any other society.

Tsukuda's (1984) work provides a useful introduction to the perspective that the two systems are quite different. In his comparison of the Japanese and American experience, three aspects of considerable differences are noted. The first is the historical and cultural tendency toward centralization or, as the writer puts it, ". . . the public sector plays a monopolizing role in Japan . . ." (p. 12), in contrast to the vigorous role of local education boards and the private sector in the United States.

A second major sociocultural difference relates to the varying sex roles for females with respect to higher education. According to Tsukuda (1984), "In Japan, females tended to be enrolled in junior colleges whereas females in the United States became equal to males, or even started exceeding males in the enrollment rate in four-year institutions in the United States" (p. 12). The role of women in higher education, although not directly related to the issue of motivation, represents a critical difference in the two systems.

Finally, Tsukuda (1984) notes the historical increase in the number of higher education institutions in Japan as compared with the United States. Unlike the elementary and secondary sector referred to earlier and dominated by public controls, the private sector has played an important role in higher education; again, this is a phenomenon peculiar to Japan.

Tsukuda (1984) concludes from an analysis of the statistical data produced in Japanese and American governmental reports that although Japan and the United States are similar to each other in terms of enrollment rates, expenditure for education, and the suicide rate, they are dissimilar in terms of the position of females in higher education, the role of the private sector in education, and the rate of juvenile delinquency. The notion that the two nations are socially and culturally unique is a pervasive aspect of this analysis. These three policy and social differences in the two educational systems illustrate the structural context in which motivation issues can be discussed.

Against this more or less factual description of Japanese and American education, three studies provide an interesting "perceptual" profile of the two systems. William Cummings (1984), in *Japanese Images of American Education* notes that "Japan has been looking at American education much longer than America has been looking at Japanese education, and Japan has far more information" (p. 1). He discusses four classes of observers of American education in Japan and their approach in conveying to the Japanese public their perceptions of American education: "Ministry of Education observers focus on aspects of finance, enrollments, and administration. Professors comment on the quality of academic life in the United States. Parents and students focus on events in the classroom and community. And politicians seem most aware of the American disease of drugs, violence, and sex" (p. 11). The view is invariably one-dimensional depending on the interest group doing the viewing.

What emerges from Cumming's (1984) study is the cultural difference in interpreting a complex phenomenon such as education. On the one hand, ". . . American education was seen as expressive, individualist, opulent, and creative; on the other as undisciplined, wasteful and hedonistic" (p. 11). These views, expressed through the Japanese media and other sources, reinforce the notion among Japanese students and parents that their system is superior and thus, in a circuitous way, contribute to a higher sense of motivation and an even greater need to achieve.

Many Western observers of Asian education have counterpoised tradition with modernity and suggested that only those nations that modernized (e.g., Japan,

China, and Korea) and set aside their traditions made progress and accomplished high levels of achievement; thereby suggesting that such achievement was associated with high motivation. Asian researchers, however, argue the opposite. Kobayashi (1984) in particular debunks many of the stereotypes held by most writers who seek to explain Japan's success economically and educationally. He acknowledges the many successes that the Japanese have achieved and the creative ways they have maintained aspects of their traditional culture in the face of rapid modernization. But he introduces an ecological, theoretical construct against which to discuss differences in American and Japanese pedagogy. What is perceived as rote learning (and therefore Confucian) by American observers is in fact part of a complex, group interaction process inherent in Japanese culture: "This rote is not really repetition since, from the practitioner's point of view, each 'repetition' is regarded as always containing learning something new, such as minuscule modifications in writing kanji (Chinese characters) each time one does it. . ." (Kobayashi, 1984, p. 110).

The thrust of Kobayashi's argument is that contrary to many thinkers in the West, tradition and modernity are not mutually exclusive. In fact, aspects of Japanese tradition may contribute to their success in education: "Thus, rote and imitation practices deemed outmoded by new scientific theories of teaching-learning which entered education in Europe and America during the time of the industrial revolution, are still maintained in the teaching-learning of traditional arts in a nation considered the most modern and industrial in Asia. Planners in developing countries sometimes argue that 'tradition' prevents modernization but this doctrine is too simplistic, as the case of contemporary Japan illustrates" (p. 113). It might further be argued that maintaining high levels of motivation is an easier task when traditional practices can be called upon both for justification of the educational effort and for group support.

What specific motivational attributes apply to the Japanese case? We have seen some broad cultural and traditional characteristics that may contribute to higher motivation but these lack the substance that we need to understand this complicated phenomenon.

One area often examined in this context is self-concept. Despite the substantial body of American literature involving judgments of one's value and abilities along a number of dimensions (primarily called self-concept or self-esteem), data on the self-concept of Japanese students is limited. Fetters et al. (1983, Table 6) report the percentage of high school seniors that agreed with three statements on self-esteem:

I'm a person of worth.
I'm satisfied with myself.
At times, I think I'm no good.

and another question about ability to enter (in Japan)/complete (in U.S.) college.

Japanese responses to the questions about worth and self-satisfaction were much less positive than Americans: Less than a third of the Japanese students agree with these statements while more than 80% of the Americans responded positively. On the third question, there was a higher percentage of negative responses for the Japanese, especially for females (71% agreeing with the statement that they felt they were no good at times in contrast to 49% for Japanese males and 51% and 41% for American females and males respectively). The question about college showed a similar Japan–U.S. pattern with over 80% of the American seniors judging themselves able to complete college while less than 40% of the Japanese stated that they had the ability to enter college (since the dropout rate from college is negligible in Japan, entering is essentially tantamount to completing college).

If the Japanese results had come from a typically American sample, there might be cause for considerable alarm. The responses to most self-concept questionnaires from United States samples are typically skewed with substantially more positive than negative replies, excepting clinical samples.

This tendency toward critical self-judgment by Japanese is apparently not an isolated event but more of a consistent pattern. Japanese students in the Harnisch and Sato study (1983; Harnisch et al., 1986) had more negative reading self-evaluations than Illinois students. In draft materials on student opinions, attitudes, and preferences, Kifer and Robitaille (1989) found that despite their high cognitive scores, Japanese students from both populations were more likely than students from other countries to consider school mathematics to be difficult and to have low opinions of their performance in that subject.

It is possible to attribute the foregoing patterns of responses to distinctive cultural tendencies in socialization regarding appropriate expressions about self-judgment. Within Japanese society, humility is valued as an essential ingredient of interpersonal harmony whereas overconfidence and public expression of beliefs that will reflect negatively on others are discouraged. American society, on the other hand, places a higher premium on self-confidence and self-assurance, and its competitive tendencies afford greater tolerance for and encouragement of public expression of one's capabilities.

What this means in terms of *true* differences in distribution of self-concept between Japanese and American students is unclear. Japanese students, as a group, may be overly self-critical, professing greater concerns about their worth and abilities than they truly believe and thus be more *realistically* motivated toward their personal educational goals. On the other hand, their self-opinions might also reflect realistic reactions to the tightly connected system of secondary and postsecondary educational stratification. In contrast, the responses of U.S. students are more likely to reflect overconfidence and weaker social linkages between school performance, opportunities, and self-esteem.

Another category of studies related to motivational attributes can be termed *locus of control*. This category of attributes deals with the tendency to judge whether the factors responsible for individual actions and performances are under one's personal control (internal) or not (external). Current emphasis in applications of the locus of control construct in academic contexts is on an individual's causal attributions for his or her success or failure. Attributions to personal ability and effort are viewed as internal (but vary on other dimensions in Weiner's [1976, 1992] theory) whereas those linked to task difficulty, luck and fate, are considered to be external factors, beyond the control of the individual. Among the internal factors, effort is considered to be a changeable behavior, whereas ability (or aptitude) is seen as a more stable personal characteristic.

Evidence from the Japanese–U.S. comparisons with respect to locus of control and causal attributions for success and failure is mixed, with variations across time and age group considered. The First International Mathematics Study included an 18-item scale intended to measure "the extent to which man is perceived as having effective control and mastery over his environment" (Husen, 1976, Vol. II, p. 45; Tables 1.15–1.19). At all three population levels considered (13-year-olds, terminal year mathematics students, terminal year nonmathematics students), Japan exhibited high means (ranked 1st or 2nd among the countries) and low standard deviations while U.S. means were much lower (close to bottom ranking) and the scores more variable. This meant that on the whole, Japanese students were more likely than students from other countries to feel that people have control over their own fate while American students were more likely to view people as helpless in the face of forces at work in the world. This finding runs counter to some popular stereotypes about "Asian fatalism" and suggests that Japanese students, at least, feel they can succeed and achieve given the effort, time and energy aimed at a task and rarely reach the conclusion that "I just can't get it."

Other studies focus on the relative prevalence of ability, effort, luck, and task difficulty in causal attributions regarding success and achievement. For example, in the Hess, Azuma et al. (1985) study (Japanese students were in the 5th grade, American students were in the 6th grade), both students and their parents were asked about their attributions for low performance in mathematics. Both Japanese children and their mothers were less likely to attribute poor performance to lack of ability and training in school and more likely to attribute it to lack of effort than American children and their mothers. American children were also more likely than Japanese children to blame poor performance on bad luck. Similar results are reported by Stevenson and Stigler (1992).

At an earlier phase of the study (when children were 4-year-olds) Japanese mothers were more likely to emphasize children's natural abilities (effort and ability were not separated in this part of the study) and less likely to emphasize parental encouragement as reasons for their children's future success in school. Hess, Azuma et al. interpret their results as supportive of a Japanese belief in individual control over success; that is, internal changeable factors such as effort are more important than either internal stable factors (ability) or external factors (luck, task difficulty, quality of teaching, etc.).

Although most studies were congruent with the Hess and Azuma (1985) study, others appear to be at odds with those findings (Fetters et al., 1983). This incongruity may be a function of differing perspectives and practices in child-rearing, socialization, religion and philosophy and work. According to Weisz, Rothbaum, and Blackburn (1984), for example, Americans emphasize and highly value primary control, whereby individuals are rewarded for influencing existing realities. Japanese, on the other hand, place greater emphasis on secondary control, whereby individuals receive "rewards by accommodating to existing realities and maximizing satisfaction or goodness of fit with things as they are" (Weisz et al., 1984, p.955). The complexity of this issue is clear and serves as a reminder that one's perception of a cultural attribute depends on both the cultural perspective from which one operates, on the structural paradigm one invokes, and on the aspects of behavior one considers.

Other more macro factors may shed additional light on what accounts for high motivation among East Asians but such factors are clearly less easy to measure. The link between education and economic development as a factor in individual student motivation has been the subject of a few inquiries, although not specifically focused on Asia. Studies such as those by Allen (1978) and Ushiogi (1984) reveal that early on, the notion that education was closely related to economic development was imbedded in the thinking of individuals in both government and business in Japan. As Allen (1978) notes: "In neither sector [government and business], however, was educational policy fashioned by men committed to the belief in the sufficiency of liberal education; it seemed essential to them that adequate provision should also be made for professional and vocational training, directed towards producing experts" (p. 33). Similar statements could be made about China and Korea (Hawkins, 1974; McGinn, 1980). It was with this early beginning that education became the route to a successful career in Japan prompting Allen (1978) to state: "Many critics have claimed that Japan has placed too much emphasis on formal educational qualifications as a path to a career, and there is a justification for such a charge" (p. 34). From that point on, most aspects of Japan's formal educational system were imbued with the concept that one studied, in preferred schools, in order to have a successful career. This *career* orientation lays the base for the manner in which schooling is viewed by all sectors in Japanese society down to and including students and their parents.

Although Allen does not link his study to student achievement and motivation it does not take a quantum leap to conclude that this rather direct relationship between education and economics is a powerful motivator. Ushiogi (1984) further elaborated on this argument with his study of the transition from school to work in Japan. In this study he traces the rapid expansion of higher education in Japan since World War II and the impact this has had on the Japanese labor market. He convincingly demonstrates that the educational experience that one has in Japan directly determines career paths and that students are motivated primarily by this knowledge. The motivation to study, and choices on what to study comes from the knowledge that large business enterprises prefer to recruit students from faculties of law, economics, business management, commerce, and engineering (highly math and science dependent fields) rather than from the liberal arts (Ushiogi, 1984). Thus, students in Japan (and China and Korea as well) are socialized from an early age to focus their studies and efforts on science and mathematics and attempt to enter the more prestigious universities, secure in the knowledge that if they are successful in this they will be recruited by the larger, more stable and lucrative Japanese businesses.

Moving further away from individual student effects and toward a more management theory (the argument that school organization and management accounts for student achievement) approach, at least two studies state that Japan's student successes are the direct result of the manner in which the schools are managed. Schiller and Walberg (1982) call Japan a "Learning Society" and state that schools are organized in such a way as to enhance what they identify as seven productive forces in school learning: (a) ability; (b) development level; (c) motivation; (d) home learning environment; (e) quantity of instruction; (f) quality of instruction; (g) classroom social environment. The authors conclude that the Japanese educational system has incentives enhancing each of these factors thus providing the institutional context in which high achievement and motivation can be fostered. Likewise, Lewis (1992) argues that the elementary and preschool experience, which "promote children's intrinsic motivation to engage in work, avoid external rewards and punishments that might undermine children's intrinsic motivation, and foster children's commitment to rules and procedures that allow the classroom to function well as a learning environment" (p. 257), all contribute to this "learning society" and enhance overall motivation.

Japanese educational television has also been singled out as a factor in promoting high levels of motivation among Japanese youth. In two articles (Tiene, 1983; Tiene & Urakawa, 1983) the authors note the effort being made in Japan to provide, nationwide, a first-rate educational television system. The Japanese have what is termed "massive TV penetration in [the] schools" (Tiene, 1983, p. 20), excellent facilities (Tiene & Urakawa, 1983, p. 19), high quality research to back up the programming (Tiene & Urakawa, 1983, p. 20), "ingenious production techniques" (Tiene & Urakawa, 1983, p. 22), and superior utilization of the media by teachers and students (Tiene & Urakawa, 1983, p. 22). The authors contend that the national and local management of educational television of such high quality is a major factor in educational achievement and high motivation especially at the elementary levels (Tiene & Urakawa, 1983, p. 21).

Although many scholars have pointed to the Japanese curriculum as a major element in Japanese successes in mathematics and science, Torrance (1982) makes a provocative argument that one unintended outcome of the curriculum is to create learning situations that stimulate high levels of motivation among Japanese students. In his article on "Education for Quality Circles in Japanese Schools" he documents how both the formal and informal school curriculum allow ". . . Japanese children to receive practice and training in group or team creativity" (p. 13). In discussing some elementary classes he visited, he noted that groups of Japanese children were doing research on health habits and problems of other students (for which they had constructed a questionnaire, administered it, and were tabulating statistics), working on problems of improving the playing fields and playground, and improving the care and nurturing of the school animals (Torrance, 1982, p. 13). He concludes: "As I observed their behavior, I had little doubt but that as adults they would be effective members of Quality Circle groups. Already they had mastered and were practicing many of the requisite skills" (p. 14). His further observations revealed that by tackling "real" life problems in their own schools they were more enthusiastic (motivated) when it came to the more structured, learning portion of the classes as well as doing homework and following through on assignments, to say nothing of the fact that they were being well prepared for life as members of Japan's industrial society.

CONCLUSION

It is doubtful that any single variable or group of variables can be isolated as definitively determining levels of motivation in the broad Asian population or, in the even more narrowly defined groups in East Asia such as Japan. What the literature demonstrates is that the cultural argument is a strong one, providing a frame of reference that allows the researcher to focus in on the pervasive philosophical system of Confucianism (in both its traditional and modern expressions) and its various attributes. Although many scholars are hesitant to link Confucianism to motivation, others, like Davis (1987) are more blunt and state flatly that children's orientations toward diligence, merit, hard work, frugality and a whole host of "motivation" values are directly related to the Confucian philosophical legacy of East Asia.

In Japan, the links between motivation and the family, self-concept, locus of control, educational management and administration, and the curriculum seem to form a chain that encompasses a more comprehensive view of what accounts for motivation, moving the discussion beyond the familiar bounds of psychology and social psychology into structural issues of school management and administration, all bound up in the uniqueness of Japanese culture. Much the same could be said for China and Korea. To the degree that "culture learning" can take place, it is likely that some of these behaviors and/or practices can be emulated (as indeed they were by the Japanese and Koreans from the Chinese) by others. Or, that characteristics that were once present in other cultures (e.g., the "Protestant

Ethic" etc.) be compared with the values and behaviors of this particular group. While a few studies of this type exist, we are lacking a systematic approach to a more holistic investigation of cross-cultural motivation and thus, this is an area for future research.

REFERENCES

Allen, G. C. (1978, March). Education, science and the economic development of Japan. *Oxford Review of Education, 4*(1), 27–36.

Amabile, T. (1983). The social psychology of creativity: A componential conceptualization. *Journal of Personality and Social Psychology, 45,* 357–76.

Anderson, A. M. (1982). The great Japanese IQ increase. *Nature, 279,* 180–181.

Anderson, R. S. (1975). *Education in Japan: A century of modern development.* Washington, DC: U.S. Government Printing House.

Chapey, G. (1983, May). Can we learn a lesson from Japan? *Clearing House, 56*(9), 394–96.

Cogan, J. J. (1984, March). Should the U.S. mimic Japanese education? Let's look before we leap. *Phi Delta Kappan,* 462–468.

Colcutt, M. (1991). The legacy of Confucianism in Japan. In G. Rozman (Ed.), *The East Asian region: Confucian heritage and its modern adaptation.* Princeton, NJ: Princeton University Press.

Cummings, W. (1984). *Japanese images of American education.* Paper presented at the East West Center Conference on Learning from Each Other, Honolulu HI.

Cummings, W. (1986). *Educational policies in crisis: Japanese and American perspectives.* New York: Praeger.

Davis, W. B. (1987). Religion and development: Weber and the East Asian experience. In M. Weiner & S. P. Huntingdon (Eds.), *Understanding political development.* Boston: Little, Brown.

DeVos, G. A. (1983). Achievement motivation and intra family attitudes in immigrant Koreans. *Journal of Psychoanalytic Anthropology, 6*(1), 25–71.

Ebrey, P. (1991). The Chinese family and the spread of Confucian values. In G. Rozman (Ed.), *The East Asian region: Confucian heritage and its modern adaptation.* Princeton, NJ: Princeton University Press.

Fetters, W. B., et al. (1983, April). *Schooling experiences in Japan and the U.S.: A cross national comparison of high school students.* Paper presented at the annual meeting of the American Educational Research Association, Montreal, Canada.

Garmon, L. (1982, July 10). Japanese jump. *Science News, 122*(2), 28–29.

Haboush, J. K. (1991). The Confucianization of Korean society. In G. Rozman (Ed.), *The East Asian region: Confucian heritage and its modern adaptation.* Princeton, NJ: Princeton University Press.

Harnisch, D. L., & Sato, T. (1983, October). *Differences in educational influences and achievement in mathematics for secondary students in Japan and the United States.* Paper presented at the ICMI-JSME Regional Conference on Mathematical Education, Tokyo.

Harnisch, D. L., et al. (1986). Mathematics productivity in Japan and Illinois. In *Evaluation in Education: International Progress* (pp. 277–284). New York: Pergamon.

Hawkins, J. N. (1974). *Mao Tse-Tung and education.* Hamden, CT: Linnet Books.

Hess, R. D., & Azuma, H., et al. (1985). Family influences on school readiness and achievement in Japan and the United States: An overview of a longitudinal study. In H. Stevenson, H. Azuma, & K. Hakuta (Eds.), *Child development and education in Japan.* New York: Freeman Publishers.

Husen, T. (Ed.). (1976). *International study of achievement in mathematics: A comparison of twelve countries* (Vol. 1 & 2). New York: Wiley.

Kifer, E., & Robitaille, D. (1989). Attitudes, preferences, and opinions. In D. Robitaille & R. A. Garden (Eds.), *The IEA study of mathematics II: Contests and outcomes of school mathematics* (pp. 178–202). London: Pergamon Press.

Kobayashi, V. N. (1984, Fall). Tradition, modernization and education: The case of Japan. *Journal of Ethnic Studies, 12*(3), 95–118.

Leestma, R., & Walberg, H. J. (1992). *Japanese educational productivity.* (Michigan Papers in Japanese Studies, No. 22). Ann Arbor, MI: Center for Japanese Studies.

Levenson, J. R. (1964). *Modern China and its Confucian past.* New York: Doubleday.

Lewis, C. C. (1992). Creativity in Japanese education. In R. Lesstma & H. J. Walberg (Eds.), *Japanese educational productivity* (pp. 225–226). Ann Arbor: University of Michigan Press.

Lynn, R. (1988). *Educational achievement in Japan: Lessons for the West.* London: Macmillan.

McGinn, N. (1980). *Education and development in Korea.* Cambridge: Harvard University Press.

Ogbu, J. U. (1987). Variability in minority school performance: A problem in search of an explanation. *Anthropology and Education Quarterly, 18*(4), 312–334.

Robinson, M. (1991). Perceptions of Confucianism in twentieth-century Korea. In G. Rozman (Ed.), *The East Asian region: Confucian heritage and its modern adaptation.* Princeton, NJ: Princeton University Press.

Rohlen, T. P. (1983). *Japan's high schools.* Berkeley: University of California Press.

Rozman, G. (Ed.). (1991). *The East Asian region: Confucian heritage and its modern adaptation.* Princeton, NJ: Princeton University Press.

Schiller, D., & Walberg, H. J. (1982, March). Japan: The learning society. *Educational Leadership, 39*(6), 411-12.

Shields, J. J. (1989). *Japanese schooling.* University Park: The Pennsylvania State University Press.

Stevenson, H. W., & Stigler, J. W. (1992). *The learning gap.* New York: Summit Books.

Sue, S. S., & Okayaki, T. (1990). Asian American educational achievements: A phenomenon in search of an explanation. *American Psychologist, 45*(8), 913–920.

Tiene, D. (1983, May). Japan sets the pace in educational television. *Educational Technology, 23*(5), 18–22.

Tiene, D., & Urakawa, T. (1983, November). Japan's elementary science series: The chemistry of successful ETV. *Educational Technology, 23*(11), 19–24.

Torrance, E. P. (1982, Winter). Education for 'quality circles' in Japanese schools. *Journal of Research and Development in Education, 15*(2), 11–15.

Tsukuda, M. (1984, December). *A factual overview of education in Japan and the United States.* Paper presented at Learning From Each Other at the East West Center, Honolulu, HI.

Ushiogi, M. (1984). *Transition from school to work: Japanese case.* Paper presented at Learning From Each Other at the East West Center, Honolulu, HI.

Weiner, B. (1976). An attributional approach for education psychology. In L. S. Shulman (Ed.), *Review of research in education,* Vol. 2(4) (pp. 179–209).

Weiner, B. (1992). *Human motivation.* London: Sage Publications.

White, M. W. (1987). *The Japanese educational challenge: A commitment to children.* New York: The Free Press.

Wiesz, J. R., Rothbaum, F. M., & Blackburn, T. C. (1984, September). Standing out and standing in: The psychology of control in America and Japan. *American Psychologist, 39*(9), 955–969.

Yao, E. L. (1985). A comparison of family characteristics of Asian-American and Anglo-American high achievers. *International Journal of Comparative Sociology, 26*(3–4), 198–208.

7 A Sociocultural Perspective on Motivation

Robert Rueda
University of Southern California

Luis C. Moll
University of Arizona

Many current school reform initiatives in the United States are motivated by concern among educators over low school achievement (Holmes Group, 1987; National Coalition of Advocates for Students, 1988; National Commission on Excellence in Education, 1983). A common element in many of these discussions is implicit or explicit reference to students' motivational deficiencies (Dunn, 1987). However, there are significant limitations with the rather narrow perspective often found in discussion of motivational factors in schooling. In this chapter, we argue that current theories of motivation are limited in that they conceptualize motivation as an individual "in-the-head" phenomenon, with little or no attention paid to the sociocultural context and the interpersonal processes within which individual activity occurs.

The purpose of the present chapter is to highlight the importance of a sociocultural perspective in understanding motivation and its impact on school performance, as an alternative to more individually based, traditional cognitive formulations. We propose a conceptualization of motivation consistent with current sociocultural, interactionist perspectives on cognitive ability as distributed and socially constructed (Forman, Minick, & Stone, in press; Salomon, in press; Wertsch, 1991). After a brief review of more traditional conceptualizations of motivation, we will outline the rudiments of an alternative sociocultural perspective. Following this, some of the key principles of this alternative perspective are illustrated with examples from our work that has focused on the acquisition of literacy with language minority (Latino) students, and implications for the structure of educational programs are discussed.

THEORIES OF MOTIVATION

The literature on motivation is extensive and growing rapidly. There are innumerable psychological variables that have been investigated as part of the general construct of motivation (Weiner, 1980, 1992), including recent attempts to develop more comprehensive models (Locke, this volume).

There has been increasing recognition that the psychological correlates of motivation are extensive. For example, relations between attributional beliefs, motivation, and perceptions of efficacy are intertwined in complex fashion (Schunk, 1990) and have been shown to be related to diverse characteristics such as learning strategies (Pintrich & De Groot, 1990; Pokay & Blumenfeld, 1990), learner characteristics (Meece, Wigfield, & Eccles, 1990), self-regulated learning (Zimmerman, 1989; Zimmerman & Schunk, 1989), social context (Ames, 1987), task design and structure (Hackman & Oldham, 1980), goals (Dweck, 1985), and teacher efficacy (Woolfolk & Hoy, 1990).

In examining this literature, there is a clear progression in the research which parallels development in the larger field of psychology. Specifically, the conceptualization of motivation has shifted from a reliance on innate drives or on operant learning to a cognitive orientation (Ames & Ames, 1989; Dweck, 1986; Dweck & Elliott, 1983; Weiner, 1980, 1984, 1985; Winne & Marx, 1989). As Winne and Marx (1989) note:

> A complete theory of motivation in the context of instruction is traditionally viewed as having to account for why students behave in classrooms as they do. This explanation of student behavior has three facets: (1) what students elect to do, (2) the temperament with which they act, and (3) their persistence in the presence of obstacles or alternatives. We postulate that these behavioral manifestations are *reflections of underlying mental events* (emphasis added). (p. 253)

Whereas early research on motivation focused on drives and personality, the cognitive emphasis currently evident in the psychological literature in learning and memory can be found in the motivation literature. In simple terms, a cognitive orientation is concerned with how incoming sensory stimulation is ". . . transformed, reduced, elaborated, recovered, and used" (Neisser, 1966, p. 4). External stimuli, as conceived in this framework, do not goad the organism or initiate mechanistic chains of thought. Rather, they are viewed as sources of information to be acted upon, such that the processed information is integrated into a "belief" that gives "meaning" to the external, physical environment.

This shift to a cognitive emphasis can be traced to some of the early work of Weiner and colleagues (Weiner, 1972; Weiner, Frieze, Kukla, Reed, Rest, & Rosenbaum, 1971) who argued that those high or low in need for achievement were likely to think differently about success and failure. By making attributions an acceptable object of study, the individual's thoughts about situations and how meanings change as contexts change were now available for scrutiny. Thoughts and cognitive processes are assumed to be the primary antecedents influencing the direction, intensity, and duration of behavior.

With the emergence of this perspective, a strong research tradition developed, with empirical findings which build upon a related set of theoretical constructs such as locus of control, causal attributions, learned helplessness, and self-efficacy. For example, Rotter's early work related to locus of control focused on individual's beliefs about whether reinforcements were under internal or external control (Rotter, 1966). In the area of casual attributions, the research suggests that children who believe that doing well in school is contingent on their own actions perform better than those who do not, as do those children who believe that good grades are caused by internal and controllable causes like effort, thus establishing a link between motivation and achievement (Seligman, 1975; Weiner, 1979). In addition, thoughts about the self have been shown to be important. This focus is most often associated with the work of Bandura's self-efficacy theory (Bandura, 1982). As an example, children who believe that they can produce the responses that lead to desired outcomes (Bandura, 1977) or who believe that they possess high ability (Harter, 1981; Stipek, 1980) perform better academically (Findley & Cooper, 1983; Stipek & Weisz, 1981).

While motivation research has incorporated a cognitive orientation for some time now, more recently there is a trend toward integrating motivation with more "learning-related" cognitive phenomenon such as metacognition, learning strategies, and self-regulatory behavior (Dweck, 1986; Pintrich, 1988, 1989; Pintrich & De Groot, 1990; Zimmerman & Schunk, 1989). As one example, Pintrich and De Groot (1990) present a model that links three dimensions of self-regulated learning (metacognitive strategies for planning and monitoring, management and control of effort, and specific cognitive strategies such as rehearsal and elaboration) with three components of motivation (students' beliefs about their ability to perform a task, students' goals and beliefs about the importance and interest of the task, and students' emotional reactions to the task). Motivational questions implied by these dimensions, which incorporate many of the existing constructs in the motivational literature, include, Can I do this task?, Why am I doing this task?, and How do I feel about this task?

As this necessarily brief and incomplete overview suggests, there is a clear trend toward integrated, cognitively based models of motivation, especially as they relate to school achievement, and as indexed by student engagement, persistence, and on-task behaviors. Even though significant and impressive progress has been made in understanding motivation and its relationship to classroom performance and academic achievement, there are some shortcomings in current theories.

One point that is evident from examining existing theoretical approaches to motivation is that there is a strong bias toward an individualistic orientation, with little attention to context or culturally based influences. That is, motivation is almost always conceptualized uniquely as a product of the intrapsychological functioning of the individual. As is apparent in the brief review presented earlier, the student is seen as the sole agent who not only processes environmental, cognitive, and affective inputs, but who generates feelings and thoughts that themselves influence actions indicative of motivation.

However, there is an emerging perspective in the psychological literature that departs from this more traditional individualistic orientation. In the mainstream literature, for example, this interest is reflected in recent work on situated cognition (Brown, Collins, & Duguid, 1989; Greeno, 1989; The Cognition and Technology Group at Vanderbilt, 1990) and more attention to sociocultural factors in learning (Belmont, 1989). These relatively recent developments can trace their roots to what is loosely termed here a sociocultural, interactionist perspective. Briefly, this framework emphasizes the impact of joint collaborative activity, features of the social context, and social negotiation on individual learning and thinking, and in addition stresses the sociocultural roots of learning and related psychological processes. This theoretical framework draws from the writings of psychologists within the sociohistorical school of psychology as described by Vygotsky (1978), among others, and further developed by his followers in the United States and elsewhere (Lave, 1988; Moll, 1990; Rogoff, 1990; Rogoff & Lave, 1984; Valsiner, 1989; Wertsch, 1985a, 1985b, 1991). The basic outline of this perspective, specifically as it relates to motivation, is presented in the remainder of the chapter along with illustrative examples and a discussion of the implications of such a perspective for designing educational programs for language minority and other students.

A SOCIOCULTURAL APPROACH TO MOTIVATION

Sociocultural theory argues for a reconceptualization of cognitive activity (and by extension, motivation) as a within-child, context-independent phenomenon towards a perspective that highlights the *interdependence* of cognitive and sociocultural activities (e.g., Laboratory of Comparative Human Cognition, 1982; Wertsch, 1991). Accordingly, from this view, motivation is not located solely within the individual without reference to the social and cultural contexts within which individual actions take place. In the field of motivation, Sivan (1986) has proposed a similar formulation:

> . . . motivation is inseparable from the instructional process and the classroom environment. The culturally determined joint activity between student and social context results in an internal state of interest and cognitive and affective engagement, and motivated behaviors, both of which can be considered cultural norms. (p. 209)

The key point, again, is the interconnectedness of social and cognitive activity, where psychological characteristics, such as motivation, are not viewed as characteristics of the individual, but of the individual-in-action within specific contexts. Minick (1985), for one, has made this point forcefully: "The individual has not psychological characteristics, the individual as an object of research does not exist, in isolation from actions and action systems" (p. 282).

This perspective, we should mention, is not necessarily new. The shift from the individual as meaning-maker to a view of collectively constructed meaning has antecedents in both sociology and psychology. As Mehan (1983) has pointed out, in sociology, *symbolic interactionists* were an early influence in the idea that consciousness (meaning) is not intrinsic to objects, people, events, and situations in the real world. Rather, it is viewed as something which is constructed. Humans are seen as symbolic beings who interpret and define their world, and their behavior must be understood with reference to this defining process.

Later, the school of thought known as *constitutive phenomenology* (Cicourel, 1973; Garfinkel, 1967; Goffman, 1963) emphasized more prominently the role of social interaction in the interpretive process. Meaning was no longer seen as being "in the privacy of one's head," but rather as a process carried out among and between people in social activities, not individual mentalistic acts.

In the school of psychology, Piaget (1954) described the individual constructivist processes (the child's interactions with the environment) which serve as the impetus for cognitive development. In particular, he emphasized the child's exploration and manipulation of the objects in the environment, facilitating the construction of reality and stable representations of the world, which he convincingly demonstrated were much different from those of adults. Most importantly, his theory assumed that development is a constructive process.

More recently, the Vygotskian influence provides a contrast to the individual constructive processes described by Piaget. Without discarding the notion of the child as an active agent in his or her own development, Vygotsky (1978) and his followers have come to emphasize culturally organized, socially mediated practices and how the child's development emerges from these practices.[1] A basic notion of this orientation is that higher order cognitive functions develop out of social actions, most prominently social interactions with more competent others in meaningful activities. Importantly, the unit of analysis is no longer the individual, but the child and more capable others engaged in meaningful activity.

Furthermore, Vygotsky also emphasized that social interactions are themselves mediated. Humans use cultural signs and tools (e.g., speech, literacy, mathematics) to mediate their interactions with each other and with their surroundings. A fundamental property of these artifacts, Vygotsky observed, is that they are social in origin; they are used first to communicate with others, to mediate contact with our social worlds; later, with practice, much of it occurring in schools, these artifacts come to mediate our interactions with self, to help us

---

[1]Much has been written about Vygotsky recently. Interested readers should consult, for example, Kozulin (1990), Moll (1990), Valsiner (1988, 1989), Van der veer and Valsiner (1991), Wertsch (1985a, 1985b), as well as Vygotsky (1978, 1987).

think, and we internalize their use (see, for example, Vygotsky, 1978, Chaps. 1–4; Wertsch, 1985b, Chaps. 2–4). Therefore, from a Vygotskian perspective, a major role of schooling is to create social contexts for mastery of and conscious awareness of the use of these cultural tools. It is by mastering these cultural technologies of representation and communication, as Olson (1986) has put it, that individuals acquire the capacity, the means, for "higher order" intellectual activity. Thus, Vygotskian theory posits a strong, dialectical connection between external (social), practical activity mediated by the use of cultural tools, such as speech and writing, and individuals' intellectual activity. As Wertsch (1985b) explains it, Vygotsky "defined external activity in terms of semiotically mediated social processes and argued that the properties of these processes provide the key to understanding the emergence of internal functioning" (p. 62).

In describing the rudiments of a sociocultural approach, then, several key elements appear to stand out: the role of social interactions, the influence of culturally based knowledge and practices, including the use of cultural technologies; the mediating role of signs and symbols, our cultural tools, as well as that of peers or more competent others: and finally, a focus on thinking as inseparable from social and cultural activities. Although this approach has focused mostly on cognition, it lends itself well to reconceptualizing motivation, especially in classroom learning situations. Not only does it take into account the effects of context (activity setting), but suggests that we examine motivation indirectly, as a mediated phenomenon, through the analysis of the activities within which kids are observed learning or not learning, motivated or otherwise, so that motivation is always a characteristic of the child in activity of a certain sort.

In order to illustrate the application and value of the preceding concepts, we provide brief examples from our work with Latino students in school settings as they attempt to gain proficiency in basic literacy. In our own and other work in this area, there are intriguing instances of wide differences in student performance (task engagement, interest, on-task behavior) as a function of context or various features of specific "activity settings." Interestingly, the lower end of these differences has often been attributed to low motivation and resulting diminished achievement. Before moving to these illustrations, a brief background on the current status of Latino students, their school achievement, and possible explanations is provided.

LATINO[2] STUDENTS AND ACADEMIC ACHIEVEMENT

The academic achievement of Latino students in the United States, especially in the area of literacy, is problematic. This is especially true of children who come from homes where little or no English is spoken. The data indicate that these

---

[2]We fully realize the enormous diversity among groups designated as Latinos; we are referring here primarily to Mexican and Puerto Rican working class children within the context of the United States.

children consistently achieve at lower levels than do their nonminority and English-speaking peers, even when bilingual instruction is provided (CTB/McGraw-Hill, 1988). This pattern of low achievement begins as early as first grade (CTB/McGraw-Hill, 1988) and continues well into higher education (Carter & Wilson, 1991; Haycock & Navarro, 1988). Especially problematic is the fact that language minority students continue to lag behind their nonminority peers throughout school, a condition that has remained stable for at least the past 20 years (Arias, 1986; Congressional Budget Office, 1987; De La Rosa & Maw, 1990; Orfield, 1986).

This pattern of educational outcomes is especially troubling in the light of anticipated demographic changes. For example, by the year 2050, the U.S. population will reach 300 million. Anglos will account for 60% of the population (dropping from 198 million in 1980 to 162 million in 2050). The Black population will account for 16% of the total, Latinos will more than double from 6.4% to 15%, and Asians will jump from 1.6% to as much as 10%. More than one in three Americans will be non-Anglo (Oxford-Carpenter, Pol, Lopez, Stupp, Gendell, & Peng, 1984). This trend is even more pronounced in certain regions. In California, for example, in 1970 the school age population was 27% minority, but by the year 2000 it will be 57% (The Tomas Rivera Center, 1991), and Latinos will comprise 35% of that total (Olsen & Chen, 1988; Vernez & Ronfeldt, 1991).

How are findings regarding low achievement to be explained? This is a complex question and an elaborate answer is beyond the scope of the present chapter. However, Sue and Padilla (1986) have suggested that existing explanations can be grouped into four categories. The first is characterized by a focus on *genetic inferiority.* That is, the claim is that minorities fail to achieve well because they are genetically inferior. A second set of explanations focuses on assumed *cultural deficits.* Specifically, the supposition is that low achievement is due to one or more cultural characteristics which are deficient, such as laziness, low self-esteem, or undependability. A third set of explanations focuses on *cultural mismatches,* that is, one or more minority group traits that clash with more traditional American cultural values and result in negative classroom interactional patterns between teacher and student. Finally, a *contextual interaction* perspective highlights the dynamic interactions which occur as cultures come into contact with one another, and how these can serve to depress or elevate the achievement of individual groups.

In line with the contextual interaction perspective, we have been struck by a rather consistent finding in our own and others' work on Latino students' acquisition and uses of literacy (see, for example, Abi-Nader, 1990, and Diaz, Moll, & Mehan, 1986). Specifically, while many of these students appear unmotivated and unable or unwilling to engage in certain tasks on one occasion or under some circumstances, on other occasions or circumstances they appear to be highly motivated and enthusiastically immerse themselves in similar or more demanding tasks. This is an important point with respect to the issue of motivation, as some investigators have suggested that in classroom learning situations, where student's choices of activities are limited, cognitive effort is an appropriate index of motivation (Corno & Mandinach, 1983).

In attempting to understand our observations, we have found ourselves forced to look beyond the particular individual psychological characteristics of the students to the interaction of the children, the task, and other features of the sociocultural context. Simply put, we view motivation not as an individual construct but as a socially and culturally mediated phenomenon, located not within the child but in the interactions of the child with others in specific activities.

A CLASSROOM ILLUSTRATION: WRITING AS "PULLING TEETH"

Our first example draws from research on the teaching of writing that has been described in detail elsewhere (Diaz, Moll, & Mehan, 1986; Moll & Diaz, 1987a, 1987b; also see Moll & Greenberg, 1990). The general goal of this line of work has been to study how writing is used in home and community settings and to explore ways of using this information to improve the teaching of writing in classrooms. We worked in collaboration with 12 teachers from three junior-high schools, all located within predominantly working-class, Latino (mostly Mexican) neighborhoods in San Diego, California. A reason for the study was that there was widespread concern from teachers and administrators about the lack and quality of the students' writing. More than one teacher described writing in her classroom as a matter of "pulling teeth": disinterested or unmotivated students, limited effort and production, especially from students being asked to write in their second language, in this case English. Getting the students to write was generally perceived by the teachers as a difficult chore.

The study's design included creating a research site, a setting within the community under study in which we met with the teachers every 2 weeks for approximately 3 hours to discuss their teaching of writing. More specifically, we met to discuss the latest research information and how this information could be used by the teachers to change or improve how they were teaching writing. We realized that very few of the students were doing any extended writing in the classrooms, a situation certainly not unique to these schools (Applebee, 1981; Hiebert & Fisher, 1991). Most classroom writing was in response to teachers' questions, to worksheets, or highly structured and inflexible routines. This was especially true for limited English proficient students, who were generally assumed not to possess the necessary English skills to participate in essay or expository writing: Therefore, teachers adjusted lessons to the students' low levels of English oral skills, common practice in these settings.

Our strategy consisted of providing teachers with instructional options that emphasized the use of writing for communication (e.g., Graves, 1983; De La Luz Reyes, 1991). We also turned to our community study to select topics or themes for writing that could potentially be interesting or relevant to the students. We wanted to change not only the process of writing, but the *motive* for writing: Classroom writing was to become an activity to communicate with someone else or with themselves about something that mattered.

We encouraged the teachers to experiment with their teaching, to keep a journal of their activities, and bring it to our sessions for discussion. The teachers agreed to develop and implement a series of writing activities in which they asked the students to write about issues of significance to them or their community (e.g., bilingualism, immigration, gangs, school life). In particular, the teachers organized prewriting discussions as a way to actively involve the students in talking about the writing topic, help them share ideas, and guide the thinking involved in developing their writing. We were surprised that these discussions, in what appeared to be relatively minor changes in instruction, had an immediate effect on student motivation. For example, 10 of the 12 teachers reported positive results, including that students had "increased enthusiasm," that there "were no moans from students when they were asked to write," and that "students who had not written anything all year stayed after class (on their own) to complete the assignment" (Moll & Diaz, 1987a, p. 206).

For our present purposes, perhaps the most interesting and revealing example in our study comes from a teacher who asked the students to write about recent violent incidents in their community: the murder of the teacher's aide a few weeks earlier, and the random shooting of people (five perished) by a man in a nearby trailer park. The two incidents combined to create the context for highly emotional discussion of violence. We quote from the teacher's journal (Moll & Diaz,, 1987a) (we have edited for brevity):

> Normally our topics are light, that is., favorite things to do, what friendship is, and so on. When I wrote "violence" on the board, I got some raised eyebrows and students shifting in their seats. . .
>
> I gave them a dictionary definition of violence and then asked them what came to mind when they thought, violence. These are the responses I initially received: killing, fighting, mugging, drugs, and guns. That was it. It was dead silent as I waited. Uncomfortable students prevailed. . .
>
> I went back and sat in my chair in the circle. I began recounting the week's trailer incident . . . I started to ask them why they thought it happened. Most felt the man just "snapped." There were many suggestions as to why, but that explanation was the prevalent one . . . I then asked them if (my aide's) murder affected them more. She was my adult aide and she was killed by her husband (earlier this year). Many of the students knew her on a personal basis. This was a difficult subject for me because she was my dear friend. The kids fell quiet when I brought up (her name). They obviously had been deeply affected by this violence. They began to relax when someone said, "Of course it affected me more, I knew her."

What followed was an emotional discussion. It was like they had been waiting for a chance to analyze how this could've happened to someone they actually knew. . ."

The teacher then used the discussion to get the students to elaborate what violence meant to them and to organize their thinking to write about the topic. The next day the students began to write. The teacher provided the students with questions to help them structure their writing. Here's how the teacher described it:

> They were slow in starting as they were in the discussion. I knew this would be the case due to the powerful emotions involved. I also tried to encourage each student to zero in on the writing problems they had [on a pretest sample] such as capitalization, proofreading, even paragraph form. At the same time, I refreshed their memories by writing on the board some of the key words from the previous day's discussion. The writing began. Many wrote frantically to pour it out.

A number of the students chose to write about personal experiences and used writing to make connections between these events and themselves. There was an increase (in comparison to the pretest samples) not only in the amount of text written, but in its coherence and organization. All the writing, we should point out, was in English, the students' second language. The students, with the teacher's assistance, were beginning to use writing as a tool of communication and as a tool to elaborate their thinking. The teacher commented on the results:

> I was impressed by the results. As I went around and discussed each paper with the students I got interesting statements, I had never questioned them directly regarding how much easier this topic was to handle regardless of the emotion, seriousness, and so on. Virginia, who wrote about a close call in a gang fight, stated, "Don't they know it's easier for us to tell them how we feel when we've been there?" I gave so many positive strokes this time around. Most knew their papers were better. I got no "Really?'s" when I pointed out especially good areas. . .
>
> This was a very successful lesson for me in many ways. I enjoyed the time to really talk to my kids. I also furthered my belief that if what's taught is important in the mind of the learner, much more will truly be learned.

Other teachers in the study organized formal inquiries that involved the students during several days in developing survey instruments, piloting them, collecting data from parents and other community members, including school personnel, analyzing and summarizing results, and incorporating results into their written products. As we analyzed the teachers' reports and the students' writings, we interpreted their experiences in relation to two factors, both related to what we could call the *social context of motivation.*

One factor was the importance of content. We deliberately tried to create links between the classroom activities and issues of life outside the classroom. The idea was for students (and teachers) to *actively* engage, through the process of writing, content that they found interesting, important, or meaningful. The introduction of this content as themes or topics for writing qualitatively changed the nature of classroom writing from a mechanical task to a thoroughly social and intellectual activity. The prewriting discussions, for example, served as vehicles for the students' interests, experiences, and opinions to become legitimate resources for writing. Similarly, the exploration of community issues showed both students and teachers that there were ample resources, including the community's bilingualism, values, and knowledge, that could be tapped for the development of classroom writing (also see Moll & Greenberg, 1990).

A second factor was the development of the teachers' role as *mediators* of learning. Here ideas from Vygotsky (1978, also see Moll, 1990), especially his concept of zone of proximal development, became very useful. Three aspects of this concept were incorporated into the lessons. First was to aim instruction beyond what the students could accomplish individually, that is, to make the writing activity reasonably challenging, within the students' reach with the teacher's assistance. The second aspect called for the teacher to provide strategic assistance in helping the students conduct and accomplish the activity, especially by providing technical support in writing and by capitalizing fully on the students' knowledge and experiences, regardless of English fluency. Third, the activity had goals that could be accomplished and the students could receive formative comments or feedback from the teacher or from peers to help them monitor their performance. The idea, then, was not only to assist or stretch the students' performance, but to help them eventually "appropriate" or take over the activity in order to perform it competently and independent of assistance. These changes in the students' performance, in turn, allowed the teachers to facilitate, to mediate, new or higher levels of performance for the students—in our theoretical language, to mediate new zones of proximal development.

It was striking that within these transformed instructional contexts, students appeared to be highly motivated; the students, with the teacher's assistance, seemed to become absorbed by the activities, willing to put in the time and effort necessary to accomplish them (cf. Csikszentmihalyi, 1991). Many of the teachers reported that the students maintained their interest over time, as they engaged in challenging and involved writing activities.

A CLASSROOM ILLUSTRATION: WRITING IN THE RESOURCE ROOM

Our second example is drawn from work that represents a long-term effort to reconceptualize the content and structure of elementary special education pull-out programs for language minority Latino students (Ruiz, 1989; Ruiz, Figueroa,

Rueda, & Beaumont, 1991). A particular emphasis of this work has been on exploring ways of fostering literacy for students in these remedial settings. A prime vehicle in this has been to create "optimal learning environments" (Ruiz, 1989), or high-level, authentic, culturally compatible instructional settings which draw on students' prior knowledge and interests in the service of basic literacy acquisition.

Our initial observations from a year-long case study of four of these elementary-level pull-out programs yielded a set of discouraging yet typically reported observations: a preponderance of low level academic drills, frequent behavior problems, general disengagement from academic work on the part of the students except under conditions of threat or material reinforcement, and a general lack of interest in academic matters (Rueda, Figueroa, & Ruiz, 1990). Because these classrooms were almost entirely populated by learning disabled students, teachers commonly ascribed students' behavioral and learning problems to pseudo-medical causes such as assumed visual-motor, perceptual-motor, and other deficits. However, the presumed lack of motivation on the part of students was also frequently mentioned as a major factor in students' poor academic outcomes.

This seeming lack of motivation was especially apparent in the language arts and writing activities that are heavily emphasized in these remedial programs. In one of the classrooms studied, writing activities consisted primarily of three types: handwriting practice of discrete letters or symbols, copying sentences, and narrative writing in response to workbook- or teacher-assigned topics. Because learning in general in this particular classroom was conceptualized as an individual activity, students were typically given instructions and then monitored as they tried to complete the assignment and finally graded but rarely provided mediation or other types of assisted performance (Tharp & Gallimore, 1988).

Esteban, a 6th-grade student in this classroom, was diagnosed as learning disabled by the school psychologist. This particular classroom is located in a low socioeconomic area, heavily impacted by gangs, violence, crime, and other common urban problems. Like most of the students in this class, Esteban demonstrated little engagement or effort in academic tasks. Writing in particular was laborious and strained, with many distractions and seat-squirming evident. Like the majority of the students in the program, the low level tasks that have comprised classroom writing activities have led to a notion of writing as "making letters pretty" and not as a communicative tool. A brief excerpt from our interview data (Rueda, 1991) illustrates this point:

Interviewer: Who is the best writer that you know?
Esteban: My friend Carlos.
Interviewer: What makes him a good writer?
Esteban: Because he always gets the words correct and his handwriting is very nice and pretty.

Interviewer: How did you learn to write?

Esteban: By writing over and over, and practicing my handwriting so that others can understand what I write. (p. 103)

His responses suggest that for him writing holds little connection to his interests or prior knowledge, an observation strengthened by the lack of engagement clearly evident in the classroom. A teacher assigned story about Abraham Lincoln during one 50-minute class period resulted in the following: "Abraham Lincoln was a good man. He was a special man. Every book that he got ahold of he read" (translated from Spanish). Our observations during this particular class period indicated the usual pattern not only with Luis but among the other students as well: distractions, teacher threats, seat squirming, talking and laughing among students, and blank stares into space. The apparent lack of motivation described by the teacher is evident.

As members of our research team were in the classroom on at least a weekly basis throughout this year-long observational period, we became very familiar both with the classroom context and with the students. One research assistant became especially friendly with several of the older (5th- and 6th-grade) boys in the classroom, Esteban in particular, to the point that these normally uncommunicative students began to confide out-of-school problems, concerns, and activities to her. Because a major goal of the project was to eventually build upon the students' out-of-school knowledge, abilities, and interests in the acquisition of basic literacy, we attempted a "natural experiment." This was occasioned by Esteban's confiding to her a tragic incident in which his cousin had been involved in a robbery-related shooting and had to be taken to the hospital with a head wound. Although such occurrences were not uncommon in this community, it was an emotionally charged issue for Esteban, who had been deeply affected.[3]

Drawing on the theoretical principles outlined in the first example, the assistant tried to reorganize the activity setting such that appropriate mediation within the zone of proximal development could be provided *through the social relationship,* building upon already existing competencies. As Esteban and the assistant discussed the student's concerns in a small side room adjacent to the classroom, the assistant suggested that Esteban write down what he wanted to say in a note to her. She strongly emphasized that this was not to be graded, and therefore he should not be concerned with handwriting neatness, spelling, etc. Because writing for purposes other than practice for correct form and evaluation were foreign to Luis, it took a bit of encouragement for him to begin the task. However, once

---

[3]Although both examples depict the consequences of violence in the communities we studied, the reader should not conclude that either community as a whole is overwhelmingly characterized by violence. Although violent incidents do occur in these communities, and deeply affects children in particular, violence is nevertheless an aberration while the existence of close, extended family networks is the norm.

he began to write, he continued for the remaining 45 minutes of the period without looking up from his page. Uncharacteristically immersing himself in the task, he produced almost three handwritten pages, and only reluctantly stopped after being convinced that the period had ended.

Neither the research assistant nor the teacher had witnessed this type of engagement or level of effort previously with this student. As in the previous example, within this transformed instructional context the apparent level of motivation was exceedingly high especially in light of past observations both by our research team as well as by the teacher. How do we account for this striking change?

As noted earlier, we draw on two key principles that have formed the foundation for our work. The first relates to creating links between literacy activities in the classroom and important issues related to students' lives outside the classroom such that students can become actively engaged with the content (McCaslin & Murdock, 1991; Wentzel, 1991). As McCaslin and Murdock (1991) have noted:

> A Vygotskian orientation is distinctive in its interest in the emergent interaction of the developing individual within and among the changing contexts of her/his multiple social/instructional environments. Thus, at a minimum, the emergent interaction of experiences within home, within school, and between home and school must be considered if we are to fully understand adaptive learning students' classroom behavior. (p. 219)

The second factor centers on the provision of strategic assistance or mediation, at an appropriate developmental level, in the context of the social relationship. In examining the contrast in Esteban's performance, the task itself had changed. Although still ostensible a classroom "writing" task, it has moved from an evaluative activity to a meaning-centered activity. Moreover, the adult has shifted roles from evaluator to mediator. As we have suggested, the conceptualization of motivation has to encompass more than individual psychological activity.

DISCUSSION

Maehr (1982) has suggested that there are five behavioral patterns that can be used as indices of motivation related to learning: (a) the direction of an individual's attention and activity, (b) persistence, or length of time engaged in an activity, (c) activity level, (d) continuing motivation, or returning to a task without apparent external incentives, and (e) performance, in many ways a consequence of the other factors. Given these criteria, we argue that the students in the preceding example show strong evidence of motivation in settings where they are often described as unmotivated. Interestingly, our observations with

Latino children's literacy are echoed elsewhere in the literature, specifically in the area of intrinsic motivation, as illustrated in the following observation by Lepper and Hodell (1989):

> It is one of the persistent paradoxes of educational psychology that so many children seem to have motivational problems in our schools. As potential educational reformers have noted time and again, the young child, outside of school, seems blessed with a seemingly limitless curiosity, a thirst for knowledge, a will to learn. Young children begin to acquire a first language, and sometimes a second and third, with remarkable facility and minimal confusion; and they do so at the tender age of two and in the relative absence of formal instruction. They learn a great deal about the social and physical environments in which they live and how to navigate through those complex environments, with limited overt tuition. Some even learn significant amounts about the process of reading or the rudiments of arithmetic without being explicitly taught these subjects. Rarely, if ever, does one find a parent complaining about his or her preschooler's lack of motivation for learning. (p. 73)

How do we explain these variations in motivation and performance? We find traditional motivational theories which focus primarily on the individual to offer little in understanding these differences. In analyzing these examples, a general pattern is evident: Children appear to be more motivated under authentic, meaningful task conditions, where they jointly construct meaning with peers and teachers, and where activities are challenging yet within their reach or zone of proximal development. The examples further suggest that learning, in order to be motivating, requires personal construction of meaning, or in other words, where the children have a sense of "owning" the task. Although academic goals are commonly described in terms of learning goals or performance goals (Dweck & Leggett, 1988), there are perhaps more basic reasons for engaging in literacy than we have heretofore routinely tapped into, such as the desire to communicate with others about something that matters.

As we have noted, these are rarely characteristics of working-class schooling. If anything, these classrooms, which help define the school experiences of the great majority of Latino and other language minority children, have been described as mechanistic, dull, and intellectually unchallenging (see, for example, Oakes, 1986). Certainly, any complete account of motivation must consider the concrete circumstances under which we ask children to learn.

IMPLICATIONS AND CONCLUSIONS

A sociocultural approach suggests that motivation is (a) socially negotiated (what it is and how it is displayed), (b) socially distributed (not just in child's head), and (c) context specific (determined by features of the activity setting). The most obvious implication of this approach is that motivation must be conceptualized as a "situated" phenomenon: located not solely within individuals, but within "systems" of activities involving other persons, environments, resources, and goals. From this perspective, motivation is accomplished, it is created, it is socially and culturally relative, and it is context-specific. It is not a unitary phenomenon, a general, invariant property of the individual mind, or an abstract property of individuals; it is manifested in activities, involving most prominently, the mediation of other human beings. In Sivan's (1986) words, ". . . the individual no longer acts as the instigator of motivation. Rather, motivation is a socially negotiated process that results in an observable manifestation of interest and cognitive and affective engagement" (p. 210).

This approach, then, requires a much more critical look at the nature of instruction, at the sorts of specific conditions that we organize for students' learning. Our work suggests that student motivation is mediated by the extent to which our pedagogy "brings learning to life." That is, motivation to learn is inseparable from our opportunities to personalize that learning, where our interests and abilities are addressed, taken into account, and incorporated into the activities. This calls for reorienting our efforts towards the development of motivational support or "scaffolding," where we fully exploit the existing resources of individuals, schools, and communities in mediating students' active engagement with classroom learning in ways that make contact with their experiences.

ACKNOWLEDGMENTS

The work in the special education classrooms referred to by Dr. Rueda was supported in part by the California State Department of Education, Dr. Shirley Thornton, Deputy Superintendent for Special Programs, by the California Office of Migrant Education, and by the University of California Linguistic Minority Research Project. Further support in the preparation of this chapter was provided to Drs. Rueda and Moll from the National Center on Cultural Diversity and Second Language Learning, University of California at Santa Cruz.

The research reported in this chapter was supported in part by the U.S. Army Research Institute for Behavioral and Social Sciences through a subcontract with Battelle Institute. However, the views, opinions and/or findings contained in this report are the authors' and should not be construed as an official ARI position, policy, or decision, unless so designated by other official documentation.

REFERENCES

Abi-Nader, J. (1990). "A house for my mother": Motivating culturally based Hispanic high school students. *Anthropology & Education Quarterly, 21,* 41–58.
Ames, C. (1987). The enhancement of student motivation. In M. Maehr & D. Kleiber (Eds.),

Advances in motivation and achievement: Vol. 6. Enhancing student motivation (pp. 123–148). Greenwich, CT: JAI Press.

Ames, C., & Ames, R. (Eds.). (1989). *Research on motivation in education. Vol. 3.: Goals and cognition.* New York: Academic Press.

Applebee, A. (1981). *Writing in the secondary school.* Urbana, IL: National Council of Teachers of English.

Arias, M. B. (1986). The context of education for Hispanic students: An overview. *American Journal of Education, 95,* 26–57.

Bandura, A. (1977). Self-efficacy: Toward a unified theory of behavioral change. *Psychological Review, 84,* 191–215.

Bandura, A. (1982). Self-efficacy mechanism in human agency. *American Psychologist, 37,* 122–147.

Belmont, J. (1989). Cognitive strategies and strategic learning: The socio-instructional approach. *American Psychologist, 44*(12), 142–148.

Brainiin, S. (1985). Mediating learning. In E. Gordon (Ed.), *Review of research in education.* Washington, DC: AERA.

Brown, J. S., Collins, A., & Duguid, P. (1989). Situated cognition and the culture of learning. *Educational Researcher, 18*(1), 32–41.

Carter, D. J., & Wilson, R. W. (1991). *Ninth Annual Status Report on Minorities in Higher Education.* Washington, DC: Office of Minorities in Higher Education, American Council on Education.

Cicourel, A. V. (1973). *Cognitive sociology: Language and meaning in social interaction.* London: Penguin.

Cognition and Technology Group at Vanderbilt. (1990). Anchored instruction and its relationship to situated cognition. *Educational Researcher, 19*(6), 2–10.

Congressional Budget Office. (1987). *Educational achievement: Explanations and implications of recent trends.* Washington, DC: The Congress of the United States.

Corno, L., & Mandinach, E. B. (1983). The role of cognitive engagement in class room learning and motivation. *Educational Psychologist, 18,* 88–108.

Csikszemtmihalyi, M. (1990). Literacy and intrinsic motivation. *Daedalus, 19*(2), 115–140.

CTB/McGraw-Hill. (1988). *SABE: Spanish Assessment of Basic Education* (technical report). Monterey, CA: CCTB/McGraw-Hill.

De La Luz Reyes, M. (1991). A process approach to literacy instruction for Spanish-speaking students: In search of a best fit. In E. H. Hiebert (Ed.), *Literacy for a diverse society: Perspectives, practices, policies* (pp. 157–171). New York: Teachers College Press.

De La Rosa, D., & Maw, C. (1990). *Hispanic education: A statistical portrait.* Washington, DC: National Council of La Raza.

Diaz, S., Moll, L. C., & Mehan, H. (1986). Sociocultural resources in instruction: A context-specific approach. In California State Department of Education, *Beyond Language: Social and cultural factors in schooling language minority children* (pp. 187–230). Los Angeles: California State University Evaluation, Dissemination, and Assessment Center.

Dunn, L. M. (1987). *Bilingual Hispanic children on the mainland: A review of research on their cognitive, linguistic, and scholastic development.* Circle Pines, MN: American Guidance Service.

Dweck, C. S. (1985). Intrinsic motivation, perceived control, and self-evaluation maintenance: An achievement goal analysis. In C. Ames & R. Ames (Eds.), *Research on motivation in education: Vol. 2. the Classroom Milieu* (pp. 289–305). New York: Academic Press.

Dweck, C. S. (1986). Motivational processes affecting learning. *American Psychologist, 41,* 1040–1048.

Dweck, C. S., & Elliott, E. S. (1983). Achievement motivation. In P. H. Mussen (Gen. Ed.) & E. M. Hetherington (Vol. Ed.), *Handbook of child psychology: Vol. IV. Social and personality development* (pp. 643–691). New York: Wiley.

Dweck, C. S., & Leggett, E. L. (1988). A social-cognitive approach to motivation and personality. *Psychological Review, 95*(2), 256–273.

Elliott, E. S., & Dweck C. S. (1988). Goals: An approach to motivation and achievement. *Journal of Personality & Social Psychology, 54*(1), 5-12.

Findley, M. J., & Cooper, H. M. (1983). Locus of control and academic achievement: A literature review. *Journal of Personality and Social Psychology, 44*, 419–427.

Forman, E., Minick, N., & Stone, C. A. (Eds.). (in press). *Contexts for learning: Sociocultural dynamics in children's development.* New York: Oxford University Press.

Garfinkel, H. (1967). *Studies in ethnomethodology.* Englewood Cliffs, NJ: Prentice-Hall.

Gergen, K. J. (1985). The social constructivist movement in modern psychology. *American Psychologist, 40*(3), 266–275.

Goffman, E. (1963). *Stigma.* Englewood Cliffs, NJ: Prentice-Hall.

Greeno, J. G. (1989). A perspective on thinking. *American Psychologist, 44*(2), 134–141.

Graves, D. (1983). *Writing: Teachers and children at work.* Exeter, NH: Heinemann.

Hackman, J. R., & Oldham, G. R. (1980). *Work redesign.* Reading, MA: Addison-Wesley.

Harter, S. (1981). The perceived competence scale for children. *Child Development, 53*, 87–97.

Haycock, K., & Navarro, S. (1988). *Unfinished business: Fulfilling our children's promise.* Oakland, CA: The Achievement Council.

Hiebert, E. H., & Fisher, C. W. (1991). Talk and talk structures that foster literacy. In E. H. Hiebert (Ed.), *Literacy for a diverse society: Perspectives, practices, and policies* (pp. 141–156). New York: Teachers College Press.

Holmes Group Inc. (1987, April). *Tomorrow's teachers. A report of the Holmes group.* East Lansing, MI: Author.

Kozulin, A. (1990). *Vygotsky's psychology.* Cambridge, MA: Harvard University Press.

Laboratory of Comparative Human Cognition. (1982). Culture and cognition. In R. J. Sternberg (Ed.), *Handbook of human intelligence.* New York: Cambridge University Press.

Lave, J. (1988). *Cognition in practice.* New York: Cambridge University Press.

Lepper, M. R., & Hodell, M. (1989). Intrinsic motivation in the classroom. In C. Ames & R. Ames (Eds.), *Research on motivation in education. Vol. 3: Goals and cognition* (pp. 73–106). New York: Academic Press.

McCaslin, M. M., & Murdock, T. B. (1991). The emergent interaction of home and school in the development of students' adaptive learning. In M. L. Maehr & P. R. Pintrich (Eds.), *Advances in motivation and achievement: A research annual* (Vol. 7, pp. 213–260). Greenwich, CT: JAI Press.

Maehr, M. (1982). *Motivational factors in school achievement.* Paper commissioned by the National Commission on Excellence in Education (NIE 400-81-0004, Task 10).

Meece, J., Wigfield, A., & Eccles, J. S. (1990). Predictors of math anxiety and its influence on young adolescents' course enrollment intentions and performance in mathematics. *Journal of Educational Psychology, 82*, 60–70.

Mehan, H. (1983). Social constructivism in psychology and sociology. *Sociologie et Societes, Vol. XIV, 2*, 77–96.

Minick, N. (1985). *L. S. Vygotsky and Soviet activity theory: New perspectives on the relationship between mind and society.* Unpublished doctoral dissertation, Northwestern University.

Moll, L. C. (Ed.). (1990). *Vygotsky and education: Instructional implications and applications of socio-historical psychology.* New York: Cambridge University Press.

Moll, L. C., & Diaz, S. (1987a). Teaching writing as communication. In D. R. Bloome (Ed.), *Literacy and schooling* (pp. 193–221). Norwood, NJ: Ablex.

Moll, L. C., & Diaz, S. (1987b). Change as the goal of educational research. *Anthropology & Education Quarterly, 18*, 300–311.

Moll, L. C., & Greenberg, J. B. (1990). Creating zones of possibilities: Combining social contexts for instruction. In L. C. Moll (Ed.), *Vygotsky and education: Instructional implications and applications of socio-historical psychology* (pp. 319–348). New York: Cambridge University Press.

National Coalition of Advocates for Students. (1988). *Barriers to excellence: Our children at risk* (3rd ed.). Boston, MA: Author.

National Commission on Excellence in Education. (1983). *A nation at risk: The imperative for educational reform*. Washington, DC: U.S. Department of Education.

Neisser, U. (1966). *Cognitive psychology*. New York: Appleton-Century-Crofts.

Oakes, J. (1986). Tracking, inequality, and the rhetoric of school reform: Why schools don't change. *Journal of Education, 168,* 61–80.

Olsen, L., & Chen, M. T. (1988). *Crossing the schoolhouse border: Immigrant students and the California public schools*. San Francisco, CA: California Tomorrow.

Olson, D. (1986). Intelligence and literacy: The relationship between intelligence and the technologies of representation and communication. In R. Sternberg & R. Wagner (Eds.), *Practical intelligence: Nature and origins of competence in the everyday world* (pp. 338–360). New York: Cambridge University Press.

Orfield, G. (1986). Hispanic education: Challenges, research, and policies. *American Journal of Education, 95,* 1–25.

Oxford-Carpenter, R., Pol, L., Lopez, D., Stupp, P., Gendell, M., & Peng, S. (1984). *Demographic projections on non-English language background and limited-English proficient persons in the United States to the year 2000 by state, age, and language group*. Rosslyn, VA: InterAmerica Research Associates, National Clearinghouse for Bilingual Education.

Piaget, J. (1954). *The construction of reality in the child*. (M. Cook, Trans.). New York: Basic Books.

Pintrich, P. R. (1988). A process-oriented view of student motivation and cognition. In J. S. Stark & L. Mets (Eds.), *Improving teaching and learning through research. New directions for institutional research* (No. 57, pp. 55–70). San Francisco: Jossey-Bass.

Pintrich, P. R. (1989). The dynamic interplay of student motivation and cognition in the college classroom. In C. Ames & M. Maehr (Eds.), *Advances in motivation and achievement: Vol. 6. Motivation enhancing environments* (pp. 117–160). Greenwich, CT: JAI Press.

Pintrich, P. R., & De Groot, E. V. (1990). Motivational and self-regulated learning components of classroom academic performance. *Journal of Educational Psychology, 82*(1), 33–40.

Pokay, P., & Blumenfeld, P. C. (1990). Predicting achievement early and late in the semester: The role of motivation and use of learning strategies. *Journal of Educational Psychology, 82*(1), 41–50.

Rogoff, B. (1990). *Apprenticeship in thinking*. New York: Oxford University Press.

Rogoff, B., & Lave, J. (Eds.). (1984). *Everyday cognition: Its development in the social context*. Cambridge, MA: Harvard University Press.

Rotter, J. (1966). Generalized expectancies for internal versus external control of reinforcement. *Psychological Monographs, 80*(1, Whole No. 609).

Rueda, R. (1991). Characteristics of literacy programs for language-minority students. In E. H. Hiebert (Ed.), *Literacy for a diverse society: Perspectives, practices, and policies* (pp. 93–107). New York: Teachers College Press.

Rueda, R., Figueroa, R., & Ruiz, N. T. (1990). *An ethnographic analysis of instructional activity settings for Mexican American learning handicapped students*. Paper presented at the Annual Meeting of the American Educational Research Association, Boston, MA.

Ruiz, N. T. (1989). An optimal learning environment for Rosemary. *Exceptional Children, 56*(2), 130–144.

Ruiz, N. T., Figueroa, R. A., Rueda, R. S., & Beaumont, C. (1991). History and status of bilingual special education for Hispanic handicapped students. In R. V. Padilla & A. H. Benavides (Eds.), *Critical perspectives on bilingual education research* (pp. 349–380). Tempe, AZ: Bilingual Press.

Salomon, G. (Ed.). (in press). *Distributed cognition.* New York: Cambridge University Press.

Schunk, D. H. (1990). Introduction to the special section on motivation and efficacy. *Journal of Educational Psychology, 82*(1), 3–6.

Seligman, M. E. P. (1975). *Helplessness: On depression, development, and death.* San Francisco: Freeman.

Sivan, E. (1986). Motivation in social constructivist theory. *Educational Psychologist, 21*(3), 209–233.

Stipek, D. (1980). A causal analysis of the relationship between locus of control and academic achievement in first grade. *Contemporary Educational Psychology, 5,* 90–99.

Stipek, D. J., & Weisz, J. R. (1981). Perceived personal control and academic achievement. *Review of Educational Research, 51,* 101–137.

Sue, S., & Padilla, A. (1986). Ethnic minority issues in the United States: Challenges for the educational system. In California State Department of Education, *Beyond Language: Social and cultural factors in schooling language minority students.* Los Angeles, CA: Evaluation, Dissemination, and Assessment Center, California State University.

Tharp, R. G., & Gallimore, R. (1988). *Rousing minds to life: Teaching, learning, and schooling in social context.* New York: Cambridge University Press.

The Tomas Rivera Center. (1991). *(Almost) 8 million and counting: A demographic overview of Latinos in California with a focus on Los Angeles County.* Claremont, CA: The Tomas Rivera Center.

Valsiner, J. (1988). *Developmental psychology in the Soviet Union.* Sussex, Great Britain: The Harvester Press.

Valsiner, J. (1989). *Human development and culture: The social nature of personality and its study.* Lexington, MA: Lexington Books.

van der Veer, R., & Valsiner, J. (1991). *Understanding Vygotsky.* Cambridge, MA: Blackwell.

Vernez, G., & Ronfeldt, D. (1991). The current situation in Mexican immigration. *Science, 251,* 1189–1193.

Vygotsky, L. S. (1978). *Mind in society: The development of higher psychological processes.* (M. Cole, V. John-Steiner, S. Scribner, & E. Souberman, Eds., and Trans.). Cambridge, MA: Harvard University Press.

Vygotsky, L. S. (1987). Thinking and speech. In L. S. Vygotsky, *Collected works, Vol. 1.* (pp. 39–285). (R. Rieber, A. Carton, & Minick, N., Eds. and Trans.). New York: Plenum.

Weiner, B. (1972). *Theories of motivation: From mechanism to cognition.* Chicago: Markham.

Weiner, B. (1979). A theory of motivation for some classroom experiences. *Journal of Educational Psychology, 71,* 3–25.

Weiner, B. (1980). *Human Motivation.* New York: Holt, Rinehart, and Winston.

Weiner, B. (1984). Principle for a theory of student motivation and its application within an attributional framework. In R. Ames & C. Ames (Eds.), *Research on motivation in education: Vol. 1. Student motivation* (pp. 15–38). Orlando, FL: Academic Press.

Weiner, B. (1992). *Human motivation: Metaphors, theories, and research.* Newbury Park, CA: Sage Publications.

Weiner, B., Frieze, I., Kukla, A., Reed, L., Rest, S., & Rosenbaum, R. M. (1971). Perceiving the causes of success and failure. In E. E. Jones, D. E. Kanose, H. H. Kelley, R. E. Nisbett, S. Valins, & B. Weiner (Eds.), *Attributions: Perceiving the causes of behavior* (pp. 95–120). Morristown, NJ: General Learning Press.

Wentzel, K. R. (1991). Social and academic goals at school: Motivation and achievement in context. In M. L. Maehr & P. R. Pintrich (Eds.), *Advances in motivation and achievement: A research annual* (Vol. 7, pp. 185–212). Greenwich, CT: JAI Press.

Wertsch, J. V. (1985a). *Culture, communication, and cognition; Vygotskian perspectives.* New York: Cambridge University Press.

Wertsch, J. V. (1985b). *Vygotsky and the social formation of mind.* Cambridge, MA: Harvard University Press.

Wertsch, J. V. (1991). *Voices of the mind: A socio-historical approach to mediated action.* Cambridge, MA: Harvard University Press.

Winne, P. H., & Marx, R. W. (1989). A cognitive-processing analysis of motivation within classroom tasks. In C. Ames & R. Ames (Eds.), *Research on motivation in education. Vol. 3: Goals and cognition* (pp. 223–258). New York: Academic Press.

Woolfolk, A. E., & Hoy, W. K. (1990). Prospective teachers' sense of efficacy and beliefs about control. *Journal of Educational Psychology, 82*(1), 81–91.

Zimmerman, B. J. (1989). Models of self-regulated learning and academic achievement. In B. J. Zimmerman & D. H. Schunk (Eds.), *Self-regulated learning and academic achievement: Theory, research, and practice.* New York: Springer-Verlag.

Zimmerman, B. J., & Schunk, D. H. (Eds.). (1989). *Self-regulated learning and academic achievement: Theory, research, and practice.* New York: Springer-Verlag.

II MOTIVATION OF GROUPS

8 Some Issues Involved in Motivating Teams

Robert W. Swezey
Andrew L. Meltzer
InterScience America

Eduardo Salas
Naval Training Systems Center

> *Team: Two or more horses, oxen etc. harnessed to the same vehicle*
> *or plow.*
> —(Webster's New World Dictionary: Second College Edition, 1980).

The nature of motivation has been of keen interest to students of human behavior for centuries. The Greek philosopher Epicurus, for instance, proposed the hedonistic view that people are motivated to seek pleasure and avoid pain, a position which, according to Franken (1982), continues as the cornerstone for various current theories of human motivation. In the 1930s and 1940s the study of human motivation attracted a great deal of interest among psychologists, resulting in the emergence of a variety of theories, including need-based conceptualizations (e.g., Maslow, 1943), and cognitive formulations (e.g., Lewin, 1938; Tolman, 1932), among many others. Later in the 1950s and 1960s, psychologists began to focus on the role of motivation in the work place, specifically in the areas of job satisfaction and job performance resulting in a variety of equity-based (e.g., Adams, 1965), instrumentality-based (e.g., Porter & Lawler, 1968; Vroom, 1964), and goal-setting (e.g., Locke, 1968) orientations. Much recent work has attempted to coordinate various theories of motivation by placing an emphasis on the diverse effects of goals (e.g., Graham, this volume; Kanfer, 1990; Locke, this volume).

The measurement of motivation is made difficult by virtue of the fact that motivation itself is not directly observable. As a result, we are left to infer motivational processes based on behavioral observations. When one speaks of motivation, one is generally concerned with the question of what arouses and energizes behavior. The direction of behavior, the intensity of action, and the persistence of behaviors over time provide raw data from which inferences about motivation can be made (Kanfer, 1990; Vinacke, 1962). According to Vroom (1964), motivation refers to the intra- and inter-individual variabilities in behavior that are not attributable to differences in ability, or to environmental demands, that coerce or force action. Vroom (1964) has further pointed out, however, that this statement is insufficient as a definition, because it fails to specify what *is* involved in motivation. Kanfer (1990) has identified three elements essential for an adequate definition of motivation.

1. The determinants or independent variables affecting the observable behavior from which motivation is to be inferred must be specified.

2. The theory must describe the nomological network of relations between latent variables and the implications of these relations for observable behaviors (Cronbach & Meehl, 1955).

3. The motivational consequences, dependent variables, or behaviors most likely to be affected by changes in the motivational system must be specified.

In this chapter we explore some of the issues involved in the motivation of teams. We discuss the nature of teams, examine the differences between individual and team motivation, review theoretical and empirical research on team motivation, specify characteristics of teams that affect teamwork and motivation, discuss research on teamwork, examine the effects of goals on groups, and discuss the concept of mental models. A brief note on terminology is warranted at this point. Although there are differences between teams and groups, group research can provide some insight into understanding teams. Therefore, while our focus is on teams, the terms *group* and *team* are used interchangeably throughout this chapter.

A fundamental question to address with regard to motivating teams (as opposed to individuals) concerns the nature of the term *team*. Just what is a team? The failure of the theoretical literature to adequately address this question has created confusion and prevented the systematic accumulation of knowledge on the subject (Salas, Dickinson, Converse, & Tannenbaum, 1992). Even after 50 years of research on the subject of teams, few principles and guidelines are available for guiding the composition or management of teams (Swezey & Salas, 1992), for distinguishing good and poor teams (Driskell, Hogan, & Salas, 1987), or evaluating teams (O'Neil, Baker, & Kazlauskas, 1992).

The identification of just what comprises a team is difficult. Team boundaries are often nebulous, with many overlapping memberships and borders (Knerr, Nadler, & Berger, 1980). Additionally, the structure and composition of a team is often unstable, and typically varies according to changes in the problems that confront the team (Glanzer, 1962). The number and variety of definitions present in the earlier literature provide ample evidence of the difficulty inherent in clearly specifying the constitution of a team (Knerr et al., 1980). Table 8.1 lists several

TABLE 8.1
A Variety of Team Definitions

Author(s)	Definition
Boguslaw & Porter (1962)	relationship in which people generate and use work procedures to make possible their interaction with machines, machine procedures, and other people in the pursuit of system objectives
Dieterly (1978)	a distinguishable set of individuals who function together to accomplish a specific objective
Smillie, Shelnutt, & Bercos (1977)	small groups, usually 2 to 11 men, who normally perform their tasks in an interactive and interdependent manner. Position or member assignment within a team must be formally defined.
Thorndyke & Weiner (1980)	set of individuals working cooperatively to achieve some common objective
Scanland (1980)	synergistic set of individuals, the sum of whose purposes is the execution of a desired function in which no individual effort is redundant of another member's effort, with no gap in the total contribution of members in fulfilling the function of the team
Daniels, Alden, Kanarick, Gray, & Reuge (1972)	three or more persons working in concert toward a common, identifiable, and relatively immediate goal
McDavid & Harari (1968)	an organized system of two or more individuals who are interrelated so that the system performs some function, has a standard set of role relationships among its members, and has a set of norms that regulate the function of the group and each of its members
Neva, Fleishman, & Rieck (1978)	two or more interdependent individuals performing coordinated tasks toward the achievement of specific task goals
Klaus & Glaser (1968)	teams are characterized by a rigid structure, organization, and communication network, well-defined assignments; and the necessity for cooperation and coordination

From Knerr, Nadler, and Berger (1980).

such definitions. In this chapter, we suggest a definition originally proposed by Salas et al. (1992). Here, a team is defined as "a distinguishable set of two or more people who interact, dynamically, interdependently, and adaptively toward a common and valued goal/objective/mission; each of whom has been assigned specific roles or functions to perform, and who have a limited life-span membership" (p. 4). This definition has been shaped by the input of many authors, including Dyer, (1984), Hall and Rizzo, (1975), Modrick, (1986), Morgan, Glickman, Woodard, Blaiwes, and Salas, (1986), and Nieva, Fleishman, and Rieck, (1978), among others; and it is viewed as being somewhat more appealing than the (1980) Webster's Dictionary definition cited in the opening of this chapter.

The central premise of our definition involves task orientation. That is, the accurate completion of a team task requires: (a) a dynamic exchange of information and resources among team members; (b) coordination of task activities; (c) constant adjustments to task demands; and (d) organizational structuring of members. From this perspective, it is clear that some form of task dependency must exist among team members in order for them to interact dynamically and adaptively to accomplish an objective. Member interdependency is one key element in distinguishing teams from groups. Although teams are essentially groups of individuals, not all groups of individuals are considered teams (Driskell & Salas, 1992; Lewis, Hritz, & Roth, 1983; O'Neil et al., 1992; Tannenbaum, Beard, & Salas, 1992).

Time is another factor for consideration in constituting teams, in that teams tend to evolve over time (Gersick, 1988; Morgan et al., 1986). That is, both roles and norms evolve, and team members develop new skills and attitudes. Further, tasks are modified, communication patterns unfold, goals are revised, and personnel may change (Tannenbaum et al., 1992).

Why are teams so important that they inspire this much concern? A recent survey of Fortune 500 companies (Stephan, Mills, Pace, & Ralphs, 1988) suggest that if American industry is to remain competitive in the world market, it must respond to global competition, manage the impact of technological developments, and produce more products without an increase in the available resources. One of the ways that industry can adapt to these challenges, is through greater use of work teams, committees, and task forces within the workplace (Tosi, Rizzo, & Carroll, 1986). In fact, American organizations do appear to be using work teams with increasing frequency (Cannon-Bowers, Oser, & Flanagan, 1992; Hackman, 1989).

From the preceding discussion it is clear that the issues of team performance and effectiveness are important ones. However, team effectiveness is very different from individual effectiveness (e.g., Yetton & Bottger, 1982). Driskell et al. (1987, p. 95) identify three input factors that may define a team's performance potential:

1. Individual-level factors: member skills, knowledge, personalities, and status characteristics.

2. Group-level factors: group size, group structure, group norms, and cohesiveness.

3. Environmental-level factors: the nature of the task, the level of environmental stress, and reward structure.

Figure 8.1 presents a recent model of team effectiveness. Included as inputs to the model, among others, are the three input factors identified by Driskell et al. (1987). In this model, team performance is the outcome of dynamic processes reflected in the coordination and communication patterns that teams develop over

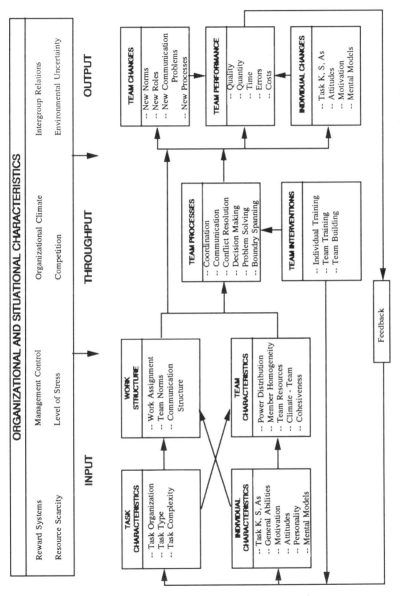

FIG. 8.1. Team Effectiveness Model. From Tannenbaum, Beard, and Salas (1992).

time (Salas et al., 1992). Note that in the model motivation appears as both an input and output. On the input side, motivation is one of the individual characteristics that influence team characteristics and work structure. On the output side, motivation is one of the individual changes that influences team performance. The team's performance serves as feedback affecting individual and task characteristics. According to Hackman (1987), teams will evaluate their performance as they work. These evaluations ultimately affect team processes and, in turn, influence future team performance.

Although there is a realization that teams may, in some situations, perform better than individuals on specific tasks (Miller, 1991), there is also some evidence to suggest that work team problems can impede performance (DeMeuse & Liebowitz, 1981). In light of the increasing importance of teams to American organizations, an improved understanding of how teams function is essential. This being the case, the motivation of teams with regard to their performance and effectiveness is an important avenue of research, especially in light of the relationships identified between individual motivation and performance (e.g., Graham, this volume; Locke, 1968; Locke, this volume; Porter & Lawler, 1968; Vroom, 1964; and others).

INDIVIDUAL VERSUS TEAM MOTIVATION

What is team motivation and how does motivating teams differ from motivating individuals? McIntyre (1988) provides input to the first part of this question. According to McIntyre (1988), team motivation refers to the extra-task characteristics of the team that make it competent, including team spirit, leadership, interpersonal skill, communication skill, work performance norms, values, and other attributes that serve to facilitate or inhibit team performance. The answer to the second part of the question however, is even more evasive. Most theories of motivation attempt to explain motivational process at the individual level (e.g., Alderfer, 1969, 1972; Graham, this volume; Herzberg, 1966; Locke, this volume; Maslow, 1943; Vroom, 1964); however, certain aspects of goal-setting theory (e.g., Locke, 1968; Locke, this volume) may be applicable to the issue of team motivation. Perhaps some insight into this issue may lie in examination of various complexities involved in the motivation of both individuals and teams in light of goal-setting theory.

According to Locke, Shaw, Saari, and Latham (1981) a goal is "what an individual is trying to accomplish; it is the object or aim of an action" (p. 126). Goals essentially represent standards of behavior (Ilgen, Shapiro, Salas, & Weiss, 1987). Research on the effects of goals on individual performance has shown that goal specificity and difficulty have a motivational impact. Specifically, goals that are challenging and specific lead to higher performance than those that are not (Ilgen et al., 1987). Ilgen et al. (1987) have also indicated that goals serve two motivational purposes at the individual level. First, they stir the person to action. In other words, they serve to influence a person's willingness to invest time and effort in an attempt to accomplish the task at hand. Second, they serve to direct time and effort in a particular direction.

At the individual level, it is clear to whom a goal applies. The individual typically is assigned, or participates in defining a goal, and then proceeds with an attempt aimed at accomplishing that goal. At the group level, however, the question to whom the goal applies, is not as clear (Ilgen et al., 1987). The goals in question may apply to several members of a team. Further, goals in team settings add at least three levels of complexity when compared to goals for individuals (Ilgen et al., 1987). First, within a team setting, one must address the issue of goals for multiple individuals. At least two sets of goals are present: the overall goals of the team, and the goals of the individuals who make up the team. Second, the source of the goals is more complex. In the case of an individual, goals could originate from the individual, or they could be assigned by an outside agent (i.e., the boss). These same sources of goals also exist in a team setting; however, individual members may not share the same goals as the team as a whole. This can result in conflict and disagreement, which does not pose a problem at the individual level. Third, multiple interdependencies exist between team and individual goals, as well as among the goals of individual team members.

The motivational effects of goals on teams may also differ from the impact of goals on individuals. In teams, goals affect individual as well as team level phenomena (Ilgen et al., 1987). Factors such as size, social pressure, and structure may also exert an influence on the motivational properties of the goals.

RESEARCH ON TEAM MOTIVATION

As mentioned earlier, much theory and research on motivation has occurred at the individual level. However, the theory and research that exists on the motivation of teams is sparse. One of the most useful theories is provided by Katz and Kahn (1978). An alternative view is provided by Rueda and Moll (this volume).

Theoretical Research of Katz and Kahn

The field of social psychology provides some theoretical grounds from which the motivation of teams may be considered. Katz and Kahn (1978), in their earlier work for instance, have identified three types of motivational patterns or frameworks in teams as follows: (a) rule enforcement, (b) external rewards, and (c) internalized motivation. In the case of *rule enforcement,* team members obey rules because they arise from legitimate sources of authority and can be enforced by legal sanctions. Rule compliance causes the acceptance of legitimate edicts and regulations to be of value within the team (Katz & Kahn, 1978). In this case, motivation bears a limited relationship to the activity being performed, since legal bases are notoriously deficient in affecting performance beyond narrow role prescriptions for quantity and quality (Katz & Kahn, 1978). Further, the potential exists for rules to become more important than the goals they were designed to accomplish, causing members to follow the rules for the sake of the rules themselves (Hall, 1991). The members in such a system may become increasingly unable to operate on their own initiative. In such cases, it is unlikely that individuals within a team will perform above and beyond the call of duty (Hall, 1991).

Within the *external rewards* framework, incentives are typically linked to desired behaviors (Katz & Kahn, 1978). In this case, actions become instrumental in achieving external rewards. This framework appears to share similarities with earlier instrumentality based models of individual motivation (e.g., Porter & Lawler, 1968; Vroom, 1964). Thus, the existence and nature of group and individual rewards can influence the level of cooperation or competition between team members, which in turn may also affect team effectiveness (Lawler, 1981; Pritchard, Jones, Roth, Stuebing, & Ekeberg, 1988). According to Katz and Kahn (1978), the external rewards offered by social systems can be broken down into four subtypes. The first is earned through membership in a system, is independent of performance, and increases with seniority (i.e., pensions, sick leave, vacation, etc.). A second type of external reward functions at an individual performance level. Such rewards include pay raises, promotions, and special recognition on the basis of individual performance. A third type of external motivation for team members can be secured from the approval members receive from team leaders. Note that in this case we are not referring to such things as pay increases or promotions, but rather to the gratification group members may find in praise provided by team leaders. Finally, a fourth type of external motivation involves the social approval of one's own team members. Characteristics of an individual's personality, such as sociability, adjustment, and likability may be related to team performance (Driskell et al., 1987). Social approval of can motivate members toward fulfilling the objectives of the team. Katz and Kahn (1978) have noted, however, that this type of motivation can either facilitate or prevent attainment of team goals depending on the nature of the team norms in operation in a specific situation.

The third motivational pattern identified by Katz and Kahn (1978) involves *internalized motivation*. The internalized motivation framework addresses both intrinsic job satisfaction and the internalization of team goals as part of an individual's value system. Within this framework, motivation is enhanced in two ways. First, an individual is motivated through the satisfaction derived from role performance. For example, an artist may gain satisfaction simply from the artistic process of painting itself; a doctor from the knowledge that he or she is helping people. The intrinsic satisfaction one derives simply by performing, can provide a potent source of motivation. Second, motivation may be enhanced through internalization of a team's goals. According to Katz and Kahn (1978):

The goals of the group become incorporated as part of the individual's value system or conception of self. As a result, satisfactions accrue to the person from the expression of attitudes and behavior reflecting his or her cherished beliefs and self-image. The reward is not so much a matter of social recognition or monetary advantage as of establishing one's self-identity, confirming one's notion of the sort of person one sees oneself to be, and expressing the values appropriate to this self-concept. (p. 407)

The norms of a work group or team can have a motivating effect on individual members. Norms act as standards or guides for people's behavior and beliefs (Penner, 1986), and teams can establish norms for their members, as well as methods for encouraging compliance with these norms (Fleishman & Zaccaro, 1992; Hackman, 1976; Nieva et al., 1978; Penner & Craiger, 1992).

As noted however, these motivational effects may or may not facilitate the attainment of a team's goals. One clear example of this is the diving phenomenon described by Mullen and Baumeister (1987). Diving refers to a situation in which, because of the norms of an immediate work group, an individual is motivated to perform at a suboptimal level. Diving can take several potential forms. In one case, team norms may discourage excellence in performance by any individual member (Penner & Craiger, 1992).In such a case, team members may tend to socialize their coworkers to this norm, and punish violators (Penner & Craiger, 1992). For example, a new employee may perform his or her task faster (out of sheer exuberance or a desire to look good) than the team norm permits. As a result, other team members may express disapproval in an attempt to get the new member to conform to existing production norms. In the other case, the team may determine whether or not excellent performance is acceptable for a particular member (Mullen & Baumeister, 1987). For example, junior members may be influenced not to do their best by members with more seniority. In such a case, excellence in performance by junior members is not acceptable based on the norms of the group. The senior members determine appropriate performance levels for lower status members.

Social Loafing and Free-Riding

The concepts of *social loafing* and *free-riding* can negatively effect team motivation. The concept of social loafing arises from social impact theory (Latane, 1981) which describes a process by which the motives, behaviors, feelings, etc., of an individual are changed by the presence or actions of others in a social setting. According to this theory, the impact of social forces that impinge upon an individual is determined by the strength of other people (i.e., status, rank, etc.), the immediacy of other people (i.e., closeness in time and space), and the number of other people. As these factors increase, a corresponding increase occurs in terms of their social impact. As Penner and Craiger (1992) have pointed out, when the size of a team increases, the social pressure on any one individual to perform well is diffused. As a result of this diffusion, motivation to perform well may also be reduced. Social loafing refers to the tendency to decrease the amount of effort one expends on a task when one is a member of a team, in the absence of any explicit demands to decrease that effort (Latane, 1986; Penner & Craiger, 1992). This social loafing effect tends to increase as team size increases, and the consequent ability to identify any one particular member decreases (Jackson & Williams, 1985; Kerr, 1983; Kerr & Bruun, 1981; Latane, Williams, & Harkins, 1979).

The free-rider effect is closely related to social loafing. In essence, the free-rider phenomenon explains social loafing as being a *rationally* or *economically* based decision to decrease one's effort. According to Penner and Craiger (1992) the mechanism that explains this behavior is an individual's belief that since a team member is but a single part of a team (with several other people also working on the task), relatively little actual work can be done while still reaping the benefits of the team's performance. Other members of the team may find the "carrying" of the free-rider to be aversive and as a result may reduce their own contributions to the team rather than play what has been termed the "sucker role" (Kerr, 1983; Orbell & Dawes, 1981). Carrying the free-rider is aversive because it violates a number of social norms (Orbell & Dawes, 1981). Free-riding violates: (a) the equity norm which calls for one's ratio of outcomes to inputs to be the same as other team members; (b) the norm of reciprocity where one is obligated to reciprocate those contributions they have received and; (c) the norm of social responsibility where every member of the team is obligated to contribute to the team.

According to Kerr (1983), rather than play the sucker role, the other team members may reduce their own efforts. Support for this "sucker effect" was found through laboratory experimentation (Kerr, 1983). Individuals who were lead to believe that their partner was able to perform the task but were consistently failing reduced their effort and their performance subsequently dropped. Thus it appears that one consequence of free-riding is a negative motivational effect on other team members. This negative motivational impact may turn into a vicious, escalating cycle (Mulvey, Klein, & Sterling, 1991) with perceptions of free-riding causing individuals to reduce their efforts which, in turn, may lead to increased perceptions of free-riding and further reductions in team motivation and performance.

Empirical Research

There is relatively little empirical research that directly addresses the issue of motivation of teams. Much of the existing research is aimed at investigating the motivation of individuals within those teams or groups. Swezey and Salas (1992), in a substantial review, have identified very few prescriptive guidelines from the research literature that have relevance to team motivation. These guidelines were originally compiled in response to a "scarcity of behavioral guidance that may be used to develop and model team training programs and devices in applied situations" (Swezey & Salas, 1992, p. 219). Several of the guidelines that are relevant to team motivation appear in Table 8.2.

Arising from these guidelines, Swezey and Salas (1992) offer some concrete suggestions for motivating teams. They suggest: (a) providing opportunities for each team member to take major responsibility for designing and directing a major task-related activity that affects the entire team, (b) employing positive reinforcement techniques and developing a system of rewards for those who exhibit supportive behaviors toward teammates, and (c) establishing both homogenous and heterogenous groupings of team members for some teamwork activities (this provides team members with a chance to work with individuals of different capabilities and backgrounds).

CHARACTERISTICS AFFECTING TEAMWORK

According to Tannenbaum et al. (1992), several characteristics of teams can be important for understanding their effectiveness. These factors include: the team's (a) structure; (b) homogeneity and/or heterogeneity; (c) cohesiveness (i.e., its sense of "teamness"); (d) size; (e) the characteristics of its task (i.e., task difficulty); (f) the organizational context and environment in which it operates; (g)

TABLE 8.2
Examples of Team Motivation Guidelines

Motivated teams will "stretch" themselves to achieve beyond what individuals, thinking about the capability of the team, might deem possible. (Ilgen et al., 1987)

Team members who do not feel central to the team's success will not feel as satisfied as members who feel central to those successes. (Ilgen et al., 1987)

Good team leaders tend to identify common factors that inhibit team member motivation. (McIntyre, Morgan, Salas, & Glickman, 1988)

Enthusiasm and the "right" attitude are often viewed by instructors as the most important differences between good and poor teams. (NATO, 1980)

Like-minded individual team members can often work together more easily, but are likely to be less creative. Members with diverse attitudes will generate more conflict, but will alsomore often hammer out more creative solutions. (Bass, 1982)

Team members should be encouraged to show verbal and physical (i.e., verbal compliments and "pats on the back") signs of support for other members and the team as a whole. (Morgan et al., 1986; Oser, McCallum, Salas, & Morgan, 1989)

Members of successful teams tend to praise the accomplishments of fellow teammates. (Morgan et al., 1986)

Team members should be supportive of teammates when the latter make mistakes. (Morgan et al., 1986)

Effective team members make positive statements to motivate the team. (Oser et al., 1989)

From Swezey and Salas (1992).

the presence of potential evaluators; and (h) the nature and sequencing of performance feedback provided to members. As we shall see, these characteristics can also affect the motivation of the team.

Group Structure

When we speak of the power distribution within a team, we refer to the hierarchical structure within the team (Nieva et al., 1978). From the leadership literature, we can identify two dimensions that appear to produce substantial effects on team performance. One is autocratic versus democratic leadership. Generally, teams with autocratic leaders perform better than teams with democratic leaders, while members of democratic teams tend to react more positively to their team (Morgan & Lassiter, 1992). A classic study that provided such group motivation data examined the effects of power distribution on performance (Lewin, Lippett, & White, 1939). These researchers performed a field experiment on clubs of 10-year-old boys and exposed these clubs to three different styles of adult leaders: autocratic, democratic, and laissez-faire. The study found that short-term productivity was highest among members of the autocratic group. However, motivation, as measured by continued work after the leader had departed, was found to be highest in the democratic group.

Another leadership dimension that appears to produce an effect on team performance is the social distance between the leader and other team members (Kahan, Webb, Shavelson, & Stolzenberg, 1985). Teams with greater social distance between leaders and followers usually perform better than teams where the social distance is smaller. In addition to the constructs of team leadership and social distance, rank structure within a team has both motivational and performance implications. Different rank structures impose different interaction requirements upon team members, which may in turn affect team performance as a whole (Morgan & Lassiter, 1992). Foushee and Helmreich (1988), for instance, found team role structure to be a powerful indictor of aircraft crew interaction. The ingrained chain of command within a cockpit may present a significant barrier to communications for team members. Crew members are often reluctant to question superiors or to assume control of the aircraft in extremis (i.e., emergency) situations (Foushee & Helmreich, 1988). The potential exists for the rank structure present in cockpit crews, especially in military aircraft, to lend itself to an autocratic style of leadership with inherent motivational effects similar to those found by Lewin and his colleagues (Swezey, 1992).

Group Homogeneity and Heterogeneity

The makeup of a team appears to have some influence on performance. Compatibility is an important factor when considering the composition of a team and its relationship to performance. It is not uncommon for high ability teams that contain incompatible members to experience difficulty in maintaining effective communications and interactions among members and, consequently, collateral difficulty in attaining goals (Bass, 1982). Indeed, Gunderson and Ryman (1967) have indicated that the makeup of a team (which includes homogeneity) is related to performance. The issues of team homogeneity and heterogeneity include such factors as personality differences, biographical differences, and individual differences in abilities.

Personality Differences. One factor involved in the homogeneity/ heterogeneity of a team is the personality characteristics of individual team members. There is debate, however, as to the magnitude of the role that personality characteristics play with regard to team performance (Morgan & Lassiter, 1992). Some have argued that findings on the subject have been inconclusive (Kahan et al., 1985). According to Morgan and Lassiter (1992), this position is based on the notion that personality traits represent constructs that are too broad to be of use in predicting specific team performance. For example, Butler and Burr (1980) investigated locus of control personality types in military teams. They found that only one of the three personality types investigated was related to performance, and it was related only weakly at that. Other research has shown that the combination of personalities within a team can exert an influence on a team's performance (Driskell et al., 1987; Hackman & Morris, 1975). Schultz (1955) for instance, found that more productive teams were homogenous with respect to several personality traits (dependence, assertiveness, and personalness). Research by Helmreich (1984, 1987) and by Chidester (1987) has indicated that attitudes and coordination behaviors among members of aircraft crews may be predicted from personality measures. Driskell et al. (1987) have proposed a taxonomy of six personality traits (intelligence, adjustment, ambition, prudence, sociability, and likability), which they believe impact team performance. According to Driskell et al. (1987), "different personality types will perform better in different task groups, because different behaviors are required in different task situations" (p. 106). This taxonomy is recommended as a guide for selecting team members on the basis of personality, and as a framework for designing investigations of the performance effects of personality in teams (Morgan & Lassiter, 1992). Referring back to the model of team effectiveness presented in Fig. 8.1, we can see that personality is one of the individual characteristics influencing team characteristics and work structure.

Biographical Differences. There is evidence to suggest that biographical variables such as age, gender, race, sex, and sociocultural background, among others, are important factors in the performance of teams (e.g., Shaw, 1976). McGrath and Altman (1966) have reported that factors such as age, gender, and education level, among others, were predictive of team performance, and Shaw (1976), has reported that gender-mixed groups tended to be more conforming and spend more time and effort on interpersonal issues than on task-relevant behaviors. Members of nonmixed teams on the other hand tended to be more task-oriented, individualistic, and competitive (Kent & McGrath, 1969; Wyer & Malinowski, 1972). Evidence also exists to suggest that the chronological age of team members may have an impact on team performance (McGrath & Altman, 1966). When generalized to teams, findings on the effects of aging on individuals suggest that younger teams will generally perform better than older teams on tasks requiring sensory/perceptual sensitivity, speed of responding, fine motor responding, or complex cognitive processing yet with age comes wisdom. Additionally, teams that are homogenous in age are more likely both to interact among themselves and to perform more efficiently than are teams that are heterogenous with respect to age (Morgan & Lassiter, 1992).

Ability Differences.   A third category of individual-difference variables that impact team performance deals with the general and task-related abilities of members. Laughlin, Branch, and Johnson (1969) found that teams that were heterogenous in ability performed better than homogenous teams on intelligence tests. Tziner and Eden (1985), in summarizing the results of prior research, noted that general abilities can produce various effects on group performance. First, the abilities of the team members may be combined in an additive fashion to increase overall team performance in proportion to the ability levels of the team members. Second, individual abilities may also be combined in such a manner as to produce an overall loss in team efficiency; and finally, the individual abilities of the team members might be combined in such a fashion that team performance is higher than the levels predicted on the basis of additivity. In an examination of three-member tank crews, Tziner and Eden (1985) reported that abilities appeared to have an additive effect when teams were heterogenous in terms of ability. Specifically, uniformly low ability teams performed poorly, while uniformly high ability teams appeared to perform well. Studies on the relationship between task-relevant abilities and team members and team performance have generally tended to indicate that team performance is improved by selecting individuals with high levels of task-specific skills (Morgan & Lassiter, 1992).

Cohesiveness

Along with homogeneity and heterogeneity, cohesiveness may play a role in a team's motivation and performance. Tannenbaum et al. (1992) have suggested that cohesiveness—which reflects a team's feeling of belongingness and sense of teamness—is related to team performance. Highly cohesive teams tend to have members who: (a) are greatly involved in the team's activities; (b) have less tendency toward absenteeism; and, (c) display high levels of coordination during team tasks.

The effects of cohesion have been related to team member interactions, satisfaction, and team performance (Shaw, 1976). A significant positive relationship between team cohesion and team member interaction has been reported by Lott and Lott, (1961). Also, positive relationships between team cohesion and member satisfaction have been reported. In general, members of cohesive teams tend to be more satisfied with their jobs and with their team situations (Morgan & Lassiter, 1992). Manning and Fullerton (1988) have reported that members of highly cohesive Army units tended to indicate greater job satisfaction than did members of less cohesive units. The general consensus, with regard to cohesiveness and performance, is that group cohesion enhances performance (Shaw, 1976). However, the reverse has also been shown: specifically, that performance enhances cohesion. Anderson (1975), for example, has demonstrated that within task-oriented teams cohesion can increase when teams are more successful.

Detractors also exist from the position that team cohesion is strongly related to team performance (e.g., Stodgill, 1972). Indeed, team cohesion may influence motivation and performance through the phenomenon known as deindividuation. Deindividuation refers to a psychological state in which a person has a decreased sense of personal identity and responsibility (Penner, 1986). Among factors that can produce deindividuation are excessive levels of physiological and psychological arousal and strong feelings of attraction to one's team (Penner & Craiger, 1992).

Team Size

In addition to the structure of a team, its homogeneity/heterogeneity, and its cohesiveness, the team's size has also been shown to have an effect on motivation and performance. As the size of a team increases, so does the size of the pool of performance resources (Shaw, 1976). According to Morgan and Lassiter (1992), larger teams have more resources available to them which, in turn, can lead to increased creativity, varieties of information processing, and increased team effectiveness. There is, however, a tradeoff. Increasing the size of a team may prove to be a double-edged sword, since increases in team size beyond a certain point may produce diminishing returns and can hinder team performance. Larger teams face problems associated with the larger number of team member interactions necessitated by size, more difficulty in coordination, and potential decreases in member participation, and increases in team size have shown a tendency to increase the coordination demands and communication workload of a team (Shaw, 1976). Indik (1965) has reported a decrease in communication with increased group size, and Gerard, Wilhelmy, and Conolley (1968) have found reduced participation among team members as the size of a team is increased. Another study (Gibb, 1951) found that as team size is increased, members report increased inhibition to participate. The increased complexity and difficulty of communication, along with changes in the team's social structure, may lead some individuals to decrease their involvement in team communications (Morgan & Lassiter, 1992).

The phenomenon of deindividuation (described earlier) may also pose a problem as the size of a team is increased. According to Penner and Craiger (1992), when a person experiences deindividuation, the person becomes relatively inattentive to previously held individual principles, and self-regulation breaks down. As a result, deindividuation can affect an individual's motivation level and, presumably, his or her performance (Penner & Craiger, 1992). Finally, with regard to motivation specifically, several studies have indicated an inverse relationship between group size and motivation (e.g., Barker, 1960, 1968; Thelen, 1949; Wicker, 1969).

Task Characteristics

Task characteristics also play a role in both team performance and motivation. The influence of the type of task on team performance has been documented by several researchers (Gladstein, 1984; Goodman, 1986; Steiner, 1972). Tannenbaum et al. (1992) have reported that task complexity is related to task performance and that task difficulty accounts for a significant amount of variance in team performance. Several researchers have also shown that task organization and task type can influence team effectiveness (Kabanoff & O'Brien, 1979; McGrath, 1984). Task demands appear to have a moderating influence on the impact of team homogeneity/heterogeneity. If successful task completion requires smooth and timely team member interactions, then homogeneity of personalities, abilities, attitudes, etc. will result in better team performance. Heterogenous teams, on the other hand, tend to perform better when the task is relatively complex and/or requires a creative solution (Morgan & Lassiter, 1992).

Organizational Context and Environment

The organizational context and environmental surroundings in which the team functions also merit consideration with respect to team performance and motivation. Organizational culture may have a motivational effect on teams. The degree of formalization in a team has profound effects on performance (Pugh, Hickson, Hinings, & Turner, 1968). If a high degree of formalization exists in team structure, team performance tends to be procedural and routinized. Highly formalized teams are therefore better suited to performing routine tasks that require little creativity (Morgan & Lassiter, 1992). Less formalized teams, on the other hand, are able to respond more effectively to situations that are less predictable. Sundstrom, Perkins, George, Futrell, and Hoffman (1990), have reported that supportive organizational cultures are associated with higher performing teams. Other organizational variables, such as an organization's reward system (Hackman, 1983; Steiner, 1972) and the nature of intergroup or lateral relations (Brett & Rognes, 1986), may also influence team behavior. The rank of a given team in relation to other teams can also influence team performance. According to Morgan and Lassiter (1992), a team's perception of its own role, status, and value to an organization is an important factor in determining the way a team interacts and performs.

Evaluation

The presence or absence of potential evaluators has been shown to have an impact on team performance (e.g., Harkins & Szymanski, 1987; Jackson & Williams, 1985). Cottrell (1972), for example, has reported that potential for evaluation may produce arousal which facilitates performance on simple tasks, but impairs performance on more complex tasks. This notion has been extended by Harkins and Szymanski (1987), who found that in order to evaluate performance, the standard of performance must be known, in addition to the quality of the performance. When an individual suspects that his or her performance may be evaluated, it is likely that he or she will be increasingly motivated and will therefore perform better (Penner & Craiger, 1992). The potential also exists for *self-evaluation* to influence individual performance (Harkins & Szymanski, 1987, 1989). A study by Harkins and Szymanski (1989) appears to confirm this potential. When individual group members were provided with a standard against which their *group's* performance could be compared, individuals increased the quantity and quality of their performance. The motivating effect of potential evaluation, however, is moderated by team size (Penner & Craiger, 1992). As a team's size increases, a given individual may feel that the probability that his or her *specific* performance will be identified and evaluated is decreased. This in turn, can result in decreased individual and team performance. The complexity of the evaluation issue is shown in Franklin's study (this volume). His data indicate a reduction in anxiety yet poorer performance in a high stakes evaluation, as compared to training evaluation, for antisubmarine warfare aircrews.

Feedback

The amount of feedback available to a team may have a motivational impact. Feedback is one way to facilitate team member performance and demonstrates the contribution of that performance to the performance of other members and to the team as a whole (Salas et al., 1992). Among researchers, there is general agreement that feedback about the effectiveness of task performance should be provided to team members in a timely manner (Dyer, 1984; Nieva et al., 1978). Feedback enhances performance on that aspect of performance about which feedback is provided (Salas et al., 1992).

In addition to feedback itself, the manner in which feedback is presented and sequenced may have motivational consequences. Sequencing feedback on various aspects of a team task is a useful method for training teams to enhance performance. Salas et al. (1992) have suggested that feedback should focus only on *one* aspect of task performance during early training sessions, but on *several* aspects of task performance during later training sessions. Briggs and Johnston (1967), found that when this sequencing strategy was employed, teams attempted to enhance performance for all aspects of a team task on which they had received feedback.

RESEARCH ON TEAMWORK

What is teamwork? Guzzo (1986) has described effective teamwork in decision-making teams as being a combination of a team's ability to monitor and gather information; to determine, assess, and select alternatives; and to evaluate the course of action selected. Despite this definition, and the apparent importance of teams to organizations, there is a general lack of understanding of the components of teamwork with regard to specific teamwork behaviors (McCallum, Oser, Morgan, & Salas, 1989). According to Dyer (1984), research is lacking with regard to such issues as how members of a team interact with one another and whether or not these interactions vary over time, by situation, and/or by team experience. While little is actually known about motivating teamwork per se (Oser, McCallum, Salas, & Morgan, 1989), an examination of some of the research on teamwork may provide insight into team motivational processes.

Several studies (McCallum et al., 1989; Oser et al., 1989) have attempted to identify behavioral constituents of teams and the effects of team evolution and maturation over time. The basis for these studies lies in the notion that successful teams exhibit specific interaction, communication, and coordination behaviors that enhance performance, whereas less successful teams display different types of specific behaviors. McCallum et al. (1989) analyzed critical team behaviors from a sample of 13 teams, each consisting of 8–12 members. They concluded that it is possible to discriminate the more effective from the less effective teams on the basis of type, frequency, and relationship of observable behaviors. More effective teams displayed more intrateam reinforcement behaviors— characterized by thanking other members for correcting errors and providing praise for work well done. According to McCallum et al. (1989) these behaviors may have fostered a sense of task competency among team members. These findings are consistent with Hackman and Walton's (1986) suggestion that providing reinforcement for good task performance, and giving assistance to members lead to effective task performance. Effective teams also tended to exhibit intrateam monitoring behaviors. Specifically, effective teams exhibited increased levels of communication and cooperative behaviors oriented toward detection and acknowledgment of errors (McCallum et al., 1989).

Oser et al. (1989) extended the work of McCallum et al. (1989). Again, their purpose was to identify critical team behaviors that can be used to differentiate more effective from less effective teams. Their results provided additional support for the findings discussed above. One of the critical team behaviors they identified was team reinforcement. Tea, reinforcement refers to the motivational and reinforcing statements made between team members. Effective teams had members who praised one another for a job well done, made positive statements to motivate each other, and thanked others for catching mistakes (Oser et al., 1989).

This concept of team reinforcement fits nicely with Fleishman and Zaccaro's (1992) categorization of team functions. They identified seven team functions in their most recent attempt to develop a taxonomy of team performance. Table 8.3 shows these functions. Of particular interest is the team motivational function as originally identified by Nieva et al. (1978). According to these authors, the dimensions of team motivation include:

TABLE 8.3
Taxonomy of Team Functions

I.   Orientation Functions
     A.   Information exchange regarding member resources and constraints
     B.   Information exchange regarding team task and goals/mission
     C.   Information exchange regarding environmental characteristics and constraints
     D.   Priority assignment among tasks

II. Resource Distribution Functions
     A.   Matching member resources to task requirements
     B.   Load balancing

III. Timing Functions (Activity Pacing)
     A.   General activity pacing
     B.   Individually oriented activity pacing

IV. Response Coordination Functions
     A.   Response sequencing
     B.   Time and position coordination of responses

V.   Motivational Functions
     A.   Development of team performance norms
     B.   Generating acceptance of team performance norms
     C.   Establishing team-level performance-rewards linkages
     D.   Reinforcement of task orientation
     E.   Balancing team orientation with individual competition
     F.   Resolution of performance - relevant conflicts

VI. Systems Monitoring Functions
     A,   General activity monitoring
     B.   Individual activity monitoring
     C.   Adjustment of team and member activities in response to errors and omissions

VII. Procedure Maintenance
     A.   Monitoring of general procedural-based activities
     B.   Monitoring of individual procedural-based activities
     C.   Adjustments of nonstandard activities

From Fleishman and Zaccaro (1992).

1. Development of team norms regarding acceptable levels of performance.

2. Generating acceptance of team performance norms.

3. Establishing performance-reward linkages for the team as an entity.

4. Reinforcement of task orientation, which includes informal rewards as well as sanctions for effective performance.

5. Balancing overall team orientation with individual competitive orientations in the team.

6. Resolution of informational, procedural, and interpersonal conflicts which interfere with task orientation.

Team motivational functions essentially involve defining team objectives related to a task and energizing the group toward these objectives.

SOME ADDITIONAL COMMENTS ON GOAL SETTING AND TEAM MOTIVATION

Research in the area of goal-setting appears to provide an opportunity for generalization from individual to team motivation. There are, however, numerous covarying factors to consider (such as social pressure, group characteristics, and inter- and intrateam competition) which occur when people are members of work teams. The effects of such factors were already discussed.

Aspects of the motivational effects of goal setting were also discussed earlier in this chapter; however, a brief amplification of this information is appropriate here. Goals serve two motivational purposes. First, they rouse people to action. That is, they influence a person's willingness to invest time and effort in an attempt to accomplish a specific goal. Second, they serve to channel a person's time and energy in a particular direction. The general finding with regard to goals and performance can be viewed in terms of goal specificity. The more difficult and specific a goal is, the greater the motivational impact. Motivational effects of goals however, appear to be moderated by task complexity. With a simple task, the energizing function of goals is of primary importance (Ilgen et al., 1987). In this case, difficult goals are more beneficial. On complex tasks, where task methods are ambiguous, difficult goals may hinder performance (Ilgen et al., 1987). In this case goal specificity becomes critical.

Goal perceptions of individual team members are an important topic to consider in light of the fact that goal perceptions of individual as team members may be different than those of individuals working alone because of the presence of a group goal (Ilgen et al., 1987). A study by Matsui, Imaizumi, Onglatco, and Kakuyama (1987), for instance, examined the effects of these differing perceptions on performance. Matsui et al. (1987) had subjects work alone under one of two experimental conditions. In one condition, subjects had an individual goal.

In the other condition, in addition to an individual goal, each subject had an assigned partner and a team goal to be attained with that partner. Matsui et al. (1987) found that individuals in teams performed better than those not in teams. The individuals with team goals perceived their individual goal as one step toward attaining the team goal. The team goal appears to have exerted a strong motivating affect. Although the team goal was unattainable for any individual, subjects in the team goal condition still strove toward it, even after having accomplished individual goals.

Another effect of team goals can be found in an examination of what occurs when a group fails to achieve its goals. In particular, responses to failure in groups tend to be the opposite of those usually found with individuals (Ilgen et al., 1987). Zander, Forward, and Albert (1969) examined team member attitudes as a function of the success of the team and found that ineffective teams continually set goals higher than previous performance indicated they should.

As is evident from this discussion, effects of performance goals on individuals are well documented. When individuals hold specific goals, performance tends to be higher than when these goals are absent (Locke et al., 1981; Locke, this volume). Further, knowledge of results (i.e., feedback) plays an important role in goal-setting. Just as feedback is crucial to individual goal-setting, so it is when goal-setting is applied to teams. Performance goals may act to structure work situations by making it possible for individuals to receive feedback about their performance relative to their goal (Ilgen, Fisher, & Taylor, 1979). This feedback may serve as a source of accomplishment and may create other effects that are interpreted as being beneficial (Ilgen et al., 1987). Indeed, Nadler (1979) has noted that team feedback provides motivational effects which influence the effort expended by team members. The comparison between the team goal and team performance feedback, may influence members' cognitive processes, which in turn impact on behavior (O'Leary–Kelly, undated). According to O'Leary–Kelly (undated), individual team members may engage in social comparison aimed at comparing their own performance levels to those of other team members in order to interpret the personal implications of team feedback.

There are caveats however, when it comes to examining the motivational effects of feedback in team situations. According to Salas et al. (1992), team level feedback provides little direct information about the quality of individual performance. It is important for team members to receive performance feedback on both individual and team levels (Matsui, Kakuyama, & Onglatco, 1987), and the provision of team feedback by itself can be dangerous when the good performance of one team member can compensate for the poor performance of a teammate (Salas et al., 1992). People performing below their individual goal level who receive only team feedback may not attempt to improve their performance if the team is succeeding. Alternatively, individuals performing satisfactorily with respect to their individual goals who receive only individual level feedback may not improve if their group is failing.

MENTAL MODELS AND TEAM MOTIVATION

A final issue to be addressed in this chapter is the concept of mental models. Again, if we refer back to the model of team effectiveness illustrated in Fig. 8.1 we see that mental models are subsumed under individual characteristics on the input side of the model and under individual change on the output side of the model. Rouse and Morris (1986) define a mental model as a "mechanism whereby humans generate descriptions of system purpose and form, explanations of system functioning and observed systems states, and predictions of future system states" (p. 360). Cannon-Bowers, Salas, and Grossman (1991) contend that in order to perform optimally, team members must be familiar with the knowledge, skills, abilities, preferences, and other task-relevant attributes of their teammates. The construct of shared mental models refers to organized knowledge shared by team members (Orasanu & Salas, in press). According to Wickens (1984), mental models provide a source of people's expectations. In a team setting, one's expectations for the behavior of one's teammates will vary as a function of the individuals who comprise the team (Cannon-Bowers et al., 1991). Based on these expectations, a team member may alter his or her behavior so that it is consistent with how he or she thinks the other team members will perform. Therefore, a team member's mental model of their team's tasks and operations could determine individual behavior and team effectiveness (Tannenbaum et al., 1992). Consequently, mental models of team tasks and operations, by virtue of their ability to determine individual behavior, can be seen as having motivational implications for the team.

SUMMARY

In this chapter, we have discussed the complex topic of team motivation and various factors which affect it. This is a difficult topic, in light of the fact that a considerable variety of motivational theories and team definitions exist. The problem is compounded by the fact that the majority of motivational theories deal with individual, rather than team or group motivation.

Differences between individual and team motivation were illustrated via goal-setting theory. The utility and functions of goals appear to be generalizable from individuals to teams. Goals in team settings are considerably more complex than those for individuals. Issues involving multiple goals, internal conflict and disagreement, and interdependencies among team members contribute to the complexity of goal effects on teams. Factors such as team size, social pressure, and structure may also have an impact on the motivational properties of goals. Potential motivation losses can occur due to social loafing and free-riding phenomena.

The research on team/group motivation is modest, however, Katz and Kahn

(1978) have identified three motivational patterns in organizations: rule enforcement, external rewards, and internalized motivation. Team norms were shown to have a motivational impact on team members. The norms of a team can both foster and inhibit individual performance. The likelihood of social loafing and free-riding behaviors are affected by the size of a team. In large teams, social pressure to perform is diffused, thus potentially reducing an individual's motivation to perform. Empirical research on this subject has mainly addressed the motivation of individuals within teams. A review of this research, however, indicates the possible impact of such factors as team structure, homogeneity/heterogeneity (with regard to biographical, personality, and ability differences), and cohesiveness on motivation. Likewise, the size of a team, the characteristics of its task, the culture/climate of the organization, and the presence of potential evaluators may have an influence on team motivation. In addition, feedback and its sequencing, have been shown to have an impact on the motivation of teams.

Research on teamwork has identified behaviors that differentiate more effective teams from less effective teams. Of particular interest from a motivational perspective, is the idea of team reinforcement behaviors. These behaviors refer to the motivational and reinforcing statements made by team members. Team reinforcement behaviors are more prevalent in effective teams. These team reinforcement behaviors are compatible with the four team functions proposed by Nieva et al. (1978), particularly the team motivational function, which involves defining a team's objectives and energizing the team toward those objectives.

The motivational effects of goals on teams has received some attention. The existence of a team goal in addition to individual goals may prove to be more motivating than the existence of individual goals alone. This motivational effect is further enhanced when failure to achieve a team goal occurs. Teams that fail to achieve a team goal will tend to set higher goals than would appear warranted based upon previous performance. With regard to goal-setting, however, a systematic model for looking at effects of goals in team settings is lacking (Ilgen et al., 1987). This may be due in part to the difficulty involved in obtaining and measuring team constructs (Dyer, 1984; Hall & Rizzo, 1975).

Recently, it has been suggested that the concept of shared mental models might be useful for the understanding and training of teamwork skills (Cannon-Bowers & Salas, 1990; Cannon-Bowers et al., 1991). The greater the accuracy and overlap among the mental models of the team members, the more likely team members will predict, adapt, and coordinate with one another (Salas et al., 1992). This construct may be important in light of the team reinforcement behaviors demonstrated by effective teams (McCallum et al., 1989; Oser et al., 1989). The shared mental model construct may be useful as an organizing concept for understanding team processes, however, considerably more work needs to be done before this construct can be applied to training teamwork behaviors (Salas et al., 1992).

So where does all of this leave us? As has been stated throughout this chapter, most of the literature on motivation has focused on individuals. Little empirical research has investigated motivation at the team or group level. Clearly, more empirical research needs to be done with regard to motivating teams. Additionally, little theory exists explaining the role and nature of team motivation. Motivation theories to date have concentrated on the individual. In light of the increasing reliance on work groups and teams by organizations and industries, theories addressing the motivation of teams need to be developed and investigated.

ACKNOWLEDGMENT

The research reported in this chapter was supported in part by the U.S. Army Research Institute for Behavioral and Social Sciences through a subcontract with Battelle Institute. However, the views, opinions and/or findings contained in this report are the authors' and should not be construed as an official ARI position, policy, or decision, unless so designated by other official documentation.

REFERENCES

Adams, J. A. (1965). Inequity in social exchange. In L. Berkowitz (Ed.), *Experimental social psychology* (Vol. 2). New York: Academic Press.

Alderfer, C. P. (1969). An empirical test of a new theory of human needs. *Organizational Behavior and Human Performance, 4,* 142–175.

Alderfer, C. P. (1972). *Existence, relatedness, and growth: Human needs in organizational settings.* New York: The Free Press.

Anderson, A. B. (1975). Combined effects of interpersonal attraction and goal-path clarity on the cohesiveness of task oriented groups. *Human Relations, 20,* 33–340.

Barker, R. G. (1960). Ecology and motivation. *Nebraska Symposium on Motivation, 8,* 1–50.

Barker, R. G. (1968). *Ecological psychology: Concepts and methods for studying the environment of human behavior.* Stanford, CA: Stanford University Press.

Bass, B. (1982). Individual capability, team performance, and team productivity. In M. Dunnette & E. Fleishman (Eds.), *Human performance and productivity: Human capability assessment.* Hillsdale, NJ: Lawrence Erlbaum Associates.

Boguslaw, R., & Porter, E. H. (1962). Team functions and training. In R. M. Gagne (Ed.), *Psychological principles in system development.* New York: Holt, Rinehart & Winston.

Brett, J. M., & Rognes, J. K. (1986). Intergroup relations in organizations. In P. S. Goodman (Ed.), *Designing effective work groups.* San Francisco: Jossey-Bass.

Briggs, G. E., & Johnston, W. A. (1967). *Team training* (NAVTRADEVCEN-1327-1, AD-608 309). Port Washington, NY: Naval Training Device Center.

Butler, M. C., & Burr, R. G. (1980). Utility of a multidimensional locus of control scale in predicting health and job-related outcomes in military environments. *Psychological Reports, 47,* 719–728.

Cannon-Bowers, J. A., Oser, R., & Flanagan, D. L. (1992). Work teams in industry: A selected review and proposed framework. In R. W. Swezey & E. Salas (Eds.), *Teams: Their training and performance*. Norwood, NJ: Ablex.

Cannon-Bowers, J. A., & Salas, E. (1990). *Cognitive psychology and team training: Shared mental models in complex systems*. In K. Kraiger (Chair), Cognitive representations of work. Symposium conducted at the annual meeting of the Society for Industrial/Organizational Psychology, Miami, FL.

Cannon-Bowers, J. A., Salas, E., & Grossman, J. D. (1991, June). *Improving tactical decision making under stress: Research directions and applied implications*. Paper presented at the International Applied Military Psychology Symposium, Stockholm, Sweden.

Chidester, T. R. (1987, April). Selection for optimal crew performance: Relative impact of selection and training. In R. S. Jensen (Ed.), *Proceedings of the fourth international symposium on aviation psychology*. Columbus, OH: Ohio State University.

Cottrell, N. B. (1972). Social facilitation. In C. G. McClintock (Ed.), *Experimental social psychology*. New York: Holt.

Cronbach, L. J., & Meehl, P. E. (1955). Construct validity in psychological tests. *Psychological Bulletin, 52*, 281–302.

Daniels, R. W., Alden, D. G., Kanarick, A. F., Gray, T. A., & Reuge, R. L. (1972). *Automated operator instruction in team tactics* (Tech. Rep. NAVTRADEVCEN 70-C-0310-1). Orlando, FL: Naval Training Device Center.

DeMeuse, K. P., & Liebowitz, S. J. (1981). An empirical analysis of team-building research. *Group and Organization Studies, 6*, 357–378.

Dieterly, D. L. (1978, October). Team performance: A model for research. In *Proceedings of the Human Factors Society—22nd Annual Meeting*, pp. 486–492. Santa Monica, CA: Human Factors Society.

Driskell, J. E., Hogan, R., & Salas, E. (1987). Personality and group performance. *Review of Personality and Social Psychology, 9*, 91–112.

Driskell, J. E., & Salas, E. (1992). Can you study real teams in contrived settings? The value of small group research to understanding teams. In R. W. Swezey & E. Salas (Eds.), *Teams: Their training and performance*. Norwood, NJ: Ablex.

Dyer, J. L. (1984). Review on team training and performance: A state-of-the-art review. In F. A. Muckler (Ed.), *Human factors review*. Santa Monica, CA: The Human Factors Society, Inc.

Fleishman, E. A., & Zaccaro, S. J. (1992). Toward a taxonomy of team performance functions. In R. W. Swezey & E. Salas (Eds.), *Teams: Their training and performance*. Norwood, NJ: Ablex.

Foushee, H. C., & Helmreich, R. L. (1988). Group interaction and flight crew performance. In E. L. Weiner & D. C. Nagel (Eds.), *Human factors in aviation*. San Diego, CA: Academic Press.

Franken, R. E. (1982) *Human motivation*. Monterey, CA: Brooks/Cole.

Gerard, H. B., Wilhelmy, R. A., & Conolley, E. S. (1968). Conformity and group size. *Journal of Personality and Social Psychology, 8*, 79–82.

Gersick, C. J. G. (1988). Time and transition in work teams: Towards a new model of group development. *Academy of Management Review, 31*, 9–41.

Gibb, J. R. (1951). The effects of group size and of threat reduction upon certainty in a problem-solving situation. *American Psychologist, 6*, 324.

Gladstein, D. L. (1984). Groups in context: A model of task group effectivness. *Administrative Science Quarterly, 29*, 499–517.

Glanzer, M. (1962). Experimental study of team training and team functioning. In R. Glaser (Ed.), *Training research and education*. Pennsylvania: University of Pittsburgh Press.

Goodman, P. S. (1986). (Ed.). *Designing effective work groups*. San Francisco: Jossey-Bass.

Gunderson, E. K., & Ryman, D. (1967). *Group homogeneity, compatibility, and accomplishment* (Report No. NNNRU-67-16). San Diego, CA: Navy Medical Neuropsychiatric Research Unit.

Guzzo, R. A. (1986). Group decision making and group effectiveness in organizations. In P. S. Goodman (Ed.), *Designing effective work groups*. San Francisco: Jossey-Bass.

Hackman, J. R. (1976). Group influences on individuals. In M. D. Dunnette (Ed.), *Handbook of industrial and organizational psychology*. Chicago: Rand McNally.

Hackman, J. R. (1983). *A normative model of work team effectiveness* (Tech. Rep. No. 2). New Haven, CT: Yale University Press.

Hackman, J. R. (1987). The design of work teams. In J. Losch (Ed.), *Handbook of organizational behavior*. Englewood Cliffs, NJ: Prentice-Hall.

Hackman, J. R. (1989). *Groups that work (and those that don't)*. San Francisco: Jossey-Bass.

Hackman, J. R., & Morris, C. G. (1975). Group tasks, group interaction process, and group performance effectiveness: A review and proposed integration. In L. Berkowitz (Ed.), *Advances in Experimental Psychology, 8*, 45–49. New York: Academic Press.

Hackman, J. R., & Walton, R. E. (1986). Leading groups in organizations. In P. S. Goodman (Ed.), *Designing effective work groups*. San Francisco: Jossey-Bass.

Hall, E. R., & Rizzo, W. A. (1975). *An assessment of U.S. navy tactical team training* (TAEG Rep. No. 18). Orlando, FL: Training Analysis and Evaluation Group.

Hall, R. H. (1991). *Organizations: Structures, processes, & outcomes*. Englewood Cliffs, NJ: Prentice-Hall.

Harkins, S. G., & Szymanski, K. (1987). Social loafing and social facilitation: New wine in old bottles. In C. Hendrick (Ed.), *Group processes and intergroup relations* (Vol. 9). Beverly Hills, CA: Sage.

Harkins, S. G., & Szymanski, K. (1989). Social loafing and group evaluation. *Journal of Personality and Social Psychology, 56*, 934–941.

Helmreich, R. L. (1984). Cockpit management attitudes. *Human Factors, 26*, 583–589.

Helmreich, R. L. (1987). Exploring flight crew behavior. *Social Behavior, 2*, 63–72.

Herzberg, F. (1966). *Work and the nature of man*. Cleveland, OH: World Publishing.

Ilgen, D. R., Fisher, C., & Taylor, M. S. (1979). Consequences of individual feedback on behavior in organizations. *Journal of Applied Psychology, 64*, 349–472.

Ilgen, D. R., Shapiro, J., Salas, E., & Weiss, H. (1987). *Functions of group goals: Possible generalizations from individuals to groups* (Tech. Rep. 87-022). Orlando, FL: Naval Training Systems Center.

Indik, B. P. (1965). Organizational size and member participation: Some empirical test of alternatives. *Human Relations, 18*, 339–350.

Jackson, J., & Williams, K. (1985). Social loafing on difficult tasks: Working collectively can improve performance. *Journal of Personality and Social Psychology, 49*, 937–942.

Kabanoff, B., & O'Brien, G. E. (1979). The effects of task type and cooperation upon group products and performance. *Organizational Behavior and Human Performance, 23*, 163–181.

Kahan, J. P., Webb, N., Shavelson, R. J., & Stolzenberg, R. M. (1985). *Individual characteristics and unit performance* (Report No. R-3194-MIL). Santa Monica, CA: Rand Corporation.

Kanfer, R. (1990). Motivation theory and industrial and organizational psychology. In M. D. Dunnette & L. M. Hough (Eds.), *Handbook of industrial & organizational psychology* (Vol. 1). Palo Alto, CA: Consulting Psychologists Press.

Katz, D., & Kahn, R. L. (1978). *The social psychology of organizations* (2nd ed.). New York: Wiley.

Kent, R. N., & McGrath, J. E. (1969). Task and group characteristics as factors influencing group performance. *Journal of Experimental Social Psychology, 5*, 429–220.

Kerr, N. L. (1983). Motivational losses in task-performing groups: A social dilemma analysis. *Journal of Personality and Social Psychology, 45*, 819–828.

Kerr, N. L., & Bruun, S. (1981). Ringelmann revisited: Alternative explanations for the social loafing effect. *Personality and Social Psychology Bulletin, 1*, 224–231.

Klaus, D. J., & Glaser, R. (1968). *Increasing team proficiency through training: Final summary report* (ONR Contract No. 2551(00). NR (154-079)). Washington, DC: American Institutes for Research.

Knerr, C., Nadler, L., & Berger, D. (1980). *Toward a Naval taxonomy* (Contract No. N00014-80-C-0781). Arlington, VA: Litton Mellonics.

Latane, B. (1981). The psychology of social impact. *American Psychologist, 36,* 343–356.

Latane, B. (1986). Responsibility and effort in organizations. In P. S. Goodman (Ed.), *Designing effective work groups*. San Francisco: Jossey-Bass.

Latane, B., Williams, K., & Harkins, S. (1979). Many hands make light the work: The causes and consequences of social loafing. *Journal of Personality and Social Psychology, 37,* 823–832.

Laughlin, P. R., Branch, L. G., & Johnson, H. H. (1969). Individual versus triadic performance and unidimensional complementary task as a function of initial ability level. *Journal of Personality and Social Psychology, 12,* 144–150.

Lawler, E. E. (1981). *Pay and organization development*. Reading, MA: Addison-Wesley.

Lewin, K. (1938). *The conceptual representation and the measurement of psychological forces*. Durham, NC: Duke University Press.

Lewin, K., Lippett, R., & White, R. K. (1939). Patterns of aggressive behavior in experimentally created "social climates." *Journal of Social Psychology, 10,* 271–299.

Lewis, C. M., Hritz, R. J., & Roth, J. T. (1983). *Understanding and improving teamwork: Concepts for understanding teams and teamwork* (Report 1) (ARI Contract No. MDA903-81-C-0198). Valencia, PA: Applied Science Associates.

Locke, E. A. (1968). Toward a theory of task motivation and incentives. *Organizational Behavior and Human Performance, 3,* 157–189.

Locke, E. A., Shaw, K. N., Saari, L. M., & Latham, G. P. (1981). Goal setting and task performance: 1969–1980. *Psychological Bulletin, 90,* 152–152.

Lott, A. J., & Lott, B. E. (1961). Group cohesiveness, communication level, and conformity. *Journal of Abnormal and Social Psychology, 62,* 408–412.

Manning, F. J., & Fullerton, T. D. (1988). Health and well-being in highly cohesive units of the U.S. Army. *Journal of Applied Social Psychology, 18,* 503–519.

Maslow, A. H. (1943). A theory of motivation. *Psychological Review, 50,* 370–96.

Matsui, T., Imaizumi, T., Onglatco, M. L., & Kakuyama, T. (1987). *Group goals lead to higher performance than individual goals*. Unpublished manuscript, Rikkyo University, Tokyo, Japan.

Matsui, T., Kakuyama, T., & Onglatco, M. L. (1987). *Interaction effects of group and individual task feedback on performance*. Unpublished manuscript, Rikkyo University, Tokyo, Japan.

McCallum, G. A., Oser, R., Morgan, B. B., Jr., & Salas, E. (1989, August). *An investigation of the behavioral components of teamwork*. Paper presented at the American Psychological Association Convention, New Orleans, LA.

McDavid, J. W., & Harari, H. (1968). *Social psychology: Individuals, groups, and societies*. New York: Harper & Row.

McGrath, J. E. (1984). *Groups: Interaction and performance*. Englewood Cliffs, NJ: Prentice-Hall.

McGrath, J. E., & Altman, I. (1966). *Small group research: A synthesis and critique of the field*. New York: Holt.

McIntyre, R. M. (1988). *Guidelines for Naval team training: A model based on a synthesis of current literature and research*. Unpublished manuscript, Old Dominion University, Norfolk, VA.

McIntyre, R. M., Morgan, B. B., Jr., Salas, E., & Glickman, A. S. (1988). Teamwork from team training: New evidence for the development of teamwork skills during operational training. *Proceedings of the 10th Interservice/Industry Training Systems Conference,* 21–27.

Miller, C. (1991). How to construct programs for teams. *Training,* Special Supplement "Reward and Recognition", pp. 4–6.

Modrick, J. A. (1986). Team training and performance. In J. Zeidner (Ed.), *Human productivity enhancement* (Vol. 1). New York: Praeger.

Morgan, B. B., Jr., Glickman, A. S., Woodard, E. A., Blaiwes, A. S., & Salas, E. (1986). *Mea-

surement of team behaviors in a Navy environment (NAVTRASYSCEN TR-86-014). Orlando, FL: Naval Training Systems Center.

Morgan, B. B., Jr., & Lassiter, D. L. (1992). Team composition and staffing. In R. W. Swezey & E. Salas (Eds.), *Teams: Their training and performance*. Norwood, NJ: Ablex.

Mullen, B., & Baumeister, R. F. (1987). Group effects on self-attention and performance: Social loafing, social facilitation, and social impairment. In C. Hendrick (Ed.), *Review of personality and social psychology*. Beverly Hills, CA: Sage.

Mulvey, P. W., Klein, H. J., & Sterling, C. L. (1991, April). *Perceived free riding in groups: An investigation of group social and goal processes and performances*. Paper presented at the Society of Industrial and Organizational Psychology Convention, St. Louis, MO.

Nadler, D. A. (1979). The effects of feedback on task group behavior: A review of the experimental research. *Organizational Behavior and Human Performance, 23*, 309–338.

NATO (1980). Oosterveld, W. J. (Chairman). *Working Group 10, AGARD-AR159 report*.

Nieva, V. F., Fleishman, E. A., & Rieck, A. (1978). *Team dimensions: Their identity, their measurement, and their relationships* (Contract No. DAHC19-78-C-0001). Washington, DC: Response Analysis Corporation.

O'Leary-Kelly, A. M. (undated). *Motivation in groups: A control theory model*. Unpublished manuscript, Texas A & M University, College Station, TX.

O'Neil, H. F. Jr., Baker, E. L., & Kazlauskas, E. J. (1992). Assessment of team performance. In R. W. Swezey & E. Salas (Eds.), *Teams: Their training and performance*. Norwood, NJ: Ablex.

Orasanu, J., & Salas, E. (in press). Team decision making in complex environments. In G. Klein, J. Orasanu, & R. Calderwood (Eds.), *Decision making in action: Models and methods*. Norwood, NJ: Ablex.

Orbell, J., & Dawes, R. (1981). Social dilemmas. In G. Stephenson & J. H. Davis (Eds.), *Progress in applied social psychology* (Vol. 1). Chichester, England: Wiley.

Oser, R., McCallum, G. A., Salas, E., & Morgan, B. B., Jr. (1989). *Toward a definition of teamwork: An analysis of critical team behaviors* (Tech. Rep. No. 89-004). Orlando, FL: Naval Training Systems Center.

Penner, L. A. (1986). *Social psychology: Concepts and applications*. Minneapolis, MN: West.

Penner, L. A., & Craiger, J. P. (1992). The weakest link: The performance of individual team members. In R. W. Swezey & E. Salas (Eds.), *Teams: Their training and performance*. Norwood, NJ: Ablex.

Porter, L. W., & Lawler, E. E. (1968). *Managerial attitudes and performance*. Homewood, IL: Dorsey Press.

Pritchard, R. D., Jones, S. D., Roth, P. L., Stuebing, K. K., & Ekeberg, S. E. (1988). Effects of group feedback, goal setting, and incentives on organizational productivity. *Journal of Applied Psychology, 73*(2), 337–358.

Pugh, D. S., Hickson, D. J., Hinings, C. R., & Turner, C. (1968). Dimensions of organization structure. *Administrative Science Quarterly, 13*, 66–105.

Rouse, W. B., & Morris, N. M. (1986). On looking into the black box: Prospects and limits in the search for mental models. *Psychological Bulletin, 100*, 349–678.

Salas, E., Dickinson, T. L., Converse, S. A., & Tannanbaum, S. I. (1992). Toward an understanding of team performance and training. In R. W. Swezey & E. Salas (Eds.), *Teams: Their training and performance*. Norwood, NJ: Ablex.

Scanland, R. (1980). Informal consultation as cited in Knerr, Nadler, and Berger (1980). *Toward a Naval taxonomy* (Contract No. N00014-80-C-0781). Arlington, VA: Litton Mellonics.

Schultz, W. C. (1955). What makes groups productive? *Human Relations, 8*, 429–465.

Shaw, M. E. (1976). *Group dynamics: The psychology of small group behavior*. New York: McGraw-Hill.

Smillie, R. J., Shelnutt, J. B., & Bercos, J. (1977). *Task report: Human factors research*. Fort Benning, GA: Litton Mellonics.

Steiner, I. D. (1972). *Group process and productivity.* New York: Academic Press.

Stephan, E., Mills, G. E., Pace, R. W., & Ralphs, L. (1988). HRD in the Fortune 500. *Training and Development Journal, 1,* 26–32.

Stodgill, R. M. (1972). Group productivity drive, and cohesiveness. *Organizational Behavior and Human Performance, 8,* 35–71.

Sundstrom, E., Perkins, M., George, J., Futrell, D., & Hoffman, D. A. (1990, April). *Work-team context, development, and effectiveness in a manufacturing organization.* Paper presented at the Fifth Annual Conference of the Society for Industrial and Organizational Psychology. Miami, FL.

Swezey, R. W. (1992). *ACT 3: Aircrew coordination training for the 90s.* Unpublished manuscript. Sterling, VA: InterScience America.

Swezey, R. W., & Salas, E. (1992). Guidelines for use in team training development. In R. W. Swezey & E. Salas (Eds.), *Teams: Their training and performance.* Norwood, NJ: Ablex.

Tannenbaum, S. I., Beard, R. L., & Salas, E. (1992). Team building and its influence on team effectiveness: An examination of conceptual and empirical developments. In K. Kelley (Ed.), *Issues, theory, and research in industrial/organizational psychology.* Amsterdam: Elsevier.

Thelen, H. A. (1949). Group dynamics in instruction: The principle of least group size. *School Review, 57,* 139–148.

Thorndyke, P. W., & Weiner, M. G. (1980). *Improving training and performance of Navy teams: A design for a research program* (Contract No. R-2607-ONR). Santa Monica, CA: Rand Corporation.

Tolman, E. C. (1932). *Purposive behavior in animals and men.* New York: Appleton-Century-Crofts.

Tosi, H. L., Rizzo, R. R., & Carroll, S. J. (1986). *Managing organizational behavior.* Cambridge, MA: Ballinger.

Tziner, A., & Eden, D. (1985). Effects of crew composition on crew performance: Does the whole equal the sum of the parts? *Journal of Applied Psychology, 70,* 85–93.

Vinacke, E. (1962). Motivation as a complex problem. *Nebraska Symposium on Motivation, 10,* 1–45.

Vroom, V. (1964). *Work and motivation.* New York: Wiley.

Wickens, C. D. (1984). *Engineering psychology and human performance.* Columbus, OH: Charles E. Merrill.

Wicker, A. W. (1969). Size of church membership and member's support of church behavior settings. *Journal of Personality and Social Psychology, 13,* 278–288.

Wyer, R. S., & Malinowski, C. (1972). Effects of sex and achievement level upon individualism and competitiveness in social interaction. *Journal of Experimental Social Psychology, 8,* 303–314.

Yetton, P. W., & Bottger, P. C. (1982). Individual versus group problem solving: An empirical test of a best-member strategy. *Organizational Behavior and Human Performance, 29,* 307–321.

Zander, A., Forward, J., & Albert, R. (1969). Adaptation of board members to repeated failure or success by their organization. *Organizational Behavior and Human Performance, 4,* 56–76.

9 The Relation Between Soldier Motivation, Leadership, and Small Unit Performance

Guy L. Siebold
U.S. Army Research Institute for the Behavioral and Social Sciences, Alexandria, Virginia

The research presented here focuses on the motivation and leadership found in 22 light infantry platoons and how the levels of these factors related to the performance of the platoons on a subsequent extended field training exercise. The research is part of a wider project to identify the "determinants" of small unit performance (Tremble & Alderks, 1991). The articulation of the relations between motivation, leadership, and performance is important for programs for improvement in these areas, for use in assessing training, and for developing models to compare the combat capabilities of various actual or hypothetical forces.

A current stream of leadership research (e.g., Blades, 1986; Fiedler & Garcia, 1987) considers how the resources available to a leader, such as his ability and leadership style, relate to group performance under varying conditions of group member motivation, cohesion, and ability. The research presented here is based on a shift of this framework. Certain characteristics of the group (e.g., group members' mean level of motivation) are treated as group resources that are related to group performance under strong or weak leadership conditions. Specifically, this human resource perspective considers that the relative performance of a small military unit is a direct function of the relative level of human resources available to the unit under positive leadership conditions (assuming equipment, tactics, and the general military situation are held sufficiently constant).

The human resource perspective is derived from this author's experience and based on personnel management, the nature of the small unit, and the function of leadership. The perspective is a way of looking at or studying the human elements that impact upon small group performance. Human resources are the collective capabilities of a group's members—their levels of motivation, cohe-

171

sion, ability, experience, and training. Generally, the small unit should perform up to the level of its members' human resources, when skilled leaders provide the purpose, direction, and focus. Without good leadership, the small unit's collective capabilities will be dissipated in multiple directions and foci. On the other hand, good leadership cannot bring a small unit to perform beyond its existing potential capabilities. As noted by Schneider (1985), early research generally supported "the thesis that management frustrates rather than facilitates the display of employee energy toward the accomplishment of organizational goals" (p. 576). Thus the human resource perspective is not without precedent in treating leadership as a facilitating condition, which can hamper or assist subordinate groups in performing up to their potential.

Motivation

Over the last decade, research on motivation reached a developmental plateau, causing Schneider (1985, p. 578) as well as Pittman and Heller (1987, p. 461) to ask, "What happened to motivation research?" Despite, or perhaps because of, this developmental plateau, a number of extensive substantive reviews or syntheses concerning motivation were published. These reviews and syntheses were presented in the context of organizational behavior (e.g., House & Singh, 1987; Ilgen & Klein, 1989; Schneider, 1985; Staw, 1984) or with a direct focus on some aspect of motivation (e.g., Brehm & Self, 1989; Ginsburg, 1990; Katzell & Thompson, 1990; Looren de Jong, 1991; Pittman & Heller, 1987; Showers & Cantor, 1985). One theme that occurred in several of these reviews was that of the need for extending motivation research across organizational levels and relating (micro-psychological) motivation to broader sets of variables.

The present research fits in with Staw's (1984, p. 658) advice to focus on middle-range theories capable of specifying and organizing the processes relevant for predicting specific types of outcomes (like unit performance). Compatible with the suggestion of House and Singh (1987, pp. 670–671), the current research takes into consideration cross-level effects. The research is targeted at the platoon level, which is above the micro (individual) level addressed by Staw but not fully at the macro (organizational) level. One may best describe small unit research as "meso level" and potentially providing clear linkages to and between micro and macro variables. These linkages can be made because individual and behavioral variables can be averaged or aggregated into small unit variables, and small unit variables can be incorporated into organizational variable categories, aggregates, or measures. The links between the micro and macro levels are an important focus of research for those interested in the intersection of individual behavior and organizations (Weick & Sandelands, 1990).

The motivation level of the unit members is considered the key group resource, assuming some middle level of training and ability. The present research adopted the more or less practical view that soldiers have of motivation; it is considered the level of effort a soldier typically makes or is likely to make to accomplish his tasks (cf. Katzell & Thompson, 1990). Three different, standard constructs in the arena of motivation or level of effort were used: (a) general job motivation, (b) motivation to do well on an upcoming major field training exercise, and (c) job satisfaction. These three constructs have been shown frequently in the literature to relate, in some fashion, to performance (e.g., see reviews cited earlier). The general hypothesis in the current research was that the more the unit members were motivated, the better a unit would perform, under positive leadership conditions (i.e., the relationship between mean group motivation and performance was direct and linear, under proper leadership facilitation). It was assumed that any differences in affordances or motivating opportunities in a unit would be reflected in different measured levels in the three motivational constructs. Likewise, it was assumed that an individual soldier's needs, desires, and proclivities would be reflected in his job motivation and satisfaction.

As research proceeds from the very micro towards the macro, broader and more stable (for the individual) variables are needed, which can relate back to the specific stimulus and individual difference variables of the micro world but which can also relate upward to the meso level and to the slower changing and structural (macro) world of organizations and cultures and populations. The three motivational constructs used in this research were chosen because they relate to much of the micro or individual level research on motivation and yet can be linked up to the meso level of the small unit. The individual soldier responses to measures of these three constructs could be averaged within a unit to become a unit characteristic.

The treatment of the average level of motivation as a key group resource is supported by the research of Tziner and Eden (1985). They examined individual motivation and ability as they related to the performance of 208 three-man tank crews. They found that both motivation and ability significantly correlated with crew performance effectiveness. Motivation had the dominant effect; only individual ability had interactive effects. Tziner and Eden concluded that for tasks requiring a large degree of interdependence, performance is "affected by summation of members' task-relevant resources." "Motivation contributed . . . additively . . . , the impact of one person's motivation on crew performance being in no way dependent on the motivation of the others" (pp. 91–92). Consistent with the results from Tziner and Eden, in the present research, each motivation construct was measured for each squad member in each platoon and aggregated to form a platoon mean for each construct. A platoon mean was considered to represent (per construct) the average level of effort available to the platoon. From this perspective, there is not a problem with aggregation bias (e.g., see James, 1982), and the three predictor constructs concerning motivation are at the same level of analysis as the criterion, platoon performance.

Leadership

Small unit leadership, of course, has been investigated for many years from many different approaches. Research has gone from focusing on leader traits, to situational leadership, to the leader-follower relationship, to, more recently, the leader's transformation of his followers (e.g., Bass, 1985). For the present research, the important aspects of leadership were: (a) the platoon leader's skills—in structuring activities, showing consideration, and being effective tactically, (b) leadership team cohesion (i.e., the extent to which a platoon's key leaders worked together in a joint, coordinated, and focused fashion), and (c) the organizational climate (i.e., the extent to which training and development were seen as primary and provided meaning and context for the actions of leaders and their relations with subordinates). These three aspects of leadership—skills, cohesion, and climate setting—in their strong or positive condition were treated as necessary for the effective utilization of group resources. Obviously, if the unit leader is unskilled or the leaders as a team are pulling in different directions or soldiers find little meaning in an activity, unit performance will not be very high (cf. Blades, 1986).

In their review, Levine and Moreland (1990) noted that group performance is the outcome of joint efforts to achieve a collective goal and that leadership facilitates that performance through carrying out organizational, directive, and motivational functions (pp. 612–613). Consistent with their perspective and that from some management literature (e.g., Peters & Waterman, 1982; Townsend, 1970), the present research treats small unit leadership in terms of its facilitative functions. While others have found a moderate direct relationship (e.g., Twohig & Tremble, 1991) between leadership and unit performance or hypothesize a contingent relationship (e.g., Blades, 1986; Fiedler & Garcia, 1987; and Vecchio, 1990; but compare Bar-Tal, 1989), they approach unit performance from a leader-centric rather than from a leader-facilitative perspective.

In terms of a sports analogy, leader-centric research would focus on the impact of the coaches on team performance; leader-facilitative research would focus on the impact of the players on team performance, as enhanced or constrained by the coaching staff. The leader-facilitative approach within the human resource perspective would not deny that there is a direct relation between the leader (or coach) and group performance. Rather the approach would posit that the dominant relation in terms of strength would be between the human resource level of the group members and group performance, under strong leadership. Further, the leader-facilitative approach would accept that leaders have broad, long-term impacts on unit performance through planning and other management functions, including those affecting human resource levels. However, these long-term impacts are not pertinent to near term unit performance within the unit's scope of action, which is the criterion of interest.

Unit Performance

The research criterion was unit performance: The level of performance demonstrated by each of 22 light infantry platoons in conducting a series of missions over a 2-week field training exercise simulating combat against an active, (about) equal size opposing force. The missions involved included movement to contact, hasty attack, deliberate attack, ambush, defense, and raid. Each of these missions requires that a platoon collectively plans, prepares, and executes multiple related tasks and subtasks, which are to be performed to prespecified standards (see Siebold & Kelly, 1988).

The training exercises were conducted at the U.S. Army Joint Readiness Training Center (JRTC), Fort Chaffee, AR. Battalion size task forces (the BLUE-FOR) were transported from their posts to the JRTC. There they operated under realistic scenarios to accomplish their assigned missions in a "free play" or open structure environment. Their opponent was a skilled opposing force (the OP-FOR), most of which was permanently assigned to the JRTC. The JRTC command center controlled the macro events and flow of scenario information to the headquarters of the OPFOR and of the BLUEFOR. Orders came from a brigade headquarters down to battalion, from battalion to company, and from company to the platoons. The training was conducted under observer/controllers (O/Cs) who monitored the activities, ensured safety, and provided training feedback through After Action Reviews and training reports. Observer/controllers were attached to each echelon level down to a platoon. Observer/controllers at the platoon level are typically a team consisting of an experienced Captain, who previously served as a company commander, and two senior noncommissioned officers (NCOs). The O/C team stays with or near its assigned platoon for the entire 2-week exercise, except for specified downtimes.

Fort Chaffee is located at the foothills south of the Ozark Mountains. The terrain varies from open field to forest to small mountains and ridges. During an initial movement to contact mission, the BLUEFOR may move in dispersed formation (soldiers about 15 feet apart) through the fields and forest area for several kilometers to try to locate enemy forces. Generally, the BLUEFOR will try to use a small element such as a squad to make contact with the OPFOR. Often a squad or platoon will be used to block the retreat of OPFOR scouts, who are likewise trying to locate BLUEFOR elements. If an OPFOR element is located, the BLUEFOR may initiate a hasty attack. The lead BLUEFOR element can call in indirect fire support from the mortars or artillery, which can be simulated by smoke grenades or small fireworks operated by JRTC personnel. The attacking BLUEFOR element will use doctrine-based tactics to engage the enemy. Soldiers on both sides have blank ammunition in their weapons. As they fire, an attachment on each weapon sends off a laser beam. When the laser beam hits a sensor on another soldier (all soldiers wear harnesses with several sensors on them), a small buzzer is set off on the harness of the soldier hit. The O/C uses a key to turn off the buzzer and declares the soldier a casualty. The extent of wounds from indirect fire or from small weapons fire is determined from a card randomly assigned to each soldier and is based on historical data from actual combat. Once a soldier is a casualty, he must be treated appropriately by unit medics and taken to a collection point for pickup for additional treatment. When hit, a soldier is "dead" for the mission if his card says so or medical treatment is not timely or proper.

A deliberate attack mission may involve BLUEFOR elements moving 10 to 12 kilometers (6 to 7 miles) through forest and along the side of ridges in the middle of the night, linking up with other BLUEFOR elements traversing by different routes, and then preparing for a predawn attack on an OPFOR command post, surrounded by barbed wire and (simulated) mine fields. Small teams will cut through the wire and clear paths through the mine fields. Others will have taken up covering or blocking positions. When the way is clear, the lead elements will proceed through to the command post area and clear the bunkers and fortified positions in a methodical manner. Care must be taken in the operation to the fields of fire of each element so that casualties by friendly fire are avoided. As one might suspect, with a skilled OPFOR, deliberate attacks may become heated and disorderly. Normally, the attacking force should have between a 3 to 1 and a 6 to 1 ratio of attackers to defenders to successfully carry off a deliberate attack mission.

A defense mission typically involves the BLUEFOR digging foxholes and protective positions to cover an approach which the OPFOR may choose. Barbed wire barriers lined with mines are laid to close roads and force the enemy to move through areas the defense is covering with their fire. The BLUEFOR may have up to a full day and night to prepare their positions; activities also include filling in sandbags, setting up fields of fire, and camouflaging their foxholes. Usually, the BLUEFOR will end up wearing their "MOPP" gear, which is the protective suit that can withstand enemy lethal agents such as gas. At some time, such as the predawn, the OPFOR will try to come through what they believe is a weakness in the defensive positions. During this mission, the OPFOR typically uses tanks and armored personnel vehicles to break through. The BLUEFOR uses the terrain and anti-armor weapons to defend. The actual battle is over in a few minutes.

METHOD

Sample

In the wider project cited (Tremble & Alderks, 1991), the full sample was 60 platoons from five light infantry battalions from three separate Army posts. Of these five battalions, two went through training rotations at the JRTC where special performance ratings were provided by the O/Cs in support of the research. In these two battalions, there were 23 platoons on which performance data were obtained. For one of these platoons, less than a majority of the soldiers provided predictor data (on motivation and leadership), which was considered an inadequate representation of the platoon for this research. Thus the sample utilized for the present analyses consisted of the soldiers in 22 light infantry platoons, 10 from one battalion at one post and 12 from another battalion at a different post. In both battalions, most of the first tour soldiers had been stationed together for over $1\frac{1}{2}$ years, although there had been turnover in the leaders at all levels.

Of these 22 platoons, 17 were line infantry platoons, 2 were scout platoons, 2 were mortar platoons, and 1 was an antitank platoon. These different types of platoons differ by function and somewhat by size, but otherwise operate under similar dynamics. A typical line infantry platoon, if fully manned, would be structured as follows: Four soldiers would make up a fire team; two fire teams plus a leader would make up a squad; three squads plus a platoon sergeant, a platoon leader, a radio man, two machine gunners, and two assistant machine gunners would make up a platoon, with 34 soldiers in total. (In practice, many of the 22 platoons were not 100% manned due to various personnel turbulence factors and the special personnel system which they were under.) The platoon is led by the platoon leader, usually a Second Lieutenant, who with the platoon sergeant and squad leaders forms a leadership team. Three line platoons plus a headquarters platoon make up a line company. The specialty platoons (scout, mortar, and antitank) were subechelons of the headquarters company. Three line companies plus a headquarters company compose a light infantry battalion.

Procedures

Under the research design of the wider project, predictor data were collected (on motivation, leadership, cohesion, and other factors) by questionnaires administered about 4 months before a battalion participated in a training rotation at the U.S. Army Joint Readiness Training Center (JRTC). Predictor data were again collected, using similar questionnaires, from soldiers 2- to 4-weeks before the battalion was scheduled for the training rotation. Criterion data on platoon performance at the JRTC were provided by the observer/controllers (O/Cs) right after the training rotation. Finally, additional criterion data on unit performance were collected by questionnaires given to the soldiers 2- to 4-weeks after the JRTC training rotation.

For the predictor questionnaire administrations, separate but similar questionnaires were given to squad members, squad leaders, platoon sergeants, and platoon leaders, together in company formations. In addition, their company commanders completed self-administered questionnaires, which included some items parallel to items in the platoon level questionnaires. For the criterion questionnaire administrations to soldiers after the JRTC training, the same questionnaire was given to all platoon members, but in groups based on member position in the platoon. The groups were: all the platoon leaders in a company, all the platoon sergeants in a company, 6- to 9-squad leaders in a company, and all the squad members from one squad in a company. In the criterion questionnaire, the soldiers were asked to rate the performance of their platoon on each mission performed at the JRTC. On self-administered questionnaires, company commanders rated the performance of their platoons on each mission a platoon performed.

The main analyses in the present research utilized only the predictor questionnaire data obtained from squad members 2- to 4-weeks before the JRTC rotation and the platoon performance ratings made by the O/Cs immediately after the completion of the rotation. However, other portions of the collected data will be cited in the context of reliability and validity.

Measures

In the predictor questionnaires administered 2- to 4-weeks prior to a battalion's JRTC training rotation, squad members through platoon leaders were asked to provide their assessments on a number of factors hypothesized to be important "determinants" of platoon performance, including: their job motivation, their motivation to do well at the JRTC, their job satisfaction, the learning climate in their unit, the degree of cohesion exhibited by their platoon's leadership team, and the effectiveness of their platoon leader. The assessments of these determinant factors, or predictor constructs, were made by responding to questionnaire items using 5-point, Likert-type response scales. The item responses were subsequently coded with the highest or most positive response coded as 5 and the less high or less positive responses coded in descending order from 4 to 1. Several questionnaire items together formed a scale for each construct. These scales with their component items are presented in Tables 9.1 and 9.2. The scale numerical data presented in the tables are based on the individual level responses of about 1,170 squad members (Tremble & Alderks, 1991). An individual respondent level factor analysis showed that of the six scales presented in the tables, only the job motivation and JRTC motivation scales loaded strongly on the same factor. Squad member scale scores were averaged together to obtain a platoon scale score, since the primary level of analysis was the platoon. In the analyses for this research, the scales were treated both by themselves and as part of either the motivational elements (set of scales) or the leadership elements.

At the end of the JRTC training rotation, each O/C team leader, as special support for the research project, rated his assigned platoon on two (questionnaire-like) rating cards. Each O/C rated the planning, preparation, and execution of each mission his assigned platoon performed, using a 4-point scale (1 = untrained, 2 = needs a lot of training, 3 = needs a little training, and 4 =

TABLE 9.1
Scales Measuring the Motivational Elements

Job Motivation Scale

4.   I don't mind taking on extra duties and responsibilities in my work with this platoon.
5.   I work hard and try to do as good a job as possible.
6.   I look forward to coming to work every day.
7.   I am very personally involved in my work.

Response alternatives for all items: Strongly agree, Agree, Neither agree nor disagree, Disagree, Strongly disagree.
Scale data: alpha = .77; item-total r range = .50 - .64.

JRTC Motivation Scale

8.   It really matters to me that we do well at the JRTC.
9.   I am putting in extra effort to prepare for the JRTC.
10.   I will learn a lot from the training at the JRTC.

Response alternatives for all items: Strongly agree, Agree, Neither agree nor disagree, Disagree, Strongly disagree.
Scale data: alpha = .84; item-total r range = .68 - .73.

Job Satisfaction Scale

25.   How useful is the work you do most of the time?
      Response alternatives:
      Very useful, Quite useful, Somewhat useful, Slightly useful, Not at all useful.

26.   How interesting is your work?
      Response alternatives:
      Very interesting, Quite interesting, Somewhat interesting, Slightly interesting, Not at all interesting.

27.   How do you like your work?
      Response alternatives:
      Like it a lot, Like it, Borderline, Dislike it, Dislike it a lot.

28.   How would you rate your overall job satisfaction?
      Response alternatives:
      Very high, High, Borderline, Low, Very low.

Scale data: alpha = .87; item-total r range = .63 - .76.

Note. Item numbers are from the questionnaire. Item-total r range is the range of correlations between each item and the scale mean with the item deleted.

trained). The missions that could have been performed included movement to contact, hasty attack, deliberate attack, raid, ambush, reconnaisance and security, defend, and retrograde. Because not every platoon performed every mission, all the (planning, preparation, and execution) ratings on the several missions conducted by each platoon were averaged to give each platoon an "overall" criterion score, or index of mission performance. Since only one O/C rated a given platoon, the use of an overall score was desirable to obtain a more stable criterion than would the use of any specific mission score.

The human resource perspective posits that there is a direct relation between platoon resources and performance, under the condition of positive leadership.

TABLE 9.2
Scales Measuring Leadership Elements

Leadership Team Cohesion

15. *Leaders* in this platoon really care about each other.
16. *Leaders* in this platoon work well together as a team.
17. *Leaders* in this platoon pull together to get the job done.

Response alternatives for all items: Strongly agree, Agree, Neither agree nor disagree, Disagree, Strongly disagree.
Scale data: alpha = .89; item-total *r* range = .73 - .85.

Learning Climate

29. Soldiers are assigned to the work they have been trained to do.
30. Soldiers are given a lot of responsibility for their work.
31. Soldiers are encouraged to do things on their own even if they sometimes make mistakes.
32. Soldiers get feedback on how they are doing.
33. The emphasis in this company is on getting things right and not just on looking good.
34. Soldiers can admit their mistakes are are helped to learn from them.
35. The leaders have confidence in the soldiers doing their jobs right.
36. When assigned new duties, soldiers are provided with quidance and direction.

Response alternatives for all items: Strongly agree, Agree, Neither agree nor disagree, Disagree, Srongly disagree.
Scale data: alpha = .87; item-total *r* range = .47 - .68.

Platoon Leader Effectiveness

(My Platoon Leader:)

(Initiating structure)
114. Maintains high standards of performance for our platoon.
115. Insists that we follow standard operating procedures (SOPs).
116. Assigns platoon members to particular tasks.
117. Takes full charge when emergencies arise.

(Consideration)

118. Treats us fairly.
119. Looks out for the welfare of his people.
120. Encourages us to work together as a team.
121. Is friendly and approachable.
122. Settles conflicts when they occur in the platoon.

(Effectiveness)

123. Knows Army tactics and war fighting.
124. Works hard and tries to do as good a job as possible.
125. Pulls his share of the load in the field.
126. Would have my confidence if we were in combat together.
127. Is an effective leader.

Response alternatives for all items: Almost always, Usually, Sometimes, Not usually, Almost never; (or Not observed/Don't know).
Scale data: alpha = .97; item-total *r* range = .79 - .97.

Note. Item numbers are from the questionnaire. Item-total r range is the range of correlations between each item and the scale mean with the item deleted.

The best way to measure this leadership condition, however, is not settled. Given that the three leadership elements (leader cohesion, climate, and platoon leader skills) were measured with 5-point rating scales, the practical question became where to make the cutoff between the strong and weak leadership conditions.

The determination of the cutoff point must take into consideration the nature of the leadership function. Soldiers look to their leaders to provide purpose and direction, to have the necessary tactical and technical skills to maneuver their unit, and to show their soldiers reasonable consideration and support. Also, soldiers look to their leaders as role models and to build soldier self-esteem and unit pride. Thus the midpoint of the 5-point rating scales (with descriptive words of "neither agree nor disagree" and "sometimes") seemed too low for a cutoff point between positive and less-than-positive (or strong versus weak) leadership. On the other hand, the next highest rating scale levels ("agree" and "usually") seemed too stringent for a cutoff point. Therefore, rather than using the rating scale levels to establish a cutoff, the median response of the soldiers to each scale was used, following the cutoff procedure established by Blades (1986). In consequence, for each scale concerning leadership, those platoons with mean scale scores above the median response (i.e., the top 11 platoons) were considered under the positive leadership condition for the scale; those platoons with mean scale scores below the median (i.e., the bottom 11 platoons) were considered under the less-than-positive leadership condition for the scale.

RESULTS

Analyses were conducted to establish the basic descriptive statistics for the measures at the platoon level for the specific sample of 22 platoons. These results are given in Table 9.3. The table shows that the overall means were towards the midpoint of each scale and there was a reasonable range of platoon level mean scores. The leadership scales did have a wider variation in platoon mean scores than did the motivation scales.

Although not shown in the table, the within platoon data were relatively similar (i.e., there was no aberrant platoon with unusually high or low standard deviations on the scale scores). Also not shown are additional data supporting the validity and reliability of the measures; some of these data are mentioned in the following. The figures in Table 9.3 are based on squad member responses. Squad members are the best source to assess their own motivation. However, the leaders in the platoon are also valid sources to assess leadership team cohesion, the platoon learning climate, and the effectiveness of the platoon leader. For these 22 platoons, the squad members' ratings of leadership team cohesion correlated significantly with the ratings of their squad leaders and platoon sergeants ($r = .59$; $p < .001$ and $r = .53$; $p < .01$, respectively), although not significantly with their platoon leaders. Likewise, the squad members' ratings of

TABLE 9.3
Basic Descriptive Statistics

Statistic	Scale or Index						
	JOBMOT	JRTCMOT	JOBSAT	LDRCOH	CLIMAT	PLTLDR	PERFORM
M of platoon means	3.42	3.83	3.06	3.24	3.18	3.58	2.10
SD of platoon means	.29	.32	.40	.59	.41	.66	.42
Individual level SD	.76	.88	.94	.99	.81	1.03	N/A
Lowest platoon mean	3.00	3.32	2.60	2.13	2.53	1.61	1.42
Highest platoon mean	4.17	4.65	4.18	4.55	4.11	4.79	3.33
Platoon level alpha	.84	.93	.95	.95	.95	.99	N/A

Note. N = 22 platoons. Scale or index titles are: JOBMOT = Job Motivation, JRTCMOT = JRTC Motivation, JOBSAT = Job Satisfaction, LDRCOH = Leadership Team Cohesion, CLIMAT = Unit Learning Climate, PLTLDR = Platoon Leader Effectiveness, and PERFORM = Index of Platoon JRTC Mission Performance (as rated by the JRTC observer/controllers). The six predictor scales are based on 5-point response scales; the criterion index (PERFORM) is based on a 4-point response scale. One-way ANOVA results indicated that there were significant differences between platoons on each of the six predictor scales at $p < .0001$. Cronbach's alpha figures at the platoon level are from Tremble and Alderks (1991) and based on the full sample of platoons (N = 60).

their learning climate were significantly correlated with their squad leaders ($r = .42$; $p < .05$), the only other position that rated climate. Similarly, the squad members' ratings of their platoon leader's effectiveness correlated significantly with the ratings of their squad leaders ($r = .45$; $p < .05$) and their platoon sergeants ($r = .42$; $p < .05$). Although the observer/controllers were the most experienced and continuous observers of platoon mission performance, their ratings of platoon performance were backed up by two other experienced soldiers observing a platoon; these other two soldiers were the company commander and the platoon sergeant, each of whose overall mission performance ratings correlated significantly with those of the O/Cs ($r = .50$; $p < .05$ and $r = .75$; $p < .01$, respectively; see Siebold & Lindsay, 1991).

The direct correlations between the six predictor scales (based on squad member responses) and the measure of performance (based on O/C ratings) were all significant, with the motivation scales more strongly related to performance than the leadership scales. The correlations among the predictor scales and with platoon JRTC mission performance, individually and jointly, are provided in Table 9.4.

Although each predictor scale was, by itself, a significant predictor of platoon performance, the mean of the motivation scales taken together or the mean of the leadership scales taken together did not substantially increase the correlation with platoon performance. The partial correlations (not shown in the table) between the motivation scales and mission performance, controlling for the effects of the leadership scales, averaged around r (partial) = .50; each partial correlation was significant at either $p < .05$ or $< .01$. The Table 9.4 correlations are direct, zero-order correlations, meant to emphasize the relations between the predictor vari-

TABLE 9.4
Correlations Among the Predictor Scales and the Platoon Mission Performance Index

Scale or Index

Scale or Index	JOBMOT	JRTCMOT	JOBSAT	LDRCOH	CLIMAT	PLTLDR	PERFORM
JRTC motivation	.76***						
Job satisfaction	.71***	.78***					
Leadership team cohesion	.72***	.48*	.70***				
Learning climate	.74***	.60**	.73***	.89***			
Platoon leader effectiveness	.73***	.43*	.46*	.72***	.75***		
Platoon mission performance	.64***	.65***	.64***	.53**	.54**	.41*	
Mean of 3 motivation scales							.70***
Mean of 3 leadership scales							.53**

Note. N = 22 platoons. Scale or index titles are: JOBMOT = Job Motivation, JRTCMOT = JRTC Motivation, JOBSAT = Job Satisfaction, LDRCOH = Leadership team cohesion, CLIMAT = Unit Learning Climate, PLTLDR = Platoon Leader Effectiveness, and PERFORM = Index of Platoon JRTC Mission Performance (as rated by the JRTC observer/controllers). The three motivation scales (elements) are JOBMOT, JRTCMOT, and JOBSAT; the three leadership scales (elementary) are LDRCOH, CLIMAT, and PLTLDR. The means of the three motivation scales correlate with the means of the three leadership scales at r = .72***.

* = p < .05.   ** = p < .01.   *** = p < .001.

183

ables and platoon mission performance. However, if one desired to focus on the relations, for example, among the three motivation variables themselves, the correlations should be corrected for any spurious covariance among the motivation variables (e.g., see O'Brien, 1991).

The human resource perspective considers the motivation level in a platoon to be directly related to platoon performance, *under the condition* of positive leadership. The data were analyzed to determine whether the human resource perspective provided a clearer view of the data than that of the simple, direct correlations between the predictors and the criterion of platoon performance. The 11 platoons with the highest scores on each of the leadership scales were considered under the condition of positive (strong) leadership for each scale. The 11 platoons with the lowest scores on the scales were considered under the condition of less-than-positive (weak) leadership. The platoon mean scores on the motivation scales for the 11 platoons with highest mean scores on each leadership scale were correlated with platoon performance separately from those of the 11 platoons with the lowest scores on each leadership scale. The resulting pattern of correlations, presented in Table 9.5, provided solid support for the value of the human resource perspective.

Under the conditions of strong leadership team cohesion, a positive learning climate, and an effective platoon leader, the platoon mean scores on the motiva-

TABLE 9.5
Correlations Between the Motivation Elements and Platoon Mission Performance Under Strong or Weak Leadership Conditions

	Leadership Scale			
Motivation Scale	LDRCOH	CLIMAT	PLTLDR	LDRMEAN
Correlation between the motivation scale and platoon mission performance under the STRONG leadership condition of each leadership scale:				
Job motivation	.91***	.88***	.89***	.89***
JRTC motivation	.73**	.93***	.75**	.79**
Job satisfaction	.77**	.82***	.76**	.76**
Mean of motivation scales	.83***	.92***	.86***	.85***
Correlation between the motivation scale and platoon mission performance under the WEAK leadership condition of each leadership scale:				
Job motivation	-.56*	-.14	-.54*	-.60*
JRTC motivation	.16	-.22	.02	.02
Job satisfaction	-.12	-.24	-.08	-.16
Mean of motivation scales	-.19	-.29	-.21	-.28

Note. n = 11 platoons for each correlation. Leadership scale titles are: LDRCOH = Leadership Team Cohesion, CLIMAT = Unit Learning Climate, PLTLDR = Platoon Leader Effectiveness, and LDRMEAN = the mean of LDRCOH, CLIMAT, and PLTLDR. The 11 platoons with the highest means on a given leadership scale were considered under a strong leadership condition for that scale. The 11 platoons with the lowest means (the bottom half) on the given leadership scale were considered under a weak leadership condition. $* = p < .05.$ $** = p < .01.$ $*** = p < .001.$

tion scales, singly and jointly, were very strongly correlated with platoon mission performance, with correlations ranging from .73 to .93. In the reverse situation, under conditions of weak leadership team cohesion, a less positive learning climate, and a less effective platoon leader, the platoon mean scores on the motivation scales, singly and jointly, were either not significantly correlated with platoon mean mission performance or were significantly but negatively correlated with platoon mean mission performance.

Table 9.5 displays the pattern of correlations in numeric form. To add visual clarity, the relations between platoon mean job motivation and platoon mean mission performance, under the strong and weak leadership team cohesion conditions respectively, are also presented graphically in Figs. 9.1 and 9.2. Figure 9.1 demonstrates the linearity of the relation between the platoon resource of mean job motivation and mission performance, under the nonlinear condition of strong leadership (i.e., for the 11 platoons with leadership team cohesion scores above the median). Figure 9.2 shows the data on the 11 platoons under the weak leadership condition. If the data were not separated by leadership condition but were presented in one figure, the clear pattern would be hidden.

DISCUSSION

The human resource perspective was a helpful approach to analyzing the data and sorting out its patterns. However, before a discussion of the strengths, weaknesses, and utility of the perspective, it is necessary to consider some alternative explanations which might have accounted for the findings.

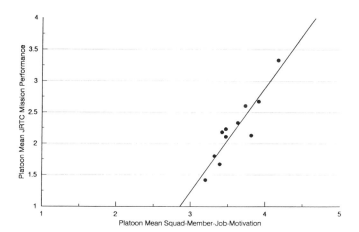

FIG. 9.1. Relation between platoon mean squad-member-job-motivation and JRTC mission performance under strong leadership-team cohesion (r = .91; n = 11 platoons; $p < .001$).

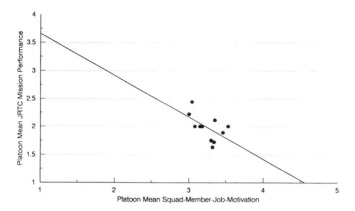

FIG. 9.2. Relation between platoon mean squad-member-job-motivation and JRTC mission performance under weak leadership-team cohesion (r = −.56; n = 11 platoons; p < .05).

Alternative Explanations

One explanation to the pattern of correlations might be that the motivation level of the leaders influenced the motivation of their squad members, the squad members' assessment of their leaders, and platoon mission performance. However, the analyses indicated that squad leader, platoon sergeant, and platoon leader scores on the motivation scales were neither significantly correlated with those of each other, the predictor scale scores of the squad members, nor with platoon performance. It appears that the motivation level of the leaders is not important in and of itself; leaders are all professionals. Rather, leaders have an impact on squad member motivation and platoon performance to the extent that they act as leaders in pulling together as a team, creating an appropriate climate, and developing their leader skills.

Another explanation to the pattern of correlations might be that the level of mission training a platoon achieved prior to its rotation to the JRTC might have influenced squad member motivation, squad member views of their leaders, and subsequent mission performance at the JRTC. Yet the analyses indicated that prerotation self-assessments of their level of mission training by the squad members, squad leaders, platoon sergeants, platoon leaders, and company commanders did not correlate significantly with the O/C ratings of mission performance and only correlated sporadically with postrotation self-assessments of mission performance by the same squad members, squad leaders, platoon sergeants, platoon leaders, and company commanders (Siebold & Lindsay, 1991). The analyses indicated that perceived level of mission training was not a strong, consistent, or frequent significant correlate of the other variables.

A third alternative explanation might be that the pattern of correlations just indicates that the O/Cs were influenced by their observation of the motivation in a platoon when they rated platoon mission performance. However, this explanation does not address why (prior) motivation was strongly related to platoon mission performance only under the strong leadership conditions. Further, the O/Cs were also asked to rate the platoons using items reflecting factors other than mission performance. These factors included leadership, motivation, and cohesion. The item on motivation ("The soldiers in this platoon were highly motivated.") was not significantly correlated with the ratings of mission performance. Rather the O/C platoon performance ratings were significantly correlated with their ratings on some of the items concerning cohesion. This pattern is not anomalous; soldiers tend to rate cohesion (displayed as teamwork and mutual help) as more important to mission performance than motivation (e.g., Julien & Siebold, 1990). Adequate motivation is taken for granted and expected to vary over an extended field exercise. Yet the lack of correlation between the O/C ratings of motivation and platoon performance does not invalidate the results which suggest motivation is an important resource for performance. The O/Cs are trained and experienced at assessing performance and looking for teamwork among soldiers, not in assessing the precise level of soldier motivation in a platoon over a 2-week period.

Strengths and Weaknesses

The main strength of the human resource perspective is not in its potential contribution to the in depth study of individual motivation, leadership, or small group performance. Rather, its strength is in its ability to suggest how these variable areas are related and how one could usefully approach the investigation of the relations among them. The perspective suggests a micro-meso link between individual level motivation, aggregate group motivation, and small unit performance. More generally, the perspective sensitizes one to a category of variables (human resources) which may have emergent properties at the group level, that is, those variables that may be without strong influence at the individual level but which in the aggregate or in the aggregate under certain conditions may impact on group performance. More specifically, the human resource perspective provides a productive way to look at the interaction of such factors as leadership, cohesion, and motivation and how they jointly relate to group performance. The latter, of course, is a major concern of the military, business, and other primary societal institutions.

Another strength of the perspective is that it brings the soldier or the worker back into consideration as a primal causal agent. Much attention has been given to the impact of leaders, technology, corporate culture, and organizational structures as drivers of productivity or performance. These are things that management can control, but are only conditions that facilitate the performance of skilled and motivated soldiers or workers.

The human resource perspective is an approach and, hence, lacks the full strength of a good theory. Much research needs to be done to further assess its value and its parameters. For example, research is desirable not only to verify the consistency of the findings in this research but to understand the tradeoffs that can be made in the main human resources (e.g., cohesion versus motivation versus training) and how the resources can best be increased (e.g., by improved selection versus increasing incentives versus increasing training funds). Also, research needs to address the issues surrounding the nonlinearity of leadership (i.e., where are the precise transition [cutoff] points between strong and weak leadership conditions; why are the points located there; and how do they operate?). Nonetheless, the human resource perspective appears to be a useful way to integrate important individual and group level variables into a common framework for a multitude of purposes.

Another strength of the human resource perspective is in its suggesting the need to expand on the current approaches to the investigation of leadership. The human resource (i.e., leader-facilitative) perspective may prove more predictive of immediate small group performance, while the leader-centric theories address more completely the intricacies of leader behavior and its impacts. Nonetheless, neither viewpoint can be said to adequately cover the full range of leader-group-performance (linear and nonlinear, direct and indirect) interactions in a systematic manner, which also encompasses time and level of analysis issues. The time element is particularly sparsely researched and underarticulated in the leader-group-performance variable cluster. For example, some leadership activities are primarily carried out prior to performance (e.g., planning); some are carried out during performance (e.g., maneuvering the unit, adjusting); and some are carried out after unit performance (e.g., after action reviews). Which, when, and how these leader activities impact on unit member resources or unit performance are not clear. In terms of usefulness, certain perspectives or theories may be better than others for distinct purposes. Thus, senior leader selection might best be based on transformational leadership theory in some form. Junior leader "school" training might best be based on competency needs and variants of cognitive resource or contingency theory. And within-military-unit leader development might best focus on using the human resource perspective for improving unit training and performance.

Utility of the Perspective

Specific applications of the perspective exist in several areas. One key problem has been how to use information on leadership, cohesion, and motivation (the human element) in the process of modeling the comparative capabilities of different actual or hypothetical military forces. The findings in the research reported earlier provide an empirically supported basis for combining information on the human element. Another key problem has been how to improve unit performance. The human resource perspective is useful in noting that improvements in group performance must focus on both the human resources and the facilitating conditions. For example, attempts to improve unit performance through an increase in soldier motivation may actually decrease performance unless any weak leadership factors are also addressed. In some cases, the problem may not be a lack of motivation but a lack of positive leadership conditions. A third key problem has been the design of leader or manager development programs. As noted in the foregoing paragraph, the perspecitve implies that different approaches to leadership be introduced in different learning environments and for different levels of leaders. Finally, a consistent problem has been the assessment of the readiness of a unit for combat. Currently, emphasis has been on "hard" numbers such as the availability of equipment and the percentage of soldiers actually filling positions in a unit. Soft factors such as motivation, morale, leadership, and level of training have been left up to the judgment of commanders. The human resource perspective posits that these soft, human elements can be adequately measured and that the measures can be combined in a meaningful way to better estimate the potential preparedness of a military unit. Unit standards for the human elements can be established and utilized. Undoubtedly, more uses for the human resource perspective will occur as research and experience confirm the strength and consistency of findings in utilizing the approach and relating human resources to small unit performance.

ACKNOWLEDGMENTS

The views, opinions, and/or findings contained in this chapter are the author's and should not be construed as an official position, policy, or decision of the U.S. Army Research Institute for the Behavioral and Social Sciences or the Department of the Army, unless so designated by other official documentation.

REFERENCES

Bar-Tal, Y. (1989). What can we learn from Fiedler's contingency model? *Journal for the Theory of Social Behaviour, 19*, 79–96.

Bass, B. M. (1985). *Leadership and performance beyond expectations.* New York: Free Press.

Blades, J. W. (1986). *Rules for leadership: Improving unit performance.* Washington, DC: National Defense University Press.

Brehm, J. W., & Self, E. A. (1989). The intensity of motivation. *Annual Review of Psychology, 40*, 109–131.

Fiedler, F. E., & Garcia, J. E. (1987). *New approaches to effective leadership: Cognitive resources and organizational performance.* New York: Wiley.

Ginsburg, G. P. (1990). The ecological perception debate: An affordance of the *Journal for the Theory of Social Behaviour. Journal for the Theory of Social Behaviour, 20*, 347–364.

House, R. J., & Singh, J. V. (1987). Organizational behavior: Some new directions for I/O psychology. *Annual Review of Psychology, 38,* 669–718.

Ilgen, D. R., & Klein, H. J. (1989). Organizational behavior. *Annual Review of Psychology, 40,* 327–351.

James, L. R. (1982). Aggregation bias in estimates of perceptual agreement. *Journal of Applied Psychology, 67,* 219–229.

Julien, T. D., & Siebold, G. L. (1990). *Unit leader assessments of a Joint Readiness Training Center rotation* (Research Report 1564). Alexandria, VA: U.S. Army Research Institute for the Behavioral and Social Sciences. (DTIC No. AD A226317)

Katzell, R. A., & Thompson, D. E. (1990). Work motivation: Theory and practice. *American Psychologist, 45,* 144–153.

Levine, J. M., & Moreland, R. L. (1990). Progress in small group research. *Annual Review of Psychology, 41,* 585–634.

Looren de Jong, H. (1991). Intentionality and the ecological approach. *Journal for the Theory of Social Behaviour, 21,* 91–109.

O'Brien, R. M. (1991). Correcting measures of relationship between aggregate-level variables. *Sociological Methodology, 1991,* 125–165.

Peters, T. J., & Waterman, R. H., Jr. (1982). *In search of excellence.* New York: Warner Books.

Pittman, T. S., & Heller, J. F. (1987). Social motivation. *Annual Review of Psychology, 38,* 461–489.

Schneider, B. (1985). Organizational behavior. *Annual Review of Psychology, 36,* 573–611.

Showers, C., & Cantor, N. (1985). Social cognition: A look at motivated strategies. *Annual Review of Psychology, 36,* 275–305.

Siebold, G. L., & Kelly, D. R. (1988). *The impact of cohesion on platoon performance at the Joint Readiness Training Center* (Technical Report 812). Alexandria, VA: U.S. Army Research Institute for the Behavioral and Social Sciences. (DTIC No. AD A202926)

Siebold, G. L., & Lindsay, T. J. (1991). Correlations among ratings of platoon performance. *Proceedings of the 33rd Annual Conference of the Military Testing Association* (pp. 67–72). San Antonio, TX: U.S. Air Force Armstrong Laboratory Human Resources Directorate and the U.S. Air Force Occupational Measurement Squadron.

Staw, B. M. (1984). Organizational behavior: A review and reformulation of the field's outcome variables. *Annual Review of Psychology, 35,* 627–66.

Townsend, R. (1970). *Up the organization.* New York: Fawcett Crest Books.

Tremble, T. R., Jr., & Alderks, C. E. (1991). *Measures for research on small unit preparedness for combat effectiveness* (Research Note 92-03). Alexandria, VA: U.S. Army Research Institute for the Behavioral and Social Sciences. (DTIC No. AD A242717)

Twohig, P. T., & Tremble, T. R., Jr. (1991). *Leadership performance measurement in a tactical environment.* (Research Report 1580). Alexandria, VA: U.S. Army Research Institute for the Behavioral and Social Sciences. (DTIC No. AD A232792)

Tziner, A., & Eden, D. (1985). Effects of crew composition on crew performance: Does the whole equal the sum of its parts? *Journal of Applied Psychology, 70,* 85–93.

Vecchio, R. P. (1990). Theoretical and empirical examination of cognitive resource theory. *Journal of Applied Psychology, 75,* 141–147.

Weick, K. E., & Sandelands, L. E. (1990). Social behavior in organizational studies. *Journal for the Theory of Social Behaviour, 20,* 323–346.

10 Psychological Resistance in Task Motivation and Performance

W. Curtis Banks
Howard University

There exists in the domain of motivation and performance an enigmatic phenomenon that is much encountered but little acknowledged. Much work in the field of psychology implicitly alludes to it. The issue is, why is it that some individuals with sufficient ability and strong motivation nonetheless do not produce under certain supervisory conditions? The name of this phenomenon is resistance.

My students and I were led to this acknowledgment by two different streams of work: one on self-concept in Blacks, which led us to some experimentation on resistance that we refer to here; the other, a program of research on comparative motivation in children, across gender and across race. This latter stream of work helped us to realize how significant such a process might be in shaping performance orientations. It had already occurred to psychologists that oftentimes an absence of performance can occur in the presence of ability. This realization, at the time, seemed like something of an ideological (if not a theoretical) breakthrough in our thinking about minority academic success. What this led to, however, was the notion that absence of performance denotes an absence of motivation. But our research suggested this might not necessarily be the case.

We had already established (Banks, McQuater, & Hubbard, 1977) that the new trait deficiency (deficiency of intrinsic motivation in Blacks) was invalid, through a cynical radical behaviorist twist of the concept of motivation. We argued that motivation, as a quality of the person, may not actually exist at all, that its existence is merely a figment of our language. As such, it is nothing more than the fiction we invoke to explain observations whose causes are not apparent—performance in the absence of reinforcers. This practice persists, we argued, largely because we are unaware of the acquired reinforcement properties of many of the stimulus features in task situations, chief among them the reinforcement value of the task itself—which in turn expresses itself in subject reports of interest.

We have argued generally that successful models of motivation and performance are likely to focus largely upon the task situation, and upon an analysis of the various stimulus features that operate in those contexts (Banks, McQuater, & Hubbard, 1978). Beginning first with an understanding of the properties of tasks themselves that impact upon the motivation of individuals to perform (Banks, McQuater, & Hubbard, 1977), such an approach would encompass a systematic examination of the social and interpersonal dynamics of task situations and the manner in which those components influence motivation and/or performance interactively with task properties.

Early approaches to understanding the bases of performance under such "nonreinforcing" circumstances as academic settings revolved around the notion of intrinsic motivation as a person-construct. Katz (1967), for example, described the critical basis of motivation as the ability of persons to sustain effort in the absence of extrinsic rewards. In this regard, persons who fail to measure up to a normative standard of success within a given environment have been described as lacking in the ability to marshall those skills of self-maintenance by which productivity is sustained under conditions of nonreinforcement.

Banks and his associates (1978) have reinterpreted that process as relying upon the acquired ability of stimuli contained within such situations to sustain the performance of different individuals. What comes to be referred to colloquially as interest, they have argued, is the tendency for certain stimulus-related behavior to be maintained in contexts from which apparent reinforcers are absent. Interest, then, represents the acquired significance of certain stimuli for a given individual, and it is largely the prior reinforcement associations that relate to highly specific classes of stimulus experiences that form the foundation of the interest-value of achievement tasks, achievement goals, and the "intrinsic motivation" by which effort toward them is maintained. Moreover, these investigators have demonstrated the predictable relationship between *intrinsic* motivational orientations and task interests, as well as the ethnic-specificity of those task orientations. Even in some early investigations where the effects of task-interest have been studied, the pattern of results anticipated this general notion (Lefcourt & Ladwig, 1965; Williams & Stack, 1972).

Williams and Stack (1972) presented Black college students with the task of preparing a persuasive statement to be delivered to another subject on one of two topics: "The contributions made by Black individuals to society" or "The role of the U.S. Vice-President in national and foreign affairs." The former task was conceived as having high interest-value, while the latter was conceived of as low in interest-value for the subject population. Consistent with the hypotheses, subjects spent more time reading and seeking information from available sources in preparation for the high-interest task than in preparation for the low-interest task.

In a study of task persistence, Lefcourt and Ladwig (1965) engaged prison inmates in a "match game" with a competitor (a confederate of the experimenters). The subjects were led to believe either that skill at the task was related to an activity of high or of low interest to them and that they could play as many games as they wished. In all instances, the "competitor" won all the games. Under these conditions of consistent failure, subjects who believed that the task related to high interest skills persisted longer than did subjects whose interest in skill-relevant activities was low.

Banks, McQuater, and Hubbard (1977) undertook an examination of the relationship of task-interest to effort orientations in adolescents. Using the cognitive paradigm employed by Weiner and Peter (1973), they asked 16- to 18-year olds to make achievement judgments in response to reports about the activities of other teenagers. Earlier, that population had been pretested for task-liking on a list of various activities. Tasks that were found to be subjectively equivalent as high or low in interest value had been selected for each sex and race subgroup. In this manner, all subjects were given an opportunity to respond with evaluative judgments in activities that were equal in high interest and in low interest value.

Black adolescents were found to be equally effort-oriented toward high-interest tasks as were White adolescents. Furthermore, effort orientations in achievement judgments were found overall to be greater in high-interest tasks than in low-interest tasks, and effort orientations in low-interest tasks were not different across the samples.

When we systematically surveyed Black and White children, from 6- to 18-years-old, male and female, about the interest value of various tasks and activities, we found a tremendous diversity. All previous research on performance motivation in children, up to that time, which had held task constant, across age, gender, and race had found significant differences among those groups in motivational orientations. What we did was hold, not task, but task interest, constant; and we found virtually no differences among groups, except for linear effects of age. In short, we found that on high interest tasks, both Black and White children were equally strong in their effort-orientations to performance. And on low interest tasks, they were uniformly weak.

But when we went further we found something else. We systematically manipulated a supervisory element in the task situation. For some tasks this was a group leader, for others a coach, or an instructor—someone whose role was that of evaluator and monitor of performance. We varied the positive or negative evaluative role of the supervisor and the racial identity as well, all under conditions of high interest tasks.

What we found was that Black adolescents responded to high interested task situations as though they had no motivation, when the supervisor was Black and nonsupportive. The results were similar when the supervisor was supportive, and White!

At the same time, a separate team of students was working on the question

"Why do Black people not have low self-esteem in the presence of racial preju-
dice and rejection?" It seemed logical, at least in theory, to Kenneth Clark and
even the Supreme Court, that they should. But we had found that Black subjects
had virtually never expressed self-rejection, preference for Whites, or low self-
esteem (Banks, McQuater, & Ross, 1979).

That led us (Banks, Stitt, Curtis, & McQuater, 1977) to develop an experimental paradigm to study psychological resistance, specifically resistance to
reinforcement. We gave subjects a novel self-monitoring task to perform, without any direct source of feedback about how well they were doing. Instead, they
were dependent upon the observation and feedback of a supervisor, who in-
structed them as to the quality of their performance and the best strategies they
could employ to improve it. We ensured that they coincidentally noticed that the
supervisor was either White or Black, since for the duration of the procedure they
would have no face-to-face contact.

When corrective feedback and down-rating came from a Black supervisor,
Black subjects' self-evaluative judgments declined, and they reported feeling less
proficient at the task. Their performance strategy changed, and they complied
with the supervisor's recommendations of increasing the use of certain techniques.

When the same feedback came from a White supervisor the results were quite
different. Self-evaluative judgments did not change. Subjects continued to hold
to their initial opinions about their proficiency at the task. Performance strategy
remained unchanged as they virtually ignored the supervisor's instruction to use
other techniques.

What this showed us was that in some task situations performance may not be
a product of either ability or motivation. In fact, where an individual's response
to supervisory intervention is one of resistance, the other reinforcement properties of the task situation may be undermined and the resultant performance may
stimulate either low ability or low motivation, or both.

For our present discussion one interesting implication of this conceptualization concerns performance in a nonsupportive (or nonreinforcing) context. As an
expression of affect toward a goal, desires, and wishes reflect the level of
significance which that goal stimulus has for the individual. If the resultant
tendency to exert behavior toward a goal is a function of the net (reinforcement)
sum of stimulus values associated with the context in which that behavior occurs,
one means of off-setting the effects of negative or nonreinforcing elements is by
elevating others that provide positive incentive. In this sense, the socialization of
extraordinarily high aspirations among those populations in which achievement
success is relatively rare, may have the purpose of providing a precompensating
incentive for sustaining efforts against a plethora of extrinsic forces likely to be
encountered in the environment. Additionally, an elevation of self-esteem could
serve two important purposes: it would provide for sustenance of the perceived
importance of self-held aspiratonal orientations, and it would serve to provide

some materially supportive basis (one's own capabilities and skills) for potentially favorable outcomes.

Cast more broadly, we may conceive of the functional roles of these elements in sustaining behavior for any individual, as well as for those particular persons beset by obstacles. From a social-learning point-of-view, an individual functions largely as a result of the stimulus forces that surround him (Mischel, 1984). However, in conjunction with those objective stimuli, the cognitive mediating processes by which the individual imparts meaning to his reinforcement experiences provide a mechanism for altering the relationships between the external stimulus events themselves and his resultant behavior (Bandura, 1986). These mechanisms play a critically important role in the adaptation of the individual. In some instances they permit the operation of remote stimulus events upon the individual's behavior as if they were proximal, and thereby facilitate the vicarious acquisition of reward-evoking appropriate behaviors (i.e., observational learning). Likewise, they can serve to buffer the individual against the effects of certain negative stimulus imposititions and preserve self-esteem and motivation, often by rendering the impact of proximal stimuli as if they were distal (see Banks, McQuater, & Hubbard, 1977).

This has led us to a reexamination of a much overlooked element in behavior—Bandura and Walters' (1963) fifth principle in social learning. In their formulation of a social learning theory of behavior, Bandura and Walters identified five essential principles: (a) the effects of rewards (or positive reinforcement) in increasing the occurrence of behavior; (b) the effects of punishment in reducing the occurrence of behavior; (c) the effects of generalization and discrimination processes; (d) the effects of observation upon learning; and (e) the effects of prior learning and situational factors on social influence attempts. The first three of these principles have, of course, received wide attention, both theoretically and empirically, in animal and human research into motivation and performance. The fourth principle, while virtually ignored in animal research, has been the focus of a large body of work, especially on the development of behavior in children. But the fifth principle, although fundamental to the human capacity for social appraisal and cognitive mediation, has received little systematic attention in the analysis of the dynamics of motivation and performance.

The phenomenon of resistance could be recast in terms of a more general theory of reinforcement systems and the social learning processes that govern behaviors within them. In this respect, social constraints may constitute negative reinforcement events, and one kind of resistance (e.g., reactance, hypothesized by Brehm (1966) may derive largely from the interactions between the incentive features that characterize task and goal stimuli and the severity of the constraints. The incentives contained within the setting may determine the severity of potential losses associated with constraints. Moreover, the compensation provided in part by elevated affect toward the goal and toward the self will come into play most clearly where "negative" reinforcement events bar access to valuable outcomes.

Banks, Stitt, Curtis, and McQuater (1977) conducted studies that lend some support to this notion. Faced with the negative reinforcement of an evaluative agent (supervisor) who was perceived to be obstructively nonobjective, Black college students showed quite different responses as a function of the severity of potential loss. Where the goal carried no clear outcome value, affect toward self was sustained at a moderately positive level by its resistance to change. However, where the goal carried valuable outcome consequences (payment), affect toward self was elevated to peculiarly high levels in anticipation of the esteem-losses that might attend compliance with an obstructive and nonobjective system of supervision. Subjects in this latter condition had no choice but to work within a system where they would be beset by constraints, in order to achieve a desired goal. Although one effect of that experience was to reduce the level of self-perceived ability, such losses (together with the potential losses associated with obstruction from the goal) were handled by a precompensation of "over-esteem."

Bandura and Walters (1963) suggested that the individual mediates the effects of reinforcements by assigning meaning to those events, perhaps through some appraisal of the intentions that they represent (Mischel, 1973). Banks, Stitt, Curtis, and McQuater (1977) have similarly argued that the primary cognitive strategy that mediates the effects of reinforcement events upon the individual derives from the need to distinguish those events that have objective information value for the individual from those that do not. They further surmise that the objective information value of any event consists of the extent to which that event is related to the behavior of the actor. In this regard, the important features of any reinforcement context are the events upon which reinforcements are contingent and the apparent events to which they are instrumental. Those reinforcement events that are contingent upon the prior behaviors of the individual provide the greatest degree of evaluative insight into the nature and proficiency of his emitted actions. Furthermore, those reinforcement events that are instrumental to some future goal object and its attainment by the acting individual provide the most information concerning the value of future behavioral alternatives.

We have found (Banks, Stitt, Curtis, & McQuater, 1977) that the social cognitive strategies by which individuals make judgments about the information value of reinforcements greatly affect the impact of such events upon esteem and behavior. Individuals were observed to engage in very little performance change in response to reinforcements perceived as neither contingent upon their behavior nor instrumental to their success goals. Likewise, there were no losses in self-esteem in connection with reinforcement events when they were perceived as contingent upon and instrumental to factors other than the recipient's behaviors and objectives.

We believe that the solution of some significant dilemmas in this field of inquiry may be accomplished by going beyond past simplistic analyses of inter-personal characteristics in task settings, and examining the underlying functional processes that mediate their effects on motivation and performance. For example, we have offered a model of the mediating processes that govern this discrimination, relying heavily upon attributional theories of social cognition. We argue that the discriminant decisions that individuals make of whether to comply with or resist supervisory direction depend on the final judgments they make about the objectivity, and resultant information value, of the feedback and directions they receive from a supervisor (Banks, Stitt, Curtis, & McQuater, 1977). The selectivity in motivation and performance reported in some research (e.g., Katz, Henchy, & Allen, 1968; Nelson-LeGall & Jones, 1990; O'Callaghan & Bryant, 1990) could therefore be understood in terms of rational judgmental processes that derive from the social information contained in task situations. One such source of information has to do with the characteristics of the supervising other; and such characteristics as race, gender, age, or expertise thereby play a significant role in shaping the performance orientations of the individual.

From this vantage point, an understanding of variations in task motivation and performance may rest upon an understanding of the social-cognitive judgments made by an individual regarding the evaluative feedback and direction received from supervisors. Notwithstanding the inherent properties of the task itself for eliciting and maintaining performance, *motivation* to perform may rise or fall with the nature of the relationship between the performer and supervisor. Furthermore, the nature of that relationship may be governed by interactive variables, not limited to simple dimensions of demographics, but including such factors as the supervisor's motives (Banks, Stitt, Curtis, & McQuater, 1977), his or her experiential similarity to the performer (Banks, 1976), or accountability to superordinate intervention.

Moreover, such an analysis of the dynamics underlying motivation could help us understand both sides of the performance supervision equation. On the one hand, why is it that some individuals with sufficient ability and strong motivation nonetheless do not produce under certain supervisory conditions? On the other hand, why is it that some supervisors make decisions to manage performance in ways that systematically undermine motivation and limit performance? Some research already provides preliminary answers to this latter question.

Banks (1976) theorized that certain dimensions of person-perception may affect the judgments individuals make about the most efficient means for managing behavior. Extending Jones and Nisbett's (1971) hypothesis regarding actor-observer differences in causal attributions, Banks hypothesized that observers will vary along a dispositional-situational continuum in their attributions concerning other individuals. Individuals dissimilar to the observer will be seen as more dispositional in the causes for their behaviors, and individuals similar to the observer will be seen as more situational. Accordingly, observers will assign more responsibility to dissimilar individuals for successful and for unsuccessful performances than to similar individuals. Some of the resultant predictions were obvious, others were counterintuitive.

Placed in the role of supervisor, subjects systematically punished the poor performance of a personally dissimilar performer more than the same performance of a personally similar performer (Banks, 1976). When the performance observed was identically successful, it was rewarded more for a performer dissimilar to the supervisor than for a performer similar to the supervisor. Not only may this help to explains systematic differences in disciplinary and corrective strategies of supervision across varying performer populations, it may explain the even more enigmatic tendency for some supervisors to overreward some performers in a systematic and discriminatory way. Aside from the broad social-ethical implications of such patterns of discrimination, the technical ramifications of such decisions for undermining motivation and performance could be significant Banks, 1976). Certainly when combined with the complex social cognitive processes that may evoke psychological resistance within performers in task situations, the judgmental phenomena governing supervisor strategies could explain some very confusing and seemingly intractible traditional problems in the management of performance.

It is important also that this approach to understanding problems of motivation and performance could help us to move from the social variables associated with resistance to an analysis of the mediating variables of cognitive judgment that most directly affect resistance behavior. Although global factors of race and/or gender may be the ostensible antecedents of resistance in some performance settings, the functional processes that are elicited by those factors may be the proximal causes of problems in performance. Insofar as that is true, the effects of social variables should be alterable through the manipulation of other factors aimed at intervening in the judgmental process by which social variables have their impact (Graham, 1988).

Moreover, aside from the theoretical implications of this discussion, there are important practical implications for the kinds of applications that are likely to benefit from the resultant insight. Our ultimate goal in understanding motivation and performance is to provide a base of knowledge that will permit the enhancement of performance, across a range of task contexts and across a range of individuals acting within them. For this purpose, analyses of task situations are more likely to yield evidence that will lend itself to programs of performance management, and the development of training and supervisory strategies that will optimize individual performance within a diverse and constantly changing population. This goal fits not only with the demands of civilian labor environments, but with military personnel applications, and even with the challenges encountered at every level of formal academic and vocational education.

ACKNOWLEDGMENTS

The research reported in this chapter was supported in part by the U.S. Army Research Institute for Behavioral and Social Sciences through a subcontract with Battelle Institute. However, the views, opinions and/or findings contained in this report are the author's and should not be construed as an official ARI position, policy, or decision, unless so designated by other official documentation.

REFERENCES

Bandura, A. (1986). *Social foundations of thought and action: A social-cognitive theory.* Englewood Cliffs, NJ: Prentice-Hall.

Bandura, A., & Walters, R. H. (1963). *Social learning and personality development.* New York: Holt, Rinehart & Winston.

Banks, W. C. (1976). The effects of perceived similarity upon the use of reward and punishment. *Journal of Experimental Social Psychology, 12,* 131–138.

Banks, W. C., McQuater, G. V., & Hubbard, J. L. (1977). Task-liking and intrinsic-extrinsic achievement orientations in blacks. *The Journal of Black Psychology, 3*(2), 61–71.

Banks, W. C., McQuater, G. V., & Hubbard, J. L. (1978). Toward a reconceptualization of the social-cognitive bases of achievement orientations in blacks. *Review of Educational Research, 48*(3), 381–397.

Banks, W. C., Stitt, K. R., Curtis, H. A., & McQuater, G. V. (1977). Perceived objectivity and the effects of evaluative reinforcement upon compliance and self-evaluation in blacks. *Journal of Experimental Social Psychology, 13,* 452–463.

Banks, W. C., McQuater, G. V., & Ross, J. (1979). On the importance of White-preference and the comparative difference of Blacks and others: A reply to Williams and Morland. *Psychological Bulletin, 85,* 33–36.

Brehm, J. W. (1966). *A theory of psychological reactance.* New York: Academic Press.

Graham, S. (1988). Can attribution theory tell us something about motivation in Blacks? *Educational Psychologist, 23*(1), 3–21.

Jones, E. E., & Nisbett, R. E. (1971). The actor and the observer: divergent perception of the causes of behavior. In E. E. Jones et al. (Eds.), *Attribution: Perceiving the causes of behavior.* Morristown: General Learning Press.

Katz, I. (1967). The socialization of academic motivation in minority group children. In D. Levine (Ed.), *Nebraska symposium on motivation.* University of Nebraska Press, *15,* 133–191.

Katz, I., Henchy, T., & Allen, H. (1968). Effects of race of tester approval-disapproval and need on Negro children's learning. *Journal of Personality and Social Psychology, 8,* 38–42.

Lefcourt, H. M., & Ladwig, G. W. (1965). The American Negro: A problem in expectancies. *Journal of Personality and Social Psychology, 1*(4), 377–380.

Mischel, W. (1973). Toward a cognitive social learning reconceptualization of personality. *Psychological Review, 80,* 252–283.

Mischel, W. (1984). Convergences and challenges in the search for consistency. *American Psychologist, 39,* 351–364.

Nelson-LeGall, S., & Jones, E. (1990). Cognitive-motivational influences on the task-related help-seeking behavior of Black children. *Child Development, 61*(2), 581–589.

O'Callaghan, K. W., & Bryant, C. (1990). Noncognitive variables: A key to Black American academic success at a military academy? *Journal of College Student Development, 31*(2), 121–126.

Weiner, B., & Peter, N. (1973). A cognitive-developmental analysis of achievement and moral judgments. *Developmental Psychology, 9*(3), 290–309.

Williams, J., & Stack, J. (1972). Internal-external control as a situational variable in determining information seeking by Negro students. *Journal of Consulting and Clinical Psychology, 39,* 187–193.

11

Stress Induced Anxiety of Individuals and Teams in a Simulator Environment

James Franken
Troy State University

Harold F. O'Neil, Jr.
University of Southern California/CRESST

Almost all elements that make up the U.S. Navy must work in team situations to "get the job done." One of the most critical of these elements today is that of Anti-Submarine Warfare (ASW). Anti-Submarine Warfare is the art of defensive or aggressive measures to neutralize enemy submarines. In our study, antisubmarine warfare focused on the use of aircraft against submarines.

As the equipment and tactics used in Anti-Submarine Warfare become increasingly complex and the importance of the submarine-hunting process increases due to the shrinking defense budget and world events, increased pressure is being applied on the teams involved. Because of the cost of actual in-flight training, the military is relying more heavily on simulators to train their aircrew teams.

Simulators are designed to be used in training and evaluation in lieu of the actual system itself. Use of simulators is safer, more economical, and more convenient than training in the real system. Simulators can also support training in a broader range of skills and functions than is possible in the real system. In general, training simulators are designed to replace the practice that would otherwise take place in the system itself plus essential practice, not possible in the real system itself (Flexman & Stark, 1987; McWilliams & Ricard, 1987; O'Neil & Robertson, 1992).

The P-3 Aircrew Tactical Trainer (Simulator) is just such a simulation, and it simulates the P-3 aircraft. It has positions (stations) for the crewmembers to sit at that are exactly like those in the real aircraft. The electronic equipment that the crewmembers operate is exactly the same as that in the aircraft and performs identically. Communication between crew members is the same and the cockpit simulator can even be connected with the tactical trainer simulator to practice with a complete aircrew complement. The simulator operator can induce problems with the equipment to simulate malfunctions the team members might experience in the aircraft. The simulator operator can also simulate most types of ship, submarine, or aircraft signatures for the crew to practice on. Weapon drops can be simulated, and actual noises that the crew would hear in the ocean are simulated. Such simulators are also used for testing or assessment, using different scenarios. Scenarios are defined as a description of the conditions in effect at the time the mission in initiated, a script of conditions and parameters that will change during the mission, and what those changes are.

There may be social implications and side effects of such simulator testing. U.S. Navy P-3 tactical teams have to successfully perform annual qualification testing (Quals) to achieve required readiness levels. Failure to do so creates severe impact on a team's social standing within their community, and the side effects of failure can be harsh. The results directly impact a squadron's readiness and reflect professional competence of the individuals and the team. Further, such performance impacts on future promotions, peer recognition, personnel evaluations, and the assigning of additional practice exercises. The loss of a team qualification may result in a change of crewmembers or geographical location, down-grading of squadron readiness, and a loss of self-esteem. These results lead to the possibility of debilitating anxiety. Consistent with this interpretation, Spielberger, Gonzalez, Taylor, Algaze, and Anton (1978) view stress as predominantly an external event that, when viewed as ego threatening, results in anxiety. It becomes a problem only when the demands or stressors exceed the individual's coping mechanism.

The problem then becomes: Does the stress associated with qualifying aircrew teams in a simulator environment increase anxiety to the point where it affects simulator performance? Is this stress-producing anxiety more pronounced in the Qualification scenarios than in the non-Qualification scenarios? What is the impact of such anxiety on cognitive processing?

A REVIEW OF THE RELEVANT LITERATURE

A recent literature search (Franken, 1991) produced only 13 studies on stress/anxiety related to team evaluation and no specific empirical studies on the effects of stress and anxiety on team evaluation in a simulator environment. An update of the review for 1991 and the first six months of 1992 revealed no further empirical studies.

Our review was based on an exhaustive computer search of several databases, for example, Education Resources Information Center (ERIC), and the National Technical Information Service (NTIS). In addition to the computer searches, manual searches of both technical and university libraries were performed. Manual searches were performed at the University of Southern California libraries and at the Lockheed Technical Library in Burbank, California. The Lockheed Technical Library is staffed by expert reference librarians who assist Lockheed employees in acquiring needed technical articles, books, and reports. The period covered by the search was 1955–1990. Over 1,900 document titles were obtained from the sources. Descriptors used included: aircrews, antisubmarine warfare, anxiety, cockpit utilization, combat air crews, emotionality, evaluation, flight, flight crews, groups, human factors, human performance, military psychology, naval training, physiology, psychology, simulator, stress, team teaching, team training, teams, teamwork, test anxiety, train, trainer, and training devices. The document titles were reviewed for salient titles and abstracts were ordered. The abstracts were reviewed and reports that were deemed applicable to the study were ordered and read. The literature discussion is organized around three major topic areas: stress and anxiety, team training, and assessing performance in simulators.

Stress and Anxiety

Stress is perceived as a threat, to which the subsequent response may be anxiety. A stressful situation is one containing stimuli or circumstances calculated to arouse anxiety in the individual (Spielberger, 1972; Spielberger et al., 1978). Spielberger (1975) has also suggested two views of anxiety—as a trait and as a state. State anxiety is viewed as a transitory emotional state that varies in intensity and fluctuates over time. It is characterized by tension and apprehension, and activation of the autonomic nervous system. Trait anxiety is conceptualized as a relatively stable difference in anxiety proneness. Trait anxiety is an individual difference variable response to situations perceived as threatening with elevations in state anxiety.

Liebert and Morris (1967), shifting test anxiety theory toward a cognitive orientation, further proposed that anxiety be broken into two components, worry and emotionality. They defined worry as the cognitive elements of the anxiety experience, such as negative expectations and cognitive concerns about oneself, the situation at hand, and potential consequences. They defined emotionality as one's perception of the physiological-affective elements of the anxiety experience, that is, indications of autonomic arousal and unpleasant feeling states such as nervousness and tension (Liebert & Morris, 1967; Morris, Davis, & Hutchings, 1981).

There are measures of both trait and state components of worry and emotionality. The Test Anxiety Inventory, developed by Spielberger (1980), is a self-report inventory developed to measure individual differences in test anxiety (trait) as a situation-specific personality trait (Spielberger, 1972, 1980). It measures both trait worry and trait emotionality. The revised worry and emotionality state scale measures both state worry and state emotionality (Morris et al., 1981).

Fiedler (1989) suggested that the findings regarding stress and anxiety also seem applicable to the area of leadership. It seems likely that this particular type of stress distracts the leader from concentrating on the job. There is ample evidence that stress plays a very important part in organizational life (e.g., Buck, 1972; McGrath & Altman, 1966). Also, Borden (1980) and Fiedler, Potter, Zais, and Knowlton (1979), among others, have pointed out that a stress-producing boss is typically seen as a critical evaluator of one's work.

Hembree (1988) reported the results of a meta-analysis of 562 studies in the area of test anxiety covering the time period from 1952 to 1988. Hembree found that test anxiety (particularly worry) causes poor performance and relates inversely to students' self-esteem and directly to their fears of negative evaluation, defensiveness, and other forms of anxiety. Other findings were: (a) The conditions that give rise to differential test anxiety levels include ability, gender, and school grade level; and (b) a variety of treatments are effective in reducing test anxiety and improving test performance and grade point average. Hembree cited no studies dealing with team anxiety or stress. O'Neil and Hedl (1990) also report that there is very little research in the area of stress induced anxiety in team training situations, either actual or simulated.

There are two major explanations of when and how anxiety interferes with test performance. It interferes either at test time or at study time. At test time, Wine (1980) proposed an attentional theory to explain how test anxiety inhibits performance: Test anxious persons divide their attention between task-relevant activities and preoccupations with worry, self-criticism, and somatic concerns (see also O'Neil & Abedi, 1992; O'Neil & Fukumura, 1992). With less attention available for task-directed efforts, their performance is depressed (a retrieval problem). An alternative "deficits" model of test anxiety has been proposed where the lower test scores obtained by test anxious students are attributable to inadequate study habits (an encoding problem) (Tobias, 1985).

One good example of the impact of stress on performance is provided by Wickens, Barnett, Stokes, Davis, and Hyman (1989). The cognitive abilities of expert and novice pilots were evaluated by a cognitive battery and assessment of a number of in-flight decisions during a simulated cross-country flight. Stress and nonstress conditions affecting pilot judgment were generated by placing the stress subjects under time pressure, dual task loading and noise stress on a simulated flight across country. It was found that stress degraded performance on those problems imposing high demand on working memory, but left unaffected performance on those problems imposing high demand on the retrieval of facts from long-term memory.

Another related aviation study by Stokes and Raby (1989) reported the effects of task-related stress on aviation-relevant cognitive skills in trainee instrument pilots using SPARTANS, an automated test battery. The battery was administered under stress and control conditions, providing data on the effects of stress manipulation upon putative cognitive components of decision making. Results found stress was related to decrements in working memory but not in declarative

memory. Both studies support the mechanism suggested in the test anxiety literature that anxiety can interfere with short-term memory; that is, one effect of
anxiety on individuals may be a retrieval problem. Finally, Larsson (1989) reported performance decrements in an antiaircraft simulator under stress induced
by noise and sleep deprivation.

Team Training

Many researchers have noted a need for prescriptive guidance in team training
and assessment as well as a lack of empirical research (Denson, 1981; Driskell &
Salas, 1992; Dyer, 1984; O'Neil, Baker, & Kazlauskas, 1992; Wagner, Hibbits,
Rosenblatt, & Schultz, 1977). This situation is cause for concern, particularly in
today's environments, where many missions and tasks require application of
coordinated teamwork for successful completion (Swezey & Salas, 1992).

   In general, different authors define teams somewhat differently. For example,
Nieva, Fleishman, and Rieck (1985) and Fleishman and Zaccaro (1992) developed a conceptual team performance model by making a clear distinction between individual task performance and team performance functions that allow
the individual members to function as a unit. Their provisional team performance
taxonomy is made up of dimensions contained within four categories of functions: orientation, organization, adaptation, and motivation. The team training
areas most often cited (Morgan, Glickman, Woodard, Blaiwes, & Salas, 1986;
Nieva et al., 1985; Shiflett, Eisner, Price, & Schemmer, 1982; Swezey & Salas,
1992) are team function, team dimensions, team performance, and team behaviors.

   In general, reviews of team training research do not cite any research on
stress/anxiety and teams. Dyer (1984) suggested that teams, especially military
teams, are under considerable stress and pressure at times and much more information is needed in these areas. However, she cited no studies of such research in
her review. Denson (1981) published a review of team training and annotated
bibliography for 1955–1979 in which nothing on stress/anxiety in teams was
cited. Another review of team training was conducted by Briggs and Johnston
(1967) with no mention of anxiety or stress in training situations. While there are
a number of studies on team/crew performance measurement systems, for instance, Obermayer, Vreuls, Muckler, Conway, and Fitzgerald (1974), they do
not address the anxiety aspect of crew performance in training situations.

Assessing Performance of Teams in Simulators

Crew (team) factors research has been greatly enhanced by the use of simulators.
Over the past 10 years, aviation research has moved from a more or less exclusive focus on ensuring and enhancing the technical proficiency of individual
pilots to a concern with the process of crew coordination and communication.

This method of performance assessment using simulators with full-mission scenarios has led to increased crew effectiveness and related safety in flying (Chidester & Foushee, 1989; Chidester, Kanki, & Helmreich, 1989; Foushee, Lauber, Baetge, & Acomb, 1991). However, we were unable to identify any empirical studies that manipulated stress and anxiety of teams in a simulator.

The purpose of this study is to determine to what degree trait and state anxiety are found in individuals and teams during high and low stress simulator scenarios and what is the effect on individual and team performance. In addition, a questionnaire was used to survey the teams to assess team attributes, and a metacognitive skill questionnaire was used to assess changes in cognition over time.

METHODOLOGY

Sample

Subjects were U.S. Navy P-3 Anti-Submarine Warfare Tactical Aircrews based at various Navy land-based air fields. P-3 aircraft are landbased, Lockheed built, 4-engine turbo-prop aircraft used for open ocean surveillance and tracking of submarines. P-3s normally hold a crew of 12, consisting of three pilots, two flight engineers, one tactical coordinator, one communicator/navigator, two acoustic sensor personnel, one nonacoustic sensor personnel, one ordinanceman, and one in-flight maintenance technician.

Tactical Team

The P-3 crew is broken down in a smaller group or tactical team. The tactical team consists of a nucleus of five team members who operate the five computerized electronic stations in the aircraft and work as a team to collect the information necessary for locating and tracking submarines. The leader of this team is the tactical coordinator (TACCO) who is an officer and coordinates the use of all electronic sensors and directs the crew efforts to perform the mission. He drops sonobuoys (devices that send sound in the ocean up to the aircraft) at strategic locations in the ocean. He also can drop weapons on the submarine or instruct the pilots to do it. The other officer of the 5-member team is the communicator/navigator (NAV) who handles mission radio communications and provides navigation services. He keeps track of where the aircraft is at all times, plots courses to take the aircraft where it has to go, and handles all of the radio communications for the aircraft except for the safety of the flight. There are two enlisted team members in acoustic stations (Sensor 1 and 2) who operate the acoustic processing stations and provide mission information to the TACCO. Acoustics is the art of determining an underwater sound source from frequencies on an electronic screen or by aurally listening (sonar). This process is the major means for detecting submarines underwater.

The Sensor 1 position is the senior of the two and usually trains the Sensor 2 position. The last member of the tactical team is the enlisted Sensor 3 position. He uses Magnetic Anomaly Detection (MAD) equipment to locate a submarine underwater with a device similar to the one geologists use to find iron ore deposits from the air. He also uses electronic equipment such as RADAR and RADAR emission findings to locate surface, land, and air targets. He operates the identification friend or foe equipment and the infra-red detection equipment.

All of the subjects who participated in this study graduated from U.S. Navy training courses before obtaining their respective positions on the aircraft. For example, the Navigation Officers attends a 5-month ground training course at the fleet replacement squadron. The course consists of classroom and simulator training. Following the ground course, the Navigation Officer flies for a month with a crew made up of other students and instructors. The Sensor position training is similar to that of the Navigation Officer. Sensors have their own ground course at fleet replacement squadrons and then, in the last month, go into the flight phase. The P-3 aircrews are made up of assigned teams who fly and work together as distinct, separate groups. Because of the necessity to maintain annual qualifications, squadrons strive to maintain consistency in aircrews. If a tactical team member is replaced on a crew, then the whole crew must redo all the qualifications or assessments (re-qual). Competition and esprit de corps among crews within a squadron is the norm.

A sample of 25 aircrews (125 subjects) participated from a population of approximately 264 active duty P-3 aircrews worldwide, for an approximate 10% sample. All subjects were male, consistent with the population which is less than 1% female. The crew members had varying amounts of experience both at their positions and on their team, which is normal for the population, as each crew has both experienced people and people in training. The Sensor 2 position is normally training for an eventual Sensor 1 position and the Navigation Officer is normally training for the TACCO position.

Qualification Process

The U.S. Navy command (Wing) had crews already scheduled for either Qual or Non-Qual scenarios. (A Wing is a naval command that controls several squadrons of aircraft, in our case, P-3 antisubmarine aircraft squadrons.) Crews have to be qualified on an annual basis. If they fail to meet the time limits on their Quals, they can be reduced in readiness level. Therefore, the Navy command assigns the crews to Qual and Non-Qual simulator exercises on an annual rotating schedule. The squadron itself and crews within it have "readiness" levels. These levels represent how trained (ready) a crew is to go out and hunt submarines. There are about a dozen qualifications (Quals) a crew must successfully pass to reach alpha level, or the top readiness level. A bravo crew would have most of the Quals but not all of them (alpha level). The squadron is rated alpha, bravo, etc., depending on how many of the crews are alpha, bravo, etc. These

Quals must be maintained on an annual basis. All crews are allowed so many Non-Qual exercises before they are scheduled for the Qual exercises.

Fourteen of the aircrews (teams) participated in Qual scenarios while the remaining 11 aircrews (teams) participated in Non-Qual scenarios. None of the crews (teams) used in this study participated in both Qual and Non-Qual scenarios. Teams used in this study were not randomly assigned to either Qual or Non-Qual simulator exercises. They were scheduled by the U.S. Navy in their normal order of rotation for these exercises. The scenario used was procedurally the same for all the crews, although the type of submarine and location in the world may have been different. For example, one crew may utilize a scenario where they are hunting a diesel submarine off the Aleutian islands in winter, and another crew may be hunting a nuclear submarine off Japan in summer. Details of equipment settings, submarine and water characteristics are classified; however, the procedures or steps taken by the crew in hunting different types of submarines in different parts of the world are basically the same. Stress is also manipulated by the following task factors: type of submarine, area of operations, equipment malfunctions, type of mission, multiple targets, and water conditions.

The annual qualifications (Qual) each aircrew must successfully master are practiced (for Non-Qual) and ultimately evaluated in a simulator. The U.S. Navy uses simulators for qualification training and testing instead of using the actual aircraft. The simulator allows the team to conduct Anti-Submarine Warfare exercises almost exactly as they would on the aircraft. Teams perform the exercises at all hours of the day or night in the simulator, just as they would in the aircraft. Although there is no motion as in the aircraft, everything else is the same. The seating, equipment, communications, and lighting are the same as found in the aircraft. A computer-generated replay system and visual monitor allows for replay of the exercise for debriefing of the aircrew following the session. Also, monitors are available for instructors to keep track of how each team member is performing during practice (Non-Qual) and evaluation (Qual) sessions. For practice sessions, the instructors can input changes and additions to the tactical scenario; however, neither Qual nor Non-Qual teams used in this study were manipulated by the operator. During the evaluation sessions, the instructors only monitor the teams' progress and evaluate them using set criteria. Evaluation forms are the same for both Qual and Non-Qual groups.

The mean number of months of experience for the Qual group (treatment group) was 57.64 (SD = 51.48), whereas the mean number of months of experience for the Non-Qual group (control group) was 41.22 (SD = 39.94). These differences were statistically significant (t = 1.95, df = 123, p = .056). With respect to how long each team member has been a member of his specific team in months, the Qual group had more time on their respective teams (M = 18.57, SD = 24.33) than the Non-Qual group (M = 11.06, SD = 9.83). However, these differences were not statistically significant (t = 1.75, df = 96, p < .10). Unfortunately, the groups differed before treatment in number of months of experience.

PROCEDURE

Simulator Session

A simulator session consists of a single team of five subjects and lasts for approximately 3 hours. When subjects arrived for the session, they were given an oral overview of the project and were given instructions for filling out the questionnaires. First, subjects were given the Team Characteristics Questionnaire (Franken, 1991), which asks direct questions about individuals and their team. Next the Test Anxiety Inventory (TAI) (Spielberger, 1980) was given, followed by the Revised Worry-Emotionality Questionnaire (Morris et al., 1981). Last was the Thinking Questionnaire (O'Neil, Baker, Jacoby, Ni, & Wittrock, 1990).

Following the filling out of the pretest questionnaires, the simulator instructor/observer and team leader conduct a prescenario briefing for the team (both Qual and Non-Qual groups). This briefing consists of (a) any problems to expect with the simulator equipment (not dissimilar from an actual aircraft brief), and (b) a tactical brief on what the team's mission consists of (what they are expected to do for the exercise). Immediately following the briefing, the team members take their positions in the simulator and begin a modified preflight check of the equipment (to ensure all simulator systems are working normally or as briefed). Once all positions are ready, the simulator instructor/observer begins the exercise.

The team's performance is monitored by the simulator instructor/observer through computer screens that reproduce what the five team members' computer screens show at their respective positions. In addition, the simulator operator has monitor screens that report the status of the computerized simulator and also what is happening with the simulated enemy submarine, surface ship, and aircraft. The team's communications between each other and with the simulated base commander are tape recorded with time marks at the same time that their computer initiated actions are stored on magnetic tape for use in reconstructing their actions. The five team members work at individual stations collecting data through electronic means. One of the five team members (TACCO) is the leader who coordinates all of the data collected from the other four team members and makes the ultimate mission decisions.

Performance/Grading

Following the simulator exercise (after the team fills out the posttest measures), the simulator instructor/observer debriefs the team on actions correct or incorrect. The simulator session itself is reconstructed by both computer and pencil-and-paper means, and the team members individually and as a whole are graded on their performance. This grade is based on a percentage basis with 100% being the highest grade possible. A break-down of the grading areas for each position is as follows:

TACCO/Mission Commander—How well was the team prepared for the mission; was mission planned to use the total capability of the aircraft; were passive systems used effectively; were active systems used effectively; were non-acoustic systems used effectively; were attack procedures used appropriately; and were general procedures utilized appropriately.

Navigator/Communicator—Were navigational procedures appropriate and effective; were communication procedures appropriate and effective; were written entries correct and appropriate; and were all contacts and bearings plotted as required.

Sensor 1 position—Was preflight performed correctly; was equipment utilized effectively; was classification and analysis of contacts appropriate; and was tactical information correct.

Sensor 2 position—Was preflight performed correctly; was equipment utilized effectively; was classification and analysis of contacts appropriate; and was tactical information correct.

Sensor 3 position—Was electronic equipment preflight performed correctly; was electronic equipment operation performed effectively; and was tactical information correct.

Mission Scenario

A typical mission would put the crew over some point in the ocean looking for an enemy submarine. For example, the Wing may assign the P-3 crew a 50-by-100 square mile area that it believes contains the submarine. The TACCO would place buoys in the water to send sound sources back to the Sensor 1 and 2 positions electronically. The Sensor personnel review the signatures to determine if they have located the enemy submarine or not. Meanwhile, the Navigation Officer is keeping track of the aircraft position and talking on the radios to other aircraft or to the base commander. The Sensor 3 position is busy monitoring for enemy electronic emissions from the RADAR emission finding device and blips on his RADAR screen. The TACCO, as the leader, is coordinating all the activity on board the aircraft and is responsible for determining the tactics to be used (what buoys to use, where to put them, what electronic equipment to use). Once the enemy submarine is located, if the mission requires it, the crew goes through the tactical procedure to track and kill the sub. All of the actions the crew makes in the simulator are the same as they would be in the aircraft.

Simulator Operation

The simulator has a freeplay option where the simulator operator can change ocean, submarine sound source and aircraft/surface ship emissions at will, or the simulator can have a preprogrammed automatic scenario that runs the length of time that the crew is using it. The Qual and Non-Qual scenarios used for the purpose of this study were all preprogrammed with slight variations as described earlier. The simulator device also tapes how the crew performed for a replay (following the exercise) of where buoys were dropped and where the aircraft was in relation to the submarine so they can be given correctional feedback after the exercise is over. Normally the crew is not given feedback during the exercise. Sometimes during the Non-Qual exercises, if the crew is having a lot of problems, the instructor may stop the scenario and give the crew some help. None of the subject crews used for this study were given help during the exercise. The simulator operator assigns performance grades to each member of the crew and an overall grade to the crew following the exercise. This overall team grade is the mean of the individual scores. Depending on how the crew performs, they would receive a passing or failing grade. One crew member could conceivably fail the whole crew. Qual crews not receiving a passing grade would have to re-qual at a later date after receiving additional simulator training. In our study, three Qual crews out of 14 failed the exercise, while none of the Non-Qual crews failed the exercise.

Test Anxiety Inventory (TAI)

The Test Anxiety Inventory was developed by Spielberger (1980). It is a self-report scale used to measure individual differences in test anxiety as a situation-specific personality trait (Spielberger, 1972). Respondents are asked to report how frequently they experience specific symptoms of anxiety before, during, and after examinations. In addition to measuring individual differences in anxiety proneness in test situations, the TAI subscales assess worry and emotionality as major components of test anxiety. Reliability and validity data are reported by Spielberger (1980). In our study, the alpha reliability was .93 for the total scale. Alpha reliability was .85 and .89 for the worry and emotionality subscales respectively.

Revised Worry–Emotionality Questionnaire

Respondents were asked to indicate their feelings, attitudes, or thoughts as they are at the moment just prior to a simulator session, or how they felt during the simulator experience, using the revised worry–emotionality questionnaire (Morris et al., 1981). Reliability coefficients of the questionnaire were found to be .81 and .86 respectively for worry and emotionality in a study on 222 college students (Morris et al., 1981). Validity coefficients were found to be .43 and .41 respectively for two groups of college students in course examination settings (Carden, 1979; Parks, 1980). Our scale had 10 items (5 worry and 5 emotionality). Subjects rated their feelings on a 5-point scale. In our study, the alpha reliability for the pretest worry and emotionality scales was .82 and .83 respectively, whereas the alpha reliability for the posttest worry and emotionality scales was .87 and .88 respectively.

Thinking Questionnaire

The state Thinking Questionnaire used in this study was developed by O'Neil (O'Neil et al., 1990). The 26-item thinking questionnaire was developed to be a measure of metacognition. Metacognition is viewed as consisting of planning, self-monitoring, cognitive strategies, and awareness. Self-monitoring is viewed as the conscious, periodic self-checking of one's goal achievement and, when necessary, selecting and applying different strategies. In order to self-monitor, one must have a goal, either assigned by someone else or self-directed, and a plan to achieve that goal. The plan requires cognitive or affective strategies, for example, finding the main idea. Finally, the process is conscious to the individual. Alpha reliability coefficients for the questionnaire were found to be .91 in a junior college sample and also .91 in a university sample (O'Neil et al., 1990). In our study, the measure had an alpha reliability coefficient of .92 for the pretest and an alpha reliability coefficient of .93 on the posttest.

Finally, we asked for information on each team member's position, time in position in months, time on the team in months, and if he had received Aircrew Coordination Training.

RESULTS

As stated earlier, the purpose of this study was to determine to what degree state and trait anxiety are found in individuals and teams during high and low stress simulator scenarios and its effect on performance. The analysis will be reported by individuals. The same statistical conclusions were reached when analyzed by teams (team measures were the mean of individual measures).

Cognitive and Affective Performance

The pretest measures were Spielberger's Test Anxiety Inventory (TAI), the Morris et al. (1981) revised worry and emotionality measure, and the Thinking Questionnaire (Franken, 1991; O'Neil et al., 1990). Results for all the pretest measures were found to be nonsignificant as expected. Thus, the qualification versus nonqualification groups were well matched on these measures.

The means and standard deviations for Qual/Non-Qual by individuals on posttest worry are reported in Table 11.1. The ANCOVA indicates that these differences were statistically significant (F = 89.17, df = 1/122, $p < .001$). Included in Table 11.1 are adjusted means to show the impact on the posttest scores when adjusted for pretest worry scores. The magnitude of the means in general indicated a low amount of worry. It was expected that the Qual group would have more state worry than the Non-Qual group, however, the reverse is true. Several reasons for this unexpected result are discussed later in the summa-

TABLE 11.1
Means and Standard Deviations of Post-Worry by Qual Group and Non-Qual Group

	N	Mean	SD
For Qual group	70	7.09	3.11
For Non-Qual group	55	8.60	4.21
		Adjusted Means	Std Err
Qual	70	7.28	0.33
Non-Qual	55	8.36	0.37

ry of this chapter. Results for the posttest emotionality measure between the Qual and Non-Qual groups were found to be nonsignificant.

The means and standard deviations for Qual/Non-Qual groups are reported in Table 11.2 for the postthinking questionnaire. An ANCOVA using the pretest measure as a covariable indicates that these differences were found to be significant ($F = 102.55$, df $= 1/122$, $p < .001$). The adjusted means are also shown in Table 11.2. The Qual group is putting more thought into the exercise scenario than the Non-Qual group.

Mission Performance. Each team member of both the Qual and Non-Qual groups was graded on performance. As the evaluation measures differ for each position, raw scores were converted to "T" scores. As seen in Table 11.3, the mean performance score for the Qual group was 47.58 and for the Non-Qual group, 53.07. These differences were statistically significant ($t = 3.54$, df $= 124$, $p < .001$). It was expected that the Qual group would have higher performance scores than the Non-Qual group. However, the Non-Qual group was

TABLE 11.2
Means and Standard Deviations of Posttest State Monitoring by Qual Group and Non-Qual Group

	N	Mean	SD
For Qual group	70	90.46	10.54
For Non-Qual group	55	85.28	12.00
		Adjusted Means	Std Err
Qual	70	89.81	.99
Non-Qual	55	86.10	1.12

TABLE 11.3
Means and Standard Deviations of Individual Performance by Qual and Non-Qual Groups

	N	Mean	SD
For Qual group	70	47.58	12.76
For Non-Qual group	55	53.07	2.04

found to have significantly higher performance scores overall. One reason for this is the fact that three of the Qual teams failed overall whereas no teams failed in the Non-Qual group. Interviews of the graders indicated that the Non-Qual teams are graded more easily so as to maintain team motivation. Team performance scores were also summed using individual scores for the respective team members. This summation is how the U.S. Navy "grades" team performance. The statistical conclusions were the same.

Up to this point statistical findings have been reported on pre- and posttest measures using individual team member scores for Qual and Non-Qual groups. We also analyzed the data using T scores by team position for TACCO, Navigator, Sensor 1, Sensor 2, and Sensor 3 positions. None of the differences were statistically significant. Thus, there were no differences on anxiety, metacognition, or relative performance by team position.

SUMMARY AND DISCUSSION

This study examined to what degree trait and state anxiety are found in individuals and teams during high and low stress simulator scenarios and the resultant effect on their performance. In addition, those attributes found to make up a team were examined. Fourteen teams took part in the high stress treatment or Qualification (Qual) scenarios while 11 teams participated in the low stress control or Non-Qualification (Non-Qual) scenarios.

Anxiety was assessed using self-report measures: The Spielberger (trait) Test Anxiety Inventory (TAI) for measuring trait anxiety and the Morris Revised Worry–Emotionality Scale for state anxiety. Also, the O'Neil Thinking Questionnaire was used for measuring self-monitoring. The Spielberger TAI and Team Characteristics Questionnaire were given before the simulator exercise as a pretest, while the state worry-emotionality and self-monitoring scales were given both before and after the simulator exercise.

The results indicate that the control (Non-Qual) group worried more than the treatment (Qual) group, while the treatment group exhibited more self-monitoring about what they are doing during the exercise. The control (Non-Qual) group was found to have higher performance scores than the treatment

(Qual) group (which was unexpected). These findings were true for both individuals and teams.

Interviews with the simulator instructors suggest this is normal due to harsher grading by instructors of Qual teams and easier grading of Non-Qual teams so as to motivate the teams. The treatment (Qual) group was found to have more experience in respective team positions and more time on the team. In general, our results were consistent with both the research literature and simulator state of practice.

As mentioned in the literature review, there is no empirical research concerning the role of stress and anxiety on individuals and teams in a simulator environment. Thus, it is difficult to decide what is ground truth. For example, in our study, it was unexpected that the Qual group would have less state worry than the Non-Qual group following the simulator experience. One explanation for this finding could have to do with the affective states of experts and novices on military tasks. All our subjects and teams could be viewed as experts. Some researchers suggest that highly skilled people are anxious prior to the day of the test or event, yet are not as anxious the day of the test or event. One such study involved paratroopers. In studying the effects of stress leading to anxiety on both expert and novice paratroopers, it was found anecdotally that the experts were more anxious on the day prior to the day of the jump, while the novices were more anxious on the day of the jump. Experimental results with novices supporting this assertion regarding the day of the jump are reported in Endler, Crooks, and Parker (1992). Wickens et al. (1989) report that the effects of stress (that induces a mild feeling of anxiety) were less on experts than on novices on the day of the flights. Stokes and Raby (1989) in a study also using expert and novice pilots came to basically the same conclusions as Wickens et al. (1989). Finally, Rachman (1982) suggested that expert military bomb-disposal operators report less stress (via physiological measures) than nonexperts.

It was further expected that the Qual teams would receive higher performance scores than the Non-Qual teams, due to the value placed on doing well; however, the data indicate the opposite. One explanation could be that the Qual teams were more anxious so they did not do as well but the state worry scores indicate that was not the case. The Non-Qual group was more anxious on the Morris posttest worry component than the Qual group. Our interviews indicated that the Qual groups are graded harder than the Non-Qual groups because they are being graded for qualification. The Non-Qual groups on practice exercises are graded slightly easier to keep up their motivation. Support for this assertion came from the instructors at both Navy field sites during interviews. Although the debriefings were very thorough for the Non-Qual groups, the percentage grading is not as harsh. The instructors feel it is more motivating for a group to receive a detailed debrief than a low score. However, for the Qual groups, once they pass the exercise, they are qualified to fly on that type of tactical mission as the need arises. They have to be judged harshly to determine that qualification.

ACKNOWLEDGMENTS

The research reported in this chapter was supported in part by the U.S. Army Research Institute for the Behavioral and Social Sciences through a subcontract with Battelle Institute. However, the views, opinions, and/or findings contained in this report are the authors' and should not be construed as an official ARI position, policy, or decision, unless so designated by other official documentation.

Partial support was also provided by the National Center for Research on Evaluation, Standards, and Student Testing (CRESST) under the Educational Research and Development Center Program cooperative agreement R117G10027 and CFDA catalog number 84.117G as administered by the Office of Educational Research and Improvement, U.S. Department of Education. The findings and opinions expressed in this chapter do not reflect the position of the Office of Educational Research and Improvement or the U.S. Department of Education.

REFERENCES

Borden, D. F. (1980). *Leader-boss stress, personality, job satisfaction and performance.* Unpublished doctoral dissertation, University of Washington, Seattle.

Briggs, G. E., & Johnston, W. A. (1967). *Team training. Final report* (Naval Training Device Center Report 1327-4). Orlando, FL: Naval Training Device Center.

Buck, V. E. (1972). *Working under pressure.* New York: Crane.

Carden, R. L. (1979). *The relationship of control and extraversion to test anxiety and impulsiveness.* Unpublished masters thesis, Middle Tennessee State University, Murfreesboro.

Chidester, T. R., & Foushee, C. H. (1989, April). Leader personality and crew effectiveness—A full-mission simulation experiment. In R. S. Jensen (Ed.), *Proceedings of the Fifth International Symposium on Aviation Psychology,* Columbus, OH.

Chidester, T. R., Kanki, B. G., & Helmreich, R. L. (1989, April). Performance evaluation in full-mission simulation: Methodological advances and research challenges. In R. S. Jensen (Ed.), *Proceedings of the Fifth International Symposium on Aviation Psychology,* Columbus, OH.

Denson, R. W. (1981). *Team training: Literature review and annotated bibliography* (AFHRL-TR-80-40). Wright-Patterson AFB, OH: Logistics and Technical Training Division.

Driskell, J. E., & Salas, E. (1992). Can you study real teams in contrived settings? The value of small group research to understanding teams. In R. Swezey & E. Salas (Eds.), *Teams: Their training and performance* (pp. 101–123). Norwood, NJ: Ablex.

Dyer, J. L. (1984). Team research and team training: A state-of-the-art review. In F. A. Muckler (Ed.), *Human factors review: 1984.* Santa Monica, CA: The Human Factors Society.

Endler, N. S., Crooks, D. S., & Parker, J. D. A. (1992). The interaction model of anxiety: An empirical test in a parachute training situation. *Anxiety, Stress, and Coping, 5,* 301–311.

Fiedler, F. E. (1989). The effective utilization of intellectual abilities and job-relevant knowledge in group performance: Cognitive resource theory and an agenda for the future. *Applied Psychology: An International Review, 38*(3), 289–304.

Fiedler, F. E., Potter, E. H., Zais, M. M., & Knowlton, W. A. R. (1979). Organizational stress and the use and misuse of managerial intelligence and experience. *Journal of Applied Psychology, 34,* 635–647.

Fleishman, E. A., & Zaccaro, S. J. (1992). Toward a taxonomy of team performance functions. In R. W. Swezey & E. Salas (Eds.), *Teams: Their training and performance* (pp. 31–56). Norwood, NJ: Ablex.

Flexman, R. E., & Stark, E. A. (1987). Training simulations. In G. Salvendy (Ed.), *Handbook of human factors* (pp. 1012–1038). New York: Wiley.

Foushee, H. C., Lauber, J. K., Baetge, M. M., & Acomb, D. B. (1991). *Crew factors in flight operations III: The operational significance of exposure to short-haul air transport operations.* Moffett Field, CA: NASA-Ames Research Center, Aeronautical Human Factors Research Office.

Franken, J. E. (1991). *The effects of stress induced anxiety on individuals and teams in a simulator environment.* Unpublished doctoral dissertation, University of Southern California, Los Angeles.

Hembree, R. (1988, Spring). Correlates, causes, effects, and treatment of test anxiety. *Review of Educational Research, 58*(1), 47–77.

Larsson, G. (1989). Personality, appraisal and cognitive coping processes, and performance during various conditions of stress. *Military Psychology, 1*(3), 176–182.

Liebert, R. M., & Morris, L. W. (1967). Cognitive and emotional components of test anxiety: A distinction and some initial data. *Psychological Reports, 20,* 975–978.

McGrath, J. E., & Altman, I. (1966). *Small group research: A synthesis and critique of the field.* New York: Holt, Rinehart & Winston.

McWilliams, E. D., & Ricard, G. L. (1987). Portable, intelligent simulation for ASW training. In R. J. Seidel & P. D. Weddle (Eds.), *Computer-based instruction in military environments* (pp. 41–57). New York: Plenum Press.

Morgan, B. B., Glickman, A. S., Woodard, E. A., Blaiwes, A. S., & Salas, E. (1986). *Measurement of team behaviors in a Navy environment* (Naval Training Systems Center Report TR-86-014). Orlando, FL: Naval Training Systems Center, Human Factors Division.

Morris, L. W., Davis, M. A., & Hutchings, C. H. (1981). Cognitive and emotional components of anxiety: Literature review and a revised worry-emotionality scale. *Journal of Educational Psychology, 73,* 541–555.

Nieva, V. F., Fleishman, E. A., & Rieck, A. (1985). *Team dimensions: Their identity, their measurement and their relationships* (Contract No. DAHC19-78-C-0001). Washington, DC: Advanced Research Resources Organization.

Obermayer, R. W., Vreuls, D., Muckler, F. A., Conway, E. J., & Fitzgerald, J. A. (1974). *Combat-ready crew performance measurement system: Final report* (DTIC #AD-8005-517). Brooks AFB, TX; Air Force Systems Command.

O'Neil, H. F., Jr., & Abedi, J. (1992). Japanese children's trait and state worry and emotionality in a high-stakes testing environment. *Anxiety, Stress, and Coping, 5*(3), 253–267.

O'Neil, H. F., Jr., Baker, E. L., Jacoby, A., Ni, Y., & Wittrock, M. (1990). *Human benchmarking studies of expert systems* (Report to DARPA, Contract No. N00014-86-K-0395). Los Angeles: University of California, Center for Technology Assessment/Center for the Study of Evaluation.

O'Neil, H. F., Jr., Baker, E. L., & Kazlauskas, E. J. (1992). Assessment of team performance. In R. Swezey & E. Salas (Eds.), *Teams: Their training and performance* (pp. 153–175). Norwood, NJ: Ablex.

O'Neil, H. F., Jr., & Fukumura, T. (1992). Relationship of worry and emotionality to test performance in a Juku environment. *Anxiety, Stress, and Coping, 5*(3), 241–251.

O'Neil, H. F., Jr., & Hedl, J. J., Jr., (1990, September). *Test anxiety and learning.* Presented to Nichinoken Second Annual International Educational Research Association, Tokyo, Japan.

O'Neil, H. F., Jr., & Robertson, M. (1992). Simulations: Occupationally oriented. In M. Alkin (Ed.), *Encyclopedia of educational research* (6th ed., pp. 1216–1222). New York: Macmillan.

Parks. S. (1980). *Self-consciousness and test anxiety.* Unpublished masters thesis. Middle Tennessee State University, Murphreesboro.

Rachman, S. J. (1982, March). *Development of courage in military personnel in training and performance in combat situations* (ARI Research Rept. 1338; Govt. Accession No. AD A 136 993). Alexandria, VA: U.S. Army Research Institute for the Behavioral and Social Sciences.

Shiflett, S., Eisner, E. J., Price, S. J., & Schemmer, F. M. (1982). *The definition and measurement of team functions* (Army Research Institute Contract MDA903-80-C-0516). Alexandria, VA: U.S. Army Research Institute for the Behavioral and Social Sciences.

Spielberger, C. D. (1972). Conceptual and methodological issues in anxiety research. In C. D. Spielberger (Ed.), *Anxiety: Current trends in theory and research* (Vol. 2, pp. 481–493). New York: Academic Press.

Spielberger, C. D. (1975). Anxiety: State-trait process. In C. D. Spielberger & I. G. Sarason (Eds.), *Stress and anxiety* (Vol. 1, pp. 115–143). Washington, DC: Hemisphere.

Spielberger, C. D. (1980). *Test Anxiety Inventory: Preliminary professional manual.* Palo Alto, CA: Consulting Psychologists Press.

Spielberger, C. D., Gonzalez, H. P., Taylor, C. J., Algaze, B., & Anton, W. D. (1978). Examination stress and test anxiety. In C. D. Spielberger & I. G. Sarason (Eds.), *Stress and anxiety* (Vol. 5, pp. 167–191). New York: Wiley.

Stokes, A. F., & Raby, M. (1989, October). Stress and cognitive performance in trainee pilots. In *Proceedings of the Human Factors Society Thirty-third Annual Meeting,* Denver, CO.

Swezey, R. W., & Salas, E. (Eds.). (1992). *Teams: Their training and performance.* Norwood, NJ: Ablex.

Tobias, S. (1985). Text anxiety: Interference, deficient skills, and cognitive capacity. *Educational Psychologist, 20,* 135–142.

Wagner, H., Hibbits, N., Rosenblatt, R. D., & Schultz, R. (1977). *Team training and evaluation strategies: State-of-the-art* (Tech. Rep. No. HumRRO-TR-77-1). Alexandria, VA: Human Resources Research Organization.

Wickens, C. D., Barnett, B., Stokes, A., Davis, T., Jr., & Hyman, F. (1989). *Expertise, stress, and pilot judgment.* Urbana: University of Illinois, Institute of Aviation, Aviation Research Laboratory.

Wine, J. D. (1980). Cognitive-attentional theory of test anxiety. In I. G. Sarason (Ed.), *Test anxiety: Theory, research, and applications* (pp. 349–385). Hillsdale, NJ: Lawrence Erlbaum Associates.

III MOTIVATION OF INDIVIDUALS

12 Curiosity and Exploratory Behavior

Charles D. Spielberger
Laura M. Starr
University of South Florida, Tampa

Tendencies to explore and investigate the environment are characteristic of the behavior of higher organisms; curiosity is generally regarded as the motivational determinant that energizes these exploratory behaviors. Both curiosity and exploration have been linked to a variety of related motivational constructs such as drives, motives, need for stimulus change, intrinsic motivation, etc. (Voss & Keller, 1983). Although many investigators have devoted their efforts to research on curiosity and exploratory behavior, the literature continues to be characterized by diverse theoretical views and contradictory empirical findings.

The goals of this chapter are to review theory and research on curiosity and exploratory behavior, and to examine the measures of these constructs as emotional states and personality traits. The chapter is divided into four sections. Theoretical conceptions of curiosity and exploratory behavior are briefly reviewed in the first section. The second section presents an optimal stimulation/dual-process theory of curiosity and anxiety. The measurement of state and trait curiosity is considered in the third section. Finally, the findings of research on the measurement of curiosity and the effects of curiosity and anxiety on classroom behavior are reported.

THEORY AND RESEARCH ON CURIOSITY

The concept of curiosity was introduced into the psychological literature as early as 1890 by William James, who considered curiosity to be one of the primary instincts. Strongly influenced by Darwin's (1965) views on evolution, James (1890) proposed an instinct theory of curiosity. He reasoned that attraction to a novel stimulus was adaptive because the new object might facilitate survival. But fear of novel objects was also adaptive because the object could prove to be dangerous or harmful. Thus, James recognized an inherent, antagonistic relationship between curiosity and fear which could result in simultaneous arousal of these two emotions by novel stimuli. However, James was especially impressed with a second type of curiosity, which he referred to as "metaphysical wonder" or "scientific curiosity." He described this type of curiosity in more cognitive terms, attributing it to the response of the "philosophic brain. . . to an inconsistency or a gap in its knowledge" (p. 430).

Greatly influenced by James' writings, William McDougall (1921) proposed a similar conception of curiosity and fear as antagonistic instincts. McDougall observed that "it is . . . not easy to distinguish in general terms between excitants of curiosity and fear. . . . .the two instincts, with their opposed impulses of approach and retreat, are apt to be excited in animals and very young children in rapid alternation, and simultaneously in ourselves" (p. 60). Also like James, McDougall (1923) described the emotional qualities that accompanied the "curiosity" instinct in terms of "feelings of mystery, of strangeness, and of wonder."

Although Freud (1933, 1936) did not directly address the origins of curiosity, he believed that exploratory behavior was determined by both instinctive biological urges and ego mechanisms designed to reduce the threat of insecurity (Aronoff, 1962). He regarded exploratory behavior as reflecting coping mechanisms that were directed toward the mastery of social forces and the problems of life. Freud's conception of curiosity was extended by Bowlby (1969), based on his investigations of the psychological processes of attachment and separation from the mother. Bowlby theorized that an infant's attachment to its mother was determined by powerful innate needs which prevented the child from engaging in exploratory behavior until it felt secure about the close proximity of the mother. While Freud and Bowlby both linked curiosity to anxiety, Freud viewed insecurity (anxiety) as the major instigator of exploratory behavior whereas Bowlby assumed that exploration occurred only after a child had developed a secure relationship with its mother.

The instinct doctrine has been strongly criticized on the grounds that instincts do not explain behavior, but merely provide a redundant description of it (Dunlap, 1919; Kuo, 1928; Watson, 1925). It has often been noted, for example, that attributing exploration to a curiosity instinct was circular and meaningless without a further description of the properties of the curiosity instinct and an explanation of how it influenced behavior. Another major criticism of instinct theory was the enormous number of instincts that were proposed to account for human behavior. It is especially interesting to note that psychologists who have worked most extensively in research on *instinctive* behavior tend to be more critical of instincts as explanatory concepts than those who lack first-hand knowledge of the behavioral evidence.

Scientific problems arising from conceptions of curiosity as an instinct have stimulated the evaluation of the alternative possibility that exploratory behavior arises from biological needs. Traditional conceptions of need or drive hold that physical or "tissue" needs stimulate behavioral activity which eventually leads to a reduction of the need. The results of a number of investigations have been interpreted as indicating that exploratory behavior is motivated by a primary drive to explore, that is, a curiosity drive, which guides and directs behavior. Moreover, some researchers have suggested that this curiosity drive is as fundamental as hunger or thirst (e.g., Cofer & Appley, 1964; White, 1961).

Dashiell (1925) regarded curiosity as an *acquired* or secondary drive and hypothesized that exploratory behaviors were learned as a result of the reduction of primary drives such as hunger or thirst. After exploratory behaviors were conditioned or learned, these behaviors could then be evoked by internal stimuli associated with primary drives, that is, the experience of hunger or thirst could activate exploratory responses that had previously resulted in the reduction of these needs.

Similarly, Dollard and Miller (1950) regarded curiosity as an acquired drive and described exploratory behaviors as instrumental responses. In essence, curiosity was a learned drive for "conceptual clarity," resulting from the fact that children are trained to detect and eliminate logical contradictions and absurdities for which they have been punished in the past. Dollard and Miller (1950) also implicitly linked curiosity to anxiety, suggesting that ". . . the cues produced by the response of labeling something as a contradiction, ambiguous or illogical tend to lead to unpleasant feelings in most people; they have a learned drive to make their explanations seem logical" (p. 120).

In contrast to interpretations of curiosity as an acquired drive, Harlow (1953) reviewed the research literature on the exploratory behavior of primates and concluded that: "The visual exploratory drive may be an unlearned and self-reinforced primary drive" (p. 38). Similarly, Nissen (1954) theorized that exploratory behavior was stimulated by a basic or primary "biogenic drive to explore." According to Nissen (1954):

> It is the function of the brain to perceive and to know...the nervous system is part of the body and as such it has homeostatic requirements comparable to those of other organs...is it then unreasonable to postulate a primary drive—a drive for one of the main organs of the body, the brain, to perform its function of perceiving and knowing? (p. 300).

Other theories of curiosity, which go beyond the assumption that exploratory behavior is motivated by primary or secondary drives, have proposed that there is an optimal level of stimulation or arousal that is maximally motivating and rewarding. This optimal stimulation viewpoint is best exemplified in the work of Daniel Berlyne, perhaps the most productive contributor to theory and experimentation on human curiosity and exploratory behavior. According to Berlyne

(1960), organisms strive to maintain a preferred level of commerce with the environment, and seek out stimuli that possess arousal potential of an intermediate or optimal level relative to the organism's state of arousal at a particular moment. Whereas optimal arousal produces feelings of pleasure, conditions of boredom and overstimulation are experienced as unpleasant.

Berlyne (1966a, 1966b) assumes that the experience of arousal as pleasant or unpleasant is determined by inputs from *reward* and *aversion* centers in the brain, which provide a neurophysiological basis for two different types of curiosity: diversive and specific. Diversive curiosity motivates exploratory behavior that increases arousal to an optimal level by increasing the novelty, change, and/or variety of the stimuli in a person's environment. In contrast, specific curiosity motivates exploratory behavior designed to obtain information that will reduce the organism's subjective uncertainty and discomfort. In situations in which an organism lacks information about the stimuli that impinge on it, specific curiosity is experienced as a mild state of discomfort and heightened physiological arousal. Stimuli with relatively high arousal potential that exceed the organism's optimal level may evoke either specific curiosity and exploratory behavior, or fear and flight, depending upon how much novelty, complexity or unpredictability is introduced. Thus, Berlyne's conception of specific curiosity seems to encompass elements of anxiety.

Optimal stimulation theories may be differentiated into two major classes: (a) Theories that emphasize the organism's physiological reaction to stimulation, and (b) Theories that are concerned with the cognitive effects of stimulation. Hebb (1955), Fiske and Maddi (1961), Leuba (1955), and Berlyne (1960) consider optimal levels of stimulation to be determined primarily by an organism's physiological reaction to stimulation. McReynolds and Bryan (1956) and Piaget (see Ginsburg & Opper, 1969) emphasize perceptual and cognitive factors as the determinants of exploratory behavior. They theorize that an optimal level of stimulation results form perceptual-cognitive incongruity, without reference to physiological arousal level. Charlesworth (1969) concisely describes Piaget's cognitive-developmental conception of curiosity as follows:

> Intellectual change or growth is the end result of a chain of events beginning with the disruption of cognitive equilibrium by a conflict between incoming information and information already stored in the central nervous system. The conflict produced by the discrepancy between these two sources of information has the capacity of motivating curiosity (exploratory) behavior, and the latter has a high probability of leading to information that can be used by the organism to reduce conflict. Conflict reduction consequently reinforces curiosity behavior, thereby insuring continued contact with novel features of the environment. (p. 273)

As previously noted, William James (1890) observed that novel objects evoked both exploratory (sensation-seeking) and avoidance behaviors. James theorized that these behaviors were motivated by curiosity and fear instincts, and called attention to the potential for an antagonistic relationship between these instincts when they were simultaneously aroused by novel stimuli. A similar conception of curiosity and fear as antagonistic instincts was also proposed by McDougall (1921). In essence, James and McDougall postulated *dual-process* theories of curiosity and anxiety to account for exploratory and avoidance reactions to novelty, ambiguity, or strangeness. Both assumed that novel stimuli evoked curiosity and fear, and that these conflicting instincts tended to activate incompatible approach and avoidance reactions.

Berlyne (1950) also observed that both curiosity and fear were aroused by novel and unexpected external stimuli, noting that the behaviors associated with these motivational systems were incompatible in that curiosity generally leads to approach whereas fear leads to avoidance and withdrawal. According to Berlyne, whether curiosity or fear is evoked will be determined by the intensity of the stimulus, with exploratory behavior being elicited by weaker stimuli and avoidance or withdrawal being more likely responses to very strong stimuli. Whiting and Mowrer adopted a similar position, suggesting that "curiosity is perhaps more closely related to anxiety than is ordinarily supposed in that novel stimuli seem to excite both fear and curiosity, often resulting in a wavering of the two" (cited by Berlyne, 1950, p. 73).

Most dual-process theories of curiosity and anxiety assume that exploration and avoidance/withdrawal are conflicting forms of behavior that are evoked by strangeness and novelty, and that the presence of both curiosity and fear results in an approach-avoidance conflict (Miller, 1961). As noted by Robert W. White (1961), a strong proponent of dual-process theory: "Fear shows itself in either freezing or avoidance, whereas exploration is clearly an instance of approach. There is hardly a more perfect example of conflict between incompatible responses than that of an animal hesitating between investigation and flight" (pp. 282–283).

Zuckerman (1969) relates individual differences in sensation seeking, including sensory, social, and thrill-seeking activities, to optimal levels of stimulation and arousal. According to Zuckerman, individuals who seek more varied, novel and complex sensory experiences are characterized by a higher optimal arousal level. Zuckerman (1975) also posits an antagonistic relationship between sensation seeking and anxiety. He views the two states as only minimally related under conditions in which arousal level is relatively low. However, as anxiety increases, sensation seeking decreases. Furthermore, Zuckerman suggests that individuals strongly motivated by a need to seek novel and varied sensations tend to be low in anxiety, whereas those who experience high levels of anxiety tend to be cautious and do not engage in sensation seeking activities. Thus, the relationship between sensation seeking and anxiety appears to be quite similar to that between curiosity and anxiety.

Building primarily on the work of Berlyne, Spielberger and Butler (1971) developed an optimal stimulation/dual process theory to account for various forms of exploratory behavior. They view curiosity and anxiety as antagonistic drives that function reciprocally to arouse and motivate behavior. These drives are conceptualized as psychobiological emotional states that vary in intensity, consisting of subjective feelings of curiosity (inquisitiveness) and anxiety (apprehension), and associated arousal of the autonomic nervous system. It is further assumed that curiosity and anxiety fluctuate over time as a function of the perceived novelty, incongruity, or ambiguity of the stimuli that a person encounters, and that people differ in their disposition to experience these emotional states. The *State-Trait Curiosity Inventory* (STCI) was developed to assess curiosity as an emotional state and individual differences in curiosity as a personality trait (Spielberger & Butler, 1971; Spielberger, Peters, & Frain, 1981).

Spielberger et al. (1981) concur with Berlyne's view that when the curiosity (or sensation seeking) drive is strong and anxiety is relatively weak, diversive exploration is motivated. They also agree that when anxiety is much stronger than curiosity, avoidance behavior (flight reactions) will occur. However, they criticize Berlyne's concept of specific curiosity because it confounds curiosity with anxiety. They argue instead that the simultaneous experience of curiosity and anxiety is symbiotic in motivating specific exploratory behavior when the physiological arousal associated with these emotional states is at or near an optimal level. Because diversive and specific curiosity can thus be explained in terms of the intensity of curiosity and anxiety as emotional states, the concept of a specific curiosity drive appears to be redundant.

Although Pearson (1970) and Langevin (1971) do not address the relation between curiosity and anxiety, they regard curiosity as a multidimensional construct. As Langevin (1971) has noted, ". . . even at the conceptual level there are a multitude of definitions of curiosity suggesting it is not a unitary construct" (p. 361). In a factor analysis of five curiosity measures, Langevin identified two major curiosity factors, which he labeled "breadth of interest" and "depth of interest." These factors, as described by Langevin, appear to be quite similar to Berlyne's concepts of diversive and specific curiosity. Breadth of interest is described as a tendency to seek stimulation from a variety of sources, whereas depth of interest involves detailed exploration of a single or small number of stimuli. However, Langevin also noted that "breadth of interest" seemed to involve an enduring personality trait whereas "depth" reflected the intensity of a fluctuating motivational state.

Ainley (1987) has also observed that the numerous scales developed to assess curiosity appear to measure different aspects of exploratory behavior. "Curiosity is in essence concerned with approach to novelty," according to Ainley (1987, p. 55), and the various scales developed to assess curiosity measure divergent aspects of breadth and depth of interest as these constructs were described by Langevin (1971). Breadth of interest involves seeking varied and changing stimulation in order to experience what a novel event is like, whereas depth of interest involves exploring and investigating new objects, events, and ideas in order to achieve an understanding of them. Although Boyle (1989) has strongly criticized Ainley's concepts of breadth and depth of interests, contending that his findings support a state-trait conception of curiosity similar to that proposed by Spielberger et al. (1981), it should be noted that only trait curiosity measures were used in Ainley's study and that different types of curiosity can be conceptualized as emotional states and personality traits.

In summary, exploratory behavior has been interpreted as resulting from an innate curiosity instinct, a fundamental (primary) drive to explore based on underlying neurophysiological structures, and as an acquired or learned drive that results from the reduction of primary drives such as hunger and thirst. More recently, it has been suggested that exploratory behavior is motivated by the simultaneous arousal of curiosity and anxiety as antagonistic motivational systems, and that curiosity itself is a multidimensional construct. On the basis of an extensive review of theory and research on curiosity and exploratory behavior, Voss and Keller (1983) concluded that although curiosity can be most meaningfully defined as a motivational prerequisite for exploratory behavior, ". . . no comprehensive framework exists that meets the standard of contemporary research and that can be used to classify the phenomena of curiosity and exploration" (p. 18).

The optimal stimulation/dual-process theory of curiosity and exploratory behavior proposed in the following section amplifies and extends our earlier conception of the effects of curiosity and anxiety on diversive and specific exploratory behavior (Spielberger & Butler, 1971; Spielberger et al., 1981). Because the development of this theory was greatly influenced by the work of Daniel Berlyne, his research on diversive and specific curiosity is discussed in some detail prior to describing the proposed theory.

AN OPTIMAL STIMULATION/DUAL PROCESS THEORY OF EXPLORATORY BEHAVIOR

Berlyne (1960) observed that exploratory behavior was intensified by situations characterized by novelty or complexity, or by lack of information, and that such conditions lead to uncertainty. If an unfamiliar situation was too disturbing, or too unpleasant, ". . . instead of eliciting exploration—which means approach and sustained contact—novel, surprising, and strange objects may provoke terror and flight" (Berlyne, 1966b, p. 30). According to Berlyne, the particular reaction that is evoked by an object "seems to depend on many things including how disturbing a stimulus pattern is, how agitated or relaxed a subject is, and what personality traits he possesses" (1966b, p. 30).

The concept of arousal, which Berlyne (1964) views primarily as a physiological activation process, is central to his theory of curiosity. Berlyne assume that level of arousal is determined by inputs from *reward* and *aversion* systems in the brain that are located in the reticular formation and certain areas of the hypothalamus. In the context of Berlyne's theory, these brain centers are assumed to mediate two different types of exploratory behavior, which Berlyne identifies as "diversive" and "specific" curiosity. Although Berlyne recognized the antagonistic relationship between curiosity and anxiety, his conceptual model does not provide for an integration of the influence of these emotional states on level of arousal or behavior. The significance of Berlyne's analysis of exploratory behavior for research on anxiety, as well as the potential importance of the state-trait distinction for research on curiosity, led us to examine Berlyne's concepts of specific and diversive curiosity from the perspective of Spielberger's (1966, 1972a) Trait-State Theory of Anxiety.

Diversive curiosity, conceptualized by Berlyne as an attempt to seek stimulation regardless of its source, appears to *increase* arousal to an optimal level by increasing the novelty, complexity, and/or variety of the stimuli in a person's environment. Diversive exploration is motivated by an environment that is boring, monotonous, or lacking in stimulation; such conditions heighten arousal and motivate stimulus-seeking behavior. In contrast, Berlyne describes specific curiosity as a state of mild discomfort, heightened arousal, and conflict among response tendencies. Specific curiosity is induced by situations in which an organism lacks information about the stimuli which impinge on it, that is, stimuli that are characterized by a high degree of complexity, novelty, and incongruity. Once aroused, specific curiosity leads to exploratory behavior designed to supply information that will reduce the organism's subjective uncertainty and discomfort. In his research on exploratory behavior, Berlyne deals primarily with specific curiosity.

Berlyne identified three groups of properties that determine the arousal or attraction value of a stimulus: (a) *Psychophysical properties,* which include size, shape, color, symmetry; (b) *Ecological properties,* which are defined as affect-laden stimuli associated with biological functions such as hunger, thirst, sex, and fear; and, most important (c) *Collative properties,* which is the generic term used by Berlyne to refer to stimulus characteristics such as novelty, complexity, incongruity, and ambiguity. The common feature of collative stimuli is that they evoke feelings of uncertainty.

Berlyne (1967) cites considerable evidence demonstrating that *increases* in stimulus intensity (arousal potential) were sometimes rewarding and, at other times, such increases generate avoidance responses so that a subsequent *decrease* in stimulus intensity was rewarding. Since small to moderate increases in arousal were often rewarding whereas extreme increases were generally aversive, Berlyne (1971) concluded that the general law of hedonic tone, posited by Wundt in 1874, adequately described the relationship between objective changes in stimulus intensity and the subjective pleasant or unpleasant feelings that were elicited by such changes. In accordance with Wundt's curve, reproduced in Fig. 12.1, small increases in stimulus intensity are experienced as pleasant whereas large changes are experienced as unpleasant.

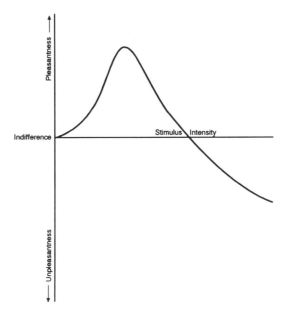

FIG. 12.1.   Wundt's Curve of changes in hedonic tone as a function of increasing stimulus intensity. Adapted from Berlyne (1967, p. 52).

On the basis of the research literature and his own research, Berlyne postulated that different physiological mechanisms underlie and mediate diversive and specific curiosity. Diversive exploration is motivated by a need to increase arousal, whereas specific exploration seeks to reduce the level of arousal. Berlyne (1967) assumed that low-intensity stimulation, generally associated with diversive curiosity, activated the portion of the brain that Schneirla (1959, 1965) has called the "A system," whereas high intensity stimulation associated with specific curiosity activates "an antagonistic 'W' system." Berlyne noted that similar models proposed by neurophysiologists were consistent with his view of separate reward and aversion systems in the brain (e.g., Olds' theory of "positive" and "negative" reinforcement systems; Grastyán's "pull" and "push" systems model).

Berlyne assumed that the threshold for the initial arousal of the reward system was lower than for the aversion system, and that the asymptotic limit for positive reinforcement (pleasantness) for the reward system is lower than the asymptotic limit of negative reinforcement (unpleasantness) for the aversion system. The hypothetical growth curves postulated by Berlyne for the reward and aversion systems are presented in Fig. 12.2 as a function of increasing arousal (collative stimulus intensity). He further suggested that the reward and aversion systems interacted to produce Wundt's curve (see Fig. 12.1).

As previously noted, Berlyne points out that stimuli with relatively high

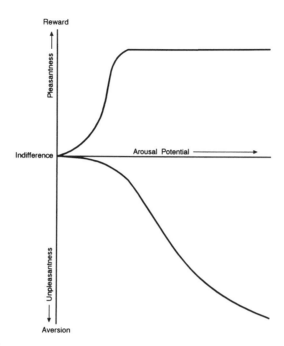

FIG. 12.2.   Curves representing the activation of reward and aversion systems as a function of increasing collative stimulus intensity (arousal potential). Adapted from Berlyne (1967, p. 88).

arousal potential may evoke either curiosity and exploration, or fear and flight, depending on how much collative stimulus intensity (i.e., novelty, complexity, unpredictability) is introduced. He also suggests that reactions to novel stimuli depend on individual differences in personality traits as well as the collative properties of the stimulus. In reviewing Berlyne's work, we were impressed with the fact that his concept of specific curiosity seemed redundant and could be integrated within a framework that takes both anxiety and curiosity into account. Assuming that the aversion system (and the physiological mechanisms which seem to underlie it) mediates anxiety, specific exploratory behavior can be explained in terms of the simultaneous influence of curiosity and anxiety.

Our analysis of exploratory behavior begins with three fundamental theoretical premises posited by Berlyne and depicted graphically in Fig. 12.2. First, we accept Berlyne's formulation with respect to the operation of reward and aversion systems in the brain, and his related assumption that the physiological mechanisms associated with these systems account for the differential arousal produced by changes in collative stimulus intensity. However, we further assume that increases in collative stimulus intensity produce increments in both curiosity (pleasantness) and anxiety (unpleasantness) with associated increments in arousal that are mediated, respectively, by the reward and aversion systems.

Second, we concur with Berlyne's assumption that the asymptotic level of arousal of the aversion system evoked by strong negative reinforcement is greater than the asymptote of arousal for the reward system evoked by positive reinforcement. From Fig. 12.2, it can be noted that Berlyne also assumes that the reward system has a lower collative stimulus intensity threshold for activation than the aversion system.

A third premise of our Optimal Stimulation/Dual Process Theory of Exploratory Behavior is based on Berlyne's assumption that Wundt's curve, as depicted in Fig. 12.1, represents the algebraic summation of the amount of pleasantness and unpleasantness associated with the arousal evoked by increasing magnitudes of collative stimulus intensity. Thus, we assume that Wundt's curve can be interpreted as reflecting the interactive effects of the reward and aversion systems on subjective feelings of pleasantness and unpleasantness that are associated with increasing levels of arousal. An important implication of this assumption is that a particular level of arousal experienced as optimally pleasurable is determined by a near asymptotic level of curiosity and a small amount of anxiety.

We differ with Berlyne (and also with Wundt) in our assumption that a state of optimal subjective pleasure will consist of strong feelings of pleasantness associated with mild feelings of unpleasantness, rather than only the former. It then follows that a person will experience an optimal level of pleasant feelings in the context of strong feelings of curiosity and mildly unpleasant feelings of anxiety. In other words, the theory posits that mild anxiety serves to accentuate subjectively experienced feelings of pleasure associated with the high level of curiosity evoked by novel stimuli.

Our major departure from Berlyne's theoretical analysis involves his concept of specific curiosity and its relation to the negative reinforcement he assumes to be associated with the aversion system and the feelings of unpleasantness that motivate specific exploratory behavior. We postulate that curiosity and anxiety are drive states mediated by physiological mechanisms and subjective feelings of pleasantness and unpleasantness, and that the interaction of these drives in response to increasing collative stimulus intensity can account for specific exploratory behavior, as well as avoidance and withdrawal. A schematic presentation of our Optimal Stimulation/Dual Process Theory of Curiosity and Exploratory Behavior is presented in Fig. 12.3.

Consistent with the foregoing discussion, six key principles may be deduced from our Optimal Stimulation/Dual Process conceptualization of exploratory behavior:

1. The curiosity drive is conceptualized as an emotional-motivational system that stimulates exploratory behavior. Subjective feelings of pleasantness are associated with the growth of the curiosity drive as a function of increasing collative stimulus intensity and activity of the positive reward system.

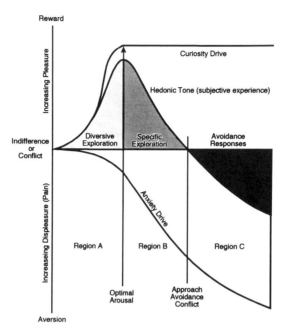

FIG. 12.3.   Schematic representation of an Optimal Stimulation/Dual Process Theory in which curiosity and anxiety have an interactive motivational effect on diversive and specific exploratory behavior.

2. The anxiety drive is conceptualized as motivating stimulus avoidance, that is, behavior that reduces stimulus intensity, physiological arousal, and unpleasant feelings. Subjective feelings of unpleasantness are associated with the growth of the anxiety drive as a function of increasing collative stimulus intensity and activity of the aversion system.

3. The arousal threshold for the curiosity drive (Berlyne's reward system) is lower (closer to zero collative stimulus intensity) than for the anxiety drive (Berlyne's aversion system).

4. The asymptotic level of the anxiety drive is assumed to be greater than that of the curiosity drive.

5. The combination of differential thresholds, different growth rates, and different asymptotic levels for the curiosity and anxiety drives produce a resultant curve that approximates Wundt's curve for hedonic tone.

6. With increasing collative stimulus intensity, subjective experiences increase in pleasantness and associated arousal up to an optimal level, then decrease in *net* pleasantness as the strength of unpleasant feelings increase, resulting in an approach-avoidance conflict. As this subjective experience becomes

increasingly unpleasant and noxious, avoidance behavior and flight reactions are generated.

At low levels of collative stimulus intensity, curiosity and diversive exploration predominate. At moderate levels, the combination of high curiosity and mild-to-moderate anxiety motivate specific exploration. At a relatively high level of arousal, there is an approach-avoidance conflict between a near-asymptotic curiosity drive that strongly stimulates exploratory behavior, and a substantially elevated level of state anxiety that motivates avoidance behavior. At very high collative stimulus intensity, high levels of anxiety are aroused that motivate avoidance behavior.

While the Optimal Stimulation/Dual Process Theory recognizes the importance of distinguishing between diversive and specific exploratory behavior as described by Berlyne, the theory posits that specific exploration can be explained in terms of the interplay of curiosity and anxiety as coacting motivational systems. The curiosity drive is assumed to have a lower threshold and a higher initial growth rate than the anxiety drive, as may be noted in Fig. 12.3, which leads to diversive exploration at relatively low levels of collative stimulus intensity. Moreover, small increments in collative stimulus intensity initially produce larger increases in positive reinforcement than in negative reinforcement, which results in stronger subjective feelings of pleasantness than unpleasantness. Diversive exploration and stimulus seeking behavior increase arousal up to an optimal level at which positive reinforcement and pleasant feelings are maximum. The portion of the collative stimulus dimension in which diversive exploration occurs is designated in Fig. 12.3 as Region A.

At moderate levels of collative stimulus intensity, specific exploration will be stimulated that motivates a person to reduce collative stimulation by seeking information that will diminish the amount of complexity, novelty, and incongruity associated with the collative stimuli that impinge on her or him. Reduction in collative stimulus intensity will increase the individual's overall experience of pleasantness by reducing the unpleasantness associated with moderately high levels of anxiety, while the pleasantness associated with high curiosity remains essentially unchanged. Thus, the anxiety drive is decreased by specific exploratory behavior, while the curiosity drive remains at a high level. The portion of the collative stimulus intensity dimension in which specific exploratory behavior occurs is defined in Fig. 12.3 as Region B.

At very high levels of collative stimulus intensity, designated as Region C in Fig. 12.3, the anxiety drive predominates and stimulus avoidance and withdrawal behaviors are motivated as a means of reducing arousal. The hedonic tone of an individual in Region C is characterized by the predominance of subjectively unpleasant feelings of state anxiety. To the extent that avoidance responses serve to reduce arousal, the anxiety state declines and the unpleasant feelings associated with it are reduced, whereas the curiosity drive remains essentially undiminished. However, specific exploratory behavior will not be initiated until collative stimulus intensity is reduced to a point where positive reinforcement effects and approach responses associated with the curiosity drive predominate over the negative reinforcement effects associated with the anxiety drive and avoidance responses, and the resulting hedonic tone shifts from unpleasant to pleasant.

The curves for curiosity and anxiety in Fig. 12.3 reflect hypothetical changes in the emotional states associated with these emotional-motivational systems that result from variations in collative stimulus intensity. It should be noted, however, that these curves do not take individual differences in trait curiosity and trait anxiety into account. The concepts of trait and state anxiety, first introduced by Cattell (1957, 1966; Cattell & Scheier, 1961) have been elaborated by Spielberger (1966, 1972a, 1972b, 1983) and his colleagues (Spielberger, Gorsuch, & Lushene, 1970; Spielberger, Lushene, & McAdoo, 1977) in considerable detail. Individual differences in trait curiosity, which may be considered as conceptually analogous to trait anxiety (Spielberger et al., 1981), are assumed to influence the thresholds, growth rates, and asymptotic levels of the feelings of pleasantness and unpleasantness that are experienced as a function of increasing levels of collative stimulus intensity.

The relation between individual differences in trait curiosity and trait anxiety and the parameters of anxiety and curiosity as drive states must be determined through empirical research. However, before this research can be undertaken, measures of state and trait curiosity must be constructed and validated. Several of the more widely used measures of curiosity and sensation seeking are described in the following section.

THE MEASUREMENT OF CURIOSITY

Differences in the theoretical orientations of curiosity researchers has resulted in the development of a variety of scales that measure one or more aspects of this multifaceted construct. One of the earliest measures, the Reactive Curiosity (RC) scale, was developed by Penney and McCann (1964) to evaluate curiosity in children. Maw and Maw (1968) also developed a self-rating instrument to measure curiosity in children, the "About Myself" scale. The items that comprise these scales were rationally selected on the basis of content validity as defined by the authors' conception of curiosity and exploratory behavior. It has been demonstrated that the RC and "About Myself" scales are useful in distinguishing between groups of children who differ in exploratory behavior.

Day (1969) designed the Ontario Test of Intrinsic Motivation (OTIM) to measure specific and diversive curiosity as these concepts were defined by Berlyne (1967). The OTIM has been used to examine relationships between curiosity and mental health, school achievement, anxiety, and creativity. Although some evidence of the validity of the OTIM has been reported (Voss & Keller, 1983), this scale has not been used extensively by other investigators. Moreover, in a study by Peters (1976), the OTIM Specific Curiosity and Diversive Curiosity subscales failed to correlate with other measures of curiosity and scores on these scales did not show the expected relationships with behavioral measures. Thus, evidence for the validity of the OTIM is limited at present.

The Sensation Seeking Scale (SSS) was developed by Zuckerman, Kolin, Price, and Zoob (1964) to "measure optimal levels of stimulation and arousal for cognitive activity, motoric activity, and positive affective tone, with the immediate objective of predicting individual differences in response to sensory deprivation" (Zuckerman, 1975, p. 1). Now in its fifth revision, the SSS consists of four separate subscales: Thrill and Adventure Seeking; Experience Seeking; Disinhibition; and Boredom Susceptibility. The Disinhibition and Boredom Susceptibility subscales appear to assess individual differences in negative aspects of diversive curiosity, whereas the Thrill and Adventure Seeking and Experience Seeking scales measure diversive curiosity as this concept is defined by Berlyne (1967).

Pearson's (1970) Novelty Experiencing Scale (NES) was designed to measure four aspects of novelty seeking behavior, each of which is defined by the relationship between the source of stimulation (internal or external) and the nature of the reaction (sensory or cognitive). Thus, the NES subscales assess four aspects of curiosity: External sensation, internal sensation, external cognition, and internal cognition. Each NES item was selected on the basis of its face validity in meeting the criteria for the novelty-seeking type being measured. On the basis of her research with the NES, Pearson (1970) concluded that curiosity and exploratory behavior cannot be regarded as unidimensional constructs.

The Academic Curiosity Inventory (ACI) was derived by Vidler and Rawan (1974) from an unpublished scale developed by Chiu (1967). They used some of Chiu's original items, modified others, and constructed new items in keeping with their conception of academic curiosity. The ACI correlated .34 with a convergent thinking test; small positive correlations of the ACI were found with measures of academic achievement. Factor analysis of the ACI yielded five factors (Vidler & Rawan, 1974, 1975), but the authors do not report the names of the factors, nor do they provide any information regarding their nature.

The ACI and the other curiosity scales that have been described all seem to measure individual differences in curiosity as a personality trait. The State-Trait Curiosity Inventory (STCI), developed by Spielberger and Butler (1971) and subsequently refined by Spielberger et al. (1976, 1981), was explicitly designed to measure the intensity of curiosity as a transitory state (S-Curiosity) and individual differences in curiosity as a relatively stable personality trait (T-Curiosity). Subjects respond to the STCI S-Curiosity and T-Curiosity subscales (each comprised of 15 items) by rating the intensity (state) and frequency (trait) of their curiosity experiences on four-point rating scales. The S-Curiosity scale requires subjects to report how they feel *at a particular moment;* the T-Curiosity scale asks subjects to report how they generally feel.

High levels of S-Curiosity reflect an intense desire to seek out, explore and understand new things in the environment. The STCI T-Curiosity subscale assesses individual differences in the disposition to experience S-Curiosity when responding to novel or ambiguous stimuli. Persons high in T-Curiosity experience curiosity states more frequently and with higher levels of intensity than persons low in T-Curiosity. The best STCI state and trait curiosity items have been included as 10-item S-Curiosity and T-Curiosity subscales in the State-Trait Personality Inventory (STPI), along with 10-item state and trait measures of anxiety and anger (Spielberger, 1979). Naylor (1981) constructed a state-trait curiosity measure, known as the Melbourne Curiosity Inventory (MCI), which is quite similar to the STCI. Factor analyses of the STCI and MCI items indicates that the STCI and MCI S-Curiosity and T-Curiosity items define correlated but relatively independent factors.

The empirical findings in studies that have endeavored to assess relationships between measures of curiosity and exploratory behavior clearly indicate that curiosity is a multifaceted construct. Research on the relations between various measures of curiosity and the implications of these findings for understanding the nature of curiosity as a psychological construct are discussed in the following section.

RESEARCH ON CURIOSITY AND CLASSROOM BEHAVIOR

Berlyne's extensive research on curiosity has provided substantial experimental evidence of the importance of distinguishing between diversive and specific exploratory behavior. Day's (1971) findings with the OTIM also indicate that diversive and specific curiosity are distinct constructs. Although Zuckerman's (1979) SSS measures individual differences in internal and external sensation seeking that are quite similar to Berlyne's concept of diversive curiosity, the SSS does not appear to assess the cognitive or intellectual aspects of curiosity that are encompassed in Berlyne's concept of specific curiosity (Boyle, 1983; Zuckerman, 1979).

Pearson (1970) examined the distinction between the sensory and cognitive aspects of curiosity. Small correlations between the NES sensory and cognitive subscales suggest that these scales measure different aspects of novelty seeking. The NES Internal and External Sensation subscales parallel Zuckerman's (1969) concepts of sensation seeking; the NES External and Internal Cognition subscales appear to measure perceptual and epistemic curiosity as these constructs are defined by Berlyne (1960).

Spielberger, Peters, and Frain (1976) investigated the relationship between curiosity as measured by the STCI and sensation seeking as measured by Zuckerman's (1979) SSS. They found correlations between the STCI T-Curiosity scale and various SSS subscales that ranged between -.08 and .35, suggesting that these scales were measuring different aspects of curiosity. This was corroborated by Frain (1977), who found, in addition, that the STCI items and the SSS subscales loaded on distinct factors. Curiosity as measured by the STCI was much more closely related to academic curiosity as assessed by the ACI (Vidler & Rawan, 1974) than to sensation-seeking. These findings suggest that sensation seeking and knowledge or information seeking (epistemic curiosity) are distinctively different curiosity constructs.

The multifaceted nature of curiosity was examined by Ainley (1987) in a factor-analytic investigation of the relations among a number of curiosity measures. These included the OTIM (Day, 1971), the MCI T-Curiosity scale (Naylor, 1981), the NES (Pearson, 1970), and the subscales of Zuckerman's (1979) SSS. Two primary factors were identified: "Breadth of Interest" was defined by the Zuckerman SSS subscales, the NES External and Internal Sensations scales, and the OTIM Diversive Curiosity scale; "Depth of Interest" had high loadings on the OTIM Specific Curiosity scale, the NES Internal and External Cognition scales, and the MCI T-Curiosity scale. Ainley concluded that the Breadth factor reflected interest in seeking out new experiences or sensations, whereas the Depth factor assessed interest in understanding and exploring new objects, events or ideas. These findings and the results of previous studies strongly indicated that measures of sensation seeking and information or knowledge seeking assess different aspects of curiosity.

Boyle (1989) has focused on an empirical investigation of the measurement of curiosity within the state-trait model. Based on his factor analysis in which state and trait factors were identified, Boyle strongly criticized Ainley's breadth vs. depth of interest conceptualization of curiosity. It should be noted, however, that all of the scales that Ainley examined were trait measures, and that her findings provide clear evidence of the existence of at least two relatively independent dimensions of curiosity. Thus, Boyle's and Ainley's findings appear complimentary, rather than contradictory.

On the basis of a review of the results of earlier factor studies of curiosity measures, Starr (1992) noted three important consistencies in these findings. First, measures of specific curiosity and cognitive novelty seeking were positively correlated, and that this facet of curiosity seems to motivate information and cognitive experience seeking. Second, she observed that measures of diversive curiosity, sensation seeking, and sensory novelty seeking appear to assess a different aspect of curiosity that motivates seeking sensory experiences. Third, the Melbourne and State-Trait Curiosity Inventories both measure distinctive state and trait aspects of curiosity. Starr hypothesized that exploratory behavior can be classified into two primary dimensions, Information Seeking and Experience Seeking, and that each of these aspects of curiosity can be assessed both as an emotional state and as a personality trait.

To assess the cognitive or information seeking aspect of curiosity, Starr administered the OTIM Specific Curiosity Scale, the NES External and Internal Cognition scales, and the STCI and MCI T-Curiosity scales. The sensory experience seeking aspect of curiosity was assessed with the SSS Thrill and Adventure Seeking and Experience Seeking scales, the OTIM Diversive Curiosity Scale, and the NES External Sensation Scale. In addition, the STCI and MCI S-Curiosity and T-Curiosity scales were administered to assess state and trait curiosity. A factor analysis (promax rotation) of the T-Curiosity scales yielded the predicted 2-factor solution, which is reported in Table 12.1.

It may be noted in Table 12.1 that the first factor, Information Seeking, was comprised of the MCI and STCI T-Curiosity scales, the OTIM Specific Curiosity scale, and the two NES Cognition scales. Each of these scales appears to measure some form of cognitive exploration or investigation. Factor II was defined by high loadings of the NES External Sensation scale and the SSS Thrill Seeking scale. The SSS Experience Seeking and OTIM-Diversive Curiosity scale also had their highest loadings on this factor. Because all scales with salient loadings on Factor II involve seeking sensory stimulation, this factor was labeled Experience Seeking. A second factor analysis, which was limited to the STPI and MCI state and trait curiosity scales, clearly identified state and trait curiosity factors. Thus, the Information Seeking trait factor has a strong state counterpart.

Peters (1978) investigated the effects of curiosity and anxiety on the classroom verbal behavior of college students. She administered the STCI and the STAI trait scales, and obtained measures of perceived instructor threat for 152

TABLE 12.1
Factor Loadings of Curiosity Scales (Promax Rotation) for Male and Female University Students

| Subscale | I. Information Seeking | | II. Experience Seeking | |
	Males	Females	Males	Females
MCI-Trait Curiosity	.76	.77	.10	.05
STCI-Trait Curiosity	.73	.74	.04	.11
OTIM-Spec. Curiosity	.72	.68	.04	.10
NES-Int Cognition	.67	.66	-.09	-.17
NES-Ext Cognition	.61	.65	-.10	-.11
NES-Ext Sensation	-.05	-.04	.75	.82
SSS-Thrill Seeking	-.06	.01	.80	.86
SSS-Exp Seeking	.24	.05	.42	.51
OTIM-Div	-.01	-.06	.21	.37

Adapted with permission from Starr (1992). Salient factor loadings are underlined.

students enrolled in four undergraduate psychology and sociology courses, each taught by a different instructor. Student-initiated questions and student responses to the instructors' questions were rated by trained observers during eight 1-hour classroom observation periods. On the basis of the Optimal Stimulation/Dual Process Theory of Exploratory Behavior (see Fig. 12.3), students high in curiosity (Region A) were expected to ask more questions than low-curiosity students whereas high trait anxiety was expected to activate avoidance responses that inhibited students' verbal behavior (Region C), especially with high-threat instructors.

Students who perceived their instructors as less threatening (Fig. 12.3, Regions A and B) asked twice as many questions as did those who viewed their instructors as threatening (Region C). Moreover, students high in T-Curiosity asked more than three times as many questions as the low curious students when the instructor was perceived as nonthreatening (Region A). In contrast, when instructors were perceived as highly threatening (Region C), the verbal responses of both high and low curious students were greatly inhibited and there was no difference between these groups in the number of questions asked in class.

Student responses to the instructors' questions were influenced by individual differences in trait anxiety, but not by curiosity. Both high and low anxious students were more likely to respond to questions from instructors whom they perceived as less threatening (Region A), and did not differ in the number of their responses. However, students with high trait anxiety gave fewer responses than low T-anxiety students to instructors perceived as threatening (Regions B and C).

Peters' results showed that individual differences in trait curiosity and trait anxiety interact with perceptions of instructor threat to influence both the number of questions asked by college students and the students' responses to instructor questions in a manner that was generally consistent with the Optimal Stimulation/Dual Process Theory of Exploratory Behavior. Perceived instructor threat and curiosity influenced question-asking behavior, whereas perceived instructor threat interacted with anxiety to influence responses to the questions asked by their instructors.

Voss and Meyer (1980) administered German adaptations of Spielberger's STCI and STAI state measures in four experimental situations that varied in the amount of perceived threat and subjects' willingness to participate in each situation. Scores on the STAI S-Anxiety scale of both males and females increased as a monotonic function of the amount of threat associated with the experimental situation. The STCI S-Curiosity scores of the male subjects increased slightly with increasing threat in the first three situations, but were lowest on the fourth (most threatening) situation. In contrast, the S-Curiosity scores of the females tended to decline as a function of increasing threat over all four experimental situations. Voss' and Meyers' results were generally consistent with the Optimal Stimulation/Dual Process Theory of Exploratory Behavior proposed in this chapter.

SUMMARY AND CONCLUSIONS

This chapter examined theory and research on curiosity and exploratory behavior, and reviewed procedures for measuring curiosity as an emotional state and individual differences in curiosity as a personality trait. An Optimal Stimulation/Dual Process Theory of Exploratory Behavior was proposed as an alternative to Berlyne's concepts of diversive and specific curiosity. In addition, the findings of several studies that investigated the relations among measures of curiosity and the interactive effects of curiosity and anxiety on classroom behavior were briefly reported.

Recent research findings indicate that curiosity is a multifaceted construct, consisting of at least two trait components that can be most meaningfully identified as information seeking and experience or sensation seeking. Three separate factor studies of a variety of curiosity measures have yielded remarkably similar findings in which such curiosity factors have been identified. Information and experience seeking are quite consistent with Berlyne's concepts of Epistemic and Diversive curiosity. As defined by Berlyne, epistemic curiosity encompasses the internal, cognitive components of curiosity that are most directly measured by information seeking scales. The desire or need to experience sensory stimulation as measured by Experience Seeking scales is consistent with Berlyne's construct of diversive curiosity and Zuckerman's concept of sensation seeking.

Recent research findings also provide evidence that individuals vary in the level of curiosity that is experienced at any particular moment (state curiosity) and in the frequency and intensity that curiosity states are experienced over time (trait curiosity). While findings on the state and trait aspects of curiosity are limited at present to the information seeking component, it is logical to assume state-trait differences in seeking sensory experience, and these need to be studied.

ACKNOWLEDGMENTS

The research reported in this chapter was supported in part by the U.S. Army Research Institute for Behavioral and Social Sciences through a subcontract with Battelle Institute. However, the views, opinions and/or findings that are reported are solely those of the authors, and should not be construed as an official ARI position, policy, or decision unless so designated by other official documentation.

An earlier version of the theoretical conception of curiosity reported herein was reported by Spielberger et al. (1981). The recent research on the assessment of curiosity is based on the Master's thesis of the second author (Starr, 1992).

REFERENCES

Ainley, M. D. (1987). The factor structure of curiosity measures: Breadth and depth of interest curiosity styles. *Australian Journal of Psychology, 39,*53–59.

Aronoff, J. (1962). Freud's conception of the origin of curiosity. *The Journal of Psychology, 54,* 39–45.

Berlyne, D. E. (1950). Novelty and curiosity as determinants of exploratory behavior. *British Journal of Psychology, 41,* 68–80.

Berlyne, D. E. (1960). *Conflict, arousal, and curiosity.* New York: McGraw-Hill.

Berlyne, D. E. (1964). Emotional aspects of learning. *Annual Review of Psychology, 15,* 115–142.

Berlyne, D. E. (1966a). Conflict and arousal. *Scientific American, 215,* 82–87.

Berlyne, D. E. (1966b). Curiosity and exploration. *Science, 153,* 25–33.

Berlyne, D. E. (1967). Arousal and reinforcement. In D. Levine (Ed.), *Nebraska symposium on motivation* (pp. 1–110). Lincoln: University of Nebraska Press.

Berlyne, D. E. (1971). *Aesthetics and psychobiology.* New York: Appleton-Century-Crofts.

Bowlby, J. (1969). *Attachment and loss* (Vol. 1: Attachment). New York: Basic Books.

Boyle, G. J. (1983). Critical review of state-trait curiosity test development. *Motivation and Emotion, 7,* 377–397.

Boyle, G. J. (1989). Breadth-depth or state-trait curiosity: A factor analysis of state-trait curiosity and state anxiety scales. *Personality and Individual Differences, 10,* 175–183.

Cattell, R. B. (1957). *Personality and motivation structure and measurement.* New York: Harcourt.

Cattell, R. B. (1966). Anxiety and motivation: Theory and crucial experiments. In C. D. Spielberger (Ed.), *Anxiety and behavior* (pp. 23–62). New York: Academic Press.

Cattell, R. B., & Scheier, I. H. (1961). *The meaning and measurement of neuroticism and anxiety.* New York: Ronald Press.

Charlesworth, W. R. (1969). The role of surprise in cognitive development. In D. Elkind & J. H. Flavell (Eds.), *Studies in cognitive development* (pp. 257–314). New York: Oxford University Press.

Chiu, L. H. (1967). *A factorial study of academic motivation.* Unpublished doctoral dissertation, Teachers College, Columbia University, NY.

Cofer, C. N., & Appley, M. H. (1964). *Motivation: Theory and research.* New York: Wiley.

Darwin, C. (1965). *Expression of the emotions in man and animals.* Chicago: University of Chicago Press. (Originally published, 1872).

Dashiell, J. F. (1925). A quantitative demonstration of animal drive. *Journal of Comparative and Physiological Psychology, 5,* 205–208.

Day, H. I. (1969). *An instrument for the measurement of intrinsic motivation.* An interim report to the Department of Manpower and Immigration.

Day, H. I. (1971). The measure of specific curiosity. In H. I. Day, D. E. Berlyne, & D. E. Hunt (Eds.), *Intrinsic motivation: A new direction in education* (pp. 99–112). Toronto: Holt, Rinehart & Winston of Canada.

Dollard, J., & Miller, N. E. (1950). *Personality and psychotherapy.* New York: McGraw-Hill.

Dunlap, K. (1919). Are there any instincts? *Journal of Abnormal Psychology, 14,* 307–311.

Fiske, D. W., & Maddi, S. T. (1961). *Functions of varied experience.* Homewood, IL: Dorsey Press.

Frain, F. J. (1977). *A study of the relationship between anxiety and curiosity.* Unpublished master's thesis, University of South Florida, Tampa.

Freud, S. (1933). *New introductory lectures in psychoanalysis.* New York: Norton.

Freud, S. (1936). *The problem of anxiety.* New York: Norton.

Ginsburg, H., & Opper, S. (1969). *Piaget's theory of intellectual developments: An introduction.* Englewood Cliffs, NJ: Prentice-Hall.

Harlow, H. F. (1953). Motivation as a factor in new responses. In M. R. Jones (Ed.), *Current theory and research in motivation* (pp. 24–49). Lincoln: University of Nebraska Press.

Hebb, D. O. (1955). Drives and the C.N.S. (conceptual nervous system). *Psychological Review, 62,* 243–254.

James, W. (1890). *The principles of psychology.* New York: Holt.

Kuo, Z. Y. (1928). The fundamental error of the concept of purpose and the trial and error fallacy. *Psychological Review, 35,* 414–433.

Langevin, R. (1971). Is curiosity a unitary construct? *Canadian Journal of Psychology, 25,* 361–374.

Leuba, C. (1955). Toward some integration of learning theories: The concept of optimal stimulation. *Psychological Reports, 1,* 27–33.

Maw, W. H., & Maw, E. W. (1968). Self appraisal of curiosity. *The Journal of Educational Research, 61,* 462–465.

McDougall, W. (1921). *An introduction to social psychology.* Boston, MA: J. W. Luce Co.

McDougall, W. (1923). *Outline of psychology.* New York: Scribner.

McReynolds, P., & Bryan, J. (1956). Tendency to obtain new percepts as a function of the level of unassimilated percepts. *Perceptual and Motor Skills, 16,* 12–24.

Miller, N. E. (1961). Some recent studies of conflict behavior and drugs. *American Psychologist, 16,* 12–24.

Naylor, F. D. (1981). A state-trait curiosity inventory. *Australian Psychologist, 16,* 172–183.

Nissen, H. W. (1954). The nature of the drive as innate determinant of behavioral organization. In M. R. Jones (Ed.), *Nebraska Symposium on Motivation.* Lincoln: University of Nebraska Press.

Pearson, P. (1970). Relationships between global and specified measures of novelty seeking. *Journal of Consulting Psychology, 11,* 199–204.

Penney, R. K., & McCann, B. (1964). The children's reactive curiosity scale. *Psychological Reports, 15,* 323–334.

Peters, R. A. (1976). *The effects of anxiety, curiosity, and instructor threat on student verbal behavior in the college classroom.* Unpublished doctoral dissertation, University of South Florida, Tampa.

Peters, R. A. (1978). Effects of anxiety, curiosity, and perceived-instructor threat on student verbal behavior in the college classroom. *Journal of Educational Psychology, 70,* 388–395.

Schneirla, T. C. (1959). An evolutionary and developmental theory of biphasic processes underlying approach and withdrawal. In M. R. Jones (Ed.), *Nebraska Symposium on Motivation.* Lincoln: University of Nebraska Press.

Schneirla, T. C. (1965). Aspects of stimulation and organization in approach-withdrawal processes underlying vertegrate behavioral development. In D. L. Lehrman, R. Hinde, & E. Shaw (Eds.), *Advances in the study of behavior.* New York: Academic Press.

Spielberger, C. D. (1966). Theory and research on anxiety. In C. D. Spielberger (Ed.), *Anxiety and behavior.* New York: Academic Press.

Spielberger, C. D. (1972a). *Anxiety: Current trends in theory and research* (Vol. 1). New York: Academic Press.

Spielberger, C. D. (1972b). Conceptual and methodological issues in anxiety research. In C. D. Spielberger (Ed.), *Anxiety: Current trends in theory and research* (Vol. 1). New York: Academic Press.

Spielberger, C. D. (1979). Preliminary Manual for the State-Trait Personality Inventory (STPI). Unpublished manuscript, University of South Florida, Tampa.

Spielberger, C. D. (1983). *Manual for the State-Trait Anxiety Inventory (STAI) (Form Y).* Palo Alto, CA: Consulting Psychologists Press.

Spielberger, C. D., & Butler, T. F. (1971). *On the relationship between anxiety, curiosity, and arousal: A working paper.* Unpublished manuscript, Florida State University, Tallahassee.

Spielberger, C. D., Gorsuch, R. L., & Lushene, R. E. (1970). *Manual for the State-Trait Anxiety Inventory.* Palo Alto, CA: Consulting Psychologists Press.

Spielberger, C. D., Lushene, R. E., & McAdoo, W. G. (1977). Theory and measurement of anxiety states. In R. B. Cattell & R. M. Dreger (Eds.), *Handbook of modern personality theory* (pp. 239–253). New York: Hemisphere/Wiley.

Spielberger, C. D., Peters, R. A., & Frain, F. J. (1976). *The State-Trait Curiosity Inventory.* Unpublished test, University of South Florida.

Spielberger, C. D., Peters, R. A., & Frain, F. J. (1981). Curiosity and anxiety. In H. G. Voss & H. Keller (Eds.), *Curiosity research: Basic concepts and results.* Weinheim, FRG: Beltz.

Starr, L. M. (1992). *Assessment of curiosity as a multifaceted construct.* Unpublished master's thesis, University of South Florida, Tampa.

Vidler, D. C., & Rawan, H. R. (1974). Construct validation of a scale of academic curiosity. *Psychological Reports, 35,* 263–266.

Vidler, D. C., & Rawan, H. R. (1975). Further validation of a scale of academic curiosity. *Psychological Reports, 37,* 115–118.

Voss, H. G., & Keller, H. (1983). *Curiosity and exploration: Theories and results.* New York: Academic Press.

Voss, H. G., & Meyer, H. J. (1980). Befindlichkeitsmasse von Angst und Neugier in Stressituationen. [Measurement of anxiety and curiosity as emotional states in stress situations]. *Psychologische Beiträge.*

Watson, J. B. (1925). *Behaviorism.* New York: Norton.

White, R. W. (1961). Motivation reconsidered: The concept of competence. In D. W. Fiske & S. R. Maddi (Eds.), *Functions of varied experience.* Homewood, IL: Dorsey Press.

Zuckerman, M. (1969). Theoretical formulations: I. In J. P. Zubek (Ed.), *Sensory deprivation: Fifteen years of research* (pp. 407–432). New York: Appleton-Century-Crofts.

Zuckerman, M. (1975). *Manual and research report for the Sensation Seeking Scale.* Unpublished manuscript, University of Delaware.

Zuckerman, M. (1979). *Sensation seeking: Beyond the optimal level of arousal.* Hillsdale, NJ: Lawrence Erlbaum Associates.

Zuckerman, M., Kolin, E., Price, L., & Zoob, I. (1964). Development of a Sensation-Seeking Scale. *Journal of Consulting Psychology, 28,* 477–482.

13 The Measurement and Teaching of Creativity

Harold F. O'Neil, Jr.
University of Southern California/CRESST

Jamal Abedi
University of California, Los Angeles/CRESST

Charles D. Spielberger
University of South Florida, Gainesville

We believe that although many education and training systems have achieved excellent results in terms of domain-specific declarative and procedural knowledge, this excellence has been at a cost of reducing students' creativity. It is clearly in the long-term interest of education and training vendors to examine the creativity of students in their environments and to develop instruction to stimulate and improve students' creativity. Such instruction could be either teacher-led or technology-based. The purpose of this chapter is to review the literature on the nature, measurement, and teaching of creativity, and to suggest some necessary research activities to facilitate the teaching of creativity.

NATURE AND MEASUREMENT OF CREATIVITY

Many psychologists, educators, and philosophers of science have endeavored to articulate commonly acceptable definitions of creativity. Sanders and Sanders (1984, pp. 24–27), for example, cite various definitions of creativity offered by well-known educators, researchers and writers; several of these are given in Table 13.1.

Inspection of this table clearly demonstrates the complexity of creativity as a scientific construct. For example, Paul Torrance (cited in Sanders & Sanders, 1984) believes that: "Creativity is a process that involves sensing gaps or disturbing missing elements, hypotheses, communicating the results and possibly modifying and retesting these hypotheses" (p. 25).

Other definitions of creativity cited by Sanders and Sanders (1984) are even less operationally defined, representing a more complex picture of creativity. For

TABLE 13.1
Definitions of Creativity

Paul Torrance	"Creativity is a process that *involves sensing gaps or disturbing missing elements*, hypotheses, communicating the results and possibly modifying and retesting therse hypotheses."
Robert Samples	*"New Know"*
Jerome Bruner	"'*Effective surprise*'-An act that is the hallmark of a creative enterprise...I could not care less about the person's intention, whether or not he intended to create. The road to banality is paved with creative intentions."
Jean Piaget	*"If you want to be creative, stay in part a child,* with the creativity and invention that characterizes children before they are deformed by adult society."
Arthur Koestler	*"The combination of previously unrelated structures* in such a way that you get more out of the emergent whole then you have put in."
S. J. Parnes	"Let us start with the premise that *the essence of creativity is the fundamental notion of the 'aha'*--meaning the fresh and relevant association of thoughts, facts, ideas, etc., into anew configuration...one which pleases, which has meaning beyond the sum of the parts."
J. P. Guilford	*"Divergent thinking* in problem solving"
Abraham Maslow	"Primary creativity comes out of the unconscious...in the source of new discovery (or real novelty) of *ideas which depart from what exists at this point."*
Clark Moustakas	*"Creativity is an abstraction that attains a concrete form only in a particular and unique relation.* The branches of a tree stretch out expansive and free, maintaining a basic identity, an essential uniqueness in color, form, and pattern. They stand out in contrast to the fixed nature of the trunk. Yet, one cannot see a tree without recognizing its essential harmony, its wholeness, and its unity. (Creativity, like the branch, has meaning only in relation to the larger system.)"
Carl Sagan	"Mere critical thinking without the search for new patterns is sterile and doomed. To solve complex problems in changing circumstances requires *the activity of both cerebral hemispheres: the path to the future lies through the corpus callosum.:*

example, George Prince in *The Practice of Creativity* (1972) defines creativity as

> an arbitrary harmony, an unexpected astonishment, a habitual revelation, a familiar surprise, a generous selfishness, an unexpected certainty, a formable stubbornness, a vital triviality, a disciplined freedom, an intoxicating steadiness, a repeated initiation, a difficult delight, a predictable gamble, an ephemeral solidity, a unifying difference, a demanding satisfier, a miraculous expectation, an accustomed amazement. (pp. vii)

Among the definitions of creativity cited by Sanders and Sanders (1984), Guilford's definition as "divergent thinking in problem solving" is clearer from a psychometrics standpoint in that it is more helpful in guiding the construction of a tool for assessing creativity. Guilford (1959) defined divergent thinking as "we think in different directions" (p. 470), and hypothesized that at least eight primary abilities constitute the structure of creativity (Guilford, 1950) (see Table 13.2). These abilities were derived from his model of the "Structure of Intellect." The eight primary abilities are: Sensitivity to Problems, Fluency, Novel Ideas, Flexibility, Synthesizing, Analyzing, Complexity, and Evaluation. But Guilford's theory of creativity has been severely criticized. For example, Brown (1989) points out that Guilford has initially constructed his Structure of Intellect model and has then tried to verify it.

Torrance, who has been involved in both the teaching and measurement of creativity, provides a more practical view of creativity. In a recent article, Torrance and Goff (1989) propose the notion that numerous abilities underlie creativity. On the basis of their review of extensive research in this field, they believe that creativity

include[s] sensitivity to problems, fluency (ability to produce large numbers of ideas), flexibility (ability to produce a variety of ideas or use a variety of approaches), originality (ability to produce new, unusual, innovative ideas), elaboration (ability to fill in the details), and redefinition (ability to define or perceive in a way different from the usual established, intended way). (p. 142).

Although some of the factors underlying Torrance's definition of creativity and his Tests of Creative Thinking are adapted from Guilford's Structure of Intellect model, Torrance views creativity in the context of an educational model. Because our goal in this chapter is to suggest some approaches to teaching and

TABLE 13.2
Guilford's "Structure of Intellect" Primary Abilities

1. Sensitivity to problems	Creative individuals see problems which are not seen by noncreative people.
2. Fluency	Creative people produce large numbers of ideas.
3. Novel ideas	Creative people have unusual ideas.
4. Flexibility	Creative people use a variety of approaches.
5. Synthesizing	Creative people organize their ideas into larger and more inclusive ones.
6. Analyzing	Creative people break down "symbolic structures" to build new ones.
7. Complexity	Creative people can work with a number of interrelated ideas.
8. Evaluation	Creative people easily define the values of new ideas.

Note. See Brown (1989, p. 14).

measuring creativity in education and training settings, we have adopted Torrance's view of creativity as the most useful. In this chapter we focus on two distinctive and different aspects of creativity: (a) the measurement of creativity, and (b) the teaching of creativity.

The number and complexity of the definitions of creativity as a psychological construct have resulted in a multitude of instruments for measuring creativity. Although the literature presents many different approaches/instruments for measuring creativity, most of these tests lack the psychometric characteristics that a good measurement device should have. Moreover, the instruments for measuring creativity are very different in their form and in what they measure. As Hocevar and Bachelor (1989) have pointed out, "When viewed as a group, the most salient characteristic of creativity measurements is their diversity" (p. 53).

Creativity tests have been categorized in the literature in four quite different ways: (a) measures of divergent thinking, personality traits, and interests; (b) autobiographical inventories, rating by others; (c) creative activities and accomplishments; or (d) real life criteria of creativity. In the *Handbook of Creativity* (Glover, Ronning, & Reynolds, 1989), Hocevar and Bachelor (1989) provide a more detailed classification based on their review of the measurement of creativity. These categories are: (a) tests of divergent thinking, (b) attitude and interest inventories, (c) personality inventories, (d) biographical inventories, (e) rating by teachers, peers, and supervisors, (f) judgments of products, (g) eminence, (h) self-reported creative activities and achievements, and (i) "other creativity assessment procedures" (pp. 53, 58).

Torrance and Goff (1989) analyzed 255 creativity tests and assigned them to 13 categories (see Table 13.3). As shown in this table, there are more personality/attitude types of tests than any other category. Rating/observations tests are the next highest in frequency, whereas measures of artistic creativity, (e.g., dance, dramatics, music, and the like) have the lowest number of tests.

An important property in measurement is its validity. As mentioned earlier, because of the complex nature of creativity constructs, construct validity has been the main concern of researchers and psychometricians in the area of creativity measurement. Before our discussion of construct validity, however, we briefly discuss various reliability issues.

Because many creativity tests use open-ended or constructed responses, the interjudge reliability method would be generally the most appropriate method to establish reliability. A potential major problem with these types of tests is the problem of subjectivity of scoring. The lack of a widely accepted definition of creative behavior and of objective scoring techniques makes the scoring of creativity tests difficult and consequently may introduce a relatively large measurement error.

For example, the test-retest, split-half, and internal consistency reliability coefficients reported for many creativity tests are low. Other factors that also influence the magnitude of reliability coefficients of creativity measures include:

TABLE 13.3
Distribution of Types of Creativity Tests From the Torrence Creativity Test Collection

Type and Focus of Instrument	Number	Percentage
Personality/Attitude	62	28
Rating/Observations	42	19
Verbal	50	22
Figural	21	9
General	28	12
Mathematical/Science	6	3
Movement/Dance	5	2
Questionnaires	5	2
Dramatics	2	1
Combinations (Personality/ Attitude & Ratings/ Observations)	2	1
Artistic	1	0.5
Musical	1	0.5
Total	225	

restriction in range of scores, level of difficulty of vocabulary in test directions, differences in the motivational levels of individuals taking the tests, and substantial heterogeneity in the cultural backgrounds of the subjects (Michael & Wright, 1989). Fortunately, our recommended test for research purposes—the Torrance Tests of Creative Thinking (TTCT)—possesses reasonable reliability. We discuss this specific test later.

Construct Validity

The recent literature on creativity measurement has increasingly used a discriminant validity approach. For example, if creativity is different from other constructs, such as intelligence, achievement, or self-esteem, then intercorrelations between different instruments measuring creativity should be higher than the intercorrelations between creativity tests and those other measures (e.g., intelligence). The multitrait-multimethod technique (Campbell & Fiske, 1959) has frequently been used as a means for assessing the discriminant validity of creativity measures. Unfortunately, the creativity literature in general indicates a serious lack of discriminant validity for many creativity measures.

Hocevar and Bachelor (1989) cited a study (Holland, 1959) in which teachers, principals, and guidance counselors were asked to rate students on 12 traits, including originality. Originality is a key dimension of creativity. It was expected that the correlation between originality and these other traits would be low. The results of this study showed that the correlations between originality and speaking and writing skills were .72 and .84 respectively, while the other nine correlations between originality and the other variables ranged from .50 to .65. The data indicate a lack of discriminant validity. Hocevar and Bachelor (1989) cited several other studies that show similar trends. The problem of lack of discriminant validity becomes even more serious when judges are asked to discriminate between various dimensions of creativity. Based on several studies, Hocevar and Bachelor (1989) indicated that "the dimensions of divergent thinking tests have questionable discriminant validity" (p. 61).

Related to the validity of creativity measures is the problem associated with the measurement of originality. Originality is the most fundamental underlying factor in many measures of creativity. Originality is defined as the ability to produce unique ideas; the criterion for scoring originality that is most commonly used is statistical rarity.

A significant problem in the measurement of originality is the high correlation that is typically found between scores on measures of originality and ideational fluency (the ability to produce a large number of ideas). For example, very high correlations have been reported between ideational fluency and originality scores (Hocevar, 1979a, 1979b, 1980). These high correlations between the two variables indicate that they may measure the same construct, or that they may be confounded in some aspect. One explanation for this might be that the more responses (high fluency score), the higher chance of expressing a unique idea (high originality score). Based on the evidence from multitrait-multimethod studies, factor analysis, and analysis of partial correlation, Hocevar concluded that current tests of originality measure little more than ideational fluency. He then explained strategies for minimizing the fluency/originality confounding problem (see Hocevar & Michael, 1979; Zarnegar, Hocevar, & Michael, 1988). Among the strategies are different scoring procedures like ratio scores, equated scores, nonoverlapping scores, noncontaminated scores, factor scores, and task-induced independent scores (see Table 13.4). He believes that equated scores and task-

TABLE 13.4
Scoring Strategies to Minimize Confounding of Fluency and Originality

---

Ratio Score equals total originality score divided by total fluency score.

Equated Score equals score obtained by scoring an equal number of responses for originality.

Non-overlapping Scores consist of two indices: number of common responses and number of uncommon responses.

Non-Contaminated Score is obtained by scoring fluency on one set of tasks and originality on another set of tasks.

Factor Scores: If an origality factor can be identified either in an exploratory or confirmatory factor analysis, then factor scores based on that factor could be obtained.

Task-Induced Independent Scores instruct the subjects to give the same number of responses.

---

induced independent scores are preferable, but he adds that more research in this area is needed.

What Tests to Use in Measuring Creativity?

As mentioned earlier, there are many tests for measuring creativity which are different in their form, number and type of questions, and difficulty of administration and scoring. Few of them can be used to measure creativity with a high degree of confidence. For more detailed descriptions of creativity tests we refer readers to the *10th Mental Measurement Yearbook* (Conoley & Kramer, 1989) and to Hocevar and Bachelor (1989).

There are, however, two tests that have been used extensively in creativity research, and both have reasonable reliability and validity: (a) Guilford Test of Divergent Thinking (Guilford & Hoepfner, 1971), and (b) Torrance Tests of Creative Thinking (TTCT) (Torrance, 1974).

Guilford Test of Creative Thinking.   Based on his factor analytic model of the structure-of-intellect (SI), Guilford and his associates in the University of Southern California Aptitudes Research Project developed tests of divergent thinking (Guilford & Hoepfner, 1971). Of the 13 tests in this battery, 9 require verbal (semantic) responses and 4 employ figural content. The 9 verbal response tests are: (1) Word Fluency; (2) Ideational Fluency; (3) Associational Fluency; (4) Expressional Fluency; (5) Alternate Uses; (6) Simile Interpretations; (7) Plot Titles; (8) Consequences; and (9) Possible Jobs. The four figural tests are: (1) Making Objects; (2) Sketches; (3) Match Problems; and (4) Decorations. Recent research has partially confirmed his factor structure (Bachelor & Michael, 1991; Michael & Bachelor, 1990).

Scorer reliability and split-half reliability coefficients are satisfactory for these tests (Anastasi, 1982). Norms in terms of percentiles and standard scores are provided in the preliminary manuals (Anastasi, 1982, p. 387). Guilford and his associates have also developed a battery of creativity tests for children, with 5 verbal (semantic) and 5 figural tests in this battery. The authors have provided test norms for Grades 4 through 6. See Guilford and Hoepfner (1971) for detailed description and sample items of these tests.

Torrance Tests of Creative Thinking.   The Torrance Tests of Creative Thinking (TTCT) are the most widely used tests of creativity: More than 2,000 studies have used these tests (Torrance & Goff, 1989). Feldhusen and Clinkenbeard (1986) point out that "the most frequently employed criterion of the effectiveness of creativity training materials is some version of the Torrance Tests of Creative Thinking (TTCT)" (p. 153). Developed within an educational context, the TTCT consist of 12 tests that are grouped under verbal, pictorial, and auditory categories. These test categories are called Thinking Creatively with Words, Thinking

Creatively with Pictures, and Thinking Creatively with Sounds and Words, re-spectively. The tests are designed to be used from kindergarten to graduate school.

In Thinking Creatively with Words, there are seven activities involved which yield three total scores, one for Fluency, one for Flexibility, and one for Origi-nality. The next battery, Thinking Creatively with Pictures, has three activities and produces four total scores: Fluency, Flexibility, Originality, and Elaboration. Thinking Creatively with Sounds and Words, which is the most recent addition to the test, consists of two tests, (a) Sounds and Images, and (b) Onomatopoeia and Images. This battery yields only an originality score, which is obtained based on statistical rarity. The test comes with manuals for instructions and scoring (An-astasi, 1982).

Based on the studies cited in the manuals, all but one of the reliabilities for the Torrance measures range from .80 to .95. However, originality is the most difficult factor to score, resulting in reliability falling below .80 (see Anastasi, 1982, pp. 389–391, for more information). The predictive validity is excellent. For example, two longitudinal studies show good predictive validity of TTCT, one with high school students initiated in 1959 and one with elementary school students initiated in 1958. For the high school group ($N = 230$), a 12-year follow up indicated an overall validity coefficient of .51 between TTCT scores and criteria of creative accomplishment (Torrance & Goff, 1989). For the elementary school group, after 20 years, an overall validity coefficient of .63 was obtained (Torrance & Goff, 1989).

Thus, based on the literature in creative measurement, the creativity test of choice is the TTCT. However, a major concern is administering and scoring this commonly used creativity test. Because many of the test items are open-ended, the TTCT takes a considerable amount of time and expense to administer and score.

A Multiple-Choice Test for Measuring Creativity.   A much-needed approach to the measurement of creativity is the development of a psychometrically sound multiple-choice test to measure creativity, using the Torrance Tests of Creative Thinking and the development of creative products to validate it. A research effort initiated by Jamal Abedi (a coauthor of this chapter) and his students to develop a multiple-choice test for estimating scores of the four traits underlying the Torrance Tests of Creative Thinking (i.e., Fluency, Flexibility, Originality, and Elaboration) (see Table 13.5) has yielded very promising results. The origi-nal Persian language, 50-item, multiple-choice version of their test was adminis-tered in Iran to a group of 600 ninth- and tenth-grade students. The test was readministered to a subgroup of students ($n = 150$) after 1 week and test-retest reliability was .85. The TTCT was also administered to a subgroup ($n = 100$) of the students. The validity correlation coefficients between the four TTCT scores and four multiple-choice scores ranged from .15 to .41. The highest correlation

TABLE 13.5
Torrance Tests of Creative Thinking: Four Underlying Traits

Fluency—ability to produce large numbers of ideas
Flexibility—ability to produce a variety of ideas or use a variety of approaches
Originality—ability to produce new, unusual, innovative ideas
Elaboration—ability to fill in the details

Note. See Torrence (1977, p. 16).

(.41) was between the fluency scores of the two tests. Although disappointing, the results clearly indicated that additional research was needed.

A 1986 revision of the scale was lengthened to 85 items and translated into English. One of the main objectives in preparing the new test items and revising existing items was to attempt to write culture-free items, that is, to avoid items that might be associated with a specific cultural background. After further revision, a 75-item test was prepared in 1991 and provided to various professional reviewers. Items were revised again based on this feedback. Abedi's plan is to examine the reliability and the construct and concurrent validity of this test. The 75-item test also has been translated into Spanish and a cross-cultural study has been completed. The development of the scale is currently being documented.

Recommended Research

For research purposes, we suggest conducting a validity study in an educational context, using Abedi's test with the Torrance Tests of Creative Thinking and the use of creative products for concurrent validity. Anxiety should be measured, as it seems to depress creativity (e.g., Smith, Michael, & Hocevar, 1990). If acceptable reliability and validity are found, then a similar study should be carried out in an Army educational or training environment. Assuming acceptable reliability and validity, a multiple-choice test then could be used to measure creativity. The major use for this test would be to validate various methods of teaching students to be more creative.

TEACHING CREATIVITY

A basic question is: Can creative thinking be taught? Torrance and Torrance (1973), in their book on teaching creativity, concluded that in their 15 years experience of studying and teaching creative thinking, "they see evidence that teaching makes a difference in creativity" (p. 6). The general conclusion in their book was that

> it does indeed seem possible to teach creative thinking. The most successful approaches seem to be those that involve both cognitive and emotional functioning,

provide adequate structure and motivation, and give opportunities for involvement, practice, and interaction with teachers and other students. Motivating and facilitating conditions certainly make a difference in creative functioning but differences seem greatest and most predictable when deliberate teaching is involved. (p. 46)

Torrance and Torrance (1973) based the foregoing generalization on their review of 142 studies on the teachability of creativity (Torrance, 1972); the studies then were classified into nine categories according to the method used for stimulating creativity. The percentage of success ranged from 50% for "curricular and administrative arrangements" to 91% for "Osborn-Parnes" and 92% for "other disciplined approaches." There are numerous other studies that provide evidence that creativity is teachable (see Torrance, 1986). Among the other researchers who have demonstrated the teachability of creativity are the following: Blank and Parker (1986); Baron and Harrington (1981); Carnevale, Gainer, and Meltzer (1990); Epstein (1991); Feldhusen and Clinkenbeard (1986); Jaben (1985a, 1985b); Marks (1989); Mayer (1989); Milgram (1989); Onda (1986); Shaw and Cliatt (1986); Stovall and Williams (1985); Torrance and Goff (1989).

A representative study was conducted by Torrance and Torrance (1973) using an "Osborn-Parnes modified procedure" with 11 tenth graders. (For detailed information about Osborn-Parnes procedures see Parnes, 1967.) They administered a pretest and a posttest to see the effect of the "Osborn-Parnes" method on students' creativity. They reported significant improvement of creative responses. For example, on the criterion "development of criteria and evaluation of ideas" they reported an average of 1 idea on the pretest as compared with an average of 5.5 ideas on the posttest. They also reported significant gains on the scores of originality and elaboration of the Torrance Tests of Creative Thinking (Torrance & Torrance, 1973, p. 21).

A more recent study by Singh (1985) also showed the effects of teaching creativity. Singh examined the effects of teaching mathematics on the basis of process-oriented, divergent thinking principles to the experimental group, while the control group was taught by the regular method. Results of math scores indicated that teacher behavior significantly helped students in the experimental group to develop creative potential (Singh, 1985).

The literature has reported numerous studies and/or curricular plans/activities for teaching creativity in specific areas or domains. Some of these studies have examined the effectiveness of existing models or activities for specific domains, and others have offered new techniques. There are many domains for which creativity models, teaching methods, or activities have been reported in the literature. Following are some examples:

Architecture (Taylor, 1989); Algebra (Kerekes, 1990); Business Communication (Golen, 1986); Chemistry (Christensen, 1988); Geography (Freseman, 1990); Dance (Stinson, 1990; Weiler, 1988); Logo Programming Language (Clements, 1991); Management (Shalley, 1991); Music (Balkin, 1985; Burns,

1988; Ludowise, 1985; Moore, 1990); Reading (Bonds & Bonds, 1990); Poetry (Craig, 1987); Social Studies (Eulie, 1984; Solomon, 1989; Subotnik, 1984); Teacher Education Curriculum (Bozik, 1990; Soriano & Eunice, 1989); Writing (McClain, 1986; Oklahoma State Department of Education, 1985; Sweeney, 1986); Problem Solving (Adamson, 1985; Davis, 1984; Disinger, 1990; Kruse, 1987; Mayer, 1989; National Council of Teachers of English, 1986; Paine, 1984; Stevens, 1985); Teaching of Thinking (Brown, 1988; Cliatt & Shaw, 1987; de Bono, 1986; Gartenhaus, 1984; Hauser, 1987; Heiman & Slomianko 1987; Kirby & Kuykendall, 1985; Petreshene, 1985; Robinson, 1987; Schuster, 1984).

How to Teach Creative Thinking

We now shift our focus to "how to teach" creative thinking and to the discussion of some well-known methods or systems for teaching creativity. Sanders and Sanders (1984), in their book *Teaching Creativity Through Metaphor,* explain hemispheric specialization and how instructional strategies that use both sides of the brain could foster creativity. Although the experimental evidence is limited for this approach, we believe that the metaphor of left brain/right brain is useful to generate ideas of how to teach creativity (see Cardinale, 1990; Deshmukh, 1985; Geske, 1992; Torrance & Rockenstein, 1987; Wess, 1985).

Sanders and Sanders believe that the left hemisphere of the brain deals mainly with logical, analytical, and verbal abilities, and that this side of the brain controls language, cognition, and sense of time in most people. In contrast, the right hemisphere is intuitive, conceptual and nonverbal, and controls spatial relationships, intuitive thinking, and imagery (Sanders & Sanders, 1984, p. 10). Sanders and Sanders believe that educational systems that put too much emphasis on facts, details, memory, and predetermined answers force a left-hemisphere dominance, which could result in a lack of development of right-brain creativity and conceptual ability (p. 19). Many scholars in both the United States and Japan believe that the Japanese educational system has this approach. They suggest that to teach creativity, rather than encouraging memorization of concepts, an alternative model should be offered of how concepts can be applied. They believe that teaching metaphors provides such a model. They also emphasize the importance of the process of imagery formation in fostering creativity. Sanders and Sanders (1987) presented a 7-step technique for using metaphors with elementary students to develop their creativity and improve their writing skills.

Literature also suggests numerous instructional strategies for enhancing creativity that are not directly tied to the issue of right/left brain hemisphere. Studies cited earlier in teaching creativity have shown effectiveness of many of these strategies. However, the instructional strategies suggested in the literature are mainly domain-specific methods (e.g., Bean, 1992; Burns & Klingstedt, 1988; Davis, 1989; Thomas, 1985).

What to Use for Teaching Creativity?

The most critical question in teaching creativity is what kind of methods, activities, or models to use. Although the literature that we reviewed on teaching creativity has reported numerous options available for this purpose, an explicit, detailed, teacher-led curriculum to teach creativity is rare.

Feldhusen and Clinkenbeard (1986) reviewed research on curriculum materials used in teaching creativity. The materials reviewed include the Purdue Creative Thinking Program (PCTP) by Feldhusen, Bahlke, and Treffinger (1969); Creative Problem Solving (CPS) by Parnes (Parnes, Noller, & Biondi, 1977; Noller, Parnes, & Biondi, 1976); the Productive Thinking Program (PTP) by Covington, Crutchfield, and Davis (1966); Image/Craft and the Ideabooks by Torrance and Gupta (1964); New Directions in Creativity by Renzulli (1973a, 1973b); the Peabody Language Development Kits by Dunn and Smith (1967); and the Imagery Training Program by Khatena (1976). We now briefly describe the best selection of curriculum materials for elementary grade students, the data on their effectiveness, and their applicability internationally.

Purdue Creative Thinking Program (PCTP). This program consists of a series of 28 lessons designed for third-, fourth-, fifth-, and sixth-grade students to foster divergent thinking abilities (see Feldhusen & Clinkenbeard, 1986, and Feldhusen et al., 1969 for a description of this program). Each lesson has three parts. The first part teaches ideas for improving creative thinking; the second part is a story about a famous American pioneer. The third part, which is a series of printed exercises, provides practice in creative thinking.

Studies of the effectiveness of this program have demonstrated very positive results (see for example, Feldhusen, Speedie, & Treffinger, 1971; Huber, Treffinger, Tracy, & Rand, 1979; Jaben, 1985a, 1985b; Pitts, 1975; Robinson, 1969; Rose & Lin, 1984; Shively, Feldhusen, & Treffinger, 1972; Speedie, Treffinger, & Feldhusen, 1971; Treffinger, Speedie, & Bruner, 1974). International studies of the PCTP approach have also shown positive results. For example, Alencar, Feldhusen, and Wicllok (1976) used the PCTP approach with Brazilian students. The results indicated that the experimental group demonstrated more creativity. Sherif (1978) used PCTP on Egyptian children and found that the experimental group performed significantly better than the control group on TTCT.

Productive Thinking Program (PTP). This program consists of a series of programmed instructional booklets for fifth- and sixth-grade students and is designed to foster creative problem solving abilities (see Covington & Crutchfield, 1965, and Covington et al., 1966, for a detailed description of this program). The lessons are presented to students in a mystery story format. The story characters stress the affective elements in problem solving. The findings on effectiveness of this program are mixed. Some studies found the PTP program to be highly effective (Covington & Crutchfield, 1965; Olton & Crutchfield, 1969). Other studies also found moderately positive results for effectiveness of PTP (Ripple & Dacey, 1967; Rose & Lin, 1984; Schuler, 1974; Treffinger & Ripple, 1969; Wardrop et al., 1969). The literature in general is supportive of the PTP program, and it is believed to be an effective tool in developing creative problem solving abilities.

Creative Problem Solving (CPS). This program is designed to foster creative problem solving. The program consists of five steps: (a) fact-finding; (b) problem-finding; (c) idea-finding; (d) solution-finding; and (e) acceptance-finding (Feldhusen & Clinkenbeard, 1986). This program has been found to be very effective in teaching creative problem solving. The literature has shown evidence on effectiveness of various components of the creative problem solving approach (see for example Biles, 1976; Biondi, 1975; Kealey, 1977; Meadow, Parnes, & Reese, 1959; Parnes 1961, 1967; Parnes & Meadow, 1959; Parnes et al., 1977; Reese, Parnes, Treffinger, & Kaltsounis, 1976; Rose & Lin 1984; Shean, 1977).

Torrance and Goff (1989) describe four curriculum programs designed to foster creativity which are (a) The Future Problem Solving Program; (b) Odyssey of the Mind; (c) Invent America; and (d) the Torrance Creative Scholars Program. Torrance and Goff (1989) indicated that "the four programs are examples of the kinds of creative programming conceived in the United States and extended out internationally" (p. 142).

Recommended Research

There is no single, off-the-shelf program that can be easily modified for teaching creativity to students. However, there are several programs that could serve as the basis for a curriculum development effort. For example, the Purdue Creative Thinking Program has been shown to be effective nationally and internationally. Other programs, like the Productive Thinking Program, Creative Problem Solving, and the four approaches suggested by Torrance and Goff (1989), are promising and should also be considered as part of a design for teaching creativity.

What is needed is a composite approach in which the best techniques would be abstracted from various approaches to the teaching of creativity. The approach and curriculum could then be field tested and revised based on student performance.

ACKNOWLEDGMENTS

The research reported in this chapter was supported in part by the U.S. Army Research Institute for the Behavioral and Social Sciences through a subcontract with Battelle Institute, and in part by the Center for the Study of Learning,

Nichinoken, Inc., Yokohama, Japan. However, the views, opinions and/or findings contained in this report are the authors' and should not be construed as an official position, policy, or decision of either ARI or Nichinoken, Inc. unless so designated by other official documentation.

Partial support was also provided by the National Center for Research on Evaluation, Standards, and Student Testing (CRESST) under the Educational Research and Development Center Program cooperative agreement R117G10027 and CFDA catalog number 84.117G as administered by the Office of Educational Research and Improvement, U.S. Department of Education. The findings and opinions expressed in this chapter do not reflect the position or policies of the Office of Educational Research and Improvement or the U.S. Department of Education.

REFERENCES

Adamson, C. (1985). Creativity in the classroom. *Pointer, 29*(3), 11–15.

Alencar, E., Feldhusen, J. F., & Wicllok, F. W. (1976). Creative training in elementary school in Brazil. *Journal of Experimental Education, 44*, 23–27.

Anastasi, A. (1982). *Psychological testing* (5th ed.). New York: Macmillan.

Bachelor, P., & Michael, W. B. (1991). Higher-order factors of creativity within Guilford's Structure-of-Intellect model: A re-analysis of a fifty-three variable data base. *Creativity Research Journal, 4*(2) 157–175.

Balkin, A. (1985). The creative music classroom: Laboratory for creativity in life. *Music Educators Journal, 71*(5), 43–46.

Baron, F., & Harrington, D. M. (1981). Creativity, intelligence and personality. *Annual Review of Psychology, 32*, 439–475.

Bean, R. (1992). *Individuality: Self-expression and other keys to creativity: Using the 4 conditions of self-esteem in elementary and middle schools*. Santa Cruz, CA: ETR Associates.

Biles, B. R. (1976). Creative problem-solving training for graduate and professional students. *DAI, 37A*, 4220.

Biondi, A. M. (1975). *Creative problem-solving: From holding patterns to free flight*. New York: Creative Educational Foundation.

Blank, S. S., & Parker, D. J. (1986). Training for figural fluency, flexibility and originality in native Canadian children. *Journal of Special Education, 10*(4), 339–348.

Bonds, C., & Bonds, L. G. (1990). Adding creativity to reading instruction. *Reading Improvement, 27*(2), 106–110.

Bozik, M. (1990). Teachers as creative decision makers: Implications for curriculum. *Action in Teacher Education, 12*(1), 50–54.

Brown, M. A. (1988, February). *Applying the S.O.I. model to curriculum development*. Paper presented at the annual conference of the California Association for the Gifted, Santa Clara, CA.

Brown, R. T. (1989). Creativity. What are we to measure? In J. A. Glover, R. R. Ronning, & C. R. Reynolds (Eds.), *Handbook of creativity* (pp. 3–32). New York: Plenum Press.

Burns, M. T. (1988). Music as a tool for enhancing creativity. *Journal of Creative Behavior, 22*(1), 62–69.

Burns, R. W., & Klingstedt, J. L. (1988). Excellence through high-quality individualization. *Clearing House, 61*(9) 417–418.

Campbell, D. T., & Fiske, D. W. (1959). Convergent and discriminant validation by the multitrait-multimethod matrix. *Psychological Bulletin, 56*, 81–105.

Cardinale, G. W. (1990). Whole brain or whole bored. *Social Studies Review, 29*(2) 36–45.

Carnevale, A. P., Gainer, L. J., & Meltzer, A. S. (1990). *Workplace basics. The essential skills employers want.* San Francisco/Oxford: Jossey-Bass.

Christensen, J. J. (1988). Reflections on teaching creativity (Award Lecture). *Chemical Engineering Education, 22*(4) 170–176.

Clements, D. H. (1991, Spring). Enhancement of creativity in computer environments. *American Educational Research Journal, 28*(1), 173–187.

Cliatt, M. J., & Shaw, J. M. (1987). *Developing thinking skills in young children: Teacher/assistant teacher staff development materials.* Jackson, MS: Mississippi State Department of Education, Jackson Bureau of School Improvement.

Conoley, J. C., & Kramer, J. J. (Eds.). (1989). *The 10th mental measurement yearbook.* Lincoln: University of Nebraska Press.

Covington, M. V., & Crutchfield, R. S. (1965). Facilitation of creative problem solving. *Programmed Instruction, 4,* 305.

Covington, M. V., Crutchfield, R. S., & Davis, L. (1966). The productive thinking program. Berkeley, CA: Educational Innovation, Inc.

Craig, C. (1987). Using creative thinking skills to enhance poetry writing. *Canadian Journal of English Language Arts, 11*(3), 64–72.

Davis, G. A. (1989). Objectives and activities for teaching creative thinking. *Gifted Child Quarterly, 33*(2), 81–84.

Davis, M. S. (1984). Time for the future. *Social Education, 48*(7), 570–571.

de Bono, E. (1986). A technique for teaching creative thinking. *Momentum, 17*(3), 17–19.

Deshmukh, M. N. (1985). Teaching the inteachable: Some pedagogical considerations of creativity. *Psycho-Lingua, 15*(1) 33–40.

Disinger, J. F. (1990). Teaching creative thinking through environmental education. *Environmental Education Digest, 3.*

Dunn, L. M., & Smith, J. O. (1967). *Peabody language development kits. Manual for level #3.* Circle Pines, MN: American Guidance Service, Inc.

Epstein, R. (1991). Skinner, creativity, and the problem of spontaneous behavior. *Psychological Science, 2*(6), 362–370.

Eulie, J. (1984). Creativity: Its implications for social studies. *Social Studies, 75*(1), 28–31.

Feldhusen, J. F., Bahlke, S. J., & Treffinger, D. J. (1969). Teaching creative thinking. *Elementary School Journal, 70,* 48–53.

Feldhusen, J. F., & Clinkenbeard, P. A. (1986). Creativity instructional materials: A review of research. *Journal of Creative Behavior, 20*(3), 153–182.

Feldhusen, J. F., Speedie, S. M., & Treffinger, D. J. (1971). The Purdue Creative Thinking Program: Research and evaluation. *NSPI Journal, 10,* 5–9.

Freseman, R. D. (1990). Improving higher order thinking of middle school geography students by teaching skills directly. Fort Lauderdale, FL: Nova University, Ed.D. Practicum.

Gartenhaus, A. R. (1984). *In pursuit of wild geese. Teaching creative thinking: A Smithsonian approach.* Washington, DC: Smithsonian Institute.

Geske, J. (1992, August). *Teaching creativity for right brain and left brain thinkers.* Paper presented at the annual meeting of the Association for Education in Journalism and Mass Communication, Montreal, Canada.

Glover, J. A., Ronning, R. R., & Reynolds, C. R. (Eds.). (1989). *Handbook of creativity.* New York: Plenum Press.

Golen, S. P. (1986). *Methods of teaching selected topics in business communication.* Urbana, IL: Association for Business Communication.

Guilford, J. P. (1950). Creativity. *American Psychologist, 5,* 444–454.

Guilford, J. P. (1959). Three faces of intellect. *American Psychologist, 14,* 469–479.

Guilford, J. P., & Hoepfner, R. (1971). *The analysis of intelligence.* New York: McGraw-Hill.

Hauser, J. (1987, February). *Stimulating critical thinking and discussion formats: Research and strategies for educators to ponder.* Paper presented at the annual meeting of the Association of Teacher Educators, Houston, TX.

Heiman, M., & Slomianko, J. (1987). *Thinking skills instruction: Concepts and techniques. Building students' thinking skills series.* Washington, DC: National Education Association.

Hocevar, D. (1979a). Ideational fluency as a confounding factor in the measurement of originality. *Journal of Educational Psychology, 71*(2) 191–196.

Hocevar, D. (1979b). The unidimensional nature of creative thinking in fifth grade children. *Child Study Journal, 9*(4) 273–278.

Hocevar, D. (1980). Intelligence, divergent thinking, and creativity. *Intelligence, 4,* 25–40.

Hocevar, D., & Bachelor, P. (1989). A taxonomy and critique of measurements used in the study of creativity. In J. A. Glover, R. R. Ronning, & C. R. Reynolds (Eds.), *Handbook of creativity* (pp. 53–76). New York: Plenum Press.

Hocevar, D., & Michael, W. B. (1979). The effects of scoring formulas on the discriminant validity of tests of divergent thinking. *Educational and Psychological Measurement, 39,* 917–921.

Holland, J. L. (1959). Some limitations of teacher ratings as predictors of creativity. *Journal of Educational Psychology, 50,* 219–223.

Huber J. R., Treffinger, D. J., Tracy, D. B., & Rand, D. C. (1979). The self-instructional use of programmed creativity training materials with gifted and regular students. *Journal of Educational Psychology, 3,* 303–309.

Jaben, T. H. (1985a). Effects of instruction for creativity on learning disabled students' drawings. *Perceptual and Motor Skills, 61,* 895–898.

Jaben, T. H. (1985b). Effects of instruction on elementary-age students' productive thinking. *Psychological Reports, 57*(3) 900–902.

Kealey, J. R. (1977). A study of the effects of training in creative problem solving on the creativity of student teachers of foreign language and on the attitudes of their students. *DAI, 37A,* 5053.

Kerekes, V. (1990). A problem-solving approach to teaching second-year algebra. *Mathematics Teacher, 83*(6), 32–35.

Khatena, J. (1976, April). *Creative imagination imagery: Where is it going?* Paper presented at the annual meeting of the American Educational Research Association, San Francisco.

Kirby, D., & Kuykendall, C. (1985). *Thinking through language. Book one.* Urbana, IL: National Council of Teachers of English.

Kruse, J. C. (1987). *Classroom activities in thinking skills.* Philadelphia: Research for Better Schools, Inc.

Ludowise, K. D. (1985). Movement to music: Ten activities that foster creativity. *Childhood Education, 62*(1), 40–43.

Marks, T. (1989). Creativity inside out. From theory to practice. *Creativity Research Journal, 2,* 204–221.

Mayer, R. E. (1989). Cognitive views of creativity: Creative teaching for creative learning. *Contemporary Educational Psychology, 14*(3), 203–211.

McClain, A. (1986, October). *I can teach, they can write. Student teachers and primary children pattern books as models for creative writing.* Paper presented at the annual meeting of the Northwest Regional Conference of the National Council of Teachers of English, Portland, OR.

Meadow, A., Parnes, S. J., & Reese, H. W. (1959). Influence of brainstorming instructions and problems sequence on creative problem solving test. *Journal of Applied Psychology, 43,* 413–418.

Michael, W. B., & Bachelor, P. (1990). Higher-order Structure-of-Intellect creativity factors in divergent production tests: A re-analysis of a Guilford data base. *Creativity Research Journal, 3*(1), 58–74.

Michael, W. B., & Wright, C. R. (1989). Psychometric issues in the assessment of creativity. In J. A. Glover, R. R. Ronning, & C. R. Reynolds (Eds.), *Handbook of creativity* (pp. 33–52). New York: Plenum Press.

Milgram, R. M. (Ed.). (1989). *Teaching gifted and talented learners in regular classrooms.* Springfield, IL: Charles C. Thomas.

Moore, J. L. (1990). Strategies for fostering creative thinking. *Music Educators Journal, 76*(9), 38–42.

National Council of Teachers of English. (1986). *Activities to promote critical thinking. Classroom practices in teaching English.* Urbana, IL: NCTE Committee on Classroom Practice in Teaching English.

Noller, R. B., Parnes, S. J., & Biondi, A. M. (1976). *Creative action book.* New York: Scribner.

Oklahoma State Department of Education. (1985). *Kaleidoscope: Focus on creative reading, writing and thinking.* Oklahoma City: Author.

Olton, R. M., & Crutchfield, R. S. (1969). Developing the skills of productive thinking. In P. Mussen, J. Langer, & M. Covington (Eds.), *Trends and issues in developmental psychology* (pp. 68–91). New York: Holt, Rinehart and Winston.

Onda, A. (1986). Trends in creativity research in Japan—History and present status. *Journal of Creative Behavior, 20*(2) 134–140.

Paine, C. (1984). Help problem solvers solve problems with problem solving. *Learning, 12*(6), 30–31.

Parnes, S. J. (1961). Effects of extended effort in creative problem solving. *Journal of Educational Psychology, 52,* 117–122.

Parnes, S. J. (1967). *Creative behavior workbook.* New York: Scribner.

Parnes, S. J., & Meadow, A. (1959). Effects of brainstorming instructions on creative problem-solving by trained and untrained subjects. *Journal of Educational Psychology, 50,* 171–176.

Parnes, S. J., Noller, R. B., & Biondi, A. M. (1977). *Guide to creative action.* New York: Scribner.

Petreshene, S. S. (1985). Ten-minute think sessions. *Instructor, 94*(5), 69–71.

Pitts, C. S. (1975). *Effects of a creativity program on the creative thinking abilities of elementary emotionally disturbed children.* Unpublished master's thesis. University of New Mexico, Albuquerque.

Prince, G. M. (1972). *The practice of creativity; A manual for dynamic group problem solving.* New York: Collier Books.

Reese, H., Parnes, S., Treffinger, D., & Kaltsounis, G. (1976). Effects of a creative studies program on Structure-of-Intellect factors. *Journal of Educational Psychology, 68,* 401–410.

Renzulli, J. (1973a). *New directions in creativity: Mark I.* New York: Harper and Row.

Renzulli, J. (1973b). *New directions in creativity: Mark II.* New York: Harper and Row.

Ripple, R. E., & Dacey, J. S. (1967). The facilitation of problem solving and verbal creativity by exposure to programmed instruction. *Psychology in the Schools, 4,* 240–245.

Robinson, I. S. (1987). *A program to incorporate high-order thinking skills into teaching and learning for Grades K-3* (Ed.D. Practicum). Fort Lauderdale, FL; Nova University.

Robinson, W. L. T. (1969). *Taped creativity series versus conventional teaching and learning.* Unpublished master's thesis. Atlanta University.

Rose, L. H., & Lin, H. T. (1984). A meta-analysis of long-term creativity training programs. *Journal of Creative Behavior, 18,* 11–22.

Sanders, D. A., & Sanders, J. A. (1984). *Teaching creativity through metaphor. An integrated brain approach.* New York: Longman.

Sanders, D. A., & Sanders, J. A. (1987). Capturing the magic of metaphor. *Learning, 15*(6), 37–39.

Schuler, G. (1974, April). *The effectiveness of the Productive Thinking Program.* Paper presented at the annual meeting of the American Educational Research Association, Chicago.

Schuster, E. H. (1984). An opportunity for divergent thinking in the classroom. *Gifted/ Creative/Talented, 34,* 30–33.

Shalley, C. E. (1991). Effects of productivity goals, creativity goals, and personal discretion on individual creativity. *Journal of Applied Psychology, 76*(2), 179–185.

Shaw, J. M., & Cliatt, M. J. (1986). A model for training teachers to encourage divergent thinking in young children. *Journal of Creative Behavior, 20*(2) 81–88.

Shean, J. M. (1977). The effect of training in creative problem solving on divergent thinking and organizational perceptions of students of school administration. *DAI, 38A,* 585.

Sherif, N. (1978). *The effects of creativity training, classroom atmosphere, and cognitive style on the creative thinking abilities of Egyptian elementary school children.* Unpublished doctoral dissertation. Purchase University.

Shively, S. M., Feldhusen, J. F., & Treffinger, D. J. (1972). Developing creativity and related attitudes. *The Journal of Experimental Education, 41,* 63–69.

Singh, B. (1985). Change in some characteristics of teacher behaviour and its effect on pupil creativity. *Indian Journal of Applied Psychology, 22*(1–2), 31–35.

Smith, K. L. R., Michael, W. B., & Hocevar, D. (1990). Performance on creativity measures with examination-taking instructions intended to induce high or low levels of test anxiety. *Creativity Research Journal, 3*(4), 265–280.

Solomon, W. (1989). Teaching social studies creatively. *Social Studies and the Young Learner, 2*(1), 3–5.

Soriano, A., & Eunice, M. L. (1989). Instructing Brazilian teachers to develop children's creative abilities. *Gifted Child Today, 12*(3), 13–14.

Speedie, S. M., Treffinger, D. J., & Feldhusen, J. F. (1971). Evaluation of components of the Purdue Creative Thinking Program: A longitudinal study. *Psychological Reports, 29,* 395–398.

Stevens, L. A. (1985). To solve or not to solve. *Instructor, 94*(8), 57–58.

Stinson, S. W. (1990). Dance education in early childhood. *Design for Arts in Education, 91*(6), 34–41.

Stovall, N. C., & Williams, R. H. (1985). A comparative study of the effectiveness of the Williams-Stockmyer creativity system in promoting the creative thinking of sixth grade children. *Creative Child & Adult Quarterly, 10*(2), 106–113.

Subotnik, R. F. (1984). Emphasis on the creative dimension: Social studies curriculum modifications for gifted intermediate and secondary students. *Roeper Review, 7*(1), 7–10.

Sweeney, J. (1986, August). *"Individual sparks": An approach to teaching the young advertising writer.* Paper presented at the annual meeting of the Association for Education in Journalism and Mass Communication, Norman, OK.

Taylor, A. (1989). Perspectives on architecture and children. *Art Education, 42*(5), 7–12.

Thomas, R. S. (1985). *Strategies for differentiating curricula.* Baltimore, MD: Baltimore County Public Schools, Department of Curriculum.

Torrance, E. P. (1972). Can we teach children to think creatively? *Journal of Creative Behavior, 6,* 114–143.

Torrance, E. P. (1974). *Norm-technical manual: Torrance Tests of Creative Thinking.* Lexington, MA: Personnel Press.

Torrance, E. P. (1977). *Creativity in the classroom.* Washington, DC: National Education Association.

Torrance, E. P. (1986). Teaching creative and gifted learners. In M. C. Wittrock (Ed.), *Handbook of research on teaching* (3rd ed., pp. 630–647). New York: Macmillan.

Torrance, E. P., & Goff, K. (1989). A quiet revolution. *Journal of Creative Behavior, 23*(2), 136–145.

Torrance, E. P., & Gupta, R. (1964). *Programmed experiences in creative thinking.* Minneapolis: University of Minnesota, Bureau of Educational Research.

Torrance, E. P., & Rockenstein, A. L. (1987). Styles of thinking and creativity. *Gifted International, 4*(1), 37–49.

Torrance, E. P., & Torrance, P. J. (1973). *Is creativity teachable?* Bloomington, IN: Phi Delta Kappa Educational Foundation.

Treffinger, D. J., & Ripple, R. E. (1969). Developing creative problem solving abilities and related attitudes through programmed instruction. *Journal of Creative Behavior, 3,* 105–110.

Treffinger, D. J., Speedie, S. M., & Bruner, W. D. (1974). Improving children's creative problem solving ability: The Purdue Creative Project. *The Journal of Creative Behavior, 8,* 20–30.

Wardrop, J. L., Olton, R. M., Goodwin, W. L., Covington, M. V., Klausmeier, H. J., Crutchfield, R. S., & Ronda, T. (1969). The development of productive thinking skills in fifth-grade children. *Journal of Experimental Education, 37,* 67–77.

Weiler, V. B. (1988). *A guide to curriculum planning in dance.* Madison: Wisconsin State Department of Public Instruction.

Wess, R. C. (1985). Creativity and composing: The composition teacher as student. *Teaching English in the Two-Year College, 12*(3) 191–197.

Zarnegar, Z., Hocevar, D., & Michael, W. B. (1988). Components of original thinking in gifted children. *Educational and Psychological Measurement, 48,* 5–16.

　　　　　　　　　　　　　　　　　　　　　　　　　　　　　　　　　　　ﾞ

14

The Effects of an Intensive General Thinking Program on the Motivation and Cognitive Development of At-Risk Students: Findings From the HOTS Program

Stanley Pogrow
Gary Londer
University of Arizona, Tucson

One of the biggest social programs facing the United States is how to solve the problem of the at-risk student. Despite major increases in educational funding, and despite increased knowledge about the nature of learning, there are a substantial number of students in public education, particularly in urban areas, that continue to fail. Levin (1986) estimates that disadvantaged students accounted for 30% of elementary and secondary students in 1982, and that percentage is increasing. It is significantly higher in urban districts. Macchiarola (1988) found the dropout rate to be 45% in New York City Public Schools. The rates are significantly higher in the poor sections of the city. In Los Angeles, 19% of the Black and Hispanic students were left back a year in 1984-1985 (Orfield, 1988). Schmidt (1992) cites 1990 census data as showing that more children than ever are falling behind grade level.

There are myriad reasons for the failures of these students and the schools that they attend. It is not known whether educational interventions by themselves can make a substantial dent in the problem of the at-risk student. At the same time, it is clear that the typical at-risk student suffers from major learning and motivational problems. It is also clear that, given the severity of the students' problem, for any educational intervention to have major effects it must be carefully designed, highly systematic and creative, and provide extensive services. The Higher Order Thinking Skills (HOTS) program is an attempt to design such an intervention. Indeed, there are few such programmatic efforts that provide researchers with an opportunity to study the effects of extended, intensive learning environments on the motivation and cognitive development of at-risk students.

This chapter focuses on conclusions about the nature of motivation and cognitive development that have been observed from experience with the HOTS program. Although research on motivation was not used in the design of the program, existing research is reviewed. The utility of this research for the design of intensive environments is also examined. We conclude with a discussion of the need to reorient future research on motivation and cognitive development to study the effects of intensive environments.

This chapter forsakes the traditional organizational pattern where the ideas presented originate from, or are justified by, a review of the literature. Such organization in this instance would not be true to what actually happened. Given the lack of research in intensive environments, the techniques used in HOTS originated largely from intuition, which was refined by large-scale observation, and key ideas from cognitive psychology. It is only recently that the research on motivation was reviewed. Therefore, the key techniques used in the HOTS program are presented first, before the literature on motivation is reviewed to see the extent to which the research on motivation and at-risk students is consistent with what has been observed in the HOTS program, and the extent to which the literature would have provided important clues had it been reviewed in the early stages of the program.

OVERVIEW OF THE HOTS PROGRAM

The Higher Order Thinking Skills (HOTS) program began as an alternative approach for helping Chapter 1 students in 1981 in a school in southern California. Chapter 1 is the largest Federal education program, amounting to $6 billion in 1992. The goal of Chapter 1 is to provide supplementary assistance to disadvantaged students who appear to have ability, but who are not succeeding in school. Traditionally, Chapter 1 services consist of providing extra drill in basic concepts in reading and math. The focus is on helping students learn vocabulary and number concepts that they do not know. A major given is that basic, remedial assistance should be linked to the specific facts being taught in regular classroom instruction.

HOTS was a dramatic departure from tradition. Instead of providing additional drill in basic factual information, HOTS focused on developing the thinking ability of educationally disadvantaged students. Thinking activities were not linked to the school's regular curriculum, or to any formal content material, such as science. Instead, HOTS focused on developing general thinking ability as opposed to thinking-in-content ability. In HOTS schools, general thinking activities replaced all other Chapter 1 supplementary help services. Chapter 1 students were pulled from their regular classroom and sent to the HOTS lab for a specified time. They received regular school instruction the rest of the day.

The key research question in designing HOTS was: "What effects would general thinking activities have on the motivation, cognitive development, and basic skill development of educationally disadvantaged students?" The key design question was: "Is it possible to develop a general thinking approach that would transfer to improvements in a wide variety of social and cognitive outcomes?"

Chapter 1 is primarily evaluated on the basis of gains on nationally normed standardized test scores. The goal of HOTS was to produce the expected gains in basic standardized test scores in reading and math for Chapter 1 students through a transfer process. It was hoped that the students would spontaneously transfer and apply their improved thinking processes to learn the content of the regular curriculum more efficiently—the first time it was taught. It was also hoped that the gains would be replicable on a large scale among students from a wide variety of cultures. As of 1993, the HOTS program has spread to 1,800 schools in 48 states, which has made it possible to study the effects of this thinking skills approach on motivation and cognitive development on a large scale.

Defining Intensiveness in Pedagogical Interventions

Given the extent of the motivation and learning problems faced by at-risk students, occasional exposure to thinking activities was not likely to have any effect. As a result, HOTS was designed to be a very intensive intervention. An intensive intervention is defined as one for which:

1. Extensive amounts of service are provided over a long term, that is, daily activities over at least a year,

2. There are carefully developed implementation procedures, and a way to determine the quality of implementation,

3. There is a carefully developed, highly detailed curriculum (or set of highly specified daily procedures) based on the latest findings from cognitive science, and

4. There is a state-of-the-art teacher training component that produces behavioral change in the teacher, and is highly individualized. This training component must train teachers to teach the curriculum and to use sophisticated questioning techniques.

Unfortunately, few interventions meet more than two of these criteria, and most do not meet more than one. In addition, most research into learning involves short-term interventions, and the researcher seldom knows, or reports, the quality of the intervention being studied.

Overview of the HOTS Program

HOTS is an example of an intensive intervention. Students are in HOTS for at least 35 minutes a day, 4–5 days a week, for 2 years. A carefully detailed, 820 page curriculum provides a detailed, daily lesson plan for the teacher. These lessons are in the form of semiscripts, a sequence of key questions that teachers are going to ask each day. Questions are built around the use of specified pieces of software. The questions, combined with the setting, create an intriguing and enjoyable learning environment for the students. We were aware that simply providing extensive amounts of interesting activities by themselves probably would not have extensive impact on learning, unless they were designed to develop key cognitive skills.

Research in cognitive psychology, particularly information processing theories of psychology, suggested that the following key thinking skills underlie all learning:

Metacognition.   Being systematic in the identification and articulation of strategies for solving problems.

Inference from Context.   Being able to tell from surrounding information what a given piece of unknown information means.

Decontextualization.   Generalizing information from one context to another.

Information Synthesis.   Applying multiple sources of information and/or variables to solve a problem.

Although there is no way of proving whether this is an optimal list of the key thinking skills, it is hard to imagine that these are not critical tools. The curriculum was designed so that when students tried to answer key questions and had their answers probed, they would be engaged in the above thinking activities. The goal of the HOTS curriculum development process was to ensure that students would be engaged in each of the key thinking skills every day.

In order to ensure that the curriculum, which is only words on paper, comes alive as a reflective environment, a detailed Socratic methodology of probing students was developed. This system prescribes general methods of probing a student's answer under a variety of key conversation events. These key events were identified by informally watching conversations between teachers and students over 8 years. Of particular concern were the general type of conversation events where ambiguity in the discussion broke down, resulting in the teacher's telling the students what to do, or giving broad hints.

To help teachers internalize the Socratic techniques, a small group-intensive, weeklong training workshop is held. The focus of the workshop is on developing teacher's instincts, as opposed to developing their knowledge base about higher order thinking, cognitive development, or Socratic techniques. The approach is behavioral rather than intellectual. Teachers learn how to identify the type of conversation event through a segment of a student's conversation, and how to improvise an appropriate followup probe. They practice teaching lessons in the curriculum to each other, and each teaching is debriefed. Teachers succeed in learning new reflexes on how to talk and listen to students, and how to probe each response for understanding.

The combination of curriculum, Socratic system, and training represents a very complex design for an instructional environment. (A detailed discussion of the curricular, Socratic, and teacher training techniques can be found in Pogrow, 1990). The complexity of the design, however, is transparent to the student; the result is a very systematic and engaging learning environment. Feedback from HOTS teachers and extensive observation in schools of the actual results in classrooms are used to refine the instructional system.

REVIEW OF THE LITERATURE ON MOTIVATION AND THE AT-RISK STUDENT

There has been a strong focus in the research literature on motivation in preadolescents on the at-risk student. Unfortunately, research focus has shifted in the late 1980s and 1990s and few recent studies have at-risk students in their samples. Because it is unclear whether motivation operates the same way in the at-risk as compared to the advantaged student, this review focuses on those studies that have had significant numbers of at-risk students in their samples— even though the data are somewhat dated.

Research on motivation in preadolescents has focused on the effects of self-efficacy (a student's beliefs or perceptions about his or her capabilities to apply knowledge and skills to academic tasks), and failure attribution (whether students attribute failure to their ability rather than their effort). There are three main theories on how motivation operates in preadolescents. The first, self-efficacy theory, hypothesizes that self-efficacy is an important variable in understanding students' motivation and achievement (Bandura, 1982). The second theory, attribution theory (Weiner, 1979), hypothesizes that student's perceived causes of outcomes affects their motivation and performance. Attribution theory hypothesizes that low achieving students will be more motivated to engage in difficult tasks or persist after failing on a task, if they attribute failure or difficulty to the need for greater effort. The third theory, self-regulated learning, hypothesizes that students are more likely to be motivated to learn when they are self-reliant in the application of planning, integration, and other cognitive skills to academic tasks (Corno & Mandinach, 1983). In this theoretical perspective, increased motivation to learn is linked to developing a way to learn.

Each of these theoretical perspectives has different implications for the design of interventions for at-risk students. A self-efficacy perspective would suggest increasing students' confidence in themselves. An attribution theorist would attempt to retrain students to attribute their failure on academic tasks to inadequate effort rather than to a lack of ability. The self-regulated learning perspective suggests developing better cognitive strategies in the students, and that such skills would lead in turn to more effort. Research on the effects of each of these perspectives follows.

Self-Efficacy Research

Teacher feedback is a significant factor in the development of self-efficacy. Schunk (1982) found that feedback linking prior achievements with effort (e.g., "You've been working hard") led to higher task motivations self-efficacy, and subtraction skill, as compared to telling students to work harder or not providing effort feedback. Schunk and Rice (1989) found that providing a combination of process goals (techniques and strategies students can use to promote learning) and progress feedback produced significantly higher performance on the self-efficacy and main idea reading skill tests than providing process goals and telling students what they should know or be able to accomplish.

Instructional techniques are also important in developing self-efficacy. Schunk (1985) found that specific performance goals, whether self-set or set by teachers, enhanced subtraction achievement and self-efficacy more than no goals. Schunk and Swartz (1991) assert that children who were given techniques for improving writing, combined with a goal of learning techniques for improving writing, reported enhanced self-efficacy and exhibited improved writing skills as compared to children who only received techniques for improving writing without goals. Schunk and Cox (1986) found that continuously verbalizing a strategy while solving problems led to higher self-efficacy and skill in solving subtraction problems.

There is conflicting evidence on the relative effect of observing peer models being successful on tasks and instructional strategies. Schunk and Hanson (1985) note that observing peer models enhanced self-efficacy for learning, along with posttest self-efficacy and skillful performance, more than observing a teacher model or not observing a model. However, there were no effects from coping and mastery strategy training. Schunk and Hanson found that the children in this study had prior successes with the experimental content, and may have used those experiences and concentrated more on what the models had in common (success with the task) than on differences (rate of learning, errors, etc.) In a follow-up study, Schunk, Hanson, and Cox's (1987) students had few prior successes with the content (addition and subtraction of fractions). In their study, coping strategies increased achievement outcomes more than observing mastery models.

Attribution Theory

Research has documented differences in how students feeling a high level of helplessness view the learning process as opposed to those who feel that they are in control. Diener and Dweck (1978) found that helpless students spend little time searching for strategies to overcome failure. Ames and Archer (1988) found that attribution in students is also a function of students' motivational patterns. Students who were primarily motivated towards process goals, that is, making progress and working hard, tended to associate failure with lack of effort. Students who were motivated to get the best grades associated failure with a lack of ability.

It also appears that attribution training works best when students experience occasional failure during the treatment. Dweck (1975) found that self-perceived helpless students who were told that their failures were due to a lack of effort did better than a control group of helpless students who only experienced success. Fowler and Peterson (1981) noted significant increases in reading persistence for those children who had received attribution retraining. Additionally, they found, that when the arrangement of sentences grouped the difficult items in multiples (multiple failure length followed by some reinforcement), reading persistence was facilitated even without the benefit of attribution training. The authors concluded that a reasonable amount of failure may be as important a variable as attribution training in increasing persistence.

Relich, Debus, and Walker (1986) assert that skill training combined with attributional retraining was effective in increasing achievement in a specific task area such as division. A path analysis found that self-efficacy was related to achievement and teacher feedback was related to efficacy.

Self-Regulated learning

There are clear differences in the learning patterns of successful and unsuccessful learners. Gray (1982, cited in Corno and Mandinach, 1983), found that higher ability students took notes that contained inferences, and other organizational patterns. Furthermore, the students prepared for testing through self-monitoring techniques. Less able students' notes seldom contained inferences or sophisticated organizational patterns. Gray found that the average size of information clusters used by learners when teaching material to others showed a significant correlation with general ability When less able students were trained to use organizing processes, their cluster sizes increased, and cluster size and task completion were highly correlated.

Rohrkemper and Bershon (1984) found that lower ability students were more likely to have difficulty knowing if they did not understand something in the first place. They also had negative expectations for eventually understanding how to solve a task, which appeared to create for them a passive role in learning. As a result, they tended to rely on outside sources for help, instead of relying on themselves. In addition, high ability students were better able to tell when they did not understand something; whereas low ability students had trouble figuring out that they did not understand something.

Mandinach and Corno (1985) investigated the cognitive engagement processes used by successful and unsuccessful learners in the computer game Wumpus. This game was used because it required the application of strategic planning and logical reasoning that are critical attributes of self-regulated learning. Both strategic planning and self-regulated learning were measured by an index of "effort avoidance" (the percentage of unnecessary risks successfully avoided during the game). A high score was considered to reflect a student's ability to think logically and consider alternative strategies. High ability students exhibited more self-regulated behavior than low ability students, and students using self-regulated learning were more successful in the game than those who use other forms of cognitive engagement. The researchers conclude that although computer games and simulations can be motivating and cognitively engaging, not all students will engage in the same manner. Low performing students will not perceive the interaction as a learning experience.

Because of these learning problems, many researchers have advocated developing self-regulated learning skills in at-risk students. Rohrkemper and Bershon (1984) conclude that low achieving students need to learn how to approach a task, stay engaged and re-engage when there are problems. Students need to learn how to rely on themselves to do this. Corno and Mandinach (1983) and Corno and Snow (1986) all suggest that developing the flexible use of higher cognitive skills across tasks needs to be a general goal of education.

Ames (1990) established strategies that teachers could use to develop a mastery achievement goal orientation. In this orientation, students want to learn something new even when obstacles are presented; students believe their efforts will lead to mastery. Although there are elements of student attribution in this work, the focus is on training the teachers in how to meet the learning needs of the at-risk students. The training and techniques had a significant effect. Ames found that when teachers used the techniques for several months, experimental at-risk students showed higher mastery scores that control at-risk students. This study is also significant because it was the only one that studied the effects of an intervention in regular classroom settings. Unfortunately, no data were collected on student achievement.

LIMITATIONS OF EXISTING MOTIVATION RESEARCH

If one were to build an intensive instructional environment for developing the motivational and cognitive development of at-risk students, the research reviewed would not be of much help. Most of the research has studied motivation and its learning effects for discrete lower level skills, such as mastering subtraction. Nor is there any evidence that any of the reported gains from the interventions transfer, or are sustained beyond the immediate intervention. It may indeed be possible to increase self-efficacy, or motivation around a specific task, but what happens when that task is changed. None of the studies give any insight into this problem. For example, Montague and Bos (1989) found that learning disabled students were as able to learn a strategy for solving a math word problem as high performing students. The problem was that the low performing students

TABLE 14.1
Characteristics of Motivation Studies

Study	Study Length	Student Type	Type of Task
Ames (1990)	Several months	at risk	mastery orientation
Schunk and Rice (1991)	15 days	at risk	main idea
Schunk (1985)	5 days	at risk	subtraction
Lee and Anderson (1993)	4 lessons	range of students	science tasks
Schunk and Swartz (1991)	160 days	middle class	writing a paragraph
Schunk and Cox (1986)	6 days	learning disabled	subtraction
Schunk and Hanson (1985)	2 days	low performing	subtraction
Schunk et al. (1987)	6 days	low performing	fractions
Schunk (1982)	3 days	low performing	subtraction
Dweck (1975)	25 days	helpless	math problems
Diener and Dweck (1978)	1 day	helpless	discrimination
Fowler and Peterson (1981)	5 days	at risk	reading sentences
Relich, Debus, and Walker (1986)	11 days	helpless	division
Rohrkemper and Bershon (1984)	12 weeks	low	division
Gray (1982)	2 1/2 hours	at risk	organizing
Mandinach and Corno (1985)	Not applicable	range of students	computer simulation

were unable to generalize and apply that strategy to a new context. As a result, it is possible that the knowledge produced from these discrete intervention studies are of no real help to students or teachers.

Table 14.1 shows how short term the cited studies were, and how discrete the tasks were. In contrast to the severity of the learning problems faced by at-risk students, the conclusions drawn by the researchers from these types of studies are at best naive. Indeed, with the exception of Ames (1990; Lee and Anderson, 1993) none of the interventions in the research occurred in real classrooms. There is no evidence that any of the conclusions drawn by the other researchers would work in actual classrooms, and Ames (1990) did not use cognitive development or achievement as dependent variables. It is not that the research is not valid, it is just that it does not offer important or useful clues for the designs of real-world interventions.

Historically, few of the interventions tried with at-risk students have been intensive in any research field. In addition, there is little research on the effect of intensive interventions on the motivation and cognitive development of at-risk students. Typically, researchers have studied very short duration interventions, or longer-term haphazardly designed interventions where no one knows whether, or to what extent, the hoped for interactions with students are actually occurring. (These are, of course, general problems with all social science research.) Although the foregoing research contains some useful hints on the nature of motivation and teaching of cognitive skills, the only way to truly understand its functioning with at-risks students is to design and study the effects of an intensive intervention.

FINDINGS FROM THE HOTS PROGRAM

The primary conclusion reached from working with at-risk students over an 11-year period on a wide variety of higher order tasks, is that there is a real learning deficit that prevents them from learning in school. This deficit manifests itself in the way that students do not seem to know how to deal with ideas, how to make generalizations, or even know what a generalization is. They are unprepared to talk to each other about ideas, or anything symbolic. They basically seem to be individuals who do not know how to deal with or understand symbolic ideas. We therefore refer to the typical at-risk student as someone who doesn't understand "understanding."

Not only is this lack of a sense of understanding very real; it is quite profound. As discuss later, the problem seems to require a long-term intensive intervention. It is unlikely that such a major learning problem can be solved by focusing on enhancing self-efficacy or motivation (although we see later, motivation does play a key role.) There is a real need to foster general intellectual capabilities. Successfully doing so, however, requires answers to the following questions: Is the lack of a sense of understanding a function of a low intellect? How does a sense of understanding evolve? How does understanding relate to motivation and vice versa?

It is clear that at-risk students have a high level of intellectual ability/potential. Our best guess as to why they come to school without a sense of understanding is that the deficit results from a lack of experience in having adults discuss ideas with them, either in the home or outside. The primary mechanism by which a sense of understanding evolves is through conversation with adults. It is a special type of conversation, however, wherein adults probe and urge children to clarify their ideas. Talk where adults simply tell youngsters what to do doesn't seem to develop that sense—no matter how much such adults love their children. Heath (1983) found that children reared in small communities where parents did not allow their children to reflect about their ideas, and where the parents did not respond to such reflections never did well in school—even though they came from a caring home environment.

However, all the blame cannot be laid solely at the child's doorstep. When we examined the type of dialogue that exists in the classroom, almost none of it was conversational. Students are almost never given an opportunity to express ideas, or to have a teacher reflect about their ideas in anything but the most simplistic ways. Ninety-six percent of the questions in classrooms we surveyed required one word answers. This was true even in small group settings. Indeed, if students did not come to school with a developed sense of understanding, there was no way that it could develop in school—if sophisticated conversation is the key mechanism for such development. Indeed, student verbalization by itself is not sufficient; it must be skillfully probed by teachers.

To date, the sophistication of student verbalization is the best indicator that we

TABLE 14.2
Manifestations of the Development of Understanding

Stages of Understanding	Time
Giving multiword answers	2 months
Understanding the difference between guessing and being systematic	4 months
Putting reasons in answers without prompting	5-6 months
Publicly disconfirming a prior hypothesis with a reason	6-8 months
Internalizing and automating all of the above	12-18 months

have been able to find of cognitive development. In addition, there seems to be a pattern in students' response to the constant probing and prodding of their verbalizations—a pattern that indicates both the extent of the understanding deficit and the need for an intensive environment to overcome it. Feedback from teachers and observation of tapes suggest that developing and internalizing a sense of understanding does through the following stages and requires the prescribed dosage of HOTS activities (35 minutes a day, 4–5 days a week). See Table 14.2.

Using the sophistication of verbal interaction as an indicator of the development of a sense of understanding is consistent with the theories of Vygotsky (1989) who concluded that changes in the social use of language presaged cognitive growth. In the beginning of HOTS, students could not express coherent ideas (either to the teacher or among themselves) or talk in general terms. As their articulation became more sophisticated, problem solving and efficiency of learning increased. It appears then, that investing time in this general cognitive development is more effective for achieving traditional goals, such as standardized test score gains, then directly drilling students. Providing 35 minutes a day of the HOTS program for 2 years in lieu of remedial activities produces greater gains in standardized test scores. HOTS students achieved spring to spring gains on standardized test scores that were 67% higher in reading and 123% higher in mathematics th an national averages. Second year gains were also greater than national averages. There were many reports from a wide variety of cultural setting of HOTS students making the honor role—close to 15%. For example, in 1991, we received a report that 10% of the HOTS students on the Navajo reservation earned straight *As* on their report cards. There are also many anecdotal reports of HOTS students winning awards at science fairs, and math and writing contests. Once a sense of understanding is developed, the HOTS students are likely to excel.

As a result of the general cognitive growth and a greater understanding of how to learn with understanding, students are now able to learn far more efficiently. They can now begin to appreciate what is being taught in the regular classroom. In addition, their motivation to learn increases. This effect is so strong, that it becomes possible to use a highly progressive approach not tied to the standardized test or regular classroom curriculum, and still produce better results than supplementary drill approaches.

It appears that once students start to develop a sense of understanding they are able to learn at a much higher level/rate than conventionally assumed. At this time we do not yet know what the upper bounds of this performance will be. We continue to increase the sophistication of the HOTS curriculum. We also continue to be amazed at the sophistication of the HOTS students. For example, by the end of two years in HOTS students are able to read classical literature, such as *The Adventures of Tom Sawyer,* with comprehension, and they are able to draw inferences about the characters.

Implications for a theory of motivation

The HOTS project is guilty of not having collected systematic data on changes in the motivation and self-efficacy levels of HOTS students over time. At the same time, impressionistic data are extensive and very robust. When one works on a national scale, maintains careful communications with teachers, and spends a great deal of time visiting classrooms in a wide variety of cultural settings, one collects a tremendous amount of information. When these impressions form stable patterns over time, they become a type of data. Although these data are not a substitute for more systematic forms of evidence, they are valuable for hypothesis generating purposes—as well as for improving the quality of the intervention.

Our impressionistic data suggest that there are two different types of motivation that play key roles in the metamorphosis of at-risk students to becoming reflective learners. The first type of motivation functions within a single learning episode. A learning episode is considered the process of mastering a single software environment, which usually translates to a single unit of the HOTS curriculum. The second type of motivation builds up gradually and functions across learning episodes. The second is, of course, the more important of the two, but the first is necessary to enable the developmental learning process to be initiated.

In order to develop the first type of motivation, it is essential for a student to be engaged in the task. The higher order the task, the more engaged the student must be. It is not just a matter of paying attention and being on task, the student must also exert substantial amounts of emotional energy. Being reflective around school tasks and engaging in Socratic forms of interaction are so counterintuitive that the student must set aside basic tendencies and respond emotionally to a new type of social situation. Many veteran teachers have indicated how shocked they have been in the early stages of HOTS when their formerly placid Chapter 1 students began to react with uncharacteristically high levels of passion, mostly negative in the early stages. At last, the student has been engaged on an emotional level.

What motivates students to persist in trying to master a difficult task in a strange and emotionally threatening situation? The only way to accomplish that is to have tasks that are highly intriguing to students so that their curiosity exceeds their anxiety. HOTS accomplishes this by providing tasks that combine the use of computers (for visual stimulation) with fantasy and drama. The tasks and interactions are carefully scripted. (At the same time, the Socratic techniques ensure a nonlinear form of interaction, with much improvisation.) What emerges is a curriculum development process that resembles the types of techniques a playwright uses to engage an audience.

The intrigued student is thus motivated to pursue the difficult and strange task despite his or her emotional discomfort. Obviously, this engagement is not sufficient. The tasks must be designed in accordance with basic learning theories as well, so that the engagement translates over time into cognitive growth. This stage also needs to be one in which students learn basic self-regulation learning techniques. There are strong parallels between the concept of self-regulated learning used by motivation theorists and metacognition used by cognitive psychologists. In addition, the more intriguing the tasks, the more difficult and higher order they can be and have students sustain their Type 1 motivation.

During the early episodes, students frustration was reflected in statements such as "I cannot solve this," or "I am too stupid to solve this." At this point it is critical for teachers not to overencourage the students or to simplify the task. Students must discover on their own that if they start to think, they can in fact solve the task. It is their ultimate success, as opposed to phony praise and encouragement, that ultimately makes Type 2 motivation possible.

After five to ten such learning episodes, which may take anywhere from 5 months to a year, students start to approach difficult tasks with an attitude that it's okay if I get stuck initially. Their attitude becomes: "I know that if I think about the problem I will ultimately solve it." Students start to enjoy challenges and to believe in themselves. As they begin to experience success in the classroom, a natural level of Type 2 motivation emerges, which they spontaneously bring to new tasks. We also suspect that related factors such as self-efficacy also increases during this period.

Implications for the Design of Interventions for At-Risk Students

It is essential that interventions designed for the at-risk student be of a long-term nature and be consistently engaging. It is not enough to have a strong theoretical perspective or a strong research base—although they are important elements. A more important starting point is to have the right metaphor as an organizing concept for curricular activities. The vision of replacing missing dinner-table conversation, and of organizing a curriculum based on how dinner-table conversation traditionally took place, is what drove the basic design and structure of the curriculum. If the same ideas from cognitive psychology had been implemented via a metaphor other than dinner-table conversation, the project probably would not have been as effective. For example, modeling the HOTS curriculum on the ad-hoc nature of dinner-table conversation provided the critical, counterintuitive clue that the HOTS activities should not be linked to the formal curriculum of the school.

This is not an argument against using research in the design of interventions to help at-risk students. We did, and continue to use research findings to improve the HOTS intervention. The data that we found most helpful in the ongoing design process was basic research on cognition, particularly research that combined knowledge of the functioning of the brain with a test on an intervention based on that knowledge. In many cases (but not always), the research findings were more valuable than conclusions the researchers drew from their data. This research was critical in identifying the four key thinking skills to focus on for general cognitive development. It is just that basic research cannot answer most of the specific development questions that arise. The metaphor then becomes critical for making the myriad development decisions, and for deciding which research is indeed critical.

Forming an effective intensive intervention requires the development of a highly creative and entertaining environment, where a high level of creativity is sustained over a long period of time. This is easier said than done. In addition, the creativity must be such that students are intrigued and drawn into a reflective state. It is not enough for the activities to be creative from an adult perspective, it is important that they be so from the cultural context of the young—a context that is shaped largely from TV. The process of converting students from the point at which the motivation is generated primarily from external stimuli and dependency on teachers to the point that they become reflective from an internally generated sense of motivation and rely more on themselves is a long weaning process. At the same time, that stage can be reached with most of the students. The best grade levels for starting this conversion seem to be from the middle of third grade to the start of sixth grade (although there has also been success starting at seventh grade).

It is also possible to design training that significantly changes how adults approach a process, such as teaching. Going from direct, linear forms of instruction, where students are told what to do, to Socratic techniques where you help students figure out on their own what something means by asking questions, is a major change. Motivating adults to change basic patterns of behavior requires: (a) a realization that what is being done now is not working, and (b) seeing results form the efforts. Getting teachers to the point that they can use Socratic techniques effectively requires: (a) bright individuals, (b) a carefully worked out technology for actually teaching Socratically, and (c) a behavioral approach to learning how to use the technology. The latter means that instead of providing highly detailed information about the nature and basis of the technology, it is more effective to let the individual learn how to use it under conditions where it is important to use it correctly.

The following are the two biggest mistakes with respect to training teachers to using new, reform techniques:

Relying Strictly on Motivation. Teachers are often given advocacy and the philosophic base to engage in something new without a technology for actually doing it. It is assumed that the main problem in getting teachers to use the new concept is motivational, when in reality the advocates have no sense of how difficult it is to actually use the techniques. Current examples of such interventions in education are: Whole language, multidisciplinary instruction, computer use, etc. No technology for actually doing those things effectively has been developed.

Using an Intellectual Development Approach. Teachers are often given research, historical and philosophical information, about something and then expected to figure out how to actually to it. It is equivalent to asking an actor to first write a Shakespearean quality play and then to perform it. A current example of such an intervention in education is the thinking skills movement.

A better approach is to train teachers in the details of how to use a sophisticated, effective, intervention.

Implications for Theories of Learning

One of the most widely debated question is "Should thinking be taught as a process or in content?" Most contemporary theorists have concluded that thinking should be taught in content, and that general transfer doesn't exist.[1] It seems obvious from the experience with HOTS that this is not true *in the case of at-risk students.*[2] There is no way that students who do not understand "understanding" can be successful in math or science curricula that places an emphasis on thinking. Nor can teachers in regular classroom settings such a fundamental problem, where students do not even know how to begin to think symbolically. Indeed, the inappropriateness of placing at-risk students into thinking-in-content is probably the single biggest cause for the failure of the science and math reform initiatives in the 1960s and 1970s. Although it was noble to place at-risk students into process forms of discovery curricula, there was no way that these students could succeed—even though they had the intellectual potential to do so.

---

[1]For example, Alexander and Judy (1988) conclude that training in general problem solving will be of benefit only after students have achieved high levels of domain knowledge. Prawat (1991), in discussing the theoretical advantages of immersing thinking in content, notes that: "The main argument against stand-alone programs is the oft-repeated and now generally accepted claim that generic thinking skills do not readily transfer or generalize to other parts of the curriculum or to out-of-school performances."

[2]At the same time, existing research conclusions may be correct for highly educated individuals engaged in advanced study in concluding that transfer does not exist.

The HOTS experience led to the formulation of the following *theory of cognitive underpinnings:*

At-risk students must first be placed in general thinking activities for 1- to 2-years before being put into sophisticated thinking-in-content activities.

The theory of cognitive underpinnings has major implications for how reform efforts are organized and implemented. For example, a major current educational reform is to eliminate tracking at the middle school level (Oakes, 1992). The current approach is to simply put all the students together, from at-risk to gifted. If, indeed, the students are placed into challenging curricula, the theory of cognitive underpinnings predicts that the at-risk students will once again fail, and well intentioned efforts will go for naught. An alternative approach being established by the HOTS project has been to create a series of middle schools wherein at-risk students are first placed into HOTS and then subsequently placed into exemplary academic curricula with other students. It is expected that with the requisite general thinking development, the former at-risk students will hold their own in thinking-in-content activities. This will provide the basis for a large-scale test of the theory of cognitive underpinnings. It will also provide greater insight into the functioning of the student's internalized sense of motivation to learn after completion of the HOTS program.

In other words, although the ultimate goal is thinking-in-content, the means for at-risk students has to include a prior general thinking development stage. In addition, the fact that the general thinking HOTS activities lead to improved academic performance suggest that general transfer does in fact exist, at least in the case of at-risk students. Pogrow (1991a, 1991b) provides a more detailed description of the implications of the HOTS experience for cognitive theory and educational reform.

Implications for Theories of Motivating the At-Risk Learner

It appears that motivation develops for at-risk students in two stages. It has been hypothesized that students must first be highly motivated across high anxiety episodes of learning before a Type 2 motivation appears, one that is possible across learning tasks in general. Most of the self-efficacy research would apply primarily to Type 2 motivation. There were, however, some insights in the motivation literature that are consistent with some of the design characteristics of the HOTS Type 1 intervention. For example, Rohrkemper and Bershon (1984) were correct in their finding that lower ability students tended to have difficulty knowing if they did not understand something in the first place. Fowler and Peterson (1981) were correct in their conclusion that occasional student failure was a key element in increasing motivation.

The best contribution of this chapter to motivation theory suggests that stimulating Type 1 motivation requires: (a) highly sophisticated curricula and teaching techniques that create an environment that promotes high anxiety and high curiosity, (b) that students ultimately be successful repeatedly on such learning tasks, and (c) that such success be done in a way that general cognitive development occurs so that students can begin to see that their success in the special environment carries over to the regular classroom.

FUTURE RESEARCH NEEDS

More research is needed on the effects of and causes of motivation in intensive environments. This is not only with respect to the study of motivation, but with respect to all pedagogical variables. The experience in the HOTS environment did confirm some of the key conclusions from the motivation research cited earlier. Yet, the findings from the HOTS intensive environment are far richer and more illuminating for practice. For example, the findings by Diener and Dweck (1978) and Rohrkemper and Bershon (1984) that student verbalization is important are correct. What they did not realize or report is that verbalization by itself is not sufficient. Such verbalization must be consistently and skillfully probed.

The findings from the HOTS environment have also generated insight into a fundamental cognition problem—the issue of the interaction between general and specific forms of thinking. These findings brought into question a position widely held by researchers. Although it cannot yet be proved if the theory of cognitive underpinnings is valid, it has been supported by basic research subsequently reported in England. Adey (1989) experimented with allocating 25% of science instruction to sixth- and seventh-graders over a 2-year period to general thinking development. After 2 years the experimental group was significantly higher on Piagetian reasoning tasks. Both groups were the same on science achievement. A year after the general thinking training was concluded, both groups were the same on the thinking measure (the experimental group had regressed), but the experimental group was significantly higher on the science achievement test. In other words, general thinking instruction maintained for a sufficient length of time seems to have a future transfer effect on science achievement. This suggests that there is at least some validity to counterintuitive findings from general observation of students in a large-scale intensive environment.

Although there is a high knowledge generation payoff from intensive environments, two major problems exist. First, it takes tremendous time to develop and refine intensive environments. Second, there is no guarantee that hard work will ultimately pay off with an intervention that works. It may take as long at 3–6 years before the developers learn if the intervention is working. The tremendous design, development, and dissemination effort has made it impossible for the HOTS project to conduct quality basic research around the intervention. A better alternative to either researchers doing basic research around limited interventions, or intensive environment designers not doing more systematic research, is for the groups to join forces. It is only by a process in which researchers join with individuals capable of, and interested in, designing intensive environments that knowledge about how to help at-risk students will advance. HOTS demonstrates that much can be learned from watching students in well crafted intensive environments. After 10 years of working with HOTS, we continue to gain new insights into the students and learn how to best implement the intervention.

There is also a need to study the interrelationship of cognitive and motivational development in intensive environments. For example, the HOTS project did not collect any systematic data on motivation, while Ames (1990) did not collect data on cognitive development. Well crafted intensive environments offer an opportunity to better understand how motivation affects the cognitive development of at-risk students and vice versa.

The HOTS project is embarking on creating a new intensive intervention, a 2-year prealgebra curriculum for all students, to be called HOTS–Math. The goal is to see whether a highly creative learning environment increases student motivation to learn mathematics. In addition, the motivation and performance of ex HOTS students will be compared to regular students and those of former Chapter 1 students not in HOTS. Finally, the performance of ex HOTS students in HOTS math will be compared to their performance in less interesting curricula. This combination of research will provide greater insight into the interaction of the hypothesized Type 1 and Type 2 forms of motivation.

CONCLUSION

It is possible to dramatically increase the motivation and cognitive development of at-risk students. In addition, it appear to be possible to define a specific, practical dose of activities needed to stimulate such improvement. It also appears that most at-risk students suffer from a major learning deficit, and that increases in motivation arise from increases in cognitive development. The increases in motivation seem to initially arise from external, highly stimulating activities. It is only after repeated success with such activities, after experiencing initial failure, over an extended period of time that at-risk students develop an internal sense of motivation for learning.

ACKNOWLEDGMENTS

Preparation of this chapter was supported in part by the U.S. Army Research Institute for Behavioral and Social Sciences through a subcontract with Battelle Institute. However, the ideas contained in this report are those of the authors and do not represent the views of ARI unless so designated by other official documentation.

REFERENCES

Adey, P. (1989). Cognitive acceleration through science education. In *Learning to think-Thinking to learn,* Paris.

Alexander, P., & Judy, J. (1988). The interaction of domain specific and strategic knowledge in academic performance. Review of *Educational Research, 58*(4) 375–404.

Ames, C. (1990). *Achievement goals and classroom structure: Developing and learning orientation to students.* Unpublished paper presented at the annual meeting of the American Education Research Association.

Ames, C., & Archer, J. (1988). Achievement goals in the classroom: Students' learning strategies and motivation processes. *Journal of Educational Psychology, Vol. 80*(3) 260–267.

Bandura, A. (1982). Self-efficacy mechanism in human agency. *American Psychologist, 37,* 122–148.

Corno, L., & Mandinach, E. B. (1983). The role of cognitive engagement in classroom learning and motivation. *Educational Psychologist, Vol. 18*(2) 88–108.

Corno, L., & Snow, R. E. (1986). Adapting teaching on individual differences among learners. In M. C. Wittrock (Ed.), *Handbook of research on teaching* (pp. 605–629). New York: Macmillan.

Diener, C. I., & Dweck, C. S. (1978). An analysis of learned helplessness: Continuous changes in performance, strategy, and achievement cognitions following failure. *Journal of Personality and Social Psychology, Vol. 36*(5) 451–462.

Dweck, C. S. (1975). The role of expectations and attributions in the alleviation of learned helplessness. *Journal of Personality and Social Psychology, 31,* 674–685.

Fowler, J. W., & Peterson, P. L. (1981). Increasing reading persistence and altering attributional style of learned helpless children. *Journal of Educational Psychology, 73*(2), 251–260.

Gray, L. E. (1982). *Aptitude constructs, Learning processes and achievement.* Palo Alto, CA: Stanford University.

Heath, S. B. (1983). *Way with words: Language, life, and work in communities and classrooms.* Cambridge, London: Cambridge University Press.

Lee, O., & Anderson, C. W. (1993). Task engagement and conceptual change in middle school science classrooms. *American Education Research Journal, 30*(3), 585–610.

Levin, H. (1986). *Educational reform for disadvantaged students: An emerging crisis.* West Haven, CT; NEA Professional Library.

Macchiarola, F. (Ed). (1988). Values, standards, and climate in schools serving students at risk. In *School Success for students at risk.* Orlando, FL: Harcourt Brace Jovanovich.

Mandinach, E. B., & Corno, L. (1985). Cognitive engagement variations among students of different ability level and sex in a computer problem solving game. *Sex Roles, 13*(3/4), 241–251.

Montague, M., & Bos, C. (1989). Cognitive and metacognitive characteristics of eighth grade students' mathematical problem-solving. Paper presented at the annual meeting of the *American Educational Research Association,* San Francisco.

Oakes, J. (1992). Can tracking research inform practice? Technical, normative, and political considerations. *Educational Researcher, 21*(5), 12–20.

Orfield, G. (1988). Race, income, and educational inequality. In *School success for students at risk* Orlando, FL: Harcourt Brace Jovanovich.

Pogrow, S. (1990). *HOTS (Higher Order Thinking Skills): A validated thinking skills approach to using computers with students who are at-risk.* New York: Scholastic.

Pogrow, S. (1991a). Converting at-risk students into reflective learners. In A. Costa & J. Bellanca (Eds.), *Mind matters.* Skylight Publishing.

Pogrow, S. (1991b). A validated approach to thinking development for the at-risk population. In C. Collins & J. Mangieri (Eds.), *Building the quality of thinking in and out of schools.* Hillsdale, NJ: Lawrence Erlbaum Associates.

Prawat, R. (1991). The value of ideas: The immersion approach to the development of thinking. *Educational Researcher, 20*(3), 3–10.

Relich, J. D., Debus, R. L., & Walker, R. (1986). The mediating role of attribution and self-efficacy variables for treatment effects on achievement outcomes. *Contemporary Educational Psychology, 11*(3), 195–216.

Rohrkemper, M. M., & Bershon, B. L. (1984). Elementary school students' reports of the causes and effects of problem difficulty in mathematics. *The Elementary School Journal, 85*(1), 127–147.

Schmidt, P. (1992). Census data find more are falling behind in school. *Education Week,* Vol. 11, June 10, p. 149.

Schunk, D. H. (1982). Effects of effort attributional feedback on children's perceived self-efficacy and achievement. *Journal of Educational Psychology, 74*(4), 548–556.

Schunk, D. H. (1985). Participation in goal settings: Effects on self-efficacy and skills of learning-disabled children. *Journal of Special Education, 19*(3), 307–317.

Schunk, D. H., & Cox, P. D. (1986). Strategy training and attributional feedback with learning disabled students. *Journal of Educational Psychology, 78,* 201–209.

Schunk, D. H., & Hanson, A. R. (1985). Peer models: Influence on children's self efficacy and achievement. *Journal of Educational Psychology, 77*(3), 313–322.

Schunk, D. H., Hanson, A. R., & Cox, P. D. (1987). Peer-model attributes and children's achievement behaviors. *Journal of Educational Psychology, 79*(1), 54–61.

Schunk, D. H., & Rice, J. M. (1989). Learning goals and children's reading comprehension. *Journal of Reading Behavior, 21*(3), 279–293.

Schunk, D. H., & Rice, J. M. (1991). Learning goals and progress feedback during reading comprehension instruction. *Journal of Reading Behavior, 23*(3), 351–364.

Schunk, D.H., & Swartz, C. W. (1991). Process goals and progress feedback: Effects on children's self-efficacy and skills. Presented at the annual convention of the *American Educational Research Association,* Chicago, IL.

Vygotsky, L. S. (1989). *Mind in society; The development of higher cognitive processes.* Cambridge, MA: Harvard University Press.

Weiner, B. (1979). A theory of motivation for some classroom experiences. *Journal of Educational Psychology, 71,* 3–25.

15

Motivated to Lead: Dispositional and Biographical Antecedents of Leadership Performance*

Fred A. Mael
Leonard A. White
US Army Research Institute, Alexandria, VA

Researchers and practitioners interested in the prediction of performance have generally favored measures of aptitude, such as physical and cognitive tests. Measures of motivation, such as temperament tests,have fared relatively poorly in the past, especially when compared to other measures (Asher & Sciarrino, 1974; Ghiselli, 1973; Reilly & Chao, 1982).

Recently, however, a reevaluation of the merits of dispositional indices as predictors of performance and as selection tools has occurred. A literature review by Kamp and Hough (1988) and meta-analysis by Barrick and Mount (1991) of the so-called "Big Five" personality dimensions (Digman, 1990; Hogan, 1986; Hough, 1991; Tupes & Christal, 1961) have demonstrated that stable and significant prediction with dispositional measures is possible, although the practical utility of the measure will vary according to the personality dimension, the type of occupation, and the job performance criterion. These personality dimensions tend to be relatively independent of cognitive ability measures as well (McRae & Costa, 1987). In addition, recent work demonstrates that individual temperaments, especially positive and negative affectivity, strongly influence job satisfaction and other job attitudes, regardless of job and organizational characteristics (Arvey, Bouchard, Segal, & Abraham, 1989; Rafaeli & Sutton, 1989; Staw, Bell, & Clausen, 1986). Even in the area of leadership prediction, where trait theory has been much-maligned, meta-analysis of previous data, as well as better focused research, has resulted in a reconsideration of previous assumptions (Lord, De Vader, & Alliger, 1986).

---

*The views expressed in this paper are those of the authors and do not necessarily reflect the views of the US Army Research Institute, the US Military Institute, or the Department of the Army.

The history of biodata and selection has been different. Generally, biodata measures have fared well in meta-analytic reviews of selection instruments (Asher & Sciarrino, 1974; Ghiselli, 1973; Reilly & Chao 1982). Ironically, though, many items termed *biodata* are indistinguishable from the types of self-report items found in temperament and attitude measures (Ashworth, 1989; Crosby, 1990). It is not uncommon to find items about internal states, opinions, and reactions to hypothetical situations in biodata measures. The confusion between the two types of measures is especially problematic in light of claimed advantages of biodata. For example, biodata items are presumed to achieve higher validities and be more resistant to socially desirable responding and faking than temperament items (Asher, 1972; Asher & Sciarrino, 1974; Mumford & Owens, 1987; Telenson, Alexander, & Barrett, 1983). However, this may be true only of certain types of biodata, such as verifiable items (Asher, 1972). Moreover, biodata measures have not been without critics. With the traditional approach, empirical keying, weights are typically assigned to each alternative based on its mean score on the criterion of interest, so that the continuum of values within the item is arranged to reflect scores on the criterion. Although purely empirical keying can lead to optimal correlations with criteria, it is highly sensitive to sample characteristics, so that when the key is cross-validated, the regression coefficient is vulnerable to shrinkage. The method has also been derided as "dustbowl empiricism" for being comparatively atheoretical and for failing to advance understanding of antecedents of successful performance (Dunnette, 1961; Pace & Schoenfeldt, 1977).

In this chapter, we present a conceptual rationale for the prediction of behavior with biodata, drawn to a great extent from Mael (1991). In this context, we clarify the distinction between dispositional/temperament items and biodata items. We then discuss a methodology for converting a validated temperament measure, the Army's Assessment of Background and Life Experiences (ABLE), into objective biodata scales in order to reap the "best of both worlds" (e.g. the interpretability and stability of validity coefficients associated with dispositional measures and the less fakable and often more palatable characteristics of objective biodata). Results of research on this methodology are then presented, and we discuss implications in our conclusion.

Although the conceptual rationale for using temperament items—that people behave and perform, or are constrained from performing, according to their personalities—is straightforward and intuitive, the rationale for biodata items, and why they are successful in predicting performance, is somewhat more complicated, and is discussed next.

A CONCEPTUAL RATIONALE FOR BIODATA

We begin with a description of what biodata items attempt to measure and why biodata items predict subsequent behavior. Toward this purpose, a conceptual rationale, integrating different theoretical perspectives on biodata, is proposed.

Past Behavior Predicts Future Behavior

Owens (1976) has stated that "one of our most basic measurement axioms holds that the best predictor of what a man *will do* in the future is what he *has done* in the past" (p. 625). Owens' dictum is often cited as the rationale behind biodata and its effectiveness. However, a strict interpretation of this axiom could limit biodata to previous actions of the same type, such as a previous job or activities which required similar skills. For the majority of background experiences in biodata instruments, such as school performance, club memberships, extracurricular activities, and relationships with family, friends, and coworkers, additional conceptual elaboration is needed.

The Ecology Model

The only comprehensive and clearly enunciated model of biodata to date has been developed by Owens, Mumford, and their associates (Mumford & Owens, 1987; Mumford & Stokes, 1991). Starting from the original Developmental-Integrative model of Owens (1976), it has been integrated with the more general ecology model of Gibson (1979) into an ecology model of biodata. A brief synopsis of the basic tenets follows.

An individual enters life with certain hereditary and environmental resources and limitations which determine initial individual differences. The person then attempts to maximize personal adaptation to his or her environment through learning and cognition. It is assumed that a person will select situations of endeavor based on the perceived reinforcement value of their outcomes. The perceived value will be based on the individual's needs and values, so that initial choices will reflect preexisting characteristics of the individual. Another frame of reference is the *template,* an idealized image about how life should proceed that encapsulates one's beliefs about the world and oneself.

However, once choices have been made, further adaptation becomes necessary as a means of attaining desired goals in the chosen situation. This begins a cycle of choice, development, and adaptation, which leads to yet more focused choices based on more clearly perceived means of need and value satisfaction. The successful person will seek out a variety of situations to satisfy all needs and values. Through this iterative process, the person develops a cohesive pattern of choices. Therefore, when attempting to predict a person's performance, a wide range of previous behaviors, even if only indirectly comparable to the criterion of interest, can contribute to prediction of subsequent choices and performance.

Owens and Schoenfeldt (1979) differentiate between two categories of variables. The first category, called *input variables,* deals with things done *to* the person, and includes all prior situational exposures such as parental warmth, parental beliefs, and school and community characteristics. These would be equivalent to the initial, nonchoice resources and limitations mentioned earlier. The second category, termed *prior behaviors,* is primarily concerned with previous activities, but could also include feelings about social relations, reactions to school, and reading preferences. This would be the primary realm of the choice-adaptation-choice cycles described before.

Because the model stresses individual choice and adaptation across time, it is strongest at providing a rationale for all items dealing with acquired skills, abilities, and knowledge. Previous experiences that have increased a person's skill level and self-efficacy in a specific realm increase the desirability of pursuing and the probability of competently repeating that type of behavior. Nevertheless, there appear to be biodata topics that are either not expressly covered or not explained in depth by the model.

First, although input variables are included, the model focuses mainly on volitional prior behaviors, but is less detailed when dealing with events that happen *to* the person, both at an early age and throughout the life cycle. Second, while the role of previous successes and accomplishments versus nonaccomplishments is addressed, the role of failures and dubious accomplishments in shaping future behavior is not clearly explicated. Finally, it seems clear that through affiliations with entities such as clubs, sports teams, and organizations, or in performing various extracurricular activities, the individual both absorbs peripheral characteristics not needed for adaptive purposes, and retains these characteristics long after the person's involvement with the entity or activity has ceased.

In order to better account for the predictive value of these specific types of events and behaviors, social identity theory (Ashforth & Mael, 1989) could serve as a useful complement to the more individualistic, choice-oriented ecology model.

Social Identity Theory

Social identity theory (SIT; Tajfel, 1978; Turner, 1981, 1982, 1984, 1987) can be summarized as follows: every person has a *self-concept,* defined as the set of cognitive representations of the self available to a person, which is comprised of two parts. The first is the *personal identity,* which denotes attributes of the person which are personal in nature and specific to the individual. These might include bodily attributes and dispositional characteristics. The second component is the *social identity,* which includes all self-defining aspects of the person expressed in terms of psychologically belonging to a perceived social category. Baumeister (1986) makes a similar distinction between the *private self* and the *collective self.* Social categories include nationality, political or social affiliation, or any number of formal and informal groups. Personal self-categorizations are not considered better representations of the "true self" than social ones (Turner, 1987). "The sum total of the social identifications used by a person to define him- or herself will be described as his or her social identity" (Turner, 1982, p. 18).

Self-definition, according to perceived category or role, results in behaviors consistent with that definition (Stryker & Serpe, 1982; Wicklund & Gollwitzer, 1982). The more intense the identification with a social identity category, the greater the perceived sharing of characteristics with other members of that "psychological group" (Mael, 1988). Furthermore, to the extent that a social category is salient, individuals undergo depersonalization and self-stereotyping (Turner, 1987). *Depersonalization* is the downplaying of one's unique characteristics and the perception of the self as a prototypical exemplar of the category's members, which leads to behaviors consistent with that prototype. Thus, a person's implicit theories about what the members of a category typically do or are expected to do will lead to embodiment of those norms. The salience of any specific component of self-categorization may be dependent on the situation (Turner, 1987). In addition, the relative weight of personal versus social identity components is also affected by cultural norms (Triandis, 1989).

A "psychological group" around which the social identity forms may even be one in which there is no face to face social interaction, and in which membership is anonymous (Turner, 1984). It is the individual's perception of oneness with the perceived entity which is sufficient. Thus, a psychological group may form around amorphous categories such as an age cohort (Caspi, 1987), cosufferers from a malady, or other people with a specific, shared characteristic. In addition, while individuals tend to seek out social identities that enhance self-esteem (Tajfel, 1978), they also identify with categories that were not joined by choice (Triandis, 1989), and they may maintain these social identities even when not reinforcing or satisfying. Indeed, identifications are often tenaciously maintained even in situations involving great loss or suffering (Brown, 1986), missed potential benefits (Tajfel, 1982), and even expected failure (Gammons, 1986). Even when identification is unintended, immersion in a psychological group's social milieu may lead to self-definition in terms of that group and adoption of its values and norms (Becker & Carper, 1956). The assertions of the SIT theorists have been supported by an extensive body of empirical work, much of it summarized in books edited by Tajfel (1982) and Turner (1987).

Application of SIT to Biodata.   From an SIT perspective, every experience or series of experiences which conceivably categorizes (or stigmatizes) a person has the potential to shape subsequent behavioral patterns, though each component's influence is mitigated by the effects of the personal identity and all other social identifications. Thus, when a person associates with a team, club, school, or any other psychological group, the person takes on (to varying degrees) the syndrome of aspirations, preferences, values, and self-perceptions that are endemic to group members. Peripheral compulsions or inhibitions ("Marines/ministers/married women don't do things like that") may also become part of the person's behavioral repertoire, even when they contradict the person's own dispositional tendencies. These influences on behavior may outlive the person's active or continued involvement in the group (Mael & Ashforth, 1992). Even failures or negative accomplishments (e.g., the inability to swim, ride a bike, or drive a car at the same age as classmates, or being fired from a job) could place a person in a self-perceived psychological group. That group's profile would provide self-definition that could lead to subsequent behaviors insuring continued alienation, rejection, or failure. The same would be true of "input variables," state variables that were part of the person's environment. A syndrome of similar behaviors may be associated with the natives of a certain place, the children of parents with similar occupations, and the students of high schools of a certain size or gender composition. Biodata items thus encompass not only the choice-based, adaptive responses of the individual, but also the effects of all characteristics internalized through identification with the myriad psychosocial entities with whom one interacts throughout life.

In summary, SIT demonstrates that a person's previous experiences, even those not occurring by choice, those involving failures or lost accomplishments, or those involving adoption of the prototypical characteristics of psychological groups (even if peripheral to personal adaptation), can strongly affect the personal and social identity, and thereby affect subsequent behavior. Thus, SIT can supplement the ecology model to provide a conceptual rationale for the use of biodata. In the next section, this rationale, as well as the views of other researchers, is utilized to determine what, if any, characteristics differentiate biodata items from temperament items.

Differentiating Between Temperament and Biodata Items

Researchers who have addressed the apparent similarity between temperament and biodata items have acknowledged that, at least in terms of content, the domains overlap (Anastasi, 1982; Mumford & Stokes, 1991), and cannot be separated into orthogonal factors (Hough, 1989). Three questions remain to be answered: (a) What content areas fit in one domain and not the other? (b) What items could be used in both, but would be interpreted or utilized differently as biodata rather than temperament items? (c) What attributes, if any, are appropriate for one domain and not the other?

Content Area Differences

Regarding the first question, biodata items appear to draw from a larger, more inclusive realm of individual differences data, including behaviors that reflect interests, values, skills, and certain aptitudes and abilities, as well as personality attributes (Mumford & Stokes, 1991). One could argue that biodata achieve higher validities partly because they cover both ability and motivational topics. In fact, Hollenbeck and Whitener (1988) have argued that the validity of personality measures for selection would be better evaluated in conjunction with ability measures. Biodata measures can accomplish this within the same instrument.

Some input variable items are appropriate for biodata, but not temperament. Items measuring behaviors or characteristics of someone other than the respondent (i.e., parents, siblings), or characteristics of work situations (Mitchell, 1990), might appear in biodata forms. By contrast, temperament items typically deal only with the respondent's disposition. In addition, while temperament items only reflect responses that could be influenced by the person's disposition, biodata items may measure aspects of the person's environment that are unaffected by, but affect, the person. In general, biodata measures attempt to capture both the personal identity and the range of social identities, while temperament measures deal primarily with the personal identity.

In other ways, however, the content realm of biodata is more restricted. Because biodata items attempt to measure the effects of actual behaviors and events on continued adaptation and self-definition, both the ecology model and the SIT model would limit biodata to behaviors that actually take place or have taken place. Conversely, temperament measures frequently utilize behavioral intent items or responses to hypothetical situations as indices of stable, underlying dispositions.

Different Interpretation of Items

Regarding the second question, it is possible for the same item to be utilized within either domain, albeit for different reasons. Even when an actual behavior is sampled in a temperament measure, the behavior is viewed as a tangible manifestation of a preexisting disposition. According to the currently ascendant interactionist perspective in personality theory, temperament items presume temporal, if not cross-situational, consistency (Kenrick & Funder, 1988; Pervin, 1985). A relatively fixed dispositional orientation is presumed to influence the behaviors sampled. From a biodata perspective, however, events and experiences may not only be indications of underlying dispositions, but more importantly *shapers* of subsequent behavior and potential modifiers of future dispositional responses. Biodata items assume that the behaviors sampled could shape or override initial dispositions.

Item Attribute Differences

The third question, regarding whether certain item attributes are unique to biodata versus temperament, is the subject of considerable controversy (Asher, 1972; Barge, 1987; Mumford & Stokes, 1991; Stricker, 1987). Some biodata researchers feel that any type of item used in other self-report measures may be profitably utilized as biodata. Others take the implicit position that because biodata is limited to actual behaviors, the genre should limit itself to behaviors that have definitely taken place. Therefore, only items whose responses are objective and potentially verifiable should be used.

This is a luxury that is generally not available to those working with temperament measures. Developers of temperament scales seek to write items that are pure measures of a single construct and that have high internal consistency with their scales and lower correlations with measures of other temperaments. To accomplish this, complex behaviors, which may be the result of numerous temperaments and other determinants, are to be avoided, while subjective items tapping specific dispositions are preferred. Because subjective items about internal states are generally utilized, temperament researchers have had to seek alternative controls on social desirability and faking (Hough, Eaton, Dunnette, Kamp, & McCloy, 1990). Thus, most biodata item attributes that have been advanced should be seen not as defining characteristics of biodata, but as higher standards for self-report fidelity, standards which could only be adhered to with biodata.

THE UNITED STATES MILITARY ACADEMY (USMA) RESEARCH

This chapter describes an attempt to achieve the conceptual benefits of measuring specific temperament constructs, while retaining the less fakable properties associated with objective biodata. The study was conducted at the United States Military Academy at West Point (USMA), an applied setting in which it was considered more acceptable to question applicants on biographical information than on temperament scales. Objective biodata were empirically keyed directly to temperament scales, and then used rationally (as scales with a priori values) with multiple criteria. The goal was to determine if biodata scales could parallel individual temperament scales, and if they would provide stable prediction of unique variance in the criteria when keyed in this fashion. No attempt was made to assign objective items exclusively to a single construct scale, and the current approach acknowledges the possibility that the behaviors or events behind each biodata item may relate to several different constructs. Thus, in this effort, temperament scales and their biodata analogs were compared in terms of their relationship with USMA cadet leadership performance, as well as their vulnerability to faking. The incremental contribution of both the temperament and biodata measures beyond that of the current USMA admissions measure was also examined.

As a precursor to describing the current research, it would be worthwhile to discuss the development and validation work that went into the temperament measure used in this research. In the following section, the Army's Assessment of Background and Life Experiences (ABLE) is discussed in depth.

The Army's ABLE

The ABLE, is a temperament measure developed and validated as part of a long-term personnel research project to improve the selection and classification of enlisted personnel Campbell & Zook, 1991; Hough et al., 1990; White, Nord,

Mael, & Young, 1993). A principal objective of this research, called Project A, was to validate the Armed Services Vocational Aptitude Battery (ASVAB) against actual job performance. The ASVAB is a cognitive test used operationally in preenlistment screening of applicants for all of the Armed Services. Previously, it had only been validated against training performance. In addition, new supplementary tests were designed to measure additional constructs beyond ASVAB for predicting performance. ABLE was developed in this research to capture the motivational element of performance ("will do"), as opposed to the ability ("can do") element. ABLE is also under consideration by the joint Armed Services to be used as part of a measure of adaptability to military life.

Scale development involved reviewing major personality inventories and then reducing the number of temperament dimensions by eliminating redundancy and focusing on stable predictors of job performance (Kamp & Hough, 1988; Hough et al., 1990). To estimate relationships between these temperament constructs and job performance, a total of 237 validity studies conducted between 1960 and 1984 were reviewed. Within the set of temperament constructs, measures of Achievement and Dominance emerged as likely predictors of leadership potential. Performance in training and the number of outstanding accomplishments on the job (e.g., awards) was also related to the Achievement construct and Internal Control. Measures of Dependability showed consistent, positive relationships with teamwork, attendance at work, and the avoidance of disciplinary problems.

Based on this meta-analysis, preliminary temperament scales were developed to measure the most promising constructs for predicting the components of enlisted job performance and overall effectiveness. This initial battery was administered to 11,000 trainees in four groups of Army jobs, known as Military Occupational Specialties (MOS). Guided by results from this Preliminary Battery, 10 content scales measuring 7 constructs were retained to form ABLE. (see Table 15.1). In addition, validity scales, which indicate whether or not the respondents answers reflect random responding, faking bad, or social desirability distortion, were included (Hough et al., 1990) The resulting form of the ABLE was administered as part of the Army's Project A Concurrent (CV) and Longitudinal Validation (LV) research. Nearly 60,000 soldiers in a representative sample of Military Occupational Specialties (MOS) participated in the Project A research and their ABLE scores were used to predict performance during training, the first term of enlistment, and entry-level non-commissioned officer (NCO) leadership. Performance during first and second tours of duty was assessed by multiple measurement methods including tests of job and training knowledge, hands-on performance tests, peer and supervisory ratings, and administrative criteria. In addition, two new methods were developed for assessing second-tour NCO performance: role-play exercises and a situational leadership measure. The role-play exercises were used to assess one-on-one interpersonal skills required for counseling and training, and a Situational Judgment Test was

TABLE 15.1
Temperament Scales by Construct in the Assessment of Background and Life Experience (ABLE)

Construct	Scale
Stress tolerance	Emotional stability
Dependability	Nondelinquency Traditional values Conscienctiousness
Achievement	Work orientation Energy level
Surgency/Leadership	Dominance Self-esteem
Physical condition	Physical condition
Locus of control	Internal control
Agreeableness	Cooperativeness
Response validity scales	Nonrandom response Social desirability Poor impression

designed to measure supervisory skill and decision-making within the constraints of a paper-and-pencil format.

Results from these large scale validation studies indicate that ABLE predicts leadership, job effort, and personal discipline (Hough et al., 1990). Higher scores on Dominance and Work Orientation were significantly related to the NCO Effort and Leadership dimension, with uncorrected concurrent validities from .30 to .34. Self-Esteem and Dominance showed positive relationships with NCO effectiveness in training and counseling subordinates (mean $r = .20$).

During the first term of enlistment, the Achievement construct of ABLE was found to be a significant predictor of job effort (for the Work Orientation scale, uncorrected $r = .23$). The ABLE Dependability construct significantly predicted discipline problems among enlisted soldiers, with (uncorrected) validities ranging from .23 to .29 for the three Dependability scales. In addition, lower scores on the ABLE, particularly Emotional Stability, were significantly related to greater rates of first term attrition, with the relationship most pronounced among those scoring low on ABLE (White, Nord, & Mael, 1990).

In research involving officers, enlisted personnel, and a small sample of cadets, the ABLE was examined as a predictor of success in Ranger training. The Ranger course is a rigorous and physically demanding training program to develop small unit leaders. Trainees are required to lead small units in combat operations across varied terrains, while under severe food and sleep deprivation. In this environment, those with higher scores on Energy Level and Emotional

Stability had higher graduation rates from the Ranger Course (White, Mael, & Sachs, 1991). In other research (DeMatteo, White, Teplitzky, & Sachs, 1991), these same measures were found to predict the successful completion of Special Forces Assessment System, which is used to select volunteers for Special Forces training. As a group, soldiers who qualify for Special Forces training scored at or above the 80th percentile on the ABLE. It is for these reasons that researchers at USMA felt that the ABLE could complement their current, academically oriented selection process and help predict leadership potential and performance.

However, ABLE has potential drawbacks for use in an enlistment or admissions package. One is the fear of extensive faking and socially desirable responding (Young, White, & Oppler, 1991). ABLE is a relatively transparent test, with no attempt to obscure desirable responses, and with virtually all items arranged in a linear continuum of desirability. In a previous administration with enlisted soldiers, faking has not contaminated ABLE's validity (Hough et al., 1990). However, the fear of faking would be increased in an admissions situation, where the instrument is often taken at home under the tutelage of parents and other advisors. A second concern was that some ABLE items concerned somewhat intrusive and "psychological" topics, such as physical symptoms, fears, anxieties, and feelings of depression and failure. USMA researchers felt that these types of items could be resented, thus driving away capable candidates.

Therefore, Mael and Schwartz (1992) sought to determine if ABLE motivational constructs could be measured with more palatable biodata items. This chapter reviews their previous work, and extends it to an additional criterion and to cross-validation work drawing on two additional samples. This effort is described next.

METHOD

The sample sizes and measures for the USMA research are shown in Table 15.2. The sample sizes and measures for the cross-validation analysis performed with the subsequent class at USMA, which is described later in this chapter, also appears in Fig. 15.2.

Sample and Instruments.   The 1,325 incoming cadets of the USMA class of 1994, of which 1,164 (88%) were men, completed questionnaires in July 1990. The following measures were included:

ABLE. An 88-item version of ABLE was assembled for this research. The measure included the following scales: a 21-item Emotional Stability scale; a 10-item Dependability scale, here composed primarily of items dealing with endorsement of traditional values, as opposed to other forms of ABLE, which also include nondelinquency items in the Dependability construct; a 14-item Work Orientation scale; a 12-item Dominance scale; and an 18-item Energy scale. An

TABLE 15.2
USMA Research Database

Samples	Predictor Measures	Criteria
Class of 1994 n = 1,334	Biodata: 73 items ABLE: 5 scales USMA Measures - Whole Candidate Score (WCS) - SAT - High School Rank - Leader Potential Score (LPS) - Physical Aptitude Exam (PAE)	Leadership Performance Ratings - Cadet Basic Training (first 6 weeks) - Fall semester - Cadet Field Training (after 1 year)
Class of 1995 n = 1,258	Biodata: 73 Items USMA Measures	- Cadet Basic Training

11-item Social Desirability scale, designed to detect persons whose responses are consistently contaminated with socially desirable responses (Hough et al., 1990), was also included.

USMA Measures. The selection measures currently used at USMA were included in the research for the purpose of determining the incremental contribution of ABLE and the biodata (Burke, 1992). The primary measure is the weighted composite called the Whole Candidate Score (WCS), which is based 60% on an applicant's standardized test scores (i.e., SAT, ACT) and graduating rank in high school; 30% on the Leadership Potential Score (LPS), derived from the School Official Evaluation (an evaluation form filled out by high school instructors), and the Candidate Activities Record (CAR), a checklist of extracurricular activities and varsity sports; and 10% on scores on the Physical Aptitude Examination (PAE). The WCS and each of it's components were evaluated individually against the criteria, in order to isolate the determinants of success on each criterion.

Biodata Questionnaire. A 73-item biographical data questionnaire was developed for this research. A number of the items or item topics appeared in previous biodata forms (England, 1971; Glennon, Albright, & Owens, 1966; Richardson, Bellows, Henry, & Co., 1985), while others were developed expressly for this research. Items were included if they addressed behaviors or events seen as relating to: (a) the criteria of interest, with leadership performance as the primary criterion, and general soldiering and attrition from USMA as the secondary ones; (b) the ABLE temperaments included in the research, especially Dominance; or (c) aspects of military adaptability and other constructs not covered on the version of the ABLE being used. Those falling into the last category included interpersonal style, preference for rugged pastimes, and quality of familial structure and relationships. Additional detail about the development of the biodata scale can be found in Mael and Schwartz (1991). Although additional items appeared on the initial biodata instrument, the aforementioned 73 items are those that were also administered to the subsequent cross-validation sample.

To attempt to minimize faking, the items used in the current research had many of the biodata attributes defined and discussed in Mael (1991), in that they were all historical, external, objective, first-person, and primarily verifiable, at least in principle. Noncontrollable items were allowed, and "job relevance" was of necessity defined broadly. Adherence to these guidelines and testing time constraints forced abandonment of other potentially useful items.

In order to utilize the biodata as analogs to the ABLE scales, the items were keyed to ABLE using an approach that was primarily empirical, while still retaining much of the theoretical and logical discretion described as "rainforest empiricism" by Mael (1991). The details of the methodology used in keying the biodata items used in this research can be found in Mael and Schwartz (1991). In the current study, each biodata item was keyed to each ABLE scale, and retained as part of a composite if significantly correlated above .075 with the scale. The five scales that emerged were: Bio-Emotional Stability (22 items); Bio-Dependability (27 items); Bio-Work Orientation (32 items); Bio-Dominance (57 items); and Bio-Energy (40 items). Because of the heterogenous nature of the objective biodata items, the item pools for each scale were not mutually exclusive, and no attempt was made to derive factorially distinct scales.

In addition, a biodata composite for the whole ABLE was created. To do this, the best codings of each item, regardless of which ABLE-keyed scale they had come from, were utilized to form a composite, representing the best of the five temperament-keyed scales. The resultant 75-item scale was called Bio-ABLE.

Criterion Measures.   Three operational criterion measures were used for this research. The first was ratings of demonstrated leadership capability from the initial six-week cadet basic training (CBT) period known colloquially as "Beast Barracks," which takes place before the onset of classes. The second criterion was ratings of demonstrated leadership capability, which were collected at the end of the first semester of classes in December, 1990. The third criterion was ratings of demonstrated leadership capability during cadet field training (CFT), which takes place during the second summer of attendance at USMA. Each rating was done with the same twelve-dimension rating form, and involved a weighted combination of ratings by peers and superiors. The moderate correlations between the criterion measures ($r = .35$ for CBT and fall leadership; $r = .39$ for CBT and CFT leadership; and $r = .23$ for fall and CFT leadership), as well as evidence of differential relationships with the predictors, served as compelling grounds not to combine the ratings or treat them as repeated measures of the same criterion.

TABLE 15.3
Descriptive Statistics and Intercorrelations for ABLE Scales, USMA Class of 1994

Variable	Items	Mean	SD	1	2	3	4	5	6	7
1. Emotional Stability	21	2.36	.30	.84						
2. Dependability	10	2.54	.28	.18	.70					
3. Work orientation	14	2.37	.37	.18	.49	.84				
4. Dominance	12	2.53	.32	.36	.17	.33	.82			
5. Energy	18	2.34	.22	.57	.38	.51	.44	.81		
6. ABLE total	75	2.40	.22	.73	.55	.69	.64	.84	.92	
7. Social Desirability	11	1.42	.25	.16	.31	.39	.09	.23	.34	.55

n = 1,324
All correlations are significant at $p < .001$.
Alpha coefficient appears in diagonal.

RESULTS

ABLE and BioABLE Analyses

Descriptive statistics and reliability estimates for the ABLE scales used in this research are shown in Table 15.3. The mean score on the Social Desirability scale was quite low, indicating that the examinees were not attempting to distort their responses by faking good. The correlations between each of individual and overall ABLE scales and their biodata analogs appear in Table 15.4. As can be seen, the correlations between each ABLE scale and its equivalent biodata scale range between .37 and .53. Only two off-diagonal correlations between ABLE scales and the biodata scales of other ABLE scales were of similar magnitude. It should be noted, however, that the ABLE scales were themselves not orthogonal, with correlations between scales as high as .57. In addition, because the same items were used on multiple biodata scales, there were large correlations between

TABLE 15.4
Intercorrelations Between ABLE-Keyed Biodata Scales and ABLE Scales, USMA Class of 1994

Variable	Items	ES	Dep	WO	Dom	EN	ABLE
Bio-Emotional stability	22	.37	.07*	.17	.31	.34	.37
Bio-Dependability	27	.03#	.42	.50	.16	.22	.33
Bio-Work orientation	32	.09	.34	.53	.29	.27	.40
Bio-Dominance	57	.20	.11	.27	.52	.29	.38
Bio-Energy	40	.28	.18	.34	.43	.44	.47
BioABLE	75	.19	.25	.44	.41	.34	.45

n = 1,314-1,334.
= n.s.; * = $p < .05$; for all others, $p < .001$.

some of the biodata scales. Thus, some degree of overlap in the off-diagonal coefficients was inevitable. In spite of this, to a great extent the biodata did manage to approximate the specific ABLE constructs that they were keyed to, and demonstrated some degree of discrimination in their relationships to the ABLE scales.

The intercorrelations between ABLE, BioABLE, WCS, and the individual USMA predictors are found in Table 15.5. Among those who are selected for USMA, high school rank has the dominant relationship with the overall WCS, while the PAE actually has a significant negative relationship.

Relationships to CBT Leadership Ratings

The correlations of the ABLE scales, the equivalent biodata scales, and the USMA predictors with CBT leader ratings appear in Table 15.6. Each of the ABLE scales was related to leadership performance, with the relationships for Emotional Stability, Dominance, and Energy Level being highest. Two of the biodata scales, Bio-Dependability and Bio-Work Orientation, did not have a significant relationship with the criterion. Each of the other biodata scales, as well as BioABLE, was related to CBT leadership, although BioABLE's relationship with the ratings was clearly pulled down by the inclusion of Bio-Dependability and Bio-Work Orientation items. The result was that BioABLE's correlation with the criterion was significantly lower than that of ABLE ($t_{1184} = 3.21, p < .01$), as computed by a formula described in Cohen and Cohen (1983, p. 56–57).

The USMA measure WCS was not related to the criterion, and the same was true of SAT and high school rank. Conversely, the PAE had a significant relationship to the ratings, and the LPS had a smaller, but still significant, relationship as well.

TABLE 15.5
Intercorrelations Between ABLE, ABLE-Keyed Biodata (BioABLE), and Current USMA Predictors, USMA Class of 1994

Variable	1	2	3	4	5	6
1. ABLE total						
2. BioABLE	.45					
3. WCS	.11	.24				
4. SAT	.01#	-.06*	.21			
5. High school rank	.09	.22	.71	-.03#		
6. LPS	.13	.37	.12	-.10	.12	
7. PAE	.12	.07*	-.11	-.09	-.11	.09

n = 1,314-1,334.
= n.s.; * = $p < .05$; for all others, $p < .001$.

TABLE 15.6
Correlations of ABLE Scales, Biodata Keyed to ABLE, and USMA Predictors With CBT, Fall, and
CFT Leadership Criteria, USMA Class of 1994

Variabale	CBT	Fall	CFT
Emotional stability	.17	.03#	.14
Bio-Emotional stability	.17	.06*	.23
Dependability	.10	.14	.08*
Bio-Dependability	-.01#	.13	.05#
Work orientation	.10	.14	.10
Bio-Work orientations	-.01#	.12	.07*
Dominance	.12	.07**	.17
Bio-Dominance	.07*	.06*	.20
Energy	.18	.06*	.20
Bio-Energy	.16	.08**	.23
ABLE total	.19*	.11	.20
BioABLE	.07*	.11	.19
WCS	.04#	.20	.06#
SAT	.01#	.02#	-.06#
High school rank	-.01#	.17	-.03#
LPS	.06*	.07*	.15
PAE	.17	.02#	.19

$n = 1,183$ (CBT and Fall); 1,076 (CFT).
= N.S.; * = $p < .05$; for all others, $p < .001$.

Incremental Validity of ABLE and Biodata.   A series of hierarchical multiple regressions was performed to determine the incremental contributions of the ABLE and biodata scales over and above the WCS. Both the ABLE and Bio-ABLE provided incremental validity when entered separately. When all three were entered together, only the ABLE had a significant value, demonstrating an expected overlap being ABLE and BioABLE.

It should be noted that because the cadets were chosen from a larger sample of applicants based on their WCS scores, there was substantial restriction of range on that predictor. It is probably that were the whole applicant sample to be assessed, the WCS would show a stronger relationship with this and subsequent criteria. Nevertheless, it is likely that there was a good deal of restriction of range on the ABLE and biodata as well among the select group of successful applicants.

Relationships to Fall Semester Leadership Ratings

The correlations of the ABLE scales, the equivalent biodata scales, and the USMA predictors with fall semester leader ratings appear in Table 15.6. Each of the ABLE scales, with the exception of Emotional Stability, was related to fall ratings, with the relationships for Dependability and Work Orientation being highest. The relationships with Dominance and Energy Level were lower than they were with the other criteria. By contrast, each of the biodata scales, including Bio-Emotional Stability, was related to these leadership ratings. In each case, the relationship to the ratings was comparable to that of the equivalent ABLE scale, with no statistically significant differences Overall ABLE and BioABLE also showed their closest proximity to each other with this criterion.

In contrast to the previous criteria, WCS had the strongest relationship of any predictor to the fall ratings. The correlation between high school rank and the fall ratings was also higher than that of any ABLE or biodata scales. The LPS had a small but significant relationship with fall ratings, while SAT and PAE did not.

Incremental Validity of ABLE and Biodata.   The same series of multiple regressions were performed with this criterion. Both ABLE and BioABLE were found to add incremental validity when entered separately with WCS. As opposed to the previous criterion, however, when BioABLE and ABLE were entered together without WCS, the biodata scale added significantly to the coefficient. Once again, though, BioABLE did not add significant variance over the combined contribution of both ABLE and WCS. By contrast, for this criterion, WCS accounted for significant variance even when entered with both ABLE and BioABLE. Apparently, the redundancy of BioABLE derives from partial overlap with both ABLE and WCS, rather than from extensive overlap with ABLE.

Relationships to Cadet Field Training (CFT) Leadership Ratings

The correlations of the ABLE scales, the equivalent biodata scales, and the USMA predictors with CFT leader ratings appear in Table 15.6. Each of the ABLE scales was related to leadership performance, with the relationships for Dominance, Energy Level, and Emotional Stability being highest. Similarly, all of the individual biodata scales except Bio-Dependability were related to leadership performance, with Bio-Dominance, Bio-Energy Level, and Bio-Emotional Stability having the strongest relationships. In fact, in each of these cases, the biodata analog had a slightly stronger relationship than did the original ABLE scale. Once again, the WCS was not related to the criterion, as was true of SAT and high school rank. Conversely, the PAE and LPS had a significant relationship to the ratings.

Incremental Validity of ABLE and Biodata.   An identical series of multiple regressions was performed to determine the incremental contributions of the ABLE and biodata scales over and above the WCS. Both the ABLE and Bio-ABLE provided incremental validity when entered separately. By contrast, the WCS did not account for significant variance when entered with either the ABLE or BioABLE. Even when entered together, both ABLE and BioABLE added significantly.

Cross-Validation Efforts

Because of a lack of testing time at USMA, it was not possible to completely replicate the original Mael and Schwartz (1991) study by readministering both the ABLE and biodata scales to a subsequent class. However, the most promising biodata items were readministered to the USMA Class of 1995, and both the ABLE and biodata measures were readministered to a sample of 1,002 new enlisted recruits stationed at Ft. Leonard Wood, Missouri. Together, the preliminary results from these data collections support the stability of the biodata-keyed-to-ABLE measures. The corroborative evidence from both of these samples follows.

USMA Class of 1995

Of the three leadership criteria discussed earlier, only ratings of CBT leadership scores were available for the Class of 1995 at the time of this writing. Correlations between the biodata scales and the USMA predictors with CBT leadership for both classes are shown in Tables 15.7. It can be seen that the same biodata scales (Bio-Emotional Stability, Bio-Dominance, and Bio-Energy Level) that were significantly related to the leadership ratings for the Class of 1994 were significant for the Class of 1995. Moreover, not only were the relationships comparable in each case, but the Bio-Dominance scale had a significantly *higher* correlation than the previous year. One plausible explanation is that because of USMA policy changes that effectively lowered the attrition rate to half that of the previous year, the variance among those remaining for the complete CBT training period was greater than before. This may also explain the larger correlations

TABLE 15.7
Biodata Scales Keyed to ABLE With Class of 1994 and USMA Predictors Correlated With CBT
Leadership for Class of 1994 and Cross-Validated With Class of 1995

Variable	1994	1995
Bio-Emotional stability	.17	.15
Bio-Dependability	-.01#	.01#
Bio-Work orientation	-.01#	.00#
Bio-Dominance	-.07*	.13
Bio-Energy	.16	.13
BioABLE	.07*	.11
WCS	.04#	.10
SAT	.01#	.05#
High school rank	-.01#	.02#
LPS	.06*	.13
PAE	.17	.20

n = 1,183 (1994); 1,198 (1995).
= n.s.; * = $p < .05$; for all others, $p < .001$.

TABLE 15.8
Descriptive Statistics and Intercorrelations for ABLE Scales, Enlisted Sample

Variable	Items	Mean	SD	1	2	3	4	5
1. Emotional stability	21	2.28	.34	.87				
2. Dependability	10	2.57	.31	.43	.72			
3. Work orientation	14	2.23	.38	.46	.47	.84		
4. Dominance	12	2.18	.41	.51	.26	.54	.85	
5. Energy	18	2.26	.34	.70	.50	.70	.58	.85

n = 1,002.
All correlations are significant at *p* < .001.
Alpha coefficient appears in diagonal.

for LPS and WCS as well, even though they were not keyed to any items in the 1994 sample. In fact, as opposed to the previous group, WCS added incremental validity even when entered together with BioABLE. In summary, though, it can be seen that shrinkage was not evidenced with this methodology, and that Bio-ABLE again increased validity over that provided by the current system.

Enlisted Recruit Sample

The readministration at Ft. Leonard Wood provided another set of correlations between the ABLE scales and their biodata analogs, albeit with a somewhat different sample. Descriptive statistics for the five ABLE scales included in the original USMA research, including intercorrelations between the scales, are shown in Table 15.8. The correlations between each of individual and overall ABLE scales and their biodata analogs appear in Table 15.9. It can be seen that the relationships between the ABLE and biodata scales for Emotional Stability, Dominance, and Energy Level were comparable in the enlisted sample. A signif-

TABLE 15.9
Intercorrelations Between ABLE-Keyed Biodata Scales and ABLE Scales, Enlisted Sample

Variable	Items	ES	Dep	WO	Dom	EN
Bio-Emotional stability	22	.34	.17	.29	.34	.36
Bio-Dependability	27	.28	.33	.40	.28	.39
Bio-Work orientation	32	.31	.25	.41	.38	.40
Bio-Dominance	57	.33	.17	.40	.47	.44
Bio-Energy	40	.38	.24	.43	.44	.45

n = 1,002.
= n.s.; * = *p* < .05; for all others, *p* < .001.

icant decrement in correlations was found for Bio-Dependability and Bio-Work Orientation; however, this decrement was well within the acceptable range of shrinkage (Mumford & Owens, 1987), and the correlations with the ABLE scales were still highly significant. It also must be remembered that because of socio-economic and aptitude differences between the enlisted and cadet samples, it is possible that substantive differences, rather than item instability, account for much of the decrement in these specific scales.

It can also be seen that the evidence for discriminant validity is not as strong as in the original USMA sample shown earlier in Table 15.4. However, it is apparent from the intercorrelation of ABLE scales shown in Table 15.8 that the ABLE scales had poorer discriminant validity than in the original USMA sample, shown in Table 15.3. Enlisted sample ABLE intercorrelations were as high as .70, with an average intercorrelation of .49, as opposed to an average of .34 in the initial USMA sample. It is understandable that the biodata scales keyed to ABLE would bear much of the same lack of discrimination for this sample, especially given the use of common items in multiple biodata scales.

Thus, overall, the combined evidence to date is that the biodata scales keyed to ABLE demonstrate a good deal of stability, both in a similar replication and with a different type of sample. Additional evidence of criterion-related validity will become available as both of these later samples mature.

Social Desirability Analyses

Returning to the initial USMA sample, an analysis of the relative relationship of the ABLE and biodata scales to socially desirable responding was undertaken (Mael & Schwartz, 1991). Table 15.10 shows the correlation between the ABLE Social Desirability scale and each of the ABLE scales, as well as the overall ABLE. The same correlations are shown for the biodata scales keyed to each ABLE scale, and the overall ABLE composite (BioABLE). In each case, the correlation with social desirability for the ABLE scale was significantly higher than the correlation for the equivalent biodata scale (Emotional Stability, $t_{1324} = 2.30$, $p < .05$; Dependability, $t_{1324} = 2.34$, $p < .05$; Work Orientation, $t_{1324} = 6.12$, $p < .01$; Energy, $t_{1324} = 3.51$, $p < .01$; overall ABLE versus BioABLE, $t_{1324} = 6.12$, $p < .01$). The sole exception was Dominance, for which both the ABLE and biodata scales had small relationships to the Social Desirability scale.

Social desirability was unrelated to summer leader ratings ($r = .04$), fall leader ratings ($r = -.01$), but did have a slight relationship to field training ratings ($r = .06$, $p < .05$). Some previous studies have shown socially desirable responding or faking to be criterion-related. When positively related, it has been interpreted as demonstrating self-esteem (Hogan & Stokes, 1989; Zerbe & Paul-hus, 1987), and when negatively related, it has been interpreted as measuring defensiveness and approval-seeking (Crosby, 1990; Crowne & Marlowe, 1960). In either case, it has been treated as meaningful variance by these researchers,

TABLE 15.10
Correlations of ABLE Scales, Biodata Keyed to ABLE, and USMA Predictors With ABLE
Validity (Social Desirability) Scale

Variabale	SD Scale	Variable	SD Scale
Emotional stability	.16	WCS	.04#
Bio-Emotional stability	.09	SAT	-.03#
Dependability	.31	High school rank	.09
Bio-Dependability	.25	LPS	.06
Work orientation	.39	PAE	-.00
Bio-Work orientations	.24		
Dominance	.09		
Bio-Dominance	.07		
Energy	.23		
Bio-Energy	.13		
ABLE total	.34		
BioABLE	.18		

n = 1,314-1,334.
= n.s.; for all others, p < .001.

rather than measurement error. Clearly, in this sample, socially desirable responding did not account for significant variance in two of the three criteria. Furthermore, partialling the effects of those scores from the ABLE and biodata predictor-criterion relationships did not affect those relationships in any way for any criterion, possibly because the overall degree of faking was low.

Although there was a significant, positive relationship between the social desirability scale and each of the ABLE and biodata scales, there was no relationship between the social desirability scale and either WCS, SAT, or the PAE. However, there was a positive relationship with the LPS. It should be noted that common method variance with the ABLE and biodata scales, both of which were administered together with the validity scale, would exaggerate their relationships. Surprisingly, the relationship with high school rank was positive and comparable to that of some of the biodata scales, even though the USMA high school rankings were not derived from self-report sources.

CONCLUSIONS

The findings of this research were highly encouraging. Five biodata scales were created to parallel temperament scales from the ABLE. In each case, the biodata scale was clearly related to the equivalent ABLE scale, and almost always had a smaller relationship to the other ABLE scales. The biodata scales were also compared to the ABLE scales in their ability to predict three leadership criterion measures Out of a total of 15 such comparisons, the biodata measures had a statistically smaller relationship to the criterion in only two cases. In some cases, the biodata scales actually had a slightly higher relationship to the criterion. These results demonstrate that it is possible to develop objective biodata measures that will be substantially analogous to valid temperament measures. Considering that the initial USMA sample was a highly select group, and that restriction of range on the predictor and criterion sides were likely, the results are even more encouraging.

Furthermore, with each criterion, either overall ABLE or BioABLE (the biodata equivalent) added incremental validity over and above the WCS measure currently used by USMA to assess leadership potential. For two of the criteria, BioABLE was redundant with ABLE and did not account for additional variance, while for the third BioABLE had a lesser overlap. Insofar as the biodata were keyed to maximize their relationship with ABLE scales in this research, this redundancy is desirable. In addition, there was some evidence that the biodata keyed to ABLE showed little shrinkage or loss of validity upon cross-validation with another sample. The results do not preclude the possibility that the biodata, keyed directly to the criterion, would show less overlap with ABLE and account for more variance in the criteria, albeit with a loss of interpretability. Preliminary evidence supports this position (Mael, Schwartz, & McLellan, 1992).

Moreover, another anticipated benefit of using biodata analogs, that of reducing vulnerability to socially desirable responding, was also realized. Four of the five individual biodata scales, as well as the overall biodata scale, each had a significantly smaller correlation with the ABLE validity scale than the equivalent ABLE scale. Thus, the use of objective biodata does seem to reduce the faking problem (Becker & Colquitt, 1992; McManus & Masztal, 1993). There are indications, however, that keying the biodata directly to the criteria would result in even less vulnerability to socially desirable responding than either the temperament scales or even these same biodata keyed to a temperament scale (Mael, Schwartz, & McLellan, 1992).

The results are also useful in pinpointing which temperament factors are most important in determining early success at West Point. Cadets rated highest in leadership performance during the initial six-week training period were distinguished most clearly by their greater emotional stability, stress tolerance, and energy level. Dependability, in the sense of endorsement of traditional values, and a strong work orientation, had the strongest relationship to leadership behavior in the ratings form the fall semester. Finally, those rated highest in field training leadership were similar to those doing best in basic training, although the additional component of dominance begins to take on greater significance.

The relatively minor role played by dominance until field training (the final leadership criterion), in spite of it's conceptual relationship to leadership orientation, is understandable upon further investigation. The primary role of the plebe (freshman cadet) is to be a good team player, rather than to direct other cadets in the accomplishment of their duties, and the fall semester ratings are dominated by academic accomplishments. Thus, the importance of dominance does not become apparent until the first real opportunities for leading, which occurs in field training. It will be important to obtain criterion measures from a cadet's last two years at USMA and beyond in order to appraise the relative importance of dominance.

Beyond the value of this methodology for applied prediction, this line of research demonstrates how use of temperament and biodata items in tandem can increase understanding of the motivational determinants of behavior. Writing biodata items with specific constructs in mind could prove a partial antidote for the shrinkage and uninterpretability criticisms which have hampered the utility of objective biodata (White & Kilcullen, 1992). Additional research needs to be done to reconcile the benefits of orienting items to a priori constructs with the benefits of allowing items to reflect the multifaceted, multiconstruct social identities that they may encompass. It is possible that a set of objective biodata items could serve dual functions, representing both specific constructs and more complex syndromes.

In addition, pairing objective biodata measures with temperament scales could enrich our understanding of the determinants and correlates of dispositional styles. Optimally, understanding of both temperament and biographical precursors of motivation and behavior could be enhanced. In order to maximize this gain, specific analyses at the objective item or item-cluster level might be more appropriate, rather than viewing each biodata scale as a unified entity, as is done in selection research.

In summary, the results suggest a potential method of capturing temperament or other constructs with biodata, while still retaining the strengths associated with objective biodata in regard to socially desirable responding. This "best of both worlds" approach may prove to be a fruitful avenue of research in the years to come.

ACKNOWLEDGMENTS

The views, opinions, and/or findings contained in this chapter are the authors' and should not be construed as an official position, policy, or decision of the U.S. Army Research Institute for the Behavioral and Social Sciences or the Department of the Army, unless so designated by other official documentation.

REFERENCES

Anastasi, A. (1982). *Psychological testing* (5th ed.). New York: Macmillan.

Arvey, R. D., Bouchard, T. J., Jr., Segal, N. L., & Abraham, L. M. (1989). Job satisfaction: Environmental and genetic components. *Journal of Applied Psychology, 74,* 187–192.

Asher, J. J. (1972). The biographical item: Can it be improved? *Personnel Psychology, 25,* 251–269.

Asher, J. J., & Sciarrino, J. A. (1974). Realistic work sample tests: A review. *Personnel Psychology, 27,* 519–533.

Ashforth, B. E., & Mael, F. (1989). Social identity theory and the organization. *Academy of Management Review, 14*, 20–39.

Ashworth, S. D. (1989, April). The distinctions that I/O psychologists have made between biodata and personality measurement are no longer meaningful. In T. W. Mitchell (Chair), *Biodata vs. personality: The same or different classes of individual differences?* Symposium presented at the annual meeting of the Society for Industrial and Organizational Psychology, Boston, MA.

Barge, B. N. (1987, August). *Characteristics of biodata items and their relationship to validity.* Paper presented at the 95th annual meeting of the American Psychological Association, New York.

Barrick, M. R., & Mount, M. K. (1991). The big five personality dimensions and job performance: A meta-analysis. *Personnel Psychology, 44*, 1–26.

Baumeister, R. F. (1986). *Public self and private self.* New York: Springer.

Becker, H. S., & Carper, J. W. (1956). The development of identification with an occupation. *American Journal of Sociology, 61*, 289–298.

Becker, T., & Colquitt, A. (1992). Potential versus actual faking of a biodata form: An analysis along several dimensions of item type. *Personnel Psychology, 45*, 389–406.

Brown, R. W. (1986). *Social psychology, the second edition.* New York: Free Press.

Burke, W. P. (1992). *Admissions variables through the Class of 1995.* Office of Institutional Research (Research Report 92-003). West Point, NY: United States Military Academy.

Campbell, J. P., & Zook, L. M. (1991). *Improving the selection, classification, and utilization of Army enlisted personnel: Final report on Project A.* Research report 1597. Alexandria, VA: U.S. Army Research Institute for the Behavioral and Social Sciences.

Caspi, A. (1987). Personality in the life course. *Journal of Personality and Social Psychology, 53*, 1203–1213.

Cohen, J., & Cohen, P. (1983). *Applied multiple regression/correlation analysis for the behavioral sciences* (2nd edition). Hillsdale, NJ: Lawrence Erlbaum Associates.

Crosby, M. M. (1990, April). *Social desirability and biodata: predicting sales success.* Paper presented at the fifth annual conference of the Society for Industrial and Organizational Psychology, Miami Beach, Florida.

Crowne, D. P., & Marlowe, D. (1960). *The approval motive.* New York: Wiley.

DeMatteo, J. S., White, L. A., Teplitzky, M. L., & Sachs, S. A. (1991, October). *Relationship between temperament constructs and selection for Special Forces training.* Paper presented at the meeting of the Military Testing Association, San Antonio, TX.

Digman, J. M. (1990). Personality structure: Emergence of the five-factor model. *Annual Review of Psychology, 41*, 417–440.

Dunnette, M. D. (1962). Personnel management. *Annual Review of Psychology, 13*, 285–314.

England, G. W. (1971). *Development and use of weighted application blanks* (Rev. Ed.). Minneapolis: University of Minnesota, Industrial Relations Center.

Gammons, P. (1986, November 3). Living and dying with the Woe Sox. *Sports Illustrated*, pp. 22–23.

Ghiselli, E. E. (1973). The validity of aptitude tests in personnel selection. *Personnel Psychology, 26*, 461–477.

Gibson, J. J. (1979). *An ecological approach to visual perception.* Boston, MA: Houghton Mifflin.

Glennon, J. R., Albright, L. E., & Owens, W. A. (1966). *A catalog of life history items.* Greensboro, NC: Creativity Research Institute of the Richardson Foundation.

Hogan, J. B., & Stokes, G. S. (1989). *The influence of socially desirable responding on biographical data of applicant versus incumbent samples: Implications for predictive and concurrent research designs.* Paper presented at the annual meeting of the Society for Industrial and Organizational Psychology, Boston, MA.

Hogan, R. (1986). *Manual for the Hogan Personality Inventory.* Minneapolis: National Computer Systems.

Hollenbeck, J. R., & Whitener, E. M. (1988). Reclaiming personality traits for personnel selection: Self-esteem as an illustrative case. *Journal of Management, 14*, 81–91.

Hough, L. M. (1989, April). Biodata and the measurement of individual differences. In T. W. Mitchell (Chair), *Biodata vs. personality: The same or different classes of individual differences?* Symposium presented at the annual meeting of the Society for Industrial and Organizational Psychology, Boston, MA.

Hough, L. M. (1991). *The "Big Five" personality variables—construct confusion: Description versus prediction.* Unpublished manuscript.

Hough, L. M., Eaton, N. K., Dunnette, M. D., Kamp, J. D., & McCloy, R. A. (1990). Criterion-related validities of personality constructs and the effect of response distortion on those validities. *Journal of Applied Psychology, 75*, 581–595.

Kamp, J. D., & Hough, L. M. (1988). Utility of temperament for predicting job performance. In L. M. Hough (Ed.), *Literature review: Utility of temperament, biodata, and interest assessment for predicting job performance* (Research note 88-02). Alexandria, VA; US ARI.

Kenrick, D. T., & Funder, D. C. (1988). Profiting from controversy: Lessons from the person-situation debate. *American Psychologist, 43*, 23–34.

Lord, R. G., De Vader, C. L., & Alliger, G. M. (1986). A meta-analysis of the relation between personality traits and leadership perceptions: An application of validity generalization procedures. *Journal of Applied Psychology, 71*, 402–410.

Mael, F. A. (1988). *Organizational Identification: Construct redefinition and a field application with organizational alumni.* Unpublished doctoral dissertation, Wayne State University, Detroit.

Mael, F. A. (1991). A conceptual rationale for the domain and attributes of biodata items. *Personnel Psychology, 44*, 763–792.

Mael, F. A., & Ashforth, B. E. (1992). Alumni and their alma mater: A partial test of the reformulated model of organizational identification. *Journal of Organizational Behavior, 13*, 103–123.

Mael, F. A., & Schwartz, A. C. (1991). *Capturing adaptability constructs with objective biodata* (Technical report 939). Alexandria, VA; U.S. Army Research Institute for the Behavioral and Social Sciences.

Mael, F. A., & Schwartz, A. C. (1992, April). *Capturing adaptability constructs with objective biodata.* Paper presented at the annual meeting of the Society for Industrial/Organizational Psychology, Montreal, Quebec.

Mael, F. A., Schwartz, A. C., & McLellan, J. A. (1992, August). Antidotes to dustbowl empiricism with objective biodata. In Rumsey, M. G. (Chair) *Biodata advances: Bridging the rational and empirical perspectives.* Symposium to be presented at the annual meeting of the American Psychological Association, Washington, DC.

McCrae, R. R., & Costa, P. T., Jr. (1987). Validation of the five-factor model of personality across instruments and observers. *Journal of Personality and Social Psychology, 49*, 710–721.

McManus, M. A., & Masztal, J. J. (1993, April). *Attributes of biodata: Relationships to validity and socially desirable responding.* Paper presented at the annual meeting of the Society for Industrial and Organizational Psychology, San Francisco, CA.

Mitchell, T. W. (1990, June). Can biodata predict personality? In M. G. Aamodt (Chair), *What does biodata predict?* Paper presented at the annual meeting of the International Personnel Management Association Assessment Council (IPMAAC), San Diego, CA.

Mumford, M. D., & Owens, W. A. (1987). Methodology review: Principles, procedures, and findings in the application of background data measures. *Applied Psychological Measurement, 11*, 1–31.

Mumford, M. D., & Stokes, G. S. (1991). Developmental determinants of individual action: Theory and practice in the application of background data. In M. D. Dunnette (Ed.), *The handbook of industrial and organizational psychology* (2nd edition). Orlando, FL.: Consulting Psychologists Press.

Owens, W. A. (1976). Background data. In M. D. Dunnette (Ed.), *Handbook of industrial psychology.* New York: Rand McNally.

Owens, W. A., & Schoenfeldt, L. F. (1979). Toward a classification of persons. *Journal of Applied Psychology, 65,* 569–607.

Pace, L. A., & Schoenfeldt, L. F. (1977). Legal concerns in the use of weighted application blanks. *Personnel Psychology, 30,* 159–166.

Pervin, L. A. (1985). Personality: Current controversies, issues, and directions. *Annual Review of Psychology, 36,* 83–114.

Rafaeli, A., & Sutton, R. I. (1989). The expression of emotion in organizational life. In L. L. Cummings & B. M. Staw (Eds.), *Research in Organizational Behavior, 11,* 1–42.

Reilly, R. R., & Chao, G. T. (1982). Validity and fairness of some alternative employee selection procedures. *Personnel Psychology, 35,* 1–62.

Richardson, Bellows, Henry, & Co. (1985). *Supervisory profile record.* Washington, D.C.: Author.

Staw, B. M., Bell, N. E., & Clausen, J. A. (1986). The dispositional approach to job attitudes: A lifetime longitudinal test. *Administrative Science Quarterly, 31,* 56–77.

Stricker, L. J. (1987, November). *Developing a biographical measure to assess leadership potential.* Paper presented at the Annual Meeting of the Military Testing Association, Ottawa, Ontario.

Stryker, S., & Serpe, R. T. (1982). Commitment, identity, salience, and role behavior: Theory and research example. In W. Ickes & E. S. Knowles (Eds.), *Personality, roles, and social behavior* (pp. 199–218). New York: Springer-Verlag.

Tajfel, H. (1978). The achievement of group differentiation. In H. Tajfel (Ed.), *Differentiation between social groups: Studies in the social psychology of intergroup relations* (pp. 77–98). London: Academic Press.

Tajfel, H. (1982). Instrumentality, identity and social comparisons In H. Tajfel (Ed.), *Social identity and intergroup relations* (pp. 483–507). Cambridge, England: Cambridge University Press.

Telenson, P. A., Alexander, R. A., & Barrett, G. V. (1983). Scoring the biographical information blank: A comparison of three weighting techniques. *Applied Psychological Measurement, 7,* 73–80.

Triandis, H. C. (1989). The self and social behavior in differing cultural contexts. *Psychological Review, 96,* 506–520.

Tupes, E. C., & Christal, R. E. (1961, May). *Recurrent personality factors based on trait ratings* (ASD-TR-61-97). Lackland Air Force Base, TX: Aeronautical Systems Division, Personnel Laboratory.

Turner, J. C. (1981). The experimental social psychology of intergroup behavior. In J. C. Turner & H. Giles (Eds.), *Intergroup behavior* (pp. 66–101). Chicago: University of Chicago Press.

Turner, J. C. (1982). Towards a cognitive redefinition of the social group. In H. Tajfel (Ed.), *Social identity and intergroup relations* (pp. 15–40). Cambridge, England: Cambridge University Press.

Turner, J. C. (1984). Social identification and psychological group information. In H. Tajfel (Ed.), *The social dimension: European developments in social psychology* (Vol. 2, pp. 518–538). Cambridge, England: Cambridge University Press.

Turner, J. C. (1987). A self-categorization theory. In J. C. Turner (Ed.), *Rediscovering the social group* (pp. 42–67). New York: Basil Blackwell.

White, L. A., & Kilcullen, R. N. (1992, August). The validity of rational biodata scales. In Rumsey, M. C. (Chair) *Biodata advances: Bridging the rational and empirical perspectives.* Symposium to be presented at the annual meeting of the American Psychological Association, Washington, D.C.

White, L. A., Nord, R. D., & Mael, F. A. (1990, April). *Setting enlistment standards on the ABLE to reduce attrition.* Paper presented at the annual Army Science Conference, Durham, NC.

White, L. A., Nord, R. D., Mael, F. A., & Young, M. (1993). The Assessment of Background and Life Experiences (ABLE). In T. Trent & J. Lawrence (Eds.) *Adaptability screening for the services.* Washington: Office of the Assistant Secretary for Defense, Force Management and Personnel.

White, L. A., Mael, F. A., & Sachs, S. A. (1991). *Selection of candidates for Ranger training.* Unpublished manuscript, U.S. Army Research Institute, Alexandria, VA.

Wicklund, R. A., & Gollwitzer, P. M. (1982). *Symbolic self-completion*. Hillsdale, NJ: Lawrence Erlbaum Associates.

Young, M. C., White, L. A., & Oppler, S. H. (1991, October). *Coaching effects on the Assessment of Background and Life Experiences*. Paper presented at the meeting of the Military Testing Association, San Antonio, TX.

Zerbe, W. J., & Paulhus, D. L. (1987). Socially desirable responding in organizational behavior: A reconception: *Academy of Management Review, 12*, 250–264.

Author Index

Subject Index